_____

Presented to

_____

From

_____

Date

HOLLYWOOD, JESUS, AND YOU
365 Days for Growing your Faith and Praying for Hollywood

Copyright (c) 2020 by Karen Covell

Published by Thrilling Life Publishers
P.O. Box 92522
Southlake, TX 76092
www.thrillinglife.com

International Standard Book Number: 978-0-9889240-4-8

Cover Design by Elaine Lanmon
Cover Photo by Cameron Covell
Back Cover Photo of Karen Covell by Cameron Covell

Hollywood, Jesus, and You

365 Days for Growing your Faith and Praying for Hollywood

by

KAREN COVELL

with Kimberly Roberts

Thrilling Life Publishers

ACKNOWLEDGEMENTS

I want to thank Phil Cooke for introducing me to the people at You Version™ and encouraging me to write an HPN devotional for them. That was the beginning of a beautiful thing. I also thank Kim Roberts who has supported me, organized me, and encouraged me all along the way. She pushed me forward when I couldn't see the end and she handled all of the technical aspects of both the You Version™ Devotional and the hard copy, for which I am forever grateful. I thank my dear husband, best friend and Pal, Jim, for always believing in me and completely supporting every crazy idea I come up with. And his love for Scripture is truly my inspiration. I thank my dear friend, Victorya Rogers, my greatest cheerleader, for jumping in and making this book a reality. And finally, I thank all of the faithful YouVersion™ devotional readers who made me realize a hard copy book was worthwhile. You have embraced our on-line HPN Devotional with zeal and I am so grateful.

DEDICATION

This book is dedicated to all the faithful prayer warriors who pray with HPN for the Hollywood entertainment industry. Thank you for having the vision and commitment to pray for the people, the projects and the issues impacting our culture because of the work and the lives of entertainment professionals. You are truly visionaries across the globe. The Hollywood Prayer Network is only as eternally effective as our praying members, so I want you to know we couldn't do our work and ministry without you! And to my best friend and husband Jim, I wouldn't do anything without you, Pal!

TABLE OF CONTENTS

INTRODUCTION

For years I have had the vision to write a devotional for the Hollywood Prayer Network to share with our whole community of pray-ers and creatives across the globe. I wanted to write it for those who desire to grow more Christ-like, as well as for those who pray for the people creating the world's culture and entertainment. My passion was to combine praying for Hollywood and personal spiritual growth in one Devotional. So, I told my friend Phil Cooke, who introduced me to some of his friends at YouVersion™, and the rest is history. After over 200,000 online readers of the YouVersion™ Hollywood Prayer Network Devotional, it was time to publish a hard copy.

At the time of printing this devotional, it is the only known personal daily devotional that dedicates one day a week to focus on praying for entertainment professionals in Hollywood. These creative leaders are creating entertainment, shaping our culture and influencing people's thoughts, dress, language and even beliefs in every people group around the world. That's why I'm including Hollywood, the world's most influential marketplace, in this personal devotional. Christians understand how Washington DC is the seat of power, but few realize that Hollywood is the seat of influence. I know it's a challenge to consistently pursue your own spiritual growth, let alone pray for the people in Hollywood. But ironically, it all ties together! Culture affects all of us. And we can positively impact our world and our own faith by praying for the culture-makers!

Christians in Hollywood are a unique group of people who love Jesus, love creativity, and believe that the creative arts, visual storytelling, music, and other forms of entertainment are all gifts from God. We want all people to grow in their faith and to celebrate CREATIVITY and the WORD. God created and Jesus spoke the Word. So, we offer to you the words to create, grow, seek God, emulate Jesus, and impact culture!

If you want the content of our films, TV shows, music, internet, and video games to change, first the hearts of the people creating them need to change. And as you grow in your faith and pray for the people in Hollywood, you become part of a spiritual shift in our society. You are inviting God to come into the hearts of our nation's entertainment creators and the global audience, drawing God's presence into Hollywood and around the world where He can transform the lives of both the pre-Christians and the believers.

I've written this devotional as a 365-day journey. We chose to omit dates and simply make it 52 weekly topics so that you can begin any time of year. Feel free to start at Week One or simply skip around by topics. It's up to you.

So grab a journal to keep alongside you as you read and pray, and write down your thoughts each day so you have a record of what the Lord is speaking to you. Thank you for joining us on this journey. And may you fall more in love with Jesus, one day at a time!

With love and thanks,

Karen Covell

Karen Covell
Producer, Author, Speaker and Founder of The Hollywood Prayer Network
Hollywood, California

PRAYER

WEEK ONE

The Hollywood Prayer Network invites you to join us this week to grow in your own faith and to pray for the people, the projects, and the impact that the Hollywood Entertainment Industry has on our culture. Prayer changes us, and it is the most important life changer of all the gifts God has given to us. Get excited about your conversations with God as you spend this week seeking Him. Your prayers make an eternal difference!

DAY 1

GOLDEN BOWLS OF PRAYER

"And when he had taken it, the four living creatures and the twenty-four elders fell down before the Lamb. Each one had a harp and they were holding golden bowls full of incense, which are the prayers of the saints."

Revelation 5:8

"To get nations back on their feet, we must first get down on our knees."

Billy Graham

PRAY: Dear Lord, I thank you that the elders in heaven are with Golden Bowls holding all of the prayers I have ever prayed and with all of the prayers ever prayed for me. Knowing that every single prayer is stored, as incense in a Golden Bowl in heaven, I pray for some of the most unlikely people in Hollywood. Lord, I pray for family members, neighbors, and especially for my enemies. May I be a Christian who fills up the bowls with prayers for others – prayers of breakthrough, hope, joy, and salvation. Lord, thank You that my prayers make an eternal difference for the people I'm praying for, and that each one is a rich and lasting incense. I pray this in Jesus' name, Amen.

REFLECT: Imagine what it would be like if no one ever prayed for you? How lonely it would feel to know that not one person ever took the time or cared enough about you to talk to God about you. Then think of the difference you can make in other people's lives by praying for them. You may be the first person to ever do so. Think about the joy of meeting Jesus in heaven and finding out how many Golden Bowls are filled with your prayers!

ACT: Start filling up the Golden Bowls of Prayer for others by praying, by name, for the people on your heart. Start with three people in Hollywood who you care about. Pray for them, asking the Lord to bless them, knowing that you have put prayers in the Golden Bowls – they are full of incense because of you! Then start praying for personal friends of yours, family members, neighbors, and keep track of who you're praying for. You are filling up heavenly Golden Bowls by taking the time to pray for the people you care about!

YOUR THOUGHTS:

DAY 2

THE LORD'S PRAYER

"This, then, is how you should pray: " 'Our Father in heaven, hallowed be your name, your kingdom come, your will be done on earth as it is in heaven. Give us today our daily bread. Forgive us our debts, as we also have forgiven our debtors. And lead us not into temptation, but deliver us from the evil one.' For if you forgive men when they sin against you, your heavenly Father will also forgive you. But if you do not forgive men their sins, your Father will not forgive your sins."   Matthew 6:9-15

"The Lord's Prayer may be committed to memory quickly, but it is slowly learnt by heart."
                                    Frederick Denison Maurice

PRAY: Dear God, I thank You that You are my heavenly Father. I do hallow Your name and thank You for sending Your kingdom down to earth for me, my family, and friends. May Your will be done in my life here on earth, just as it is in heaven. Thank You that You supply my daily bread and that You forgive me for all of my sins. Help me to forgive others. Please protect me from temptation and from the enemy. For Yours is the kingdom, the power, and the glory forever! AMEN

REFLECT: As you pray through each line of this amazing prayer, personalize it and notice that He is talking directly to you. He is your Father. You are to praise His name and ask Him to bring His heavenly kingdom down to you. Realize that He promises to supply you everything you need for each day and He forgives everything that you do. Can you even fathom that truth? He will not lead you into temptation because He loves YOU so much!

ACT: Praise God that His name is powerful, hallowed, and glorious, and worship Him now, out loud, with your favorite Christian song, hymn, or chorus. Then read the prayer out loud and hear the promises that God gives you. Read it again and ask Him to reveal what every word means and to help you embrace all of the truths and love that He is pouring down upon you as you read it as a hymn.

YOUR THOUGHTS:

DAY 3

GOD HEARS EVERYTHING

"This is the confidence we have in approaching God: that if we ask anything according to his will, he hears us. And if we know that he hears us—whatever we ask—we know that we have what we asked of him."
$\qquad\qquad\qquad\qquad\qquad\qquad\qquad\qquad\qquad$ 1 John 5:14-15

"Prayer does not prepare us for the greater work; prayer is the greater work."
$\qquad\qquad\qquad\qquad\qquad\qquad\qquad\qquad\qquad\qquad$ Oswald Chambers

PRAY: Oh heavenly Father, would you please give me confidence that You are hearing every word I pray. Help me to understand and truly know that You are listening and answering everything I tell You! Thank You that when I pray, I know that I have what I asked of You. I need Your help to trust that Your answers are coming and that You know what is best for me. Thank you, Father. Amen.

REFLECT: Reflect on what you talk to God about and realize that He is actually hearing and responding to everything you say. Does that realization change what you say, how you say it, or how often you talk to Him? It's profound how He allows us to have conversations with Him – the Creator of the universe, and He tells us He is responding to the desires of our hearts. That's awesome.

ACT: Would you make a list of the bold, seemingly impossible, and even outrageous prayers you would like to pray for other people and then pray those prayers. If you keep a journal of your prayers, you can see how the Lord has responded to you. He is listening and wants to answer all of the prayers that you have talked to Him about. Pray BIG, don't limit God, and keep track of those prayers. For He WILL answer!

YOUR THOUGHTS:

DAY 4

THE IMPORTANCE OF PRAYER

"If my people, who are called by my name, will humble themselves and pray and seek my face and turn from their wicked ways, then will I hear from heaven and will forgive their sin, and will heal their land."   2 Chronicles 7:14

"What do you really care about?"
   God (Morgan Freeman) telling Bruce (Jim Carrey) how to pray in Bruce Almighty

PRAY: Jesus, would You please give me a heart and life of humility? Would you give me a hunger to seek Your face and to turn from all the sins I'm struggling with now? Thank You so much for listening to me and hearing my prayers and forgiving my sins. And I praise You for not only healing me, but for healing my family, my neighborhood, my workplace, my city, my region, and my land – my country! True humility and heartfelt prayer can only come from You, oh God. I pray this in Your mighty name, Amen.

REFLECT: Have you thought that when you pray, you are not only impacting your own life, but you are potentially changing your world – or "healing your land"? Have you thought about the far-reaching power of your prayers? If you truly understood that your prayers could heal your family, your city, and your country, how would you pray differently? Imagine how your prayers for Hollywood can change our world – both in the content which is produced and in the lives of the people creating it.

ACT: Including your physical body in prayer is a common practice in many cultures around the globe. More and more people are raising their hands, kneeling, and even laying prostrate. What can you do physically to humble yourself and to seek His face in prayer? Take a chance, with no one around, to seek God in a new way.

YOUR THOUGHTS:

DAY 5

GOD ANSWERS EVERY PRAYER

"Therefore I tell you, whatever you ask for in prayer, believe that you have received it, and it will be yours."
                                         Mark 11:24

"If only God would give me some clear sign! Like making a large deposit in my name at a Swiss bank."
                                         Woody Allen

PRAY: Lord, please help me to believe that when I talk to You, You're not only listening but You are with me and are answering. Don't let me doubt You or Your love and faithfulness to me. Let me know that You are answering every prayer in Your way, in Your time, and with unconditional love. Let me look forward to Your answers. I pray in Jesus' name, Amen.

REFLECT: Reflect on how many times you pray about something and then are completely surprised when it's answered. Or when you pray about something you really want, and you don't get it. What does it mean to know, with confidence, that God is answering every prayer? Can you honestly believe that, regardless of what the answer is?

ACT: Write down one "unanswered prayer" and then ask the Lord to reveal to you how He actually did answer it. Be open to His response, and do not doubt that He will make it clear to you or give you peace about it. Then choose one person in Hollywood whom you think will never become a Christian and start praying for the Lord to touch that person's heart. And have no doubt that He's answering your prayers. The more you do it, the less you will doubt and the bolder your prayers will become.

YOUR THOUGHTS:

DAY 6

SEEK GOD IN PRAYER

"Ask and it will be given to you; seek, and you will find; knock and the door will be opened to you. For everyone who asks receives; he who seeks finds; and to him who knocks the door will be opened."
Matthew 7:7-8

"Prayer may not change things for you, but it for sure changes you for things."
Samuel M. Shoemaker

PRAY: Lord, I seek You through my prayers by asking You not for stuff but for more of You. I'm knocking on the door of Your heart and asking You to allow me to see people the way You see them, to hear them the way You hear them, to love them the way You love them, and to show me how much You love me. And I trust that as I keep knocking, You will open the door of my heart so that I can experience You more richly, deeply and lovingly. Thank You for listening, for loving me, and for wanting me to experience You more intimately. Selah! Amen.

REFLECT: Reflect on how many times you've asked for something and felt like God wasn't listening, or you didn't get what you asked for. Think about what you asked for. Could it be that getting it wouldn't be best for you? Do you have to wait longer? What does it mean to knock on the door of God's heart? Can you continue to turn to Him without giving up, getting discouraged, frustrated, or angry with Him? Do you believe that He is listening and answering? There is a lot to think about in this verse.

ACT: As an exercise in prayer, ASK God for something you believe would be His will for you, then SEEK Him to learn more about Him, keep KNOCKING until you feel you're really in conversation with Him, and then FIND Him by pursuing Him until you feel a door has been opened. God loves our perseverance and He is faithful.

YOUR THOUGHTS:

DAY 7

GOD GIVES YOU PEACE

"Do not be anxious about anything, but in everything, by prayer and petition, with thanksgiving, present your requests to God. And the peace of God, which transcends all understanding, will guard your hearts and your minds in Christ Jesus." Philippians 4:6-7

"You pray for rain, you gotta deal with the mud too. That's a part of it."

Denzel Washington

PRAY: Dear Jesus, I pray that You give me peace today. Please guide my steps, order my day, and show me what is most important on Your agenda for me. I want Your will to be done in my life. Please fill me to overflowing with Your peace. Guard my heart and my mind as I talk to people, make decisions, finish deadlines, and take care of my work and my family. I don't want to just give You a list of requests. I want to seek You for Your peace, Your joy, Your priorities, and Your heart for other people. Thank You, Jesus, for answering my prayers and filling me up new and fresh every day. Amen.

REFLECT: Reflect on how your whole day can change, just by letting go of your agenda and truly asking the Lord to guide you, direct your path, and even choose what words you are to say and not say. Think of the pressure that Hollywood celebrities have as they are watched, even hounded, with every step they take and every word they say. If you could be aware of the Lord hearing your every word and following your every step, how would you change? Step out of your comfort zone in prayer today.

ACT: Spend one whole prayer time just thanking God – for your life, family, friends, and your job, your gifts, talents, creativity, and your passions, your personality, character traits, and your joy, your humor, wisdom, favor, and even how you love. Don't ask Him for anything. Just thank Him and praise Him. Try it now and see how long you can go. Notice how you are feeling. You are probably experiencing more peace right now.

YOUR THOUGHTS:

GOD'S HEART FOR HOLLYWOOD

WEEK TWO

For God So Loved Hollywood – This week we're focusing on understanding and praying for Hollywood, the world's most influential mission field. Christians in Hollywood are on the front lines of ministry and they need prayer and support. So, our prayer is that you will catch the vision of the importance and global impact of Hollywood and choose to pray for the people there as you watch films and TV shows, hear music, and play video games.

"For God so loved HOLLYWOOD that He gave His only son, that WHOEVER in Hollywood would believe in Him, should not be destroyed, but have eternal, everlasting life."

Check out the video "Hollywood Prayer Network on God's Heart for Hollywood" on YouTube <u>https://youtu.be/5-7HyhR_Qxo</u>

Day 1

GOD LOVES CREATIVE PEOPLE

"In the beginning God created the heavens and the earth...So God created man in his own image, in the image of God he created him; male and female he created them."

Genesis 1:1,27

"Then the Lord said to Moses, "See, I have chosen Bezalel son of Uri, ... and I have filled him with the Spirit of God with skill, with ability and knowledge in all kinds of crafts—to make artistic designs for work in gold, silver and bronze, to cut and set stones, to work in wood, and to engage in all kinds of craftsmanship."

Exodus 31:1-5

"Imagination is the beginning of creation. You imagine what you desire, you will what you imagine, and at last, you create what you will."

George Bernard Shaw

PRAY: Lord, I thank You that Your first act was creation. You created the universe and then mankind in Your image, and it was "very good." You made us creative and You chose Bezalel as the first artist in the Bible. You have also given us creative gifts and the desire to be creative. Help me to celebrate the creative leaders in Hollywood, for You made them and they have given us beauty and powerful stories through entertainment. Amen.

REFLECT: For decades, Christians have boycotted TV shows, films, and studios. They have talked against Hollywood and even stopped their children from pursuing careers there. Why so much animosity toward this industry? God's first act was creation and He honors creative people throughout the Bible? It's because the enemy recognizes the impact of TV, films, music, and video games on our culture. Are you allowing the enemy to convince you that Hollywood is evil, or can you embrace God's love and support of those creative people? What are your feelings? Can you see it as the world's most influential mission field?

ACT: Evaluate your attitude about the Hollywood entertainment industry. To you, is it a reflection of God's creativity or is it evil and full of sinners? If you don't like Hollywood professionals, ask God to change your mind and your heart to reflect His view of them. Pray now for Him to reveal to you the importance of entertainment and then to change your heart.

YOUR THOUGHTS:

DAY 2

THE WORLD'S MOST INFLUENTIAL MISSION FIELD

"This is what the Lord Almighty, the God of Israel, says to all those I carried into exile...: "Build houses and settle down; plant gardens and eat what they produce. Marry and have sons and daughters... Increase in number there; do not decrease. Also, seek the peace and prosperity of the city to which I have carried you into exile. Pray to the Lord for it, because if it prospers, you too will prosper."　　　Jeremiah 29:4-7

"Film and entertainment are a pervasively important part of our culture, an extremely significant influence on the way our society operates... But, for better or worse, the influence of the church, which used to be all-powerful, has been usurped by film. Film and television tell us the way we conduct our lives, what is right and wrong." George Lucas

PRAY: Dear Lord, You told the Israelites exactly what they needed to do in exile. And You've also called Christians into Hollywood – a place often considered "exile." Help me understand this mission field and to pray for the Christians there to settle down, plant gardens and have children, so that there will be future generations of Christians in Hollywood. Lord, help them to seek the peace and prosperity of the city to which You have carried them. Please bless it, because if Hollywood prospers then the Christians there, too, will prosper. Amen.

REFLECT: Have you ever considered Hollywood to be a place of exile? It's very hard to live in Los Angeles – U.S.'s third most expensive city. The entertainment industry is extremely competitive, with high unemployment and divorce rates. They need us to pray for the Christians there because of the enemy's attacks of discouragement, isolation and despair. We should pray for favor, income, friends, Christian community, and work. Please pray for the peace and prosperity of Hollywood, for both the Christians and the pre-Christians.

ACT: Commit today to pray for the Christians who have been sent to Hollywood. Make a list of 5 people—friends, family, or celebrities—and pray for each of them every day this week. Pray for favor, work, and for them to make an eternal difference in the world's most influential mission field. Your prayers can change lives, give hope, and open doors for people in Hollywood needing to experience God.

YOUR THOUGHTS:

DAY 3

JESUS WAS THE BEST STORYTELLER

"Jesus spoke all these things to the crowd in parables; he did not say anything to them without using a parable. So was fulfilled what was spoken through the prophet: "I will open my mouth in parables, I will utter things hidden since the creation of the world."

Matthew 13:34-35

"There is no greater agony than bearing an untold story."

Maya Angelou

PRAY: Dear Jesus, thank You for Your example of speaking to the crowds through parables, so we can see the importance of storytelling. You fulfilled prophecies that said You would speak in parables and utter things hidden from man's heart since the creation of the world. You know exactly what we need to understand Your gospel. Thank You for speaking to us through paintings, stories, music, and parables so we can grow more Christ-like. Amen.

REFLECT: Jesus was the best and most powerful storyteller ever. He used parables, props, and referred to cultural issues and politics of the day to get His points across. Even God's prophets were artists and foretold, through stories and performance, that Jesus would come, Today's artists are prophets, for they profess either what's to come or what is happening now in society. And artists have always been upstream of the politicians, for they prophetically reflect our world, while the politicians just respond through legislation. God reminds us that artists, prophets, and storytellers are a crucial part of our society, and Jesus is our role-model. Does that make you look at movies, TV shows and songs in a new light? How do you need to adjust your beliefs about Hollywood to embrace these truths?

ACT: Look for TV programs, current films or songs that are parables. Whether you agree with them or not, can you see how they are either reflecting or commenting on our society and our culture? Even radio talk show hosts often prophetically talk about our world. Choose two of those shows, films, or songs and commit to pray for the writers, directors and producers of those shows. Ask the Lord to touch their hearts and lead them to Him, so that their lives and their work reflects His values, desires, and passions. As you pray, know that you are changing not only people's lives, but our entertainment and our culture.

YOUR THOUGHTS:

DAY 4

DON'T HATE THE PEOPLE IN HOLLYWOOD

"Do not seek revenge or bear a grudge against one of your people, but love your neighbor as yourself. I am the Lord ."   Leviticus 19:18

"To love our neighbor as ourselves is such a truth for regulating human society, that by that alone one might determine all the cases in social morality."   John Locke

PRAY: Dear Father, help me focus on the needs and brokenness of the creative community in Hollywood. Help me to love these people and to stop the Christians who talk against the creators, actors and executives in entertainment. Help me not to seek revenge or bear a grudge against anyone, but to love all my "neighbors" as myself. May we Christians not get angry at Hollywood or hold a grudge against them for what they produce or how they act. Let me love them with Your non-judgmental, unconditional love – for You are the Lord! Amen.

REFLECT: When you see an offensive TV show or a film with bad language or explicit sex, or you read an article about the broken people in Hollywood, what do you do? Can you remember, Hollywood is full of creative, intelligent people who are leaders and global influential culture-shapers – they just don't know Jesus! They need your prayers for the Lord to redeem their brokenness so they can experience life-transforming salvation. Your heart needs to break for the people who don't know God, His hope or salvation. You can't seek revenge or bear grudges, but love these "neighbors" as yourself.. How can you change your heart so that you respond to this people group with loving prayer and compassion?

ACT: Make a mental list of the films, TV shows, songs, and video games from Hollywood that have gotten you angry. Also list the people in Hollywood you have talked against after reading a magazine article or hearing the news. Ask the Lord to soften your heart and start praying for these people. Invite the Lord into their lives to bless them and give them His hope. Every time you judge someone in Hollywood, stop yourself and pray for them instead. They are God's creation and are influencing people across the globe who listen to their music, watch their films or TV shows, or play their video games. So, instead of holding a grudge, choose instead to pray. Your prayers can lead them to Jesus.

YOUR **THOUGHTS:**

DAY 5

THE CHRISTIAN COMMUNITY IN HOLLYWOOD

"May God Almighty bless you and make you fruitful and increase your numbers until you become a community of peoples."   Genesis 28:3

"I pray to be a good servant to God, a father, a husband, a son, a friend, a brother, an uncle, a good neighbor, a good leader to those who look up to me, a good follower to those who are serving God and doing the right thing."   Mark Wahlberg

PRAY: Almighty God, please bless the Christians who live and work in Hollywood. May You continue to make them fruitful and increase their numbers until they become a powerful, visible, loving community. Lead the thousands of young creative Christians who arrive in Hollywood every month to find a church and a Christian small group, in order to grow spiritually. Let them develop deep relationships, be discipled and grow strong in their faith, and create projects of truth and beauty. Lord, only You can gather the Christians, and grow them into an eternally influential community of Christ followers and great artists. Amen!

REFLECT: Artists all over the world need strong communities, for they need one another, just as you need your church family, small group, or Bible Study group. Living in a Christian community helps people grow spiritually, get empowered to share their faith, increase in numbers, bear more fruit, and become more prayerful. Christians in Hollywood need a Christian community in order to develop friendships and be in discipleship. Praying for creative professionals is powerful, for God made each of us with the same needs, struggles, and hearts. Wherever we are, Christians need other believers to bear fruit, grow, and thrive!

ACT: Take out a piece of paper and write a prayer that you would like someone to pray for you. Maybe it includes having close Christian friends and family, bearing fruit in all you do, growing deep roots or being impactful in your community, being a part of an active, loving church, etc. After you're done, pray that same prayer for the Christians in Hollywood. They are all God's children with the same desires, hopes and dreams that you have. Also pray that the Christians in Hollywood impact people around the world with their lives and their TV shows, films, music, and games. Your prayers can make that happen and they need you!

YOUR THOUGHTS:

DAY 6

THE NON-BELIEVERS IN HOLLYWOOD

"For God did not appoint us to suffer wrath but to receive salvation through our Lord Jesus Christ. He died for us so that, whether we are awake or asleep, we may live together with him. Therefore encourage one another and build each other up, just as in fact you are doing." 1 Thessalonians 5:9-11

"The underlying message of the Neighborhood is that if somebody cares about you, it's possible that you'll care about others. 'You are special, and so is your neighbor' – that part is essential: that you're not the only special person in the world. The person you happen to be with at the moment is loved, too." Fred Rogers

PRAY: Dear Jesus, how do I pray for the people in Hollywood who don't know You? I know that You don't want them to suffer wrath, but to receive salvation through You. You died for them, as well as for me, so those who choose You may all live together with You for eternity. Help me to pray for the people who influence me and my children with the entertainment they create. Help me to see the people in Hollywood with Your eyes and Your heart, and to learn how I can be loving, supportive, and compassionate towards them. Amen.

REFLECT: What a struggle it is for human beings to separate our emotions and our limited understanding with the truth of the gospel. God does not appoint wrath, anger, or judgment on anyone, but rather salvation. Jesus died for every one because He wants us all to have eternal life, and that includes Hollywood professionals. Pray for them to be transformed by your loving God. Replace any anger, frustration, or judgment with compassion, patience, and prayer. People in Hollywood are just as worthy of experiencing God's love as we are.

ACT: Commit a few minutes now to one celebrity in Hollywood who is a pre-Christian. Write his or her name on a piece of paper and ask the Lord to break your heart for that person. Pray that they don't suffer wrath, but experience God's hope, joy, peace, kindness, and salvation. Ask God to take away their suffering and to allow them to live in community with believers who can love them with Christ's love. Can you love them from afar, with the pure love of Jesus? Keep praying until you feel breakthrough.

YOUR THOUGHTS:

DAY 7

THE GLOBAL AUDIENCE

"Do not conform any longer to the pattern of this world, but be transformed by the renewing of your mind. Then you will be able to test and approve what God's will is – his good, pleasing and perfect will."

Romans 12:2

"We are so conformist; nobody is thinking. We are all sucking up stuff; we have been trained to be consumers, and we are all consuming far too much." Vivienne Westwood

PRAY: Lord, today I want to focus on the Christians around the globe who consume entertainment. Don't let them, or me, conform to the pattern of this world, but be transformed by the renewing of our minds. May they be able to test and approve what Your will is, and not be influenced or changed by the media or entertainment they're watching. I also want to enjoy my entertainment, but not let it influence Your good and perfect will for me. We all need discernment for what to watch and listen to. Please help me enjoy but not to be conformed by entertainment. Amen.

REFLECT: How many hours do you spend watching or listening to entertainment? Do you think and talk about it and process what you are consuming as much as you think and talk about what you read or listen to at church or in your quiet times? Most people spend more time consuming media than they spend with their families and God combined. So, what impact is that having on your heart and brain? It's not bad to watch and listen to films, TV shows, music, or video games. It's a matter of how you evaluate and process the messages. What do you like about them and how do they influence you? Ask God to show you how to evaluate your entertainment and how to challenge others around you to do the same.

ACT: What is the TV show, film, or music that has most influenced you? Do you know why? Evaluate what's good and bad about it. Start talking about the entertainment you consume so that you become more discerning. Don't conform to the pattern of this world, but have it inform you, so you can better evaluate God's perfect will for your life. Ask the tough questions about your entertainment consumption, tell someone else what you're thinking, and choose to start a new pattern of processing, evaluating and talking about it to others.

YOUR THOUGHTS:

PEACE is an emotion we all hunger for and yet it is so difficult to attain, especially for long periods of time. Join us this week as we seek PEACE in our daily lives, in our decisions, and in our relationships. May you find God's peace that surpasses your understanding as you spend time with Him.

DAY 1

THE LORD GIVES YOU PEACE

"The Lord bless you and keep you; the Lord make his face shine upon you and be gracious to you; the Lord turn his face toward you and give you peace."   Numbers 6:24-26

"Imagine all the people living life in peace. You may say I'm a dreamer, but I'm not the only one. I hope someday you'll join us, and the world will live as one."   John Lennon

PRAY: Lord, I ask that You do shine through me. Please make my face shine because Your face is shining on me. Be gracious to me, bless me and keep me, and let me be a light to the world. And, Lord, may You give me peace, in all circumstances, all conversations, and in all of my relationships. I hunger to feel Your peace that surpasses all understanding, so thank You for Your graciousness, care and love. I can feel Your peace and Your blessing! Amen.

REFLECT: Has anyone ever commented that you are a blessing, your face was shining or you are gracious? Or, has someone noticed the Lord in you through your graciousness or through the joy on your face? Have you ever been a source of peace for someone else? Think about how the Lord touches the lives of other people through you and ponder how you can be a peacemaker and a blessing to others.

ACT: Choose to shine in one person's life today. Who can you reach out to, talk to, smile at, serve, or care for today that would be as God's light shining graciously into their life? And pray, right now, for one celebrity or decision-maker in Hollywood to be touched by God's shining light. The Lord wants to bless all of us with His light and peace – through us!

YOUR THOUGHTS:

DAY 2

LET PEACE RULE

"Let the peace of Christ rule in your hearts, since as members of one body you were called to peace. And be thankful." Colossians 3:15

"I have to keep reminding myself: If you give your life to God, he doesn't promise you happiness and that everything will go well. But he does promise you peace. You can have peace and joy, even in bad circumstances." Patricia Heaton

PRAY: Lord, thank You that in yesterday's devotional You said that Your peace would shine through my face, and today You are telling me You will rule in my heart! As a member of your body, may Your peace be in and through my whole body so that I will be a peacemaker and be thankful. Amen.

REFLECT: Christ's peace is supposed to rule in our hearts. What rules in your heart? Since you are a member of one body, the body of Christ, the church, you were called to peace. That's a commandment. Our job is have Christ's peace rule in our hearts and be thankful. How are you doing at being peaceful and thankful?

ACT: Take 10 minutes to sit silently with God and ask Him to reveal His peace in your heart. Can you truly feel His peace? Try to push aside other distracting thoughts and focus on the peace of God through Jesus. May it fill you from head to toe. After your time of silence and as you continue with your day, try to stay aware of embracing God's peace in every moment, every conversation, and every decision. Check yourself today, stop, take a breath, and ask Jesus to fill you, new and fresh, with His divine peace. It will make a difference for you will start becoming more thankful!

YOUR THOUGHTS:

DAY 3

FIX YOUR EYES ON JESUS

"I have set the Lord always before me. Because he is at my right hand, I will not be shaken. Therefore my heart is glad and my tongue rejoices; my body also will rest secure,"

Psalm 16:8-9

"If you're missing joy and peace, you're not trusting God."   Joyce Meyer

PRAY: Lord, please help me to keep my eyes on You. Don't let me be shaken, but please fill my heart with gladness and my tongue with praise. I want my whole body to be at peace, loving You, trusting You, and being used by You to bring peace to others. Thank you for showing me that in trusting You, my heart will be glad, my tongue will rejoice, my body will rest secure, and I will experience peace! Amen.

REFLECT: Think about how often you feel gladness and praise. And have you ever felt your whole body at peace? What do you need to do to feel His peace more often? It says in Psalm 16 that we have to set the Lord always before us in order to "rest secure." What do you need to do to have the Lord always before, understanding that He is always at your right hand. Wouldn't it be amazing to be so secure, and find so much peace from the Lord's presence that you will not be shaken? That will make your heart glad.

ACT: Write down three things that you may need to change to feel more gladness and praise and peace in your life. It may be an attitude change, it may be spending more time with the Lord, or choosing not to complain...whatever it is, take steps right now to experience more of God's peace, gladness, and praise on a daily basis. Only then will your body rest secure.

YOUR THOUGHTS:

DAY 4

TAKE EVERY THOUGHT CAPTIVE

"You will keep in perfect peace those whose minds are steadfast, because they trust in you."   Isaiah 26:3

"Peace does not dwell in outward things, but within the soul; we may preserve it in the midst of the bitterest pain, if our will remains firm and submissive. Peace in this life springs from acquiescence to, not in an exemption from, suffering."   Francois Fenelon

PRAY: Lord, please show me how to stay in perfect peace with You. I need Your help to trust You more and to have my mind be steadfast. I also ask that You show me how to put my trust in You. I need perfect peace when thinking about the people in Hollywood. Most of them don't know You, and I want them to experience Your perfect peace as well. Would You stretch my heart and theirs to fall more in love with You, to trust in You and to live in peace? In Jesus' name, Amen.

REFLECT: Reflect on what it would be like to have a steadfast mind and to live in absolute perfect peace. What areas of worry do you have to let go of? What fears do you need to breakthrough? And what would it take to have perfect peace about the people creating and performing in the entertainment industry? Can you trust God to lead them to Him? Can you embrace the concept of praying for the people, the projects, and the issues of the Hollywood Entertainment Industry, and consider it the world's most influential mission field? Would you ask the Lord to help you do that?

ACT: Make TWO lists: One lists the things that you need to let go of and give to the Lord, so that you can live in more perfect peace. The other is to list the people in Hollywood whom you don't believe can become Christians. You have to trust Him for that. Would you ask the Lord to take care of both of your lists and check-in each week to see how He and you are doing?

YOUR **THOUGHTS:**

DAY 5

PEACE GUARDS YOUR HEART AND MIND

"And the peace of God, which transcends all understanding, will guard your hearts and your minds in Christ Jesus."   Philippians 4:7

"Blessed are the single-hearted, for they shall enjoy much peace... If you refuse to be hurried and pressed, if you stay your soul on God, nothing can keep you from that clearness of spirit, which is life and peace. In that stillness you know what His will is."
                                                            Amy Carmichael

PRAY: Dear Lord, I thank You that You are the God of peace! I believe that Your peace surpasses ALL understanding, and I ask that You show me how it is guarding my heart and my mind, because of my love for Christ Jesus. I want both my heart and my mind to be transformed by Your peace, and to gain all understanding in my life. Lord, would you guard my heart and my mind in Christ Jesus because of this promise from You. Thank you for Your faithfulness. Amen.

REFLECT: Think about what the PEACE OF GOD really means to you. Do you experience it daily? And is God's peace guarding your heart and your mind – in Christ Jesus? It's transformative to be enveloped in God's supernatural peace. It surpasses all of our understanding. Think about what that means and how it only works through your belief in, and love for, Jesus.

ACT: Ask God every day, for ONE WEEK, to guard your heart, and your mind, with peace. Ask Him to show you how you can be more peaceful as you seek Jesus and expect to experience His answer. You will see that His peace will transcend all understanding and will bring you closer to Jesus!

YOUR THOUGHTS:

DAY 6

PEACE IN GOD'S PRESENCE

"For God is not a God of disorder but of peace."   1 Corinthians 14:33

"In the secret of God's tabernacle no enemy can find us, and no troubles can reach us. The pride of man and the strife of tongues find no entrance into the pavilion of God. The secret of his presence is a more secure refuge than a thousand Gibraltars. I do not mean that no trials come. They may come in abundance, but they cannot penetrate into the sanctuary of the soul, and we may dwell in perfect peace even in the midst of life's fiercest storms."

Hannah Whitall Smith

PRAY: Oh, God, I know that You are not a God of disorder but of peace. May I see Your peace in Your people all around me, and especially may it shine in and through me. I want to be a living example of Your order, and of peace in the world around me. May it start in my heart, in my home, and in my personal relationships. Amen.

REFLECT: Where do you see disorder in your life? Is it in relationships, in the tidiness of your car, your home, or your office? Look honestly at anything or any place where you have created or have allowed disorder. The Lord can come into our hearts and minds and bring order to thoughts, actions, words and even beliefs, that can strengthen your relationship with Him and make your life cleaner and more peaceful. What's steps would you take to fully experience God's peace in your life?

ACT: Ask the Lord to clean up your heart, mind and soul, to bring peace, and to be more present in your thoughts, words, actions and beliefs. Ask Him to reveal to you anything that's out of place or disorderly in your life, and to replace it with His peace. As you ask Him, be aware that He will be subtly shifting things in your life in order to reach that peace that surpasses understanding. Don't miss it for He wants you to life in peace.

YOUR THOUGHTS:

Day 7

PROCLAIM PEACE

"How beautiful on the mountains are the feet of those who bring good news, who proclaim peace, who bring good tidings, who proclaim salvation, who say to Zion, 'Your God reigns'!"
                                                                        Isaiah 52:7

"You use your money to buy privacy because during most of your life you aren't allowed to be normal."
                                                                        Johnny Depp

PRAY: Dear Heavenly Father, help me to share my faith each day, either through a conversation, through serving others, or praying for someone. Help me to bring Your good news to the people around me. And help me to pray for people in my life so that they can come to know You as well. I want to be someone who proclaims peace and salvation and brings good tidings to the world. Help me to make an eternal difference by proclaiming peace, good tidings and salvation in this world because I believe that You reign! Amen.

REFLECT: Reflect on what it means to be someone who proclaims peace and brings good news. Be creative to include your attitude, your willingness to listen to others, to be a friend to a difficult person, to tell the truth to someone, to go out of your way to serve someone, to do a good deed. And most of all, to get out of your comfort zone! How often do you do that? How would it alter your life to do it more often? We should all bring good news and proclaim peace and good tidings. And that leads others to salvation.

ACT: Choose to go out of your way today to bring good news to someone, to proclaim peace, bring good tidings and offer salvation to the people in your life. Share your faith with someone today. Choose one person and do something divinely radical for him or her. Maybe they don't yet know that you are Christian, or you haven't served them, prayed for them, showed loved to them or proclaimed peace over them. Today is the day.

YOUR THOUGHTS:

PRIDE

WEEK FOUR

"Pride cometh before the fall." What a well-known quote that we have all used at one time or another to judge prideful people. We're going to spend this week looking into pride and how we can be proud of our choices, proud of God, and proud of others, yet not prideful about our accomplishments, traits, etc. Let's celebrate that God is proud of us while changing our prideful thoughts...

DAY 1

DESTRUCTIVE PRIDE

"Pride goes before destruction, a haughty spirit before a fall."   Proverbs 16:18

"For those who exalt themselves will be humbled, and those who humble themselves will be exalted."
                                                                    Matthew 23:12

"Pride, the first peer and president of hell."
                                                                    Daniel Defoe

PRAY: Dear God, I don't want to be prideful. You say pride goes before destruction and a haughty spirit comes before a fall, so help me to humble myself before You and others. And if I am exalted may it be because You lifted me up. I don't want to lift myself up, before You or other people. Please give me a humble heart, God, and help me to keep my eyes on You every day. I pray this in Jesus' name, Amen.

REFLECT: As the Church, we have certain sins that we think are better or worse than others. We can almost make a list of sins, from "not so bad" to "horrible". And then we judge others based on which sins of theirs are the "bad" or "worse" ones. And we tend to ignore the "not so bad" sins in ourselves and in others. But do we ever look at, respond to, or try to change the sin of "pride" in ourselves? God tells us pride leads us to destruction and yet aren't we prideful when we judge others, when we talk against others or decide that their sins are worse than ours? The world could be a completely different place if we just eradicated the sin of pride in our hearts. Ponder that thought. How does that start with you?

ACT: When was the last time you talked against someone, or you judged someone's words or actions? When did you last feel superior to someone else because they dressed inappropriately, acted poorly, had messy hair, or used bad language? Think of each occasion and then, without condemnation, notice your pride in that situation. Could it be that if you try to check your pride, you'll end up not pointing a finger at other people? How many examples of that have you thought of right now? How can you respond to others with more humility? Make that a priority this week as you study pride. That's the hardest sin to see in ourselves!

YOUR THOUGHTS:

DAY 2

PRIDE SEPARATES US FROM GOD

"In his pride the wicked does not seek him; in all his thoughts there is no room for God."
Psalm 10:4

"Who is it you have insulted and blasphemed? Against whom have you raised your voice and lifted your eyes in pride? Against the Holy One of Israel!"   Isaiah 37:23

"Pride is an independent, me-oriented spirit. It makes people arrogant, rude and hard to get along with. When our heart is prideful, we don't give God the credit and we mistreat people, looking down on them and thinking we deserve what we have."   Joyce Meyer

PRAY: Father in Heaven, I can't imagine ever turning from You, or blaspheming You. But You say our pride can get us to turn from You. Who is it that I have insulted or blasphemed? Against whom have I raised my voice or lifted my eyes in pride? Lord, have I ever turned against You, because of pride? Please help me to always keep my eyes on You and never get too prideful. I need you and Your Holy Spirit to keep my heart pure. Father, keep me humble every moment of every day. Thank You for helping me walk humbly in Your sight. Amen.

REFLECT: Most Christians say that we would never turn from God. We can't imagine ever committing the most horrible sin, of blaspheming God or the Holy Spirit. But we must do it or the Lord wouldn't be warning us about it. What subtle things could you be doing in your own pride that would get you to turn from God, or worse yet, blaspheme Him. It sounds impossible but reflect on these verses and consider how the enemy makes you prideful, and keep your eyes away from God. All of us are just one choice away from being prideful.

ACT: Seek God and ask Him to show you if, or how, pride is in the way of getting closer to Him, or of loving other people. Ask Him if there is any area of your life where pride is causing you are turn from Him, or worse yet, blaspheme Him. Take 10 minutes to lay out all of your thoughts and concerns, and ask God to humble you and reveal where your pride has become a barrier between you and Him. We can't see our own pride, only the Holy Spirit can. Take time to seek Him and ask Him to show you how to make more room for Him.

YOUR THOUGHTS:

DAY 3

DON'T LET WEALTH MAKE YOU PROUD

"By your great skill in trading you have increased your wealth, and because of your wealth your heart has grown proud....Your heart became proud on account of your beauty, and you corrupted your wisdom because of your splendor..."   Ezekiel 28:5,17

"In the midst of a world of light and love, of song and feast and dance, Lucifer could find nothing to think of more interesting than his own prestige."   C.S. Lewis

PRAY: Dear Lord, help me not to get so much wealth, fame, beauty, success, or status that it becomes more important than You. Let me stay humble with all that You've given me and never think that I achieved it myself. I don't want my pursuit of splendor to corrupt my wisdom. Let me be wise and know that anything good I have is because of You and Your splendor. Keep my human pride humbled and may only You be exalted in my life. Thank You for all I have, and may I always know that everything I have comes from You! Amen.

REFLECT: Reflect on the fact that nothing we do, who we are, or what we think or say is because we're smart, clever, funny, or wise on our own. All of the good in us comes from the Lord. He created us, He gives us our gifts, talents, and character traits. He had a plan from when we were in our mother's womb. So, as we work hard, make money, and gain success, we must never forget that it's a gift from God and it's all His. We are the stewards of what He gives us, from material things to intelligence, to humor, and joy, and we have to stay humble "for the Lord alone, is to be exalted." (Isaiah 2:17)

ACT: Make a list of your successes, your accomplishments, joys, attributes, and even great qualities. Then pray through that list and thank the Lord for each one, giving Him the glory, appreciating that He alone has given you everything; your abilities, achievements and intelligence. Ask Him to take away any pride that would allow you to take credit for what you have, do, say, or accomplish, and praise Him for everything in your life that He has graciously given you. Keep that list and occasionally review it, with thanks and praise!

YOUR THOUGHTS:

DAY 4

DON'T LET THE PROUD OPPRESS YOU

"My adversaries pursue me all day long; in their pride many are attacking me."
Psalm 56:2

"Better to be lowly in spirit and among the oppressed than to share plunder with the proud."
Proverbs 16:19

"None are more unjust in their judgments of others than those who have a high opinion of themselves."
Charles Spurgeon

PRAY: God, I need You. I feel attacked, for my adversaries are pursuing me and in their pride, they are attacking me. It's so hard to respond to people who treat others terribly or who take credit for things they haven't done. Help me to remember that it's better to be lowly in spirit, and oppressed, rather than to share the plunder with the proud. I don't want to be jealous of evil, prideful people. Let me choose to be righteous, even though others treat me unfairly. Give me strength to find joy in my lowly position and thank You for lifting me up and blessing me. Amen.

REFLECT: It's difficult to accept being treated unfairly or being the victim of injustice. We all want justice, and we want the unjust to be punished for their sins. So how do we handle prideful people gain success, money, and status through their wicked ways, while we are pushed aside as we live with integrity, honesty, and humility? In our hearts, we know that the Lord does not let anyone ultimately get away with wrongdoing and abusive behavior. In what situations have you felt wrongly treated by prideful people? How did you respond?

ACT: Write down these verses and then pray through them so that you can completely embrace the humility it takes to live them out. Ask the Lord to let your heart believe that as your adversaries pursue you, it is better to be lowly in spirit, along with the oppressed, than to share in the plunder with the proud. Memorize these until they're in your heart and will never leave you. You will become more Christ-like as you ponder this truth in your heart.

YOUR THOUGHTS:

DAY 5

APPROPRIATE PRIDE

"Each one should test their own actions. Then they can take pride in themselves alone, without comparing themselves to someone else,"   Galatians 6:4

"That's what Rocky is all about: pride, reputation, and not being another bum in the neighborhood."
                                                          Sylvester Stallone

PRAY: Dear Lord, would You help me to keep my eyes on my own heart, my own work, and my own progress. Help me not compare myself to other people or to the celebrities I look up to in Hollywood. Paul tells me that I should test my own actions so that I can be proud of my accomplishments – what You've done in and through me. But I need You to help me to not compare my works with others. Lord, I understand that it is OK to actually take pride in who You've made me to be. When I talk against Hollywood, I'm being prideful in judging them because I'm comparing their sinful ways to my righteous way, and that's wrong. Let me not judge with pride those I'm praying for. In Jesus name, Amen.

REFLECT: Reflect on the difference between being proud and taking personal pride in what we've accomplished or become. God wants us to be proud of our lives, knowing that He gets the glory. He wants us to celebrate what He's doing in us and through us. But when we become prideful in our own accomplishments then we are taking God out of the equation. We must try not to decide who is better or worse than we are, such as when we judge the creative decision-makers in Hollywood. We can be proud of being a follower of Jesus but not prideful that our way is right and their way is wrong. The bottom line is, we should test our own actions alone, and not compare our choices with "those immoral Hollywood celebrities," or anyone else.

ACT: Get a piece of paper and make two columns. On the top left side write PRIDEFUL OF: On the top right side write PROUD OF: Draw a line down the middle of the page and then start thinking of everything you have and all you've accomplished, or with whom you compare yourself. Be honest with yourself and write details of your life on one side or the other. What do you give yourself credit for achieving or becoming and what do you give God credit for doing in your life? Look at the columns and ask the Lord to show you how He feels about your list. This is how you can test your own actions and reveal your own pride.

YOUR THOUGHTS:

DAY 6

DON'T TAKE PRIDE IN WHAT YOU SEE

"We are not trying to commend ourselves to you again, but are giving you an opportunity to take pride in us, so that you can answer those who take pride in what is seen rather than in what is in the heart."   2 Corinthians 5:12

"If you are humble nothing will touch you, neither praise nor disgrace, because you know what you are."   Mother Teresa

PRAY: Jesus, I want You and Your followers to be proud of me because of what I see in people's hearts, not by being impressed by what people do, say, or appear to be. I don't want to praise myself or other people, as if I or they are better than You. I want to live a life of integrity, wisdom, and Christlikeness so that I can answer those who take pride in what is seen rather than in what is in the heart. Thank you for teaching me how to be wise, not full of pride, and how to live a Christ-like life. Amen.

REFLECT: Paul is trying to teach the people in Corinth that he wants to be an example to them of someone who cares about what's in their hearts, not how they appear to be on the outside. And he wants us to do the same thing. Do you try to become friends with the cool people and be seen with the "in" crowd? Or are you trying to choose friends who live Christ-like lives and to pursue people of strong moral integrity? Does human pride lead you to the most successful or the wealthiest people in your company, school, or church group? We have to understand the subtlety of pride and commend ourselves to people of truth, goodness, honesty, purity, kindness, and love. What kind of people do you hang around?

ACT: Think of your best friends at work, in your neighborhood, at school, or in your community. Are they the cool people, the wealthiest and most prestigious, or, regardless of their status, are they the most Christ-like people of integrity? Are you friends with people who accept you for exactly who you are, yet encourage you to grow? Evaluate your friends and business acquaintances and see if you choose them out of pride, or out of a hunger to be around people who will make you a better person. Then decide if you're on track with what Paul is saying and check your own pride.

YOUR THOUGHTS:

DAY 7

GOD IS PROUD OF YOU

"I have spoken to you with great frankness; I take great pride in you. I am greatly encouraged; in all our troubles my joy knows no bounds."   2 Corinthians 7:4

"At the end of the day, everything is God's plan, and he cares about what we do. He cares about our hearts, how we play the game, and how we treat people. He's definitely involved with how we handle sports and not just the outcome of it. I'm proud when athletes mention God in any way."

Tim Tebow

PRAY: Dear Lord, just as Paul loved the Corinthians and was proud of them, I want You to be proud of me and my family! I want You to be greatly encouraged by me and that my life can be proof of Your love for me. Help me to be a good Ambassador and in all my troubles let my joy know no bounds, so that people can see You in me. Thank You for Your frank words. I love You, Lord. Amen and Amen

REFLECT: We all want to hear the words, "I'm proud of you!" That fills up our hearts and our souls. Paul was very generous with his words of praise to the people he wanted to encourage. In fact, he told the Corinthians that it didn't even matter what he has suffered, his pride in them superseded anything that he had to go through to see them grow in their relationship with Jesus. Can people say that about you? Are you living a life that makes other people proud? If not, what can you do to change your reputation? Are you living a life that not only Jesus and Paul would be proud of, but also everyone around you would be proud of?

ACT: What are qualities in others that make you proud of them? Who are the people in your life whom you take great pride in? Right now, choose someone whom you're proud of. Tell them that you're proud of them and why. Tell him or her that you are greatly encouraged by them. Even in your troubles your joy will know no bounds if you focus on all of your friends, family members, and co-workers who you're proud of! What a beautiful way to end your week. And make sure God is proud of you!

YOUR THOUGHTS:

SIMPLICITY

WEEK FIVE

Oh, how complicated and stressful our lives can be! Yet God tells us He wants us to live simpler, more peaceful lives. He MAKES us lie down in green pastures, which shows we're not very good at it on our own. Let's spend this week seeking simplicity in our lives and be free of the things that are weighing us down. He's offering us a simple life. Let's accept it!

DAY 1

GOD'S SIMPLICITY AND GRACE

"For our boast is this, the testimony of our conscience, that we behaved in the world with simplicity and godly sincerity, not by earthly wisdom but by the grace of God, and supremely so toward you."   2 Corinthians 1:12 **(ESV)**

"Jesus invites us to a life of joyous trust – a way of living in which everything we have we receive as a gift, and everything we have is cared for by God, and everything we have is available to others when it is right and good. This reality frames the heart of Christian Simplicity. It is the means of liberation and power to do what is right and to overcome the forces of fear and avarice."   Richard Foster

PRAY: Dear Father, I want to live a simple yet profound life, and I ask for You to teach me how. May You give me simplicity and godly sincerity. I don't want to follow earthly wisdom, but to be wise through Your grace. I know that if I can just rely on Your grace, then I will trust You and not complicate my life with trying to do all that the world tells me I need to do to be smart, successful, beautiful, and wealthy. I want my testimony to be simply that I completely trust in You. Amen and Amen

REFLECT: How do we live a life of simplicity? Could it be to separate which of our Christian beliefs are cultural and which are truly biblical? The Lord doesn't want us to live by earthly wisdom, but to rely on His grace! Begin by seeking Him, learning more about His ways, and stripping away anything in our life that is not simple and sincere. Let's spend this week doing just that as we embrace God's grace and wisdom.

ACT: Start this week in prayer – ask the Lord to reveal to you the difference between earthly wisdom and Godly wisdom. Ask Him to fill you with His grace and to strip away anything that is complicating your life unnecessarily. Start writing down what you think God is telling you and be willing to let go of any beliefs, actions, activities, habits, or words that are not full of grace. This could be the start of developing a simple, child-like faith that frees you up to become less stressed and more like Christ! Commit yourself simply to prayer.

YOUR THOUGHTS:

DAY 2

DO JUSTICE, LOVE KINDNESS, AND WALK HUMBLY

"He has told you, O man, what is good; and what does the Lord require of you but to do justice, and to love kindness, and to walk humbly with your God." Micah 6:8 (ESV)

"The point of simplicity is not efficiency, increased productivity or even living a healthier, more relaxed life. The point is making space for treasuring God's own self." Jan Johnson

PRAY: Lord, Thank You for showing me the basics of what You require of me and what is good in Your eyes. You say that I should do justice, love kindness, and walk humbly with You. That seems too simple, and yet I ask that You show me how. I need You so that I don't over-complicate my life with a long list of rules, laws, obligations, and responsibilities. Help me to simply do what's right, find joy in loving others, and walk with You every moment of every day in joyful humility. It sounds beautiful and it's all You ask. I just need You to help me do it. Thank you, Lord! Amen.

REFLECT: Reflect on these four concepts from today's verse: 1) God has told you what is good 2) The Lord requires you to do justice 3) He requires you to love kindness and 4) The Lord requires you to walk humbly with Him. How would your life change if you implemented these four truths into your daily activities and goals? What would you have to give up? Focus on? Re-think? This one verse is life-changing if we could live it out fully. How would it change you?

ACT: Today, choose to practice each of these concepts from Micah 6:8. You may need to write these down: First of all, find out what God means when He says to "do good." Then do one thing today that is "just"; Do or say something "kind" to someone; and then decide what needs to change for you to walk "humbly with Him". At the end of the day it might be fun to write down how your day was different because of practicing these commandments. Notice whether you feel more peaceful and satisfied, even if this is the only thing you accomplish today. By following the few things that God "requires" of you, your life will not only be simpler, but you will be living by godly wisdom, not earthly wisdom.

YOUR THOUGHTS:

DAY 3

BE SATISFIED WITH YOUR DAILY BREAD

"Keep falsehood and lies far from me; give me neither poverty nor riches, but give me only my daily bread."
                                                                    Proverbs 30:8

"People who pride themselves on their "complexity" and deride others for being "simplistic" should realize that the truth is often not very complicated. What gets complex is evading the truth."
                                                                    Thomas Sowell

PRAY: God, in my quest for simplicity this week, I want to keep falsehood and lies far from me. I know that keeping up with lies is not only complicated, but stressful and exhausting. Also, please give me neither poverty nor riches for I don't want too little, which is scary and stressful, but I don't want too much, for that is also stressful and will make my life much more complicated. God, please just give me only my daily bread and keep me honest, for I know this is all I need to live a simple life. Amen.

REFLECT: Have you ever thought about how much more complicated life is for people who lie, especially to get rich? They have to keep up with the lies to stay consistent, and remember past lies so as not to get caught, and who they said what to, so as not to be exposed. It's exhausting, it's scary, and it can lead to not only embarrassing but also legal consequences. Our lives are always so much simpler when we follow God's ways and keep falsehoods, lies, and greed far from us!

ACT: What is the last lie that you told? Did it have to do with getting more money? Who did you tell it to? How can you stop that lie right now so that you don't have to keep perpetuating it in the future and so that you don't have to remember what you said and to whom you said it? Would it need an apology to end it? What can you do right now to simplify your life, end that lie and greed and never say another lie again?

YOUR THOUGHTS:

Day 4

I LACK NOTHING

"The Lord is my shepherd, I lack nothing. He makes me lie down in green pastures, he leads me beside quiet waters, he refreshes my soul."   Psalm 23:1-3

"Jesus invites us to a life of joyous trust – a way of living in which everything we have we receive as a gift, and everything we have is cared for by God, and everything we have is available to others when it is right and good."   Richard Foster

PRAY: Dear Lord, my shepherd, I thank you that because of You, and loving You, I lack NOTHING. Thank You that You make me lie down in green pastures because You want me to rest; You lead me beside quiet waters because you want me to slow down, enjoy the beauty around me, and simplify my life. Thank You that You refresh my soul, therefore I don't need to strive for peace, calm, and joy. Lord, I want to live a simpler life and I know I can only do that by depending on You, trusting You, and turning to You in times of need. I love You. In Jesus' name, Amen.

REFLECT: When you get overwhelmed, stressed, and feel that you'll never catch up, have you ever thought to read through Psalm 23 and just meditate on God's promises? He wants us to be peaceful and not complicate our lives with deadlines, huge projects, events, meetings, etc. He wants us to love Him, love others, and enjoy the world around us that He has given to us as a gift. He wants us to live an abundant life, not a busy life. Have you ever heard the quote: "If the devil can't make you bad, he'll make you busy!" That's something to think about......

ACT: How can you make your life simpler? What are you doing that might be good, but it's not BEST for you in this season of life? What are you doing just because it's an obligation or you feel guilty if you don't do it? Are you spending time with anyone who might not be healthy for you? Lie down in a "green pasture" or "beside quiet waters" right now and evaluate how you spend your time. What can you eliminate in order to live a simpler life with more space for God. Cut out busyness and let the Lord refresh your soul.

YOUR THOUGHTS:

DAY 5

CALM AND QUIET MY SOUL

*"My heart is not proud, L*ORD*, my eyes are not haughty; I do not concern myself with great matters or things too wonderful for me. But I have calmed and quieted myself, I am like a weaned child with its mother; like a weaned child I am content."*   Psalm 131: 1-2

"While the impostor draws his identity from past achievements and the adulation of others, the true self claims identity in its belovedness. We encounter God in the ordinariness of life: not in the search for spiritual highs and extraordinary, mystical experiences but in our simple presence in life."   Brennan Manning

PRAY: O Lord, I come to you to get more balance in my crazy life. I need to calm and quiet my soul, like a weaned child with its mother. I need to know I'm OK as I am and that I don't have to concern myself with greatness. I don't want to occupy myself with things that are unreasonable, unattainable, and not a priority to You. So, please quiet me now and refocus me on only what You know is important and best for me. Thank You and Amen.

REFLECT: We know the famous verse, "With God, all things are possible." But Psalm 131 tells us not to confuse that with taking on too much, expecting unrealistic goals, and striving for accomplishments that are beyond what the Lord has in store for us. Where is your heart? Is it lifted up to the Lord or full of stress, busyness and striving? Are your eyes lifted up too high or are they focused right on Jesus? Ask yourself where you are with the Lord vs. your ambition, goals, and accomplishments. Do you need to simplify your life and quiet your soul?

ACT: Choose a trusted friend or mentor and set up a meeting to have them help you to evaluate your life. We're all too busy and often with things that appear urgent but ultimately aren't important. Sit down with this respected person and talk through your life. How can you improve the balance between your goals, time, relationships, and accomplishments, with your walk with the Lord, your spiritual growth, your time in scripture, and making sure your heart is lifted up to Him and your soul is peaceful and quiet. This will be an important meeting for you!

Y**OUR THOUGHTS:**

DAY 6

LEAD A QUIET LIFE

"Make it your ambition to lead a quiet life, to mind your own business and to work with your hands, just as we told you, so that your daily life may win the respect of outsiders and so that you will not be dependent on anybody."   1 Thessalonians 4:11-12

"It is not a daily increase, but a daily decrease. Hack away at the inessentials." Bruce Lee

PRAY: Father in Heaven, I ask that You not only make it my ambition to lead a quiet life, but that You help me to mind my own business when it comes to the people around me. I pray that you will keep my eyes focused on You and not on my neighbors or the celebrities I watch and talk about from TV, Films, and music. I ask that I live a life that will win the respect of outsiders and that I won't get my identity from others' comments or from comparing myself to the beautiful people in Hollywood. Help me to be content with who You've made me to be and not idolize anyone else whom I think has more. Thank You for creating me to find peace and simplicity in You alone. Amen.

REFLECT: We often complicate our lives by watching people in the news or media who are bigger than life and appear to have more money, more fame, more beauty and more fun than we do. But it's all an image. People are never what they appear to be, and the glitz and glamour of Hollywood seems wonderful, but it's often an empty shell covering up very lonely, sad, confused people. So, catch yourself when watching others and figure out how to make it your ambition to lead a quiet, simple life and to fulfill all that the Lord has planned for you, without comparing yourself with someone else. That will win us the respect from outsiders as we walk each day with Jesus.

ACT: Pray right now for the celebrities you follow in the news or on the screen and ask the Lord to help them fall more love with Jesus. Pray that they make it their ambition to lead a quiet peaceful life, amidst the horrible pressures and invasion of their privacy that they deal with as rich or famous people. They need our prayers to handle this unnatural situation that makes their lives horribly complicated and public. Our prayers for them, as we work toward the same goal, can be life-changing for someone you admire but don't even know.

YOUR THOUGHTS:

DAY 7

LIVE SIMPLY AND BE CONTENT

"But godliness with contentment is great gain. For we brought nothing into the world, and we can take nothing out of it. But if we have food and clothing, we will be content with that."
1 Timothy 6:6-8

"My God will supply every need of yours according to his riches in glory in Christ Jesus."
Philippians 4:19 (ESV)

"See how nature – trees, flowers, grass – grows in silence; see the stars, the moon and the sun, how they move in silence..."
Mother Teresa

PRAY: Dear God, for the last day of this week, I pray for simplicity in my life. I ask for godliness and contentment, for You say that is great gain! It's true that I brought nothing into this world, and I will take nothing out of it. So, I want to be deeply grateful for the food and clothing You supply and be content with that. You promise me that You will supply every need of mine, according to Your riches in glory in Jesus Christ, so I stand on that promise and will not complicate my life with worry, busyness, or a lack of contentment. I have so much, and I thank You for supplying it for me. I pray this in Jesus' name, Amen

REFLECT: Reflect on godliness and contentment versus busyness and striving. God doesn't want us to be unproductive. He wants us to accomplish things, to work hard, and to do what He has put on our hearts to do. But He also doesn't want us to be discontent with the life that He's given us or striving for more, for better, bigger, and greater things. How do we find that balance? A simple life doesn't mean an unproductive life. It means trusting God to accomplish through us what He wants us to do, and waiting on Him for His perfect timing.

ACT: Define three clear goals that you believe the Lord has put on your heart to accomplish. Then give each one to the Lord, relinquish control over those and ask Him to lead you every day to do what He wants you to do to accomplish them. Continue to trust Him for direction, answers, and open doors. Turn over your fears to Him, knowing that your only job is to fulfill His will for you. "Rejoice always, pray constantly, and give thanks in all things!" The rest is up to Him. Congrats! You have now just begun to live a life of simplicity.

YOUR THOUGHTS:

JEALOUSY/ENVY

WEEK SIX

How many times a week do you feel jealous? Either a quick thought about your neighbor's cool car, the raise your co-worker got, or wanting a loving spouse like all of your friends have... Whatever it is, it's a struggle that can lead to sin. This week let's delve into the meanings of jealousy and plan our attack to beat it, embrace it, or use it for God's glory.

DAY 1

ENVY & JEALOUSY COME FROM THE HEART

He went on: "What comes out of a person is what defiles them. For it is from within, out of a person's heart, that evil thoughts come—sexual immorality, theft, murder, adultery, greed, malice, deceit, lewdness, envy, slander, arrogance and folly. All these evils come from inside and defile a person."   Mark 7:20 – 23

"O, Jealousy, thou ugliest fiend of hell! thy deadly venom preys on my vitals, turns the healthful hue of my fresh cheek to haggard shallowness, and drinks my spirit up."
                                                                        Hannah More

PRAY: Dear Jesus, Your words warn me that my sins, including jealousy and envy, come straight out of my heart. Please, give me strength and courage, to keep going when I make mistakes or when my emotions get out of control. Lord, I realize that only with You can I resist sin. I need You desperately every moment, because I am weak on my own. But when I am weak, then You are strong in me. So, thank You for reminding me that I have a sinful heart, deep within, but, I also know You are always there for me. Amen.

REFLECT: In Mark, Jesus lists jealousy and envy with other horrible sins, like murder and adultery, that come out of our heart and defile us. Jesus' list of sins shows that any sin is bad and separates us from God. He just doesn't tell us which ones are less bad and which sins are worse. He lists them all and tells us they defile others and ourselves. That is very humbling. We need God desperately, for otherwise, our dark hearts will do terrible things. Jealousy and envy are hard to control but they don't seem so bad until they are listed with theft, sexual immorality, greed, murder and adultery. But with God, ALL things are possible.

ACT: Look inside your own heart right now and ask the Lord what He sees. Do you see any of these sins that Jesus lists in Mark 7? Are you jealous of anyone right now? Do you envy the co-worker who just got a promotion, or the friend who gets all the lucky breaks? Do you wish you had your neighbor's car? Look at your own jealously and envy by being honest with yourself and being willing to look deep into your heart. This is the moment to face your jealous thoughts and nip them in the bud.

YOUR THOUGHTS:

DAY 2

ENVY IS NOT FROM THE HOLY SPIRIT

"For where you have envy and selfish ambition, there you find disorder and every evil practice."   James 3:16

"A heart at peace gives life to the body, but envy rots the bones."   Proverbs 14:30

"If someone is leaving you behind, and you are becoming jealous and embittered, keep praying that he may have success in the very matter where he is awakening your envy; and whether he is helped or not, one thing is sure, that your own soul will be cleansed and ennobled."   William Law

PRAY: God, my heavenly Father, You tell us very clearly in the Bible that being envious is wrong in Your eyes. You then say that wherever we have envy there will be every other evil practice as well. And in Proverbs You say that envy will rot my bones. So, Lord, the only way I can have life is to clear my heart of jealousy and envy and cry out to You for mercy. I need to take Your words more seriously. God, thank You for Your clear warning. Amen.

REFLECT: Jealousy and envy are sinful acts of the flesh. We read yesterday that jealousy comes out of our hearts. So, if a peaceful heart gives life to our body, we have to extract every form of jealousy and envy from it. We should want to live victoriously with peaceful hearts. We don't want selfish ambition or rotting bones, disorder and every evil practice. This reminds us that there are consequences to sin but there are rewards to righteousness. How would you choose to handle envy and selfish ambition?

ACT: Here's a discipline to break a habit every time you have jealous thoughts, before they ever turn into actions: The moment you feel envy towards a friend, co-worker, or even a stranger, choose instead to compliment that person. Celebrate his or her achievement or success by telling them how great it is. At first you will be merely choosing to act and speak in obedience. But if you keep doing it, you'll soon actually mean what you say and feel good about celebrating the other person, instead of thinking about yourself. Remember to turn every jealous thought into a kind word and your heart will begin to transform.

YOUR THOUGHTS:

DAY 3

BE CAREFUL NOT TO SLIP

"Surely God is good to Israel, to those who are pure in heart. But as for me, my feet had almost slipped; I had nearly lost my foothold. For I envied the arrogant when I saw the prosperity of the wicked."   Psalm 73:1-3

"You are still worldly. For since there is jealousy and quarreling among you, are you not worldly? Are you not acting like mere humans?"   1 Corinthians 3:3

"Envy blinds men and makes it impossible for them to think clearly."   Malcolm X

PRAY: God, You are so good to me, knowing that I'm going to mess up. Please be there to catch me when I slip. When I lose my emotional or spiritual foothold and start envying other people, I need Your help to pull me back. I don't want to be worldly. Please help me to avoid jealousy and quarreling so that I don't act like a mere human. I want to be Christ-like in all that I do, so that I stand out as a Christian who is heavenly minded. Help me Lord when I slip, and forgive me when I notice the prosperity of the wicked. Amen.

REFLECT: These Old and New Testaments verses show us that we struggle today with the same temptations that the Israelites did thousands of years ago. We need to understand the power of sin instead of being shocked by it. We will be jealous. We will covet what others have, and we will envy those who are smarter, more beautiful or more successful **than** we are. The issue is how to handle it? That's where prayer, planning, and purpose are important. Christians have to live on the offense, prepared for any sin or temptation that slips us up, and know exactly what to do about it when, not if, it happens. Do you have a plan?

ACT: It's time to make a plan! Sin is coming. What will you do about it? First, you must pray. Ask the Lord to prepare you for what's to come and to give you wise steps to avoid falling into temptation. Next, be prepared for how jealousy and envy sneak up on you. If you envy someone, hold your tongue and turn that negative thought into a smile, a compliment, a celebratory remark, or even a hug. Remember your purpose: You are a Christ follower who wants to please Him by loving other people and putting God and others first!

YOUR THOUGHTS:

DAY 4

THE RIGHTEOUS JEALOUSY OF GOD

"Do not worship any other god, for the Lord, whose name is Jealous, is a jealous God."
Exodus 34:14

Jealousy is a "feeling or showing envy of someone or their achievements and advantages."
or "Of God demanding faithfulness and exclusive worship."   Oxford English Dictionary

PRAY: Lord, I want to fully understand more about jealousy by learning how You're a jealous God. According to these scriptures, You love me so much that You get jealous when I spend more time, effort, and emotion on other things or people, and You want me to worship You alone. Help me to keep my eyes on You, to spend more time with You, to study the Bible more, memorize Your Word and obey You. Help me to love You more so that You don't have to fight for my attention or time. Thank You for loving me SO MUCH. Amen.

REFLECT: By definition, the word Jealous can be used in different contexts to be either a negative or a positive emotion. We need to learn the full meaning in order to better understand God. Here, God is demanding that we are completely faithful to Him and that we worship Him exclusively. He gets jealous when we worship other gods, or have other priorities that take us away from Him. That's actually amazing how much He loves us, but jarring enough to re-evaluate our time, our focus, and our priorities, making sure He really is first in our lives. What do you need to do to satisfy a jealous God?

ACT: It's time for self-evaluation: How much of your time and your heart are spent on the things of this world so that you're not fully committed to God? How can you satisfy a jealous God? Do you worship Him alone? God is a gentleman and will never demand that you put Him first, but He longs after us and rewards us for our faithfulness in ways that the world can never do. What is one thing you would change to please your God? Tell Him what that is so He knows your intentions and can help you focus more on Him. The world will never satisfy you, but your jealous God is waiting patiently for you with open arms and a loving heart. Tell Him one thing you're going to change right now. He is zealous for you!

YOUR **THOUGHTS:**

DAY 5

GET RID OF ENVY AND JEALOUSY

"Anger is cruel and fury overwhelming, but who can stand before jealousy?"

Proverbs 27:4

"Therefore, rid yourselves of all malice and all deceit, hypocrisy, envy, and slander of every kind."

1 Peter 2:1

"Our envy of others devours us most of all."   Alexander Solzhenitsyn

PRAY: Lord, these verses help me to understand the severity of being jealous and to see the difference between feeling jealous and acting out on those feelings. Help me see that jealousy is worse than cruel anger and overwhelming fury. Lord, would You expose my jealousy and envy and help me to control my jealous feelings, so that I don't act out in sin. If I feel any jealousy, malice, deceit, or envy then have Your Holy Spirit respond through me with patience, wisdom, and discernment. I pray this in Jesus' name, Amen.

REFLECT: Ponder the difference between having a jealous thought and acting upon that thought. God says that He's jealous when we worship other things instead of Him. A jealous thought is not the sin, but the sin is in how we respond to that thought. We must immediately bring it to the Lord and ask Him for understanding and perspective. Watch the Lord take that negative emotion and turn it into good. The danger comes when our jealousy becomes selfish and sinful, worse than cruel anger and overwhelming fury! It leads us to all kinds of other awful sins and ends up destroying us. So, God's response is to rid ourselves of these things. If we can't divinely discern and control our thoughts, then we can't get rid of them!

ACT: Here are three possible steps to get control over jealousy and envy: 1. We have to die to ourselves and live only for Christ; 2. We need to pray for the Lord and seek His face to help us overcome these powerful temptations: and 3. We need strong, mature Christians around us to advise, support and pray for us. Do you have these in place? If not, what do you need to do to make all three of these happen? Act pro-actively in order to avoid sin, for you won't avoid or overcome jealousy on your own. It sneaks in when you least expect it. But if you commit to these steps, you can experience freedom and joy.

YOUR THOUGHTS:

DAY 6

DO NOT COVET

"You shall not covet your neighbor's house. You shall not covet your neighbor's wife, or his male or female servant, his ox or donkey, or anything that belongs to your neighbor."

Exodus 20:17

"The worst part of success is trying to find someone who is happy for you." Bette Midler

PRAY: Father in Heaven, please help me to not covet what other people have, but be satisfied with what You've given me. You say not to covet our neighbor's house, wife, servants or property because we shouldn't compare our possessions or success with the people around us. Let me celebrate the people around me, or those I see on TV or in the movies, and be thankful for everything I have. Help me to keep my eyes only on You for You are all that matters. I thank You and pray this in Jesus' name, Amen.

REFLECT: When you compare your life to others, notice that your scope of comparison isn't very big. It's usually just with the people in your neighborhood, work, or whom you read about and watch on TV shows or in movies. We can easily find people around us who have more money, better relationships, more fame, or power. But if we had a heavenly perspective, we would also see the world's poverty, crime, brokenness and hopelessness. Our jealousy would suddenly be replaced by compassion, humility, and a desire to help! Watching the rich, famous, and beautiful people makes us compare their perfect image with our out of shape bodies and worn out clothes, because it's not God's full perspective. How will you stop coveting what other people have and get an eternal view your life?

ACT: Now is the time to stop being covetous, jealous, or envious of what someone else has. You can manage these emotions right now by watching less news and analyzing what you're watching on television or in the movie theatre. Start being honest about the impact media and entertainment is having on you. It's telling you how much you should weigh, what you should wear, who's cool, and what's important. Don't let it lead you to covetousness, jealousy, or envy. Be stronger than all of the worldly influences around you and seek out God's perspective, which is very different than what the world is telling you!

YOUR THOUGHTS:

DAY 7

GOD LOVES YOU MORE THAN YOU CAN IMAGINE

"Place me like a seal over your heart, like a seal on your arm; for love is as strong as death, its jealousy unyielding as the grave. It burns like blazing fire, like a mighty flame."

Song of Solomon 8:6

"God is jealous for your heart, not because he is petty or insecure, but because he loves you . . . He loves you too much to share you."

Kyle Idleman

PRAY: Dear Lord, I want to spend my last day of this week praising You for helping me with jealousy, envy, and covetousness. I can celebrate selfless, heavenly jealousy and not confuse it with worldly, selfish jealousy. Your love for me burns like blazing fire, like a mighty flame, and I can express that selfless love to others. I want Your mighty flame of love to motivate everything I am, do, and say. And I want to share that love with others so that they can experience Your jealousy, unyielding as the grave. Amen!

REFLECT: Wow – God's ways are the opposite of man's ways and that makes life so exciting. Our goal is to identify, understand and control our feelings of jealousy toward others and catch ourselves when we become covetous of things or people. We need, instead, to celebrate the power of God's jealous love for us and offer that to others. Our love for God should always be first, for then we can share His jealous love to the people in our lives. Have you experienced God's love burning like a blazing fire for you? Have you placed a seal on your heart to hold in His unconditional love? Let's get jealous for His love and not for the things of the world. It will lead us on an adventure that we never imagined possible...

ACT: Let's end your week on jealousy with two goals: 1) Identify, define, and then turn over to God any feelings of envy, covetousness, and jealousy, the moment it creeps up and leads to sin. 2) Embrace God's jealous love for you with such understanding and passion that it overflows to the people around you. Then, we will experience God's love to such a degree that it will be like a burning fire, and draw people to Him because of its power and light. Right now, ask the Lord to walk you through the steps to break old habits and embrace His love in ways you have never experienced before. Your life is about to change forever!

YOUR THOUGHTS:

LOVE
WEEK SEVEN

LOVE is the most beautiful word and emotion when it's used for good. GOD IS LOVE. We're all hungry for love. This week we'll look at God's promises and learn how to love people more, love God more, and be more Christ-like, because of God's amazing, unconditional, unending love for us.

DAY 1

HOW MUCH GOD LOVES US

"This is how God showed his love among us: He sent his one and only Son into the world that we might live through him."

1 John 4:9

"A new command I give you: Love one another. As I have loved you, so you must love one another."

Christ Jesus

PRAY: Dear Lord, I'm excited to spend a week focused on Your love for me, my love for You and my love for others. Please help me to learn more about the unconditional love that You offer us and please help me to love more selflessly. Thank You that You showed us Your love through sacrificing Your only Son, Jesus, and that I can live abundantly through Him. That's the greatest gift of all. I praise You, in Jesus' name, Amen.

REFLECT: Reflect on the overwhelming concept that God loves each and every one of us SO MUCH that He sacrificed His only Son for us. He let Jesus be abused, suffer, and die just to show us how much He loves us. And He loves His own Son so much that He then raised Him from the dead. And then, because Jesus was willing to die, we can live forever because of His resurrected life. It's such a wild and crazy concept that it's almost impossible to grasp, and yet it's true. What an awesome God we follow! And it's ALL about LOVE!

ACT: Tell someone today how much God loves them. Or tell someone about how amazing it is that you have eternal life just because God sent Jesus into this world and then let Him die on the cross for you. Tell them it's a crazy concept but you actually believe it. What a fun conversation that will be. Or just tell at least one person today that you love them because God first loved you! You can show others your love for them just like God continually shows each one of us His love for us!

YOUR THOUGHTS:

DAY 2

WE MUST LOVE OTHERS

"Do everything in love."   1 Corinthians 16:14

"This is my command: Love each other."   John 15:17

"Did I offer peace today? Did I bring a smile to someone's face? Did I say words of healing? Did I let go of my anger and resentment? Did I forgive? Did I love? These are the real questions."
                                                                       Henri Nouwen

PRAY: Father, I want to do EVERYTHING in love and I want to love other people. You have commanded it and I want to do it. But how do I love everyone around me? I need Your help to think loving thoughts, say loving words and act lovingly toward all of the people You have put in my life. Fill up my heart, new and fresh, with Your love. I look forward to how I can show Your love to someone else today. Amen and Amen.

REFLECT: Do everything in love. What does that really mean? It doesn't mean that we're door mats, that we let others abuse us or that we don't speak the truth, even if it's not pleasant. Loving others is hard and tough love is harder. In fact it often takes more effort, more wisdom, and more self-control to love other people than not caring at all. But God commanded it, so we have to do it. What would it take for you to be more actively loving to the people closest to you?

ACT: Choose a person close to you, who is very hard to love, and choose to do something loving for them. It might be serving them, listening to them or encouraging them. Or, it might be speaking the truth to them, in a loving but honest way. Ask God how you can love that person by doing or saying something that will help them, even if it's hard or uncomfortable for you.

YOUR THOUGHTS:

DAY 3

HOW TO LOVE GOD, OURSELVES, AND OTHERS, PART I

"Love is patient, love is kind. It does not envy, it does not boast, it is not proud."

1 Corinthians 13:4

"I realized that the deepest spiritual lessons are not learned by His letting us have our way in the end, but by His making us wait, bearing with us in love and patience until we are able to honestly pray what He taught His disciples to pray: Thy will be done."

Elisabeth Elliot

PRAY: Dear God, in order to truly love, the way You want me to, I have to change. Will You show me how to be more patient and kind, and how to not be envious of my friends who do more or have more than I do. And don't let me boast about the things I have or do. I don't want to be proud or impatient or mean. I need You to deal with my human emotions that stop me from being more loving and help me to be more like You. I love you. Amen.

REFLECT: It's so hard to love! But that's the whole point of us being here. God created us for one thing – to have loving relationships, with Him and with other people! That's it. But love requires more of us than we are capable of being, doing, or saying on our own. We can't possibly be patient, kind, or never be envious, boast, or be proud, without God. He has created us and the world so that we need Him desperately, and that's just where He wants us – needing Him, turning to Him, and depending on Him for all of our relationships. Are you ready to let Him change you?

ACT: Which is your greatest weakness: Patience, kindness, envy, boasting, or pride? Pick one, tell God you need Him desperately to help you change in that area, and then start planning how to tackle it. Your goal is to love more freely and you don't want any of these human weaknesses to get in your way. So, pray, pray, pray, with the goal of being a more loving person. It will be worth it!

YOUR THOUGHTS:

DAY 4

HOW TO LOVE GOD, OURSELVES, AND OTHERS, PART II

Love... "it does not dishonor others, it is not self-seeking, it is not easily angered, it keeps no record of wrongs."   1 Corinthians 13:5

"Love God and He will enable you to love others even when they disappoint you."

Francine Rivers

PRAY: Jesus, today's verse is tough. I need You to show me if I dishonor others, if I am self-seeking, easily angered, or if I keep records of others' wrongs. Reveal to me where I need to change and how to become a more loving person. I know I need You desperately and I'm seeing how hard it is to be more loving, but I thank You that You are there for me and You love me so much that You are excited to help me become more like You. Let's do this together! I pray in Your name, Amen.

REFLECT: How do we dishonor others? And how do we see if we're self-seeking? Do we justify our anger or keep mental records of who has hurt us or treated us badly? Let's ponder this verse and ask the Lord to pour His love into us so that our hearts are so filled up that we can't possibly say or do things to hurt others or puff ourselves up. Love is always the answer. Can you see it in this verse?

ACT: Today you get to honor somebody; do something selfLESS, hold your temper, or let go of anger or something negative about that person that you've been holding on to. Write down the name of the person you're going to honor so that you're not self-seeking, easily angered or keeping a record of wrongs. And be sure to reach out somehow by the end of the day. How are you going to accomplish this by the time you go to bed? Ready, set, GO!

YOUR THOUGHTS:

DAY 5

HOW TO LOVE GOD, OURSELVES, AND OTHERS, PART III

"Love does not delight in evil but rejoices with the truth."   1 Corinthians 13:6

"To love someone means to see him as God intended him."   Fyodor Dostoevsky

PRAY: Lord, would You help me to love other people and not think evil thoughts, say words that can hurt, or do anything harmful. Fill me with Your love, which rejoices with the truth. And help me to pray that same prayer for others who haven't yet experienced Your love. I want to pray for the celebrities in Hollywood today, who influence our children and our culture. May they find Your love so that they will live lives of truth and rejoice in that truth! I pray for them in Jesus' name, Amen.

REFLECT: Instead of getting angry at people who do evil, have you thought that they just don't know God's love. If they did, they would rejoice with the truth and not hurt others or themselves. That perspective will give you a compassion that can replace your anger or annoyance, and you can more easily understand them and pray for them. Reflect on the people in your world who do not delight in the truth, but delight in evil. Maybe they need to discover God's love so that they can rejoice with the truth. Some of the people in Hollywood delight in evil because they have never experienced God's love. But they are no different than anyone in the world. We should pray for them to find the love of Jesus.

ACT: Think of one person in Hollywood right now whom you don't like, you're angry at their choices, or you've judged their behavior. Now ask the Lord to come into their heart and fill them with His love so that they can repel evil. rejoice in the truth and become a new person..... You have just made an eternal difference in that person's life! And you may be the first person who has ever prayed for them. Do it again tomorrow!

YOUR THOUGHTS:

DAY 6

HOW TO LOVE GOD, OURSELVES, AND OTHERS, PART IV

"It always protects, always trusts, always hopes, always perseveres." 1 Corinthians 13:7

"What does love look like? It has the hands to help others. It has the feet to hasten to the poor and needy. It has eyes to see misery and want. It has the ears to hear the sighs and sorrows of men. That is what love looks like."
Augustine

PRAY: Abba Father, I feel Your protection, I know I can trust You, I have hope because of You and I persevere because I want to please You and I'm excited about heaven. But I need You to help me to protect others, to trust other people, to hope for someone who can't feel hope right now, and to persevere in hard relationships. I want to be more loving. I want to be more like You! Teach me how to love with Your unconditional love. Amen.

REFLECT: Have you noticed that the definitions of love in verse 7 are not usually what we think of when we're trying to be more loving? Read it again and ask God to show you how protecting and trusting someone, hoping for them, and persevering for them, is a way to show your love for them. Who do you protect? Who do you trust? Is there a person you have great hopes for? Do you have someone who helps you to persevere? Because this is exactly how God loves us, thinking about loving others this way takes love to a whole new level.

ACT: These expressions of love in verse 7 are the most intimate ways to show someone you love them. Choose a person close to you, maybe the same one as two days ago, and commit to telling them or showing them how you will protect them, and how you trust them. Then tell them what you are hoping for, for them. And then commit to persevere through a hard time, a difficult decision, or a broken relationship, with them. This is a deep commitment of love that will deepen and enrich your relationship.

YOUR THOUGHTS:

DAY 7

NOTHING CAN STOP LOVE

"For I am convinced that neither death nor life, neither angels nor demons, neither the present nor the future, nor any powers, neither height nor depth, nor anything else in all creation, will be able to separate us from the love of God that is in Christ Jesus our Lord."

Romans 8:38–39

"There is no pit so deep, that God's love is not deeper still."   Corrie Ten Boom

PRAY: Dear Lord, I am amazed how I have been stretched to love others through the devotions this week – especially through the 1 Corinthians verses. I realized that I need to show my love for others in all these ways because You do that for me. And I praise You and am humbled that NOTHING can separate me from Your love; nothing, nowhere, no how can separate me from Your love through Jesus. Nothing in all of creation will keep me from You. Oh Lord, I open my heart to You, new and fresh today, and run into Your unconditionally loving arms. Thank You that You love me no matter what I do, who I am, or what I say. You love me SO much that I can't even fully embrace it. I praise You, God! Amen!

REFLECT: Reflect on these truths:
- Not even death can stop God from loving you
- No spiritual beings can come between you and God
- Nothing you've done in the past or in the future can change God's love for you
- No mountain, ocean, forest, jail, or dungeon can keep Him from loving you
- Nothing in the entire universe can separate you from the love of God!

Can you believe that God loves you that much?

ACT: Proclaim God's love for you by reading all of I Corinthians 13 out loud to God, one line at a time. And thank Him for every truth in every sentence throughout the entire chapter. By the end, you will be more convinced that His love for you is real, powerful, and unending. Then memorize **Romans 8:38 – 39.** As you accept His love for you, you will have more love to give away to others. Enjoy this exercise and you will be ending this week a more loving, Christ-like person!

YOUR THOUGHTS:

CHARACTER & INTEGRITY

WEEK EIGHT

God wants us to place great value on our character. He wants us to be people of integrity, to be Christ-like, so that we can be good examples, strong Ambassadors of His, and people that others can trust. What is your moral compass? Let's look into what it takes to be a person of strong integrity and good character.

DAY 1

INTEGRITY GUIDES US

"The integrity of the upright guides them, but the unfaithful are destroyed by their duplicity."

Proverbs 11:3

"The road to becoming such a person – a child of light – involves abandoning everything to God: what others think of us, what others' harmful motives might be, fears about what others might do to us, hopes for getting ahead. We come to truly believe that God "knows what He's doing and He'll keep on doing it"

Jan Johnson

PRAY: Lord, I pray for the Christians who are creating films, TV shows, music, and video games, to stay strong in character and integrity. For You promise us that the integrity of the upright will guide us and our decisions. I ask that the people who create the world's media and entertainment will come to know You so that they won't be unfaithful, for their unfaithfulness will destroy both them and the audiences they are serving. Fill our creative leaders with Your character and integrity, in Jesus' name, Amen.

REFLECT: Reflect on what type of people you want our media, news and entertainment leaders to be. Since they produce all of the TV shows you watch, all the movies you go to and all the songs that you listen to, have you thought how their hearts guide their creativity? If they have dark hearts without a knowledge of the Lord or His hope, joy, and truth, what type of entertainment will they be creating? Did you ever consider that the content of our world's entertainment can only change if the hearts of the people creating it change.

ACT: Think of any entertainment industry decision-maker or cultural influencer you may know or watch, and pray specifically for them by name, asking the Lord to give them strength, wisdom, and to be a person of integrity and of strong character. Pray that they will not be duplicitous people as they impact the world with the media they create, produce, and distribute around the world. Ask the Holy Spirit to fill them with the integrity of Jesus.

YOUR THOUGHTS:

DAY 2

INTEGRITY PROTECTS US

"May integrity and uprightness protect me, because my hope, Lord, is in you."

Psalm 25:21

"The true measure of a man is how he treats someone who can do him absolutely no good."   Samuel Johnson

PRAY: Heavenly Father, please make me a person of integrity and uprightness, for I want You to protect me from evil. I don't want to compromise my integrity even though there are temptations every day that can get me off track and I want my uprightness to protect me. Let me be known for being a person of integrity. Lord, my hope is in You and You alone, so make me upright in all I do, say, and think. Amen.

REFLECT: How can we be protected by integrity and uprightness? Could it be that being filled with integrity puts a shield around us, protecting us from evil or even from the temptation to do evil? And how do we get there? It seems that having our hope in the Lord is the first step to becoming a person of integrity and uprightness. And Samuel Johnson's quote helps us remember to treat people well who can do absolutely nothing for us. That kind of integrity gives us some big thoughts to ponder.

ACT: With the goal of being a person of deep integrity, here are the steps to help you get there. You need to begin with hoping in Him, and then ask the Lord to fill you with integrity and uprightness in every choice you make, and in all that you do. The last step is to trust in His protection. These steps are moment-by-moment decisions that you can start implementing right now in order to reach the goal of pure, deep, beautiful, integrity and uprightness in all you do, say, and think. Because your hope is in the Lord!

YOUR THOUGHTS:

DAY 3

EVERYONE WILL GIVE AN ACCOUNT

"But I tell you that everyone will have to give account on the day of judgment for every empty word they have spoken."   Matthew 12:36

"The foundation stones for a balanced success are honesty, character, integrity, faith, love and loyalty."   Zig Ziglar

PRAY: Dear Father, don't let me speak any empty words. Guide my tongue and keep my heart pure so that I say what I mean and mean everything I say to others and to You. Don't let me give empty promises, empty flattery, or foolish advice. Let me build others up, praise You, and speak truth filled with grace. For on the day of judgment when I have to give an account, I don't want to have spoken any empty words. I pray this in Jesus' name, Amen.

REFLECT: Have you ever thought that every single one of us will be judged someday, not only on what we do but on what we say? How will you do on judgment day? Have you spoken empty words? Reflect on any time that you were careless with your words. Have you disappointed someone with something you said that wasn't fully true, or was insensitive, or unnecessary? How can you watch your words so that you don't waste them or use them unwisely? How can you catch yourself from saying empty words?

ACT: Choose to be a person of great character through the choice of your words. Right now, imagine that you are standing before the Lord, having to give an account for the words you've spoken. Is there anything you can recall that you need to acknowledge and ask forgiveness for saying? Go ahead and do that! Then know that you are forgiven, and your heart is again as white as snow, and you are starting again, this moment, with a clean slate.

YOUR THOUGHTS:

DAY 4

BE TRUSTWORTHY

"Whoever can be trusted with very little can also be trusted with much, and whoever is dishonest with very little will also be dishonest with much."   Luke 16:10

"It's very important that you have a good support system, no matter what you do in life. And just because one friend says jump, it doesn't mean you need to jump as well. Be careful of not being led in the wrong direction. And make sure you pick your friends wisely. You don't want to hang out with the wrong crowd."   Demi Lovato

PRAY: Holy Spirit, Thank you for making me aware of the importance of integrity in my life. I want to be known as a person of great character, one who can be trusted, even with very little things. Would You protect me from the temptation to be dishonest in both little things and big things. I need You to help me with every choice so that I become a completely trustworthy person. In Jesus' mighty name, Amen.

REFLECT: Do you know what your reputation is amongst your family, your friends, your co-workers and even your neighbors? Do people trust you with information, with their struggles, and with their lives? Do people come to you in confidence? What could you do to be more trustworthy, even in little, tiny thoughts and choices? Remember that being dishonest in even the smallest things will lead you to be dishonest with much.

ACT: Has someone confided in you recently? If so, what can you do right now to confirm to them that they can trust you completely? Maybe it's to pray for them, check in on them, or do something to help them in their situation. Take a step right now to give someone a reason to trust you more deeply. Start with being trusted with very little so that you can soon be trusted with much!

YOUR THOUGHTS:

DAY 5

THE VALUE OF NOBLE CHARACTER

"A wife of noble character who can find? She is worth far more than rubies."

Proverbs 31:10

"I don't care about money, I just want to be wonderful."

Marilyn Monroe

PRAY: Lord, I want to be a person of noble character, whether or not I am a wife, husband, child, or sibling. I want to be worth more than rubies because of my Christ-like character. I ask that You make me that kind of person. Thank You for all that You're doing in me and through me. And I pray for all the wives I know. May they all be women of noble character. And I pray for my mother as well. May she be worth far more than rubies in Your eyes. I pray this in the name of Jesus. Amen.

REFLECT: If you are a wife, do you consider yourself a woman of noble character? If you're a husband, do you consider your wife a woman of noble character? And how about your mother and your grandmother? Are there women in your life whom you feel are worth far more than even rubies, or diamonds or gold? It's wonderful to think about yourself or the people in your life that way. And what a gift to pray for the mothers we know to be women of noble character.

ACT: Pray for the women in your life right now, and for yourself if you are a wife, and ask the Lord to make you and them women of noble character. Pray for them to heal, to grow, and to transform into people of great integrity. Pray for their hearts to be pure and for them to be as beautiful on the inside as precious rubies. And wives, be sure to pray this for yourself as well. And know that when these women whom you are praying for get to heaven they will thank you!

YOUR **THOUGHTS:**

DAY 6

BAD COMPANY CORRUPTS CHARACTER AND INTEGRITY

"Do not be misled: "Bad company corrupts good character."   1 Corinthians 15:33

"The third-rate mind is only happy when it is thinking with the majority. The second-rate mind is only happy when it is thinking with the minority. The first-rate mind is only happy when it is thinking."   A.A. Milne

PRAY: Dear Jesus, stop me from being misled by the people I've chosen to be around. Would You reveal to me anyone who may be "bad company" for I don't want to open myself up to anything or anyone who could corrupt my character. I want to be a person of good and strong character so that You are proud of me, and if I am being influenced by anyone who is hindering that, I ask for You to show me who it is and what I need to do about it. Amen.

REFLECT: Wow, it's hard to start evaluating our friends and deciding which ones may be bad company. We're not supposed to judge others but opening ourselves up to negative influences is wrong as well. So, how do you decide if you need to clean house and step away from anyone who may be leading you astray, or encouraging you to compromise on your character and integrity? We can pray not to be misled and to be protected from people of bad character and ask God to reveal the truth to us. That's something to pray about!

ACT: Be honest with yourself right now and make a tough choice. Are you completely sure that the people closest to you make you a better person, or is there anyone you've let in to your inner circle who is a bad influence on you? It's time to determine your influences right now and know whom you could be allowing to mislead you. Do you need to separate yourself from any bad company? If so, this is the moment! If not, then praise God for all of the great people in your life!

YOUR THOUGHTS:

DAY 7

DON'T BECOME WEARY IN DOING GOOD

"Let us not become weary in doing good, for at the proper time we will reap a harvest if we do not give up."
Galatians 6:9

"Movies can and do have tremendous influence in shaping young lives in the realm of entertainment towards the ideals and objectives of normal adulthood."   Walt Disney

PRAY: Dear God, help me to not become weary in trying to do good and remind me that if I depend on You, that at the right time I will reap a harvest from my efforts. Help me to trust You for strength and never give up in my journey in life. I need Your Holy Spirit to fill me up with all I need each day, including energy, vigor and the commitment to never give up. Thank You and Amen.

REFLECT: We all want to live a life that has eternal significance. That's what it means to "reap a harvest". Are there things in your life you need to do that you know are divinely important, but you're weary in your pursuit of them? Are you discouraged, or are you just not getting enough sleep and you need a nap, or a deep rest and healing time with the Lord? What changes do you need to make to avoid becoming weary in doing good?

ACT: Is there anything you have given up on that you know you should be doing? Ask the Lord to reveal it to you so that you can get back up and start again. Ask Him to renew your strength and then commit now to keep forging ahead so that you will reap a harvest of eternally significant fruit from your labor. Never give up, never surrender!

YOUR THOUGHTS:

ANGER
WEEK NINE

This week we're focusing on an emotion that has swept our culture, and especially our roadways: ANGER! God tells us not to be angry, not to let the sun go down on our anger, and that anger turns us into "mockers" and fools. So, we want to be honest about our own anger, and ask the Lord to change us, heal us, and transform us into peacemakers and wise, calm followers of Jesus. Join us this week in letting go of our anger and embracing God's promise to find wisdom and peace in Him!

DAY 1

GET RID OF ANGER

"But now you must also rid yourselves of all such things as these: anger, rage, malice, slander, and filthy language from your lips."   Colossians 3:8

"Until the will and the affections are brought under the authority of Christ, we have not begun to understand, let alone to accept, His lordship."   Elisabeth Eliot

PRAY: Lord, I need You desperately each moment to keep me holy. Please help me get rid of any anger, any rage, malice, or slander. And please help me to hold my tongue when I'm about to use filthy language. Keep my heart pure so that the words from my lips will stay pure and help me to rid myself of all such things. Thank You for giving me strength in times of weakness so that I don't let anger, or any bad word, come out of my mouth. I'm depending on You to help me, Lord! Amen.

REFLECT: Reflect on the culture today and how accepted it is to swear, get angry, have road rage, or use slander against others. We are in an angry culture. How can you live differently than everyone around you? How can you raise your children to be Christ-like, not "cool." Our real home is heaven, and there will be no slander, malice, rage or anger there. So, can you start right now and keep your lips pure? Do you need to give up swearing, talking against others, or let go of your anger? The Holy Spirit will help to rid yourself of all such things as these. Just ask Him!

ACT: Pray now for the people in Hollywood who struggle with anger. It's a difficult life to work in the entertainment industry. Either the artists can't make a living, so they grow angry through constant rejection and financial struggles, or, they reach "the top" and everyone wants something from them. The paparazzi, fans, and the press hound them, and they have no privacy. Anger is a problem on both ends of the spectrum, and both are a common reality. As cultural role models, these people desperately need your prayers. Thank you for making an eternal difference by praying for the Hollywood entertainment professionals.

YOUR **THOUGHTS:**

DAY 2

BLESS YOUR PERSECUTORS

"Bless those who persecute you; bless and do not curse. Rejoice with those who rejoice; mourn with those who mourn. Live in harmony with one another. Do not be proud, but be willing to associate with people of low position. Do not be conceited. Do not repay anyone evil for evil. Be careful to do what is right in the eyes of everybody. If it is possible, as far as it depends on you, live at peace with everyone."   Romans 12:14-18

"Throughout life people will make you mad, disrespect you and treat you bad. Let God deal with the things they do, 'cause hate in your heart will consume you too."   Will Smith

PRAY: Lord, we live in an angry world and I want to be different. Help me to bless others, to be compassionate with those around me, and to live in peace. Please don't let me get angry at others when I don't know their story. I want to be Christ-like in all I do and say. Thank You for Your scriptures, which guide my thoughts, words, and actions. Selah! Amen.

REFLECT: Think about when you get angry. What triggers your anger? What can you do to stop getting angry? What people make you angry? Can you ask the Lord to help you to pray for those people every time any anger arises? Are you mad at Hollywood, or any of the people here? If so, pray for the Lord to fill those people up with His unconditional love, hope, joy, and salvation. And then see if your anger subsides or disappears...

ACT: Memorize Romans 12:14-18 and commit to saying it over and over every time you feel angry. Start blessing people, rejoice with friends, mourn with those who have lost a loved one and live in harmony with everyone. Pray now about anything that angers you, asking the Lord to soften your heart, heal your hurt, and melt your anger. You don't want to be proud, conceited or repay anyone evil for evil. Be careful to do what it right in the eyes of everyone, especially the Lord. Then, as far as it depends on you, you will live in peace with everyone. Commit to learning Romans 12 and then watch what the Lord has in store for you!

YOUR THOUGHTS:

DAY 3

BE ANGRY BUT DON'T SIN

"'In your anger do not sin', do not let the sun go down while you are still angry, and do not give the devil a foothold."   Ephesians 4:26-27

"Anger is an acid that can do more harm to the vessel in which it is stored than to anything on which it is poured."   Mark Twain

PRAY: Lord, don't let the sun go down on my anger tonight. Help me to be honest about what angered me today, and then let go of it and place that issue, that person, or that situation at Your feet. Please let me sleep peacefully, knowing that I am laying down with a clean heart, a pure mind, and a peaceful soul. I don't want to give the devil a foothold. I pray this in Jesus' name, Amen.

REFLECT: Anger is an indication of many things – but all of them are warnings from God that something is not right. It could be a righteous anger in response to an injustice, or you could be reacting to something that triggered your own weakness or insecurity, or you may be misunderstanding someone or something. Each time you detect anger in your heart, your words, or your actions, stop and ask God to reveal the true reason behind that anger. Only then can you do something about it. And only then do you stop the devil from getting a foothold.

ACT: In God's world, light represents something beautiful, and darkness represents something scary, wrong, or evil. So how wise it is of God to tell us not to let the sun go down on our anger, for our anger will only get worse in the dark. Right now, check your heart and tell God anything that angers you, and as you memorize Ephesians 4:26-27, ask Him to get rid of your anger and help you fix your mind on this scripture before the sun goes down.

YOUR THOUGHTS:

DAY 4

WISDOM TURNS AWAY ANGER

"Mockers stir up a city, but the wise turn away anger." Proverbs 29:8

"I have a very strict gun control policy: if there's a gun around, I want to be in control of it." Clint Eastwood

PRAY: Lord, I see such brokenness and anger in our world. And I see that some cities, such as Hollywood, always have unrest because so many of the people there don't know You. Would You please stop mockers from causing chaos, anger, and even violence in our nation? Allow the wise leaders to turn our cities away from anger and bring Your divine peace into my city, in Hollywood, and in the nation. Every city needs Your presence to stop mockers and to keep wise men away from anger. I pray this in Jesus' name, Amen.

REFLECT: As you read the paper and listen to the news, can you look deeper into the cause of our world's unrest, killings, crime, and violence? Isn't it a spiritual issue more than a human problem (Eph.6:12)? Can you pray for the heart of the "mockers" and ask the Lord to transform them into new creatures, so that they can turn away from their anger and find peace and wisdom through the Holy Spirit, thus bringing peace to our world?

ACT: Commit to pray for each criminal, broken celebrity, politician or "mocker" whom you read about in the newspaper or listen to on TV. Ask the Lord to transform their hearts and heal their brokenness. Don't talk against them or get angry at them, they just need Jesus! Be sure that you are the wise one who turns away from anger. You can be a role model to others who don't know how to respond to mockers. The world needs less anger and more compassion and prayer, and it can start with you.

YOUR THOUGHTS:

DAY 5

DON'T BE QUICKLY PROVOKED

"Do not be quickly provoked in your spirit, for anger resides in the lap of fools."

Ecclesiastes 7:9

"My dear brothers and sisters, take note of this: Everyone should be quick to listen, slow to speak and slow to become angry."

James 1:19

"Take your time. Think it through. Find the will of God." Henry Parsons Crowell

PRAY: Lord, I want to be wise. I want to hold my tongue so that I am not a fool. And I want to be quick to listen, slow to speak and slow to become angry. Would You give me the strength, wisdom, and discernment to know when righteous anger is appropriate, and when I am reacting with a destructive anger? I need the Holy Spirit to guide me and handle my anger so that I don't become a fool. I pray this in Jesus' name, AMEN!

REFLECT: We often think that many of the people around us are fools. Could it be that they are just angry, and as their anger resides in their laps they appear to be fools? Maybe they are just slow to listen and quick to speak. And how often have you gotten angry, and become foolish in your response? Our anger creates a need for us to depend on the wisdom of God to guide us in our responses, so that we are not fools, but wise followers of Christ.

ACT: What makes you provoked in your spirit? And is it making you a fool? Write down anything that you know is making your spirit angry. Then identify the root of that anger, and pray about changing or fixing that root. Make it a goal to practice listening and not speaking so quickly so that you don't become angry. Pray not to be quickly provoked in your spirit so that you will be WISE!

YOUR THOUGHTS:

DAY 6

GIVE A GENTLE ANSWER

"A gentle answer turns away wrath, but a harsh word stirs up anger."　　Proverbs 15:1

"Did I offer peace today? Did I bring a smile to someone's face? Did I say words of healing? Did I let go of my anger and resentment? Did I forgive? Did I love? These are the real questions. I must trust that the little bit of love that I sow now will bear many fruits, here in this world and the life to come."
　　　　　　　　　　　　　　　　　　　　　　　　　　　　　Henri Nouwen

PRAY: Lord, I want to be as gentle as a dove, yet as wise as a serpent (Matt. 10:16). Help me to always answer with gentle, wise words so that I can be Your vessel to turn away wrath in others. Lord, hold my tongue if I am tempted to say a harsh word. Let me be wiser than the person I'm talking to, so that I can stay calm and thus have more authority. Teach me to be Christ-like with my words and my emotions. Thank You for molding me into a peacemaker so that I can answer gently, avoid harsh words and turn away wrath. Amen.

REFLECT: Why do we want to say angry words when we're told in scripture that it's the gentle word that turns away wrath? We need Divine intervention to understand there is great wisdom in controlling our tongue. What would it take to make you absolutely convinced that getting angry is not the answer and will only make things worse! Do you truly believe that a gentle answer turns away wrath but a harsh word stirs up anger?

ACT: Commit to answering the next argument, disagreement, or nasty comment with a kind word, a word of encouragement, or a word of forgiveness. Decide right now how you're going to respond to the next conflict you're in, so that when it happens you don't just react. Avoid harsh words and just use gentle words of love. When you've succeeded that first time, then commit to doing it again, and again, and again, until you've mastered it! When you mess up, don't get discouraged, just pick yourself up and begin again with a gentle answer.

YOUR THOUGHTS:

DAY 7

THE LORD IS SLOW TO ANGER

'The Lord passed in front of Moses, calling out, "Yahweh! The Lord! The God of compassion and mercy! I am slow to anger and filled with unfailing love and faithfulness. I lavish unfailing love to a thousand generations..."'   Exodus 34:6-7a (NLT)

"I really believe that all of us have a lot of darkness in our souls. Anger, rage, fear, sadness. I don't think that's only reserved for people who have horrible upbringings. I think it really exists and is part of the human condition. I think in the course of your life you figure out ways to deal with that."
                                                                    Kevin Bacon

PRAY: I praise You, God, for Your love for Your children, for Your compassion, Your mercy, graciousness, and Your patience with us. I praise You for Your abounding love and Your truth, mixed with grace. I thank You for filling me with Your peace and giving me the strength to become more Christ-like every day. I praise You for being slow to get angry with me! I praise You, my Lord and Savior for Your unfailing love and faithfulness! Amen.

REFLECT: Stop and think about what an AWESOME God we serve, follow, and love! He forgives us, strengthens us, gives us peace, takes away our anger and frustration, fills us with hope, guides us, comforts us, and LOVES us unconditionally for a thousand generations. We should be overflowing with joy every moment knowing how great He is. Do we praise Him enough? Do we really understand how awesome He is?! Why would we ever get angry?

ACT: Don't let a day go by without Praising God for who He is and what He's done for you. If you get in the habit of praising Him every day, you won't feel anger, frustration, hate, or even discontent. Choose a time every day – whether it be first thing in the morning, or the last thing at night – to PRAISE OUR GOD. Then watch your anger disappear...

YOUR THOUGHTS:

HUMILITY / A HUMBLE HEART

WEEK TEN

This week let's tackle the pure, child-like heart of HUMILITY as we spend time with our God. We know that pride comes before the fall, so humility must come before we are lifted up. Only the Holy Spirit can truly give us a humble heart, so may that be our prayer this week.

DAY 1

HUMILITY BEFORE HONOR

"Before a downfall the heart is haughty, but humility comes before honor."

Proverbs 18:12

"The truth is that everyone pays attention to who's number one at the box office. And none of it matters, because the only thing that really exists is the connection the audience has with a movie."

Tom Hanks

PRAY: Dear Heavenly Father, I don't want pride to make me fall. I don't want to be haughty or arrogant. I want to be humble and solid in my own identity because I know that I am perfectly and wonderfully made by You and You even honor me. Please protect me from any attitude that does not allow me to honor You and others with a humble heart. Amen.

REFLECT: It's been said that "Pride must die in you before Heaven can live in you." What does that mean to you? Is your pride getting in the way of letting God and His ways permeate your life? How can you reflect Heaven in all you do and say? If a haughty heart comes before a downfall, but humility comes before honor, where are you right now?

ACT: Choose one person, a close friend, brother or sister, spouse, parent, or mentor, and ask him or her where they see pride in you. Talk about where that may come from and how to get rid of it. Ask them to join you in tackling this area of pride so that you won't fall or cause others to fall. Also ask them where they see humility in you? Celebrate that, for in humility you will experience honor – both from others and from God.

YOUR THOUGHTS:

DAY 2

THE LORD REQUIRES HUMILITY

"He has told you, O man, what is good; and what does the Lord require of you but to do justice, and to love kindness, and to walk humbly with your God."   Micah 6:8 (ESV)

"Every now and again, Our Lord lets us see what we would be like if it were not for Himself; it is a justification of what He said – "Without Me you can do nothing." That is why the bedrock of Christianity is personal, passionate devotion to the Lord Jesus."

Oswald Chambers

PRAY: Dear God, thank You for showing me what is good in me. Thank you for also laying out for me what is required of me. Would You help me to learn Your ways so that I can act justly, love mercy, and walk humbly with You? Would You give me that supernatural balance of caring about the wellbeing of other people, staying focused on You, and putting myself second, without judging myself or others? I want to do good; I want to be full of justice and to love kindness and I want to walk humbly with You, God. Amen.

REFLECT: God asks us some tough questions: What is good? And what does the Lord require of you? How do we truly know that we are walking humbly or need to learn how to walk humbly, without focusing just on ourselves? Is this all we need to become more Christ-like so that our identity is solid in the Lord, and not in our accomplishments, our looks, the length of our Quiet Times, or based on what other people say about us? What does it actually take to do all that the Lord requires?...

ACT: Check out the website I AM SECOND at www.iamsecond.com and watch a few of the short videos by people who learned what it means to walk humbly with the Lord. It's a wonderful way to understand if your heart is clear on your own sense of humility, brokenness, and strength in the Lord. The people telling their stories on this site have had to learn justice, kindness and humility and those lessons have transformed them forever.

YOUR THOUGHTS:

DAY 3

THE REWARDS OF HUMILITY

"Humility is the fear of the Lord; its wages are riches and honor and life." Proverbs 22:4

"The point of the death of Christ is that Christ took on the sins of the world, so that what we put out did not come back to us, and that our sinful nature does not reap the obvious death. That's the point. It should keep us humbled... It's not our own good works that get us through the gates of Heaven."

Bono

PRAY: Lord, please show me a healthy fear of You, an awe and respect for You that I've never experienced before. Show me how much richer my life would be if I embrace honor in a new way. I want the abundant life and I want to walk humbly with You, so will You teach me to fear You? Oh, how I want to have Your riches, and honor, and Life. Thank You, Jesus, Amen.

REFLECT: What does it mean to "fear the Lord"? Are we really to be afraid? Are you ever afraid of God? "Fear the Lord" actually refers to a specific sense of awe, respect, and submission, like you would give to a military commanding officer, or a film director, or your pastor, because you know they have the power, and the decisions they make can affect you directly. If you truly "fear the Lord" you respect His awesome greatness, and submit to His will, while understanding His love for you. When you do, you will experience a rich life, you will honor God and know that He honors the humble attitude of your heart. And others will honor you, not by what you do, but by your fear of the Lord.

ACT: Can you say that you have a "rich" life? If so, think about or list what makes it rich: Is it money, comfort, and adventures, or is it also a deep sense of love and comfort in the Lord, fabulous relationships, and an understanding of living the "abundant life"? If you want more spiritual richness, and a greater understanding of honor, then ask God to make you humble. We can't make ourselves humble, but God can transform our hearts and minds in Christ Jesus.

YOUR THOUGHTS:

DAY 4

DON'T THINK TOO HIGHLY

"For by the grace given me I say to every one of you: Do not think of yourself more highly than you ought, but rather think of yourself with sober judgment, in accordance with the faith God has distributed to each of you."   Romans 12:3

"Talent is God given. Be humble. Fame is man-given. Be grateful. Conceit is self-given. Be careful."   John Wooden

PRAY: Lord, would You reveal to me the difference between false self-esteem and confidence in You, based on sober judgment, and in accordance with my faith? I want to have true humility, but a clear understanding of who I am in You, how valued I am in Your eyes, and that I'm here on this earth to make an eternal difference. Thank You for the grace You have given me and for insight into true, beautiful humility in my heart! Amen.

REFLECT: Think about what it means to be humble, versus feeling that we are worms, or we aren't good enough, compared to other people. Try to define humility through God's eyes and know that loving ourselves is important because we are made in God's image. However, thinking we're better than other people is pride. Ask God for wisdom in this tough area of true identity, confidence, and character. We all should have sober judgment, in accordance with the faith God has distributed to each of us. Can you say you do?

ACT: Make a list with two columns: On the left list who you think you are, with your strengths, weaknesses, character traits, etc. On the right list who God says you are in His eyes. See the similarities and differences between these two lists, side by side. Do you understand HUMILITY, or do you need to study God's word more to see clearly who you are in Christ? At the bottom of the lists can you list what you enjoy about yourself? Which of your traits, beliefs or actions do you like? Those are what you thank God for, because He gave them to you and He is enjoying them as well!

YOUR THOUGHTS:

DAY 5

HE HUMBLES US

"He humbled you, causing you to hunger and then feeding you with manna, which neither you nor your ancestors had known, to teach you that man does not live on bread alone but on every word that comes from the mouth of the LORD."   Deuteronomy 8:3

"God allows us to experience the low points of life in order to teach us lessons we could not learn in any other way. The way we learn those lessons is not to deny the feelings but to find the meanings underlying them."   Stanley Lindquist

PRAY: Lord, I pray that You will show me where I need to be humbled. I also pray that You would humble the Hollywood professionals so they can recognize their need for You in their lives, as we all do. Show me and the Hollywood professionals who are creating our culture, that Your Word is true and that all of our efforts are meaningless without You. We can't live on bread alone, but on every word that comes from Your mouth. We all need to realize that this place of need is just where You want us, so that You can work in us. Amen.

REFLECT: Reflect on the artists or creative people whom you know. Artists, and all creative professionals have so much going on in their heads that they sometimes forget there is a world of people with needs and hurt around them. They become narcissists in their thinking and only the Lord can pull them out of themselves and trigger a desire in us to reach out to others, and to depend on Him. But if people don't know Jesus they won't understand about humility or that we can't live on bread alone, but only on His words of truth.

ACT: When you hear yourself, or anyone else, talking against a Hollywood professional, will you stop and tell yourself, or others, to pray instead for that person, believing only prayer can change their hearts and their lives. Your prayers matter! The concept of humility is spiritually discerned, so how can we expect others to understand it, if neither you nor your ancestors had understood. Choose now to study humility until you truly understand it for yourself and you can lovingly pray for it in others. Don't judge Hollywood or anyone else for humility doesn't allow it.

YOUR THOUGHTS:

DAY 6

WITH HUMILITY COMES WISDOM

"When pride comes, then comes disgrace, but with humility comes wisdom."

Proverbs 11:2

"You come of the Lord Adam and the Lady Eve,' said Aslan. 'And that is both honour enough to erect the head of the poorest beggar, and shame enough to bow the shoulders of the greatest emperor in earth.' "   C.S. Lewis

PRAY: Please God, protect me from pride. I know that pride will lead to disgrace, and I want to truly be humble so that I will gain wisdom. I need You to change my heart and my mind, to transform me to be more Christ-like, so that You can strip away my pride, and allow me to live a life of grace and wisdom. I so look forward to what You are going to change in me. Oh, make me wise - In Jesus' name, Amen.

REFLECT: Be honest with yourself and look deep into your heart – how are you prideful? Do you get defensive or angry? Do you compare yourself with other people? Do you think you're unworthy? Do you think you're better than anyone in your life? Do you judge others? Are you hard on yourself? All of these are signs of Pride. Reflect on how pride is impacting your life before it leads you to disgrace, for with humility comes wisdom.

ACT: Pick one area in your life where you struggle with pride and ask God to change it. Allow Him to reveal to you what you need to let go of in order to protect you from disgrace, and instead fill you with wisdom. Be willing to acknowledge your weakness, for that's the first step toward change. And then don't get discouraged by the time it may take to conquer your pride, for God's timing is perfect.

YOUR THOUGHTS:

DAY 7

VALUE OTHERS ABOVE YOURSELF

"Do nothing out of selfish ambition or vain conceit. Rather, in humility value others above yourselves, not looking to your own interests but each of you to the interests of the others."

Philippians 2:3-4

"The only humility that is really ours is not that which we try to show before God in prayer, but that which we carry with us in our daily conduct." Andrew Murray

PRAY: Lord, would You help me to love others above myself, to honor others for who You created them to be, and to get my selfish ambition out of the way in my mind, body, and soul? I need Your help to get rid of my vain conceit, for I know my identity comes through You, not by my own actions, words, looks, or accomplishments. Lord, do I put my own interests before the interests of others? I need Your help to celebrate others over myself because I know who I am in You, and it's wonderful! Amen.

REFLECT: What do you do that looks like it's selfless, but it actually is fueled by selfish ambition? We all do that, but we all aren't honest about it. Can you track any vain conceit in your life? If so, what can you do about it? Take some time for self-reflection and ask God to reveal His truths to you – not out of condemnation, but out of love and the desire to help you learn, grow, and become more humble.

ACT: Choose one person in your life whom you would like to honor and value. Write them a note, compliment them in front of others, celebrate them with others, call them and tell them what they mean to you, or throw them a party! And be sure to pick someone who will not help you, make you look better, or earn you points by reaching out to them. Choose someone you care about who will be honored by your words and actions, and who will be touched because you put their interests above your own.

YOUR THOUGHTS:

COURAGE

WEEK ELEVEN

We all want to be brave and we all have heroes. It's because God has given each of us the Divine desire to be courageous. But we can only get courage through Him. This week we're looking at how to push through our fears with His courage. And with God ALL things are possible!

DAY 1

DO NOT BE AFRAID, THE LORD IS WITH YOU

"Have I not commanded you? Be strong and courageous. Do not be afraid; do not be discouraged, for the Lord your God will be with you wherever you go."   Joshua 1:9

"Courage is going from failure to failure without losing enthusiasm." Winston Churchill

PRAY: Lord, thank You that I can turn to You for strength and courage. I don't want to be afraid of anything, but I know that You are the only one who can take fear away from my mind and heart or help me to push through my fear and discouragement. Would You fill me with courage so that I can start this day with confidence and have strength through You, with no hesitation for anything that You have for me today. Thank you for being with me wherever I go. I pray this in Jesus' name, Amen.

REFLECT: It's amazing how all throughout the Bible God gives us words of encouragement. He knows that all human beings are weak and afraid without Him. We need to know that He's here for us, that He will give us strength and courage that we don't have on our own. He is gentle but strong in His reminders, and even through His commandments He tells us not to be discouraged. We need Him desperately, and that's just where He wants us – to depend on Him each day for courage and strength. He is an awesome God to promise us that He will be with us, wherever we go!

ACT: Choose one current situation where you are either afraid or discouraged. Now put Jesus in that situation, walking with you, holding you up, giving you wisdom and guidance... Trust Him to give you the strength and courage you need to face that situation head on. Isn't that empowering to know that you're not walking through this alone? He is not only here with you to give you strength and courage, but He commands you to think this way! Now, even if you feel afraid, forge ahead and conquer that situation!

YOUR THOUGHTS:

DAY 2

BE STRONG, TAKE COURAGE, WAIT FOR THE LORD

"Be strong, and let your heart take courage, all you who wait for the Lord!"

Psalm 31:24 (ESV)

"I learned that courage was not the absence of fear, but the triumph over it. The brave man is not he who does not feel afraid, but he who conquers that fear." Nelson Mandela

PRAY: Dear Jesus, my courage and my strength, I turn to You each morning to fill me up with Your strength. Please take away my fear and show me how to push through the situations where I feel weak and afraid and am unable to proceed. Let me wait for You to deliver me, so that I will handle each day with confidence, wisdom, and with a heart full of courage. Help me to wait for You to give me what I need. Amen.

REFLECT: God tells us to be strong, knowing that we can't do anything on our own. Could this be one of God's ways to make us turn to Him, depend on Him, lean on Him, and wait for Him? He wants, more than anything, for us to put our lives completely in His hands. Then, and only then, can He fill us with the courage and strength we need to handle each day. But it only happens when we wait on Him and His timing. Isn't it ironic that we only get stronger and braver when we wait on God.

ACT: Are you afraid? Wait for the Lord. Seek His face, tell Him what you need or what you're afraid of, and then wait. Do you need courage? Wait for the Lord. Seek His face, tell him why you need Him and then wait. Wait for the Lord, wait to hear His voice, to get guidance from Him. Wait for Him to take away your fear and to fill you with strength. Today is a day to patiently wait for the Lord. Or it may be the week or the month to wait. Embrace waiting for the Lord and He will give you the courage you need to carry on!

YOUR THOUGHTS:

DAY 3

STAND FIRM, DO ALL IN THINGS IN LOVE

"Be on your guard; stand firm in the faith; be courageous; be strong. Do everything in love."
                                                        1 Corinthians 16:13-14

"I can do everything through him who gives me strength."   Philippians 4:13

"Courage is being scared to death... and saddling up anyway."   John Wayne

PRAY: God, my heavenly Father, You tell me to be on my guard and yet be strong and courageous. I need You to show me how to stand firm in my faith and especially how to do everything in love. I believe that I can do all things through You, who gives me strength, but I don't know how. Will You help me? Thank you, my God. Thank you! Amen.

REFLECT: From what are we on our guard? Against whom do we have to stand firm in the faith? Why do we have to be courageous and strong? And how do we do everything in love? None of us truly knows, but that's why we need God the Father, Jesus and Son AND the Holy Spirit. It takes a trinity to give us strength, and to prepare us for the battles of life with courage and love. Believe, in complete humility, that you can only do all things through Him who gives you strength. That's the most courageous thing you will ever do!

ACT: Make a short list of five things you need God for today.
- I need to be on my guard from this:
- I need to stand firm in the faith in this situation:
- I need to be courageous in this instance:
- I need to be strong in this:
- I need to do this in love:

Now tell the Lord you commit to do everything in love. Tell Him you believe you can do all this through Him who strengthens you. Then wait on Him to supply all that you need!

YOUR **THOUGHTS:**

DAY 4

DO NOT FEAR, THE LORD WILL UPHOLD YOU

"I took you from the ends of the earth, from its farthest corners I called you. I said, 'You are my servant'; I have chosen you and have not rejected you. So do not fear, for I am with you; do not be dismayed, for I am your God. I will strengthen you and help you; I will uphold you with my righteous right hand."   Isaiah 41:9-10

"Failure is unimportant. It takes courage to make a fool of yourself."   Charlie Chaplin

PRAY: Dear Lord, You have brought me right where I am in order to serve You here, amongst this particular people group because You have chosen me to be your courageous servant. So, don't let me judge Your servants whom You have brought to serve You in Hollywood, in Las Vegas, or in any other cities I'm afraid of. You need courageous servants to be salt and light in all the farthest corners of the earth and I pray for those in tough places, to get strength from You and to do Your work in the place they've been called to. You have sent Your people to the ends of the earth so help me to support all of them in prayer. Amen.

REFLECT: Have you ever thought that God loves every single person on the earth and in His perfect plan, has sent His people to the ends of the earth to reach every one of His creations. That truth should stop us from ever judging or disliking any people group. We all need the Lord and He loves each one of us, no matter who we are, where we are, or what we do. Could you courageously pray for the lost people in Hollywood who need to hear the saving grace of Jesus and pray for courage for His servants, whom God has sent there?

ACT: Right now, pray for the Christians in Hollywood who have been sent by God to minister, pray for, and love the media professionals who are creating the world's entertainment. Pray for these servants to have courage, wisdom, love, and grace towards that people group at "the farthest corner" of our country. Ask the Lord to give them courage so they won't feel dismayed as they share the gospel of hope to their co-workers, friends, and associates. Hollywood is a hard place to be and as they faithfully serve God there, they need your prayers of love and support. God has chosen them and not rejected them, so we can't reject them either!

YOUR THOUGHTS:

DAY 5

YOU ARE MORE THAN A CONQUEROR

"Who shall separate us from the love of Christ? Shall trouble or hardship or persecution or famine or nakedness or danger or sword? As it is written: 'For your sake we face death all day long; we are considered as sheep to be slaughtered.' No, in all these things we are more than conquerors through him who loved us. For I am convinced that neither death nor life, neither angels nor demons, neither the present nor the future, nor any powers, neither height nor depth, nor anything else in all creation, will be able to separate us from the love of God that is in Christ Jesus our Lord."　　　　　　　　Romans 8:35-39

"It is curious – curious that physical courage should be so common in the world, and moral courage so rare."

　　　　　　　　Mark Twain

PRAY: Jesus, these verses fill me with courage. I don't have to hesitate or be afraid of anything after reading Your promises. Thank You that You are with me and no one is too strong against me. And nothing can ever separate me from Your love. You loved me so much I am overwhelmed by these incredibly loving promises and truths, and for that I am full of courage to face anything today. Thank You more than I can ever express for all You've done for me, given to me and are to me. I pray this in Your mighty name. Amen.

REFLECT: Can we ever completely fathom these truths in Romans 8? It says that NOTHING will be able to separate us from His love. Even in death and life, sickness, or danger, absolutely nothing can stop God from loving us, protecting us, and caring for us. Anywhere we are, whatever we're doing, God is protecting us and giving us strength and courage. By believing that you will be more than a conqueror!

ACT: Write the extended verses, Romans 8:31-39, down on an index card, or highlight them in your Bible App, and commit them to memory. They put into perspective not only who God is, but what He does for you. Just take it one verse at a time, and don't be intimidated by the length. It is powerful and life changing. If you can get these verses planted in your mind and in your heart, you will be a person of great courage. Be a conqueror!

YOUR THOUGHTS:

DAY 6

WHEN YOU ARE AFRAID, TRUST IN THE LORD

"When I am afraid, I put my trust in you. In God, whose word I praise—in God I trust and am not afraid. What can mere mortals do to me?" Psalm 56:3-4

"Mistakes are always forgivable, if one has the courage to admit them." Bruce Lee

PRAY: Lord, would You help me to put all of my trust in You when I'm afraid. I know that when I fully put my trust in You, I am never afraid, but it's often hard to do that. Thank You that when I have courage, it's because it comes from You. And then I don't have to worry about any mere mortal! Thank you, Lord that I don't ever need to flee any situation, but I can be bold as a lion and stand firm in Your promises. Oh Lord, please let me always live by that truth and get my courage from You. In Jesus' name, AMEN and AMEN.

REFLECT: It's such a mind game sometimes to get our brains to believe what we know to be true, but what is so hard to emotionally embrace. We know that when we trust in God we won't be afraid. We know that God promises to fill us with courage that will give us the strength to face any mere mortal or any situation. But, to actually live that out is a challenge. What would it take to get both your heart and your brain to give you the courage to live every day as bold as a lion; full of courage and confidence in Him? Maybe you need to praise Him.

ACT: Define one situation where you feel fear. Now, ask the Holy Spirit to take away any fear, doubt, or concern and to fill you, instead, with a boldness to face whatever it is, head on, with courage! Ask the Lord to teach you what it takes to put your trust in Him, and NOT in yourself or your circumstances. Praise Him and His word. Then you won't be afraid! That exercise is worth repeating!

YOUR THOUGHTS:

DAY 7

TAKE COURAGE!

"The following night the Lord stood near Paul and said, 'Take courage! As you have testified about me in Jerusalem, so you must also testify in Rome.'"   Acts 23:11

"Courage is contagious. When a brave man takes a stand, the spines of others are often stiffened."
                                                                Billy Graham

PRAY: God, my faithful Father, give me courage to share my faith! Help me to be confident in my relationship with You and to testify to my friends, my family members, and co-workers about my love for You. And let me be gentle, truthful, full of grace and sensitivity, so that I can reach people where they are and say or do what is best to move them a step closer to You. Lord, it is not only a commandment, but a privilege to be salt and light in this world, so why am I so afraid? I need You to give me courage so that I can testify to others what someone once gave to me – the gift of having You as my Savior. Amen.

REFLECT: Why are we all so afraid to share our faith with others? Why don't we have the courage to tell others about the best thing that's ever happened to us? It is spiritual battle. The enemy doesn't want Christians to be talking about the Good News of Jesus or everyone would start believing in Him. But we must do what Jesus tells us. And if He says to "Take courage!" then we need to take that seriously. What's stopping you from sharing your faith with the people around you?

ACT: Choose one person in your life whom you are afraid to talk to about Jesus. Start praying for that person and asking the Lord to both prepare his/her heart to accept the truth about Him, and to give you the courage to talk confidently about the amazing love, hope, joy, and salvation of the Lord. Soon, an opportunity will arise or the Holy Spirit will start nudging you, so don't let fear stop you from the chance to make an eternal difference in that person's life. And remember, courage comes when you step out and do the right thing, especially when you're afraid!

YOUR THOUGHTS:

FAITHFULNESS

WEEK TWELVE

What do you think of when you hear the words "be faithful"? Faithfulness includes consistency, integrity, being a person of your word and honoring God. We'll look at the definition and God's Word to focus on how to be a faithful person. God tells us that if we are faithful we will "end well."

DAY 1

GOD IS FAITHFUL

"He is the Rock, his works are perfect, and all his ways are just. A faithful God who does no wrong, upright and just is he."   Deuteronomy 32:4

"Yes, thou art ever present, power divine; not circumscribed by time, nor fixed by space, confined to altars, nor to temples bound. In wealth, in want, in freedom, or in chains, in dungeons or on thrones, the faithful find thee."   Hannah More

PRAY: Dear God, You are my rock and Your works are perfect! Thank You that all Your ways are just. You are such a faithful God. I'm so grateful that You do no wrong, but that I can turn to You, who is upright and just. You are not only my creator, you are also my faithful helper, guide, comforter, and my source of strength and wisdom. Praise You for being so faithful! I pray this in the mighty name of Jesus, Amen!

REFLECT: Have you ever thought of all the names of God? He defines Himself through His deeds, His personality, and His promises. But His most amazing quality is that through all of life's disappointments, tragedies, joys, and desert times, He is FAITHFUL! He never turns away or forgets and He's never too busy. He is ALWAYS there for us, even when it doesn't feel like it, or when our circumstances don't seem to reflect that. Are you walking through a dark time now? Even Jesus cried out, "Why have You forsaken me?" before God raised Him from the dead. Hang in there. He is faithful.

ACT: Can you remember times when you felt that God was far away? Look back now and see that He has been with you all along. Make a list of:
1. When God was your ROCK -
2. When you experienced His PERFECT WORKS -
3. When you experienced or saw His JUST WAYS -
4. When He was FAITHFUL to you -

And remember in the days ahead that God does no wrong, He is upright, and He is just and He is always with you! He is a faithful God!

YOUR THOUGHTS:

DAY 2

GREAT IS YOUR FAITHFULNESS

"Because of the Lord's great love we are not consumed, for his compassions never fail. They are new every morning; great is your faithfulness."   Lamentations 3:22-23

"As I look back over fifty years of ministry, I recall innumerable tests, trials and times of crushing pain. But through it all, the Lord has proven faithful, loving, and totally true to all his promises."
David Wilkerson

PRAY: Lord, when I feel discouraged, scared, or overwhelmed, please help me to remember Your great love for me and that You will never let me get consumed. I am so grateful that Your compassions NEVER fail, but they are new every single morning. Oh Lord, great is Your faithfulness. Amen and Amen.

REFLECT: It's sometimes hard to take God at His word, especially when we don't feel His love or His presence. When He seems distant it's hard not to feel consumed. But if our faith is real and His word is true, then we will not feel consumed because we are completely engulfed in His great love. How would you get to the place where you not only believe, but you feel His never-ending compassion and love every morning, every afternoon, and every evening? How would you fully rest in the truth that He is always faithful?

ACT: Because of the Lord's great love for us we are not consumed. So, take a few minutes just to sit in the presence of your God and talk to Him. Tell Him how much you appreciate and are thankful for His faithfulness. Take this time to remind Him of all the times that He has been so faithful to you. Then praise Him for His never-ending compassion on you that is new every morning. Just bask in the memories of His great love and thank Him for His faithfulness.

YOUR THOUGHTS:

DAY 3

RELY ON HIS FAITHFULNESS

"Teach me your way, Lord, that I may rely on your faithfulness; give me an undivided heart, that I may fear your name."   Psalm 86:11

"I know of nothing which I would choose to have as the subject of my ambition for life than to be kept faithful to my God till death, still to be a soul winner, still to be a true herald of the cross, and testify the name of Jesus to the last hour."   Charles Spurgeon

PRAY: Heavenly Father, I need You every moment and yet I know that's right where You want me, for only then can You teach me Your ways. And only then will I rely on Your faithfulness. Oh Father, give me an undivided heart. I want to fear Your name with awe, embrace Your teaching, and trust that regardless of my circumstances You are faithful. In Jesus' name, Amen.

REFLECT: We should never stop learning and growing in our walk with the Lord. We should always be asking Him to teach us His way, so that we can learn to completely rely on His faithfulness. Otherwise, it's just a concept or a Bible verse. Do you think it might be that the only way to have an undivided heart and to fear His name is through practice, and through constantly asking Him to teach us, change us, strengthen us, and give us wisdom? Maybe only then will we not have a divided heart and, in the most beautiful way, truly fear His name. Only in relying on His faithfulness to us can we remain faithful to Him.

ACT: Ask God right now to teach you how to rely on His faithfulness. Ask Him to give you an undivided heart for Him, without anyone or anything distracting you or pulling you away from Him. Ask God to bring you to the point in your love for Him that you actually fear Him. And don't stop asking until you know you have learned these truths. He is faithful.

YOUR THOUGHTS:

DAY 4

THE LORD IS FAITHFUL TO PROTECT YOU

"But the Lord is faithful, and he will strengthen you and protect you from the evil one."

2 Thessalonians 3:3

"Often times God demonstrates His faithfulness in adversity by providing for us what we need to survive. He does not change our painful circumstances. He sustains us through them."

Charles Stanley

PRAY: Lord, will You help me to believe that You are faithful to all people, in all parts of the world – whether they believe in You or not? Give me strength to believe that You will protect all Christians from the evil one, regardless of where they live or what they do? Thank You for protecting me from the enemy. And thank You that You are faithful to the people in Hollywood. Would you also protect them from the evil one? You are faithful so help me and the Hollywood professionals to be faithful to You and Your promises. Amen.

REFLECT: Many Christians around the world honestly believe that God loves some people more than others, or that He will just help the people who believe in Him. That's why so many Christians hate Hollywood and judge and talk against people who work in the entertainment industry. We Christians must remember that God loves and is faithful to all people. And that's why we should pray for the people in Hollywood. We must also believe that God protects all His people from the evil one, so there is no place too dark or scary to be – even Hollywood.

ACT: If you think negatively about the people and the projects created in Hollywood, would you now ask God to show You that He loves those people just as much as He loves you, and every single person He has created across the globe. Ask Him to change your heart so that you're not afraid of Hollywood. And if you've ever told a talented young person not to go to Hollywood because it's evil, would you ask for forgiveness, because God protects all of His children from the evil one, regardless of where they are. So, we should never be afraid. God is faithful, even to the people in Hollywood.

YOUR THOUGHTS:

DAY 5

DO GOOD AND FIND LOVE AND FAITHFULNESS

"Do not those who plot evil go astray? But those who plan what is good find love and faithfulness."   Proverbs 14:22

"Be faithful in small things because it is in them that your strength lies." Mother Teresa

PRAY: Jesus, I pray today for myself and my loved ones to keep our hearts and minds away from plotting evil, for I don't want any of us to go astray. I ask that You help me and my family and friends to plan only what is good so that we will find and experience Your love and faithfulness. I need You to protect me from doing anything that could cause me to go astray. I want to find love and faithfulness by planning only what is good. Thank you, Jesus. Amen.

REFLECT: There is a belief amongst some people that God will punish anyone who goes astray or sins. But there is also the truth that God created a world with built-in consequences so that when we sin or plot evil, we will naturally experience the consequences of those actions. This verse says that those who plot evil will go astray. Could it be that this fact is not punishment but merely a natural result of disobeying God's plan for our lives? The positive result of doing God's will, or here, to plan what is good, is to find love and faithfulness. That is the natural consequence of obeying God's commands.

ACT: Have you ever plotted evil against someone? That sounds extreme, but it may be a subtle choice that seems inconsequential, like telling a lie. Make the commitment right now to only "plan what is good." Choose to obey God's word in everything you say and do, especially in the little things. Because of the way God created us and this world, only then will you live in love and faithfulness – two of the most important gifts that God has given us.

YOUR THOUGHTS:

DAY 6

WELL DONE, GOOD AND FAITHFUL SERVANT

"His master replied, 'Well done, good and faithful servant! You have been faithful with a few things; I will put you in charge of many things. Come and share your master's happiness!'" Matthew 25:21

"This job has been given to me to do. Therefore, it is a gift. Therefore, it is a privilege. Therefore, it is an offering I may make to God. Therefore, it is to be done gladly, if it is done for Him. Here, not somewhere else, I may learn God's way. In this job, not in some other, God looks for faithfulness." Elisabeth Elliot

PRAY: Dear Father in Heaven, I want to hear the words "Well done, good and faithful servant" from You some day. Please help me to be faithful with everything You give me; every relationship, and every responsibility in my walk with You. I want to experience Your joy and happiness and I know that will only be possible if I learn to be faithful to You, to other people, and to Your word. I will start with a few things and prove worthy so that You can put me in charge of many things. Oh Father, I want to come and share in Your happiness! Amen.

REFLECT: One of the best things a child can hear from his or her parent or teacher is, "Well done!" And isn't that what we also want to hear from God? How can we earn that compliment? It's not by our accomplishments or our titles, or by how much money we make or success we achieve. It's merely by being faithful, which is defined in the dictionary as "loyal, constant, steadfast." God doesn't expect us to do the impossible. He says that if we have been faithful with a few things, that He will put us in charge of many things. If we keep our eyes on Him and ask Him for help, we too can share in our Master's happiness.

ACT: Make a list of a few things that you know you are faithful in or with. Are you satisfied? Is there anything else you can add or work on? Ask God to help you become faithful in more things in your life. Expand your list so that you can be working toward hearing His beautiful words, "Well done, good and faithful servant!"

YOUR THOUGHTS:

DAY 7

LET LOVE & FAITHFULNESS NEVER LEAVE YOU

"Let love and faithfulness never leave you; bind them around your neck, write them on the tablet of your heart."

Proverbs 3:3

FAITHFULNESS, noun

1. Fidelity; loyalty; firm adherence to allegiance and duty; as the faithfulness of a subject.

2. Truth; veracity; as the faithfulness of God.

3. Strict adherence to the duties of a station; as the faithfulness of servants or ministers.

4. Strict performance of promises, vows or covenants; constancy in affection; as the faithfulness of a husband or wife. Constant; not fickle; as a faithful lover or friend.

Webster's 1828 Dictionary

PRAY: God, I want to end this week with the commitment to never let love and faithfulness leave me. Would You bind them around my neck and write them on the tablet of my heart. Would You make me a faithful person, overflowing with love. I want to be more like You, staying faithful to the truth and walking in it. And I pray this in Your name. Selah. Amen.

REFLECT: God says many times in the Bible that He is faithful and that He wants us to be faithful. Faithful to what? To whom? What do you think it means to be a faithful person? Are you a loyal friend? Are you constant in your love, joy, peace, patience, goodness and faithfulness? Are you steadfast in your walk as a Christian, being a good example and role model? Think about what it means to bind faithfulness around your neck and write it on the tablet of your heart. Sometimes it seems impossible, but with God all things are possible.

ACT: What is one situation or relationship to which you can be more faithful? Is it to a loved one? A job? A project you need to finish on time? Is it to spend more time with God, or memorize scriptures? Define that one area of life where you know you need to be more faithful, then write it down and commit to it. Write it on the tablet of your heart. Take one step to become more faithful. God will honor your choice and your commitment. You are ending the week one step closer to being a faithful person and God is pleased.

YOUR THOUGHTS:

GOSSIP

WEEK THIRTEEN

Gossip. It permeates every part of every society across the globe. Human beings love to talk about other people. But God is saddened by gossip. This week the focus is on the temptations to gossip, the dangers of gossip, and how to make our words wholesome and encouraging, building people up and leading people to Jesus. Find out how changing your words can change others' lives!

DAY 1

GOSSIPS, GOD-HATERS AND MURDERERS

"They have become filled with every kind of wickedness, evil, greed and depravity. They are full of envy, murder, strife, deceit and malice. They are gossips, slanderers, God-haters, insolent, arrogant and boastful; they invent ways of doing evil; they disobey their parents; they are senseless, faithless, heartless, ruthless. Although they know God's righteous decree that those who do such things deserve death, they not only continue to do these very things but also approve of those who practice them."   Romans 1:29-32

"Nothing is a greater, or more fearful, sacrilege than to prostitute the great name of God to the petulancy of an idle tongue."
                                                            Jeremy Taylor

PRAY: Dear Lord, I have become filled with every kind of wickedness and I ask that You clean out my heart, my mind, and my soul right now. I want to be washed as white as snow so that no gossip comes out of my mouth and no evil thoughts go into my head. I know Your righteous decree so I don't want to continue to do these evil things that displease You. Please allow me to start fresh today with a pure and contrite heart. Thank you, Lord. Amen.

REFLECT: In Romans 1:29-32, not only do we allow every kind of wickedness, evil, greed, and depravity to come into us, but Paul lists horrible things that we think and do, including GOSSIP, with God-haters, infidelity, and having no love. People often wrongly prioritize sins according to what we think is better or worse. We know turning against God is bad but seeing that Paul put gossip in the same list as God-haters is humbling and thought-provoking. Are you careful with your words? Do you talk about or against others? Although we know God's righteous decree, why don't we stop doing such things that deserve death?

ACT: Read this verse out loud and listen carefully to the list of sins that Paul defines as evil and wicked. What a variety of offenses. Go through them again and ask the Lord to take each one away from you. And for Gossip, ponder its dictionary meaning: "someone who likes to talk about someone else's private or personal business." It's not just mean words, but also private issues. Ask the Lord to reveal to you when you've gossiped and to help you hold your tongue when you're tempted. It takes commitment to break the habit.

YOUR THOUGHTS:

DAY 2

GOSSIP IS A HABITUAL SIN

"Besides, they get into the habit of being idle and going about from house to house. And not only do they become idlers, but also gossips and busybodies, saying things they ought not to."   1 Timothy 5:13

"Some say our national pastime is baseball. Not me. It's gossip."   Erma Bombeck

PRAY: Father, I'm sure I have lots of habits I don't even think about. But I ask You now to help me to see if I have a habit of gossiping. Or maybe I am idle, which makes me become a gossip. I don't ever want to talk nonsense or say things that I shouldn't. I want to have pure thoughts and say only words that bless, encourage, and honor other people. May this be the week that I break all gossip and I refocus and recommit to You and Your ways. Thank You for allowing me to start fresh every day. I love You, my heavenly Father. Amen.

REFLECT: Reflect on this insightful progression of sins that Timothy warns us about. If we get in the habit of being idle, then we start going about from house to house bothering our neighbors, and then we become busybodies who talk nonsense, saying things we ought not to. Wow, look how that creeps up on us. So, first of all, we can't become idle. We have to be wise, resourceful, and purposeful with our time, giving every moment to the Lord, for His glory, so that we don't waste our time, bother other people around us, or gossip. So, gossip can come from liking to feel powerful by talking about people behind their backs, or it could be just because we are not using our time purposefully for God's glory and for the good of others. How do you spend your time? And are you talking about others during your day?

ACT: Think about your days just this week. Have you been purposeful in using them to the best of your ability, to be productive and contemplative, and to serve God and others around you? Think through your conversations: Have you talked about people? Or have you talked about ideas, experiences, concepts, and Godly wisdom? How do you spend your time and what do you talk about in your conversations? Maybe today is the day to evaluate your days and start to break habits of being idle or of gossiping. There is no better time than the present. Recommit right now to become more Christ-like in all that you do and say.

YOUR **THOUGHTS:**

DAY 3

THE POWER OF WORDS

"A gossip betrays a confidence, but a trustworthy man keeps a secret." – "The words of a gossip are like choice morsels; they go down to the inmost parts."

Proverbs 11:13 & 18:8

"Few friendships would survive if each one knew what his friend says of him behind his back."

Blaise Pascal

PRAY: Dear God, I want to understand the power of words and how I can choose my words to avoid betraying the confidence of others. I want to be a trustworthy person who can keep a secret, instead of a perverse person, stirring up conflict. Lord, You tell me that a gossip separates close friends. I never want to do that. I want to be known for stopping quarrels and building closer friendships, not gossiping and fueling fires. Please help me to only speak words of love, kindness, encouragement, and integrity. Thank You, God! Amen.

REFLECT: Contemplate the power of words expressed in Proverbs. They are completely contradictory to the old adage, "Sticks and stones may break my bones, but words will never hurt me." How did that phrase ever become popular? Kids say it to one another and actually believe it. But words are like choice morsels. They down to the inmost parts of our soul and stay there to either flourish or fester. Words can be a weapon, gossip, or a salve, depending on which we choose to use. We can either bless or hurt other people, in one sentence. How can we become more aware of the words we use, especially when we're joking or being flippant? Don't let your words come out so quickly that it's too late to take them back.

ACT: Today's assignment is to be focused and aware of every word you say. You can either make a mental note or write down all of your questionable jokes, conversations, comments, and responses. Watch what you say and how you say it. And notice if you're saying anything that you wouldn't say if you were writing a letter. Try to heighten your awareness of your words and see if you're pleased or surprised at how you use them. Most people don't think about their words and cause more damage than they mean to. Start to evaluate everything you say. How are you doing?

YOUR THOUGHTS:

DAY 4

GOSSIP COMES OUT OF THE HEART

"For out of the heart come evil thoughts, murder, adultery, sexual immorality, theft, false testimony, slander."   Matthew 15:19

"Notice, we never pray for folks we gossip about, and we never gossip about the folk for whom we pray! For prayer is a great deterrent."   Leonard Ravenhill

PRAY: Heavenly Father, I understand that we can only know our true selves by examining our hearts, for out of the heart comes the evil thoughts listed in Matthew. Today I want to give You my heart so that I won't gossip, slander or think awful thoughts. Sometimes I can be so mad, so silly, or so carefree that I say things I don't mean. To help me avoid gossip, would Your Holy Spirit purify my heart? Thank You for giving me the strength to control everything that comes out of my mouth because I have a clean heart. Amen.

REFLECT: This verse in Matthew calls out our hearts as the problem causing us to sin. "Out of the HEART come evil thoughts" Our body is a temple, and we are in charge of that Temple, so if it is left unkempt, it can attract all kinds of sin. And if our heart is dirty, then it is free to spew out evil. It's our responsibility to protect our heart, so we must ask God to purify us so that we don't break His commandments. Our deceitful hearts love sin, but our souls long for goodness, purity, and love. Surrender control of ALL of your heart and let the Holy Spirit take control and transform your thoughts, words and actions.

ACT: Whatever time it is in your day right now, since you got up this morning, have you had any evil, mean, selfish, or gossipy thoughts? Have you said any harmful words? If not, praise God and keep going, trying to keep your heart pure for the rest of the day. If you have already slipped, then ask forgiveness and pray to start fresh, believing that as of the moment your prayer ends, you are as white as snow and ready to begin again. Do this as many times as you need to before the end of today. And as you lie down to sleep, either thank the Lord for a successful day, or ask Him to help you again tomorrow, and the next day, until you have broken the habit of gossip and you are transformed!

YOUR THOUGHTS:

DAY 5

GOSSIP AND SLANDER AGAINST YOU

'Though rulers sit together and slander me, your servant will meditate on your decrees."

Psalm 119:23

"Keeping a clear conscience, so that those who speak maliciously against your good behavior in Christ may be ashamed of their slander." 1 Peter 3:16

"The best way to deal with slander is to pray about it: God will either remove it, or remove the sting from it. Our own attempts at clearing ourselves are usually failures; we are like the boy who wished to remove the blot from his copy, and by his bungling made it ten times worse."

Charles Spurgeon

PRAY: Lord, today I pray for our political leaders, and for the leaders and decision-makers in Hollywood who don't know You and don't understand the sin of gossip and slander. Many of them see nothing wrong with speaking maliciously against other people and against You. As I meditate on Your decrees, I ask the Holy Spirit to convict those who speak maliciously and make them feel ashamed of their slander and gossip. Help me not judge our country's political and cultural "rulers", but to pray for them to find You. Amen.

REFLECT: God has told us to pray for our leaders, whether we agree with them or not, and ask Him to renew, transform and guide them. You may pray for your political leaders, but have you ever thought to pray for your cultural leaders? The leaders in Hollywood who are creating our world's media and entertainment need prayer. Many of them slander others, gossip, lie, and hurt others. It's our job to pray for them to discover and embrace the healing and transforming love of Jesus that can change their hearts and tongues.

ACT: Think of two Hollywood leaders who don't yet know Jesus and might be known for slander. Whether they are decision-makers or celebrities, they are impacting our culture through their lives, projects and even their words. Instead of gossiping about them, stop right now and pray for the Holy Spirit to come in and change their hearts, words, and actions. This keeps your conscience clear and leads these leaders closer to Jesus. That's a Win/Win!

YOUR THOUGHTS:

DAY 6

HOLD YOUR TONGUE

"Gossip betrays a confidence; so avoid a man who talks too much." "Even a fool is thought wise if he keeps silent, and discerning if he holds his tongue." Proverbs 20 &17:28

"Gossip needn't be false to be evil—there's a lot of truth that shouldn't be passed around."

Frank A. Clark

PRAY: Oh Lord, help me to be wise. Make me a trusted person of integrity. Help me to hold my tongue and listen more than talk. I never want to be a gossip or to betray anyone's confidence. Help me to choose my words and not over-talk. Give me self-discipline, regardless of the circumstances. Thank You for helping me, guiding me, and molding me into the person whom You've created me to be. I need You desperately, every moment, Lord, and I know that with wisdom comes silence. I pray this in Jesus' mighty name. Amen.

REFLECT: There is a lot to unpack in these two Proverbs. We learn that a gossip betrays a confidence, which is why we have to be so careful not to talk against anyone. As believers, we should be people whom others can turn to and trust. Those traits are rare commodities, so we must hold our tongues. "Even a fool is thought wise if he keeps silent." We can choose to act wisely just by holding our tongues. That's a start. But we also need the Holy Spirit to give us guidance on what to say, whom to say it to, and what to keep to ourselves. Holding our tongues is an important discipline for Christians and makes us wise and discerning.

ACT: Let's step out in faith and do something radical, just like Jesus. Choose someone close to you whom you have gossiped about. Did you tell too much information or reveal some secret that you should have kept silent about? Whatever form of gossip you are guilty of, now is the time to make amends. Meet with that person or call them on the phone and apologize for talking too much, even if it wasn't a serious offense – just a slip of the tongue. Let them know that you're working on controlling your words and you want to start by apologizing for this one mistake. Taking this first step in breaking any possible habit of gossip and practicing wisdom and discernment will make your heart feel so good!

YOUR THOUGHTS:

DAY 7

BUILD UP OTHERS WITH YOUR WORDS

"Do not let any unwholesome talk come out of your mouths, but only what is helpful for building others up according to their needs, that it may benefit those who listen... Get rid of all bitterness, rage and anger, brawling and slander, along with every form of malice."

Ephesians 4:29 & 31

"I resolve to speak ill of no man whatever, not even in a matter of truth; but rather by some means excuse the faults I hear charged upon others, and upon proper occasions speak all the good I know of everybody."   Benjamin Franklin

PRAY: Thank You, Lord, that I am ending my week on Gossip with Paul's mandate to only talk about what is helpful for building others up according to their needs, only what benefits those who listen. I want to keep my eyes on You, and control my tongue, so that I can stop all unwholesome talk and only benefit others and lead non-believers to You. Lord, thank You that You never give up on me, and that I can always turn to You for help, strength and wisdom. Lord, direct my words and let me make an eternal difference in the world. Amen!

REFLECT: We often focus on what we should do, act upon, or accomplish to be great Christians. But Paul tells us to focus on what we say. Embrace His words and be empowered to make an eternal difference by the words that you say. Do you only use words that are helpful for building others up according to their needs and benefit those who listen— encouraging them and not saying anything unwholesome— including gossip? People might even notice and try to follow your example. Some might ask why you're so encouraging and not angry or slanderous. Then you'd get a chance to share your faith and offer them a new hope, new ideas, and a more positive view of the world!

ACT: Ready for a new commitment to end your week? Say something nice, kind, encouraging, helpful, uplifting, or loving to one person EVERY DAY. Call a friend just to tell them you love them, or tell someone you don't know that you'd like to meet them! Start practicing wholesome talk, so you won't be tempted to get idle and gossip. You'll have so much fun that you'll notice when you miss a day. Go make the world a better place!

YOUR THOUGHTS:

REJECTION

WEEK FOURTEEN

One of the hardest hurts to overcome is the feeling of rejection. Nobody wants to be rejected and God doesn't want us to reject Him as well. This week we'll look at all of the ways we can handle rejection and learn what God says about acceptance and rejection. As cherished children of God, let's have an un-offendable heart and embrace the joy of never feeling rejected again.

DAY 1

GOD DOES NOT REJECT HIS PEOPLE

"Praise be to God, who has not rejected my prayer or withheld his love from me!"

Psalm 66:20

"For the Lord will not reject his people; he will never forsake his inheritance."

Psalm 94:14

"Don't misinterpret God's silence as rejection."

T.B. Joshua

PRAY: Dear God, I praise You, for You have not rejected my prayer or withheld Your love from me! I know, Lord, that You will not reject Your people and You will never forsake me, for I am Your inheritance. I praise Your holy name and embrace You as You have embraced me, in Jesus' name, Amen.

REFLECT: Oh, if only we could live our lives in a constant state of praise to our almighty and awesome God! That may only be possible if we don't reject ourselves, through having bad self-esteem, insecurity, or even depression. If we look at ourselves through God's eyes, and not through our own distorted mirror, then can we be free to praise Him and truly believe in our heart that the Lord will NOT reject us as one of His people. He loves you so much that you are His inheritance. Can you praise Him for that and truly believe it?

ACT: Take a look at how you feel about yourself. Are you too hard on yourself? Do you have a low self-esteem? Do you genuinely believe that God is crazy in love with you? If not, you may be rejecting God's inheritance for you. You could believe that God is rejecting you or your prayers because you think He doesn't consider you worthy. That's not true! Is there any area of your life where you are rejecting God's truths and thus not believing that you are valued, loved, and that you can make a positive difference in this world just by being you? Look deep within yourself and start praising God for who He made you to be, believing that you are His rich inheritance!

YOUR THOUGHTS:

DAY 2

DON'T REJECT PEOPLE BY THEIR APPEARANCE

"But the Lord said to Samuel, "Do not consider his appearance or his height, for I have rejected him. The Lord does not look at the things man looks at. Man looks at the outward appearance, but the Lord looks at the heart.""   1 Samuel 16:7

"For every successful actor or actress, there are countless numbers who don't make it. The name of the game is rejection. You go to an audition and you're told you're too tall or you're too Irish or your nose is not quite right. You're rejected for your education, you're rejected for this or that and it's really tough."   Liam Neeson

PRAY: Dear Heavenly Father, please give me the wisdom to not judge, accept, or reject people by their outward appearance, but to be like You and look at people's hearts. Thank You that nothing is more important to You than my heart and my intentions. How sobering that You reject people who appear to be great in our eyes but whom You can see as hypocrites, phonies, or liars. Don't let me reject anyone whom You see as beautiful on the inside! Amen.

REFLECT: It's so easy to reject people based on their appearance. That's one of the main reasons Christians reject Hollywood entertainment celebrities. They think they are arrogant, selfish, narcissistic, too rich or immoral. And yet the Lord does not look at the things people look at. He loves EVERYONE, even the Hollywood celebrities, or anyone else you have trouble loving. How do you change your negative views of people? Maybe it's to pray that you can see them through God's eyes and have His heart for them.

ACT: Think of someone in Hollywood whom either you have rejected, or you think God has rejected, or whom you have idolized because of what you see on the outside, and start praying for them. Ask the Lord to see that person's heart and to embrace them with His unconditional love. Don't let the outward appearance of anyone in Hollywood stop you from praying for them, with love, to find Jesus. You can start right now!

YOUR THOUGHTS:

DAY 3

WHOEVER REJECTS US REJECTS GOD

"Whoever listens to you listens to me; whoever rejects you rejects me; but whoever rejects me rejects him who sent me."
Luke 10:16

REJECTION: The act of throwing away; the act of casting off or forsaking; refusal to accept or grant.
Webster's 1828 Dictionary

PRAY: Dear Jesus, In Luke 10 You tell us that You equipped 72 people and sent them out to tell others about You, giving them the power and authority to speak truth to the masses. Your promise to them is the same as it is to me today. Thank You that You empower me to represent You and to live a Christ-like life, and if anyone rejects me they will be rejecting You. Please remind me that I can't take people's responses personally, as long as I'm living for You. It's all about You, Jesus! Amen.

REFLECT: The Dictionary defines rejection as: *"the dismissing or refusing of a proposal, idea, etc."* That means that if you're feeling rejected, it's because that person is dismissing or refusing your proposal or idea. Jesus says if you talk to others about Him and they reject your truths, then they are rejecting Him, not you. So, you shouldn't be afraid of rejection if Jesus isn't! And, it's even more serious than that. If they reject your words and truths about Jesus, then they are dismissing or refusing not only Jesus, but God the Father as well. It's our job to bring the love and truth of the gospel to others, regardless of being rejected.

ACT: Choose one person in your life who doesn't know Jesus and choose to pray about how to share your faith with them. Ask the Lord to take away your fear of rejection. It's not about you, it's about them and the message of salvation through Jesus. He was rejected so we can expect to be rejected at times, especially when talking about Him. So don't give up. You are offering them a relationship with the Creator of the Universe, the One who offers us unconditional love, joy, peace, hope, and salvation. Push through your concern about being dismissed, or that person will refuse to believe your story, and remember that God already knows what will happen and has told us how to handle it in Luke 10:16.

YOUR THOUGHTS:

DAY 4

DON'T REJECT JESUS AS OTHERS HAVE

"The stone the builders rejected has become the capstone;"   Psalm 118:22
"As you come to him, the living Stone-- rejected by men but chosen by God and precious to him—"   1 Peter 2:4

"When Christ was in the world, He was despised by men; in the hour of need He was forsaken by acquaintances and left by friends to the depths of scorn. He was willing to suffer and to be despised; do you dare to complain of anything? He had enemies and defamers; do you want everyone to be your friend, your benefactor? How can your patience be rewarded if no adversity test it? How can you be a friend of Christ if you are not willing to suffer any hardship? Suffer with Christ and for Christ if you wish to reign with Him."
                                                                     Thomas a Kempis

PRAY: Lord, it's sobering to know that You were rejected by the people You loved and that we too can be rejected by people. But thank You that You are the living Stone, that I am chosen by You and I'm precious to You. Don't ever let me reject You, Lord, for You, the living Stone, have chosen me! Amen and Amen.

REFLECT: We all know people who have rejected the truth of the Gospel and live for themselves; family members and friends who love us and know what we believe, but reject Jesus. Keep praying for these people, and also check to see what part of God's Gospel you might be rejecting. Do you lie or cheat? Are you prideful, jealous, angry? God wants you to be living stones that are acceptable to Him. If you are rejected by other people because of your faith, remember that you are chosen by God and precious to Him!

ACT: Think about something in your life that you are compromising on because you don't want others to reject you? Look at the possible sins you could be committing on today's *Reflect* and then ask God to make you more precious to Him. Spend some time in worship, draw close to Jesus and let Him transform you from the inside out. Ask Him to take away any fear of rejection as you commit fully to Him. Do a check list of how you're doing in God's eyes and then recommit every part of your life to Him right now.

YOUR THOUGHTS:

DAY 5

REJECT EVERY KIND OF EVIL

"Avoid every kind of evil."   1 Thessalonians 5:22

"To reject this inhuman Communist ideology is simply to be a human being. Such a rejection is more than a political act. It is a protest of our souls against those who would have us forget the concepts of good and evil."   Aleksandr Solzhenitsyn

PRAY: Jesus, I pray in Your name, to avoid every kind of evil in my life. I want to love people but I want to see where the enemy is working, reject His evil deeds and avoid his fiery darts. Please give me wisdom to see evil for what it is and the discernment to know when to turn away and flee and when to stand up against it. Help me to fight the spiritual battles, without fear, in Your name. Thank You for protecting me against evil and showing me how to reject it, but not fear it, so I can stand strong against the spirits and principalities in the heavenly realms. Amen.

REFLECT: "Reject every kind of evil." That's a powerful statement, but what does it really mean? Does it mean to flee every time we approach evil? Or do we reject people who are sinning? In reading the fuller context of the verse, it tells us not to quench the Spirit, not to treat prophecies with contempt, but to test everything against the scriptures. God wants us to hold on to what is good and to avoid every kind of evil. That's a wide and far reaching command, which requires us to study the scriptures, understand the spiritual battle between good and evil, and then avoid evil as a godly response, not an emotional reaction.

ACT: Reread all of I Thessalonians 5 and prayerfully study how to wisely understand evil. Understand that it's not avoiding people, but it is avoiding the devil's lies that come out of people. False prophets are not to be avoided, but what they say is to be rejected. So, as you read the chapter, ask God to teach you how to discern evil so that you can avoid the work of the devil and yet not avoid the people whom the enemy is using, for God loves them and they need His love through us. Maybe you'll want to start memorizing scripture by learning these five words from I Thessalonians 5:22: "Avoid every kind of evil."

YOUR THOUGHTS:

DAY 6

DON'T REJECT ONE ANOTHER

"Accept one another, then, just as Christ accepted you, in order to bring praise to God."

Romans 15:7

"The greatest gift that you can give to others is the gift of unconditional love and acceptance." Brian Tracy

PRAY: Oh Lord, teach me how to accept all people, regardless of their color, education, background, attitudes, lifestyles, or personal choices. Please help me to remember that You have accepted me, just as I am, so, I need Your help to understand that this isn't about me, but I need to accept others so that it can bring praise to You. I pray this in the precious name of Jesus, Amen.

REFLECT: It's hard to be totally accepting of other people. We all have prejudices, and some people force us out of our comfort zones by being difficult or even evil. But God tells us to accept one another. We don't have to be close friends with everyone, and we don't have to hang out with just anybody. But in our words, our attitudes, and our actions, we are to accept everyone, just as Christ accepted us. How can you bring praise to God by accepting someone whom you don't like, or whom you see is making bad choices? And what would that look like, practically?

ACT: Identify one person in your life whom you don't like. It may be someone close to you who has hurt you or someone you have written off because you have nothing in common with them and don't like them. Now pray about how you will change your attitude about them. Even if you don't have personal contact with them, in your heart, you don't want to reject them as a child of God. You want to bring praise to God by praying for them, being kind to them, even encouraging them, or just accepting them in your heart. Ask the Lord to change you, from the inside out, so that you don't reject anyone! And start with the one person you've identified today.

YOUR THOUGHTS:

DAY 7

NOTHING IS REJECTED WITH THANKSGIVING

"For everything God created is good, and nothing is to be rejected if it is received with thanksgiving, because it is consecrated by the word of God and prayer." 1 Timothy 4:4-5

"Every time I thought I was being rejected from something good, I was actually being re-directed to something better."
Dr. Steve Maraboli

PRAY: God in heaven, I know that everything You have created is good and nothing is to be rejected. I want to receive everything You give me, with thanksgiving, even if it doesn't appear to be good. I know that everything that happens to me, everything You give me and everything around me, is consecrated by Your word and my prayers. So, let me embrace everything that comes my way as good, or as something that You can turn into good. Amen.

REFLECT: It's hard to imagine that we are not to reject anything that comes at us, but we need to receive it with thanksgiving – because it is consecrated by the word of God and prayer. My husband taught me years ago to thank God for everything that comes our way – whether it be good or bad. We started thanking Him for the rejections, the jobs we didn't get, the financial stresses, the emotional hurts, and the physical pains, because we wanted to live lives of thanksgiving. It totally changed me as I learned that what I thought was a curse, turned into a blessing, and that God really is in control of everything. I Timothy 4:4-5 opens up the challenge to not reject things that don't make sense, but to thank God for them.

ACT: Choose to thank God for something bad in your life right now. Don't reject a mean person or an unfair situation or a heavy burden, as bad or evil, but choose to embrace it, thank God for it and then see how He will consecrate it by His Word and by your prayers. Don't give up on thanking Him for whatever it is and wait to see how He will change your heart, your perspective and your pain, into something beautiful!

YOUR THOUGHTS:

JOY

WEEK FIFTEEN

This week we are excited about finding JOY in the midst of sorrow and experiencing the joy of the Lord in all circumstances. We desire to live a life of joy and yet how many of us know that the joy of the Lord is our strength? God's will for our life is to rejoice and be joyful!

DAY 1

REJOICE ALWAYS!

"Be joyful always; pray continually; give thanks in all circumstances, for this is God's will for you in Christ Jesus."   1 Thessalonians 5:16-18

"The secret of gospel change is being convinced that Jesus is the good life and the fountain of joy. Any alternative we might choose would be the letdown."   Tim Chester

PRAY: Dear God, I want to always be in an attitude of rejoicing, prayer and thanksgiving. Please have Your Holy Spirit fill me up with supernatural joy and thanks so that I am living in Your will every day. And what a freeing thought, Lord, to know that if I am always rejoicing, praying, and thanking You for all the details of my life, that I am living in the center of Your will. Thank You for helping me to choose joy and do with me what is needed to make that happen. In Jesus' name, AMEN.

REFLECT: So often we are asking God what His will is. Should I take this job? Is she the right one for me? Is this where I should live? Lord, what is Your will for my life? And now we know—it's simply to rejoice always, pray constantly, and give thanks in all circumstances. That's a freeing thought to know that we can let go of the details of our life and trust that they will work out, as long as we're keeping our hearts, minds and souls focused on the Lord, with rejoicing, prayer and thankfulness!

ACT: See if you can last all day today without asking God for anything! Just choose to rejoice in everything, pray about everything, and thank Him for everything—regardless of whether it is bad or good! At the end of the day you will feel more joyful, prayerful and thankful. Joy is a choice. Give it a try!

YOUR THOUGHTS:

DAY 2

TEARS TURNED TO JOY

"Those who sow in tears will reap with songs of joy. He who goes out weeping, carrying seed to sow, will return with songs of joy, carrying sheaves with him."   Psalm 126:5-6

"Laughter dulls the sharpest pain and flattens out the greatest stress. To share it is to give a gift of health, because, as someone pointed out: Ulcers can't grow while you're laughing."
                                                            Hunter "Patch" Adams

PRAY: Lord, help me to find joy in my sorrow. I know that as I weep tears, I will reap songs of joy because You turn my sorrow into dancing. Will You please do that for me now? I need You to find joy in my sadness and experience the joy that only You can give me. I'm here Lord and calling for You. In Jesus's name, Amen.

REFLECT: The ways of the Lord are so often opposite of man's ways. Think about how you can find joy in your sorrow. Could it be that if you don't experience the darkness of sorrow you can't fully experience the lightness of joy? We will never know what real joy is if we don't know what sadness feels like—in the contrast is where we gain understanding. Have you felt both extremes—dark sorrow and total joy? Can you say that one helps you to understand the importance of the other?

ACT: Can you pray for the people in Hollywood who make the world laugh and cry?!? They need our prayers in order to serve the world with their stories, gifts, and talents so that we can experience both joy and sorrow in the movie theaters, on television, on our iPads, and through listening to our favorite songs. The people in the entertainment industry feel deep sorrow, loneliness, isolation, judgment, and fear. But that's how they write rich stories and complex characters. Would you pray that they are able experience the joy of the Lord and that they know the source of that joy! Your prayers for them will not only make an eternal difference but also bring you joy.

YOUR THOUGHTS:

DAY 3

JOY: A FRUIT OF THE SPIRIT

"But the fruit of the Spirit is love, joy, peace, patience, kindness, goodness, faithfulness, gentleness and self-control. Against such things there is no law."   Galatians 5:22-23

"If happiness is what you're after, then you are going to be let down frequently and be unhappy much of your time. Joy, though, is something else. It's not a choice, not a response to some result, it is a constant. Joy is the feeling we have from doing what we are fashioned to do, no matter the outcome."   Matthew McConaughey

PRAY: Lord, would You fill me with all of the fruits of the Spirit so that I can be overflowing today with love, peace, patience, kindness, goodness, faithfulness, self-control and, especially, joy. I need You to help me to live out these traits in my life. I want to experience Your joy today, so please fill me up new and fresh with all the fruit of Your Spirit. Selah! Amen.

REFLECT: Wouldn't it be amazing to be known for living out all of the fruits of the Spirit in your life every day? Since God defines these fruits so specifically then He makes them all available to us. Reflect on each one and ask the Lord to show you how to embrace them, or show you what transformation needs to happen for you to become more loving, joyful, peaceful, patient, kind, good, faithful and self-controlled. With God nothing is impossible.

ACT: What one fruit of the Spirit do you want to have more of in your life? Choose one fruit of the Spirit and commit to become more like that. Whichever one you choose, you may need to pray more about it, read more scriptures that deal with that, and change your thoughts to focus more on that particular fruit. Just take one at a time and ask the Lord to understand it, embrace it and have it transform you.

YOUR THOUGHTS:

DAY 4

GOD TURNS ANXIETY TO JOY

"When anxiety was great within me, your consolation brought joy to my soul."

Psalm 94:19

"When we are powerless to do a thing, it is a great joy that we can come and step inside the ability of Jesus"

Corrie ten Boom

PRAY: Dear Father in Heaven, I ask for You to take away my anxiety and fill me with joy. My anxiety is great within me as I worry about the cares and concerns in my life, but I know that Your consolation will bring me joy. Please Father, fill me up with Your consoling joy so that my anxiety will melt away. I need You every hour and thank You for your faithfulness. Amen.

REFLECT: We don't often think of God as a consoling God. But what a great truth to know that the God of the Universe consoles us and brings us joy. We often try on our own to deal with our anxiety, but this verse says that He is the one who brought me joy by His consolation. That same consolation is available to you any time and it brings joy to your soul.

ACT: Ask God right now to console you. Ask Him to take away your anxiety so that you can physically, tangibly, emotionally, and spiritually feel the worry melt away and joy fill you up. Can you concentrate? Can you believe that's possible? Can you feel His presence and His consoling? Just sit in silence for a few minutes and think of God filling up your every cell and pore with His consoling JOY.

YOUR THOUGHTS:

DAY 5

REJOICE WITH OTHERS

"Her neighbors and relatives heard that the Lord had shown her great mercy, and they shared her joy."
                                          Luke 1:58

"There is not one blade of grass, there is no color in this world that is not intended to make us rejoice."
                                          John Calvin

PRAY: Lord, help me to have joy when others are blessed. I want to feel Your joy when my family members, friends, co-workers, neighbors and even my enemies experience joy. It's hard to feel true joy, without any jealousy, when others experience Your mercy and blessings, but I want to be that person. Help me to rejoice with others and share their joy with them, as You tell us to. Amen.

REFLECT: When have you felt complete joy for someone else when they experienced a blessing, a great answer to prayer, or even an earthly success? Is that hard for you? Can you remember when the Lord has shown someone else mercy and you got a twinge of jealousy? Be honest with the Lord and yourself about how you respond to the successes and blessings of others. Can you say that you are joyful?

ACT: Choose one friend, family member or acquaintance who has just had a great thing happen to them. To intentionally experience joy, write them a congratulations note, or call them to say how happy you are for them, or email some kind and loving words. Celebrate with them! Take that step as the first in many to rejoice with others who are joyful. It will fill them up with God's love, feed your soul, and bring you more joy as well.

YOUR THOUGHTS:

DAY 6

FIND JOY IN YOUR TRIALS

"Out of the most severe trial, their overflowing joy and their extreme poverty welled up in rich generosity." 2 Corinthians 8:2

"If we can just let go and trust that things will work out the way they're supposed to, without trying to control the outcome, then we can begin to enjoy the moment more fully. The joy of the freedom it brings becomes more pleasurable than the experience itself."

Goldie Hawn

PRAY: Lord, it's easy to feel joy when everything is going well, but I don't know how to experience joy in the midst of severe trials. I want to feel "the joy of the Lord" all the time—despite my circumstances or the events in the world around me. I want my extreme poverty financially, emotions, or faith, to well up into rich generosity in my spirit, so that I can overflow with joy in any and every situation. I ask that You show me how to experience Your joy all the time, and I look forward to it. Amen.

REFLECT: Have you thought about how difficult it is to feel joy when you're going through hard times? It's impossible without the Lord. How can you live such a Christ-like life that you can experience joy in the midst of hardship, sickness, poverty, brokenness, pain or severe trials? God tells us it's possible with Him, so reflect on what changes you would need in your life to have more joy?

ACT: Assuming you have some trial in your life right now, can you define it and then choose to seek joy in the midst of it? There may be many areas of disappointment, pain, frustration, sadness or stress, but choose one and ask the Lord to help you, change you, and mold you into a joyful person while dealing with that situation. Don't get discouraged if it doesn't happen right away. You are choosing to change a lifetime habit by seeking joy in moments when you usually feel a negative emotion. Give yourself permission to let go of the worry and choose to feel joy. May it well up in rich generosity.

YOUR THOUGHTS:

DAY 7

DANCE WITH JOY

"You turned my wailing into dancing; you removed my sackcloth and clothed me with joy, that my heart may sing to you and not be silent. O Lord my God, I will give you thanks forever."   Psalm 30:11-12

"Do not abandon yourselves to despair. We are the Easter people and hallelujah is our song."   Pope John Paul II

PRAY: God, I know that You can turn my wailing into joy, so I praise You for pulling me out of my struggles and filling me with joy. I need You to take away the pain, struggle, fear or anger and replace it with dancing! I don't feel joyful, but I know You can change my heart and my mind so that my heart can sing Your praises. I don't want to be sad and silent, Lord. I will praise You and give You thanks forever and ever. Amen.

REFLECT: When we're sad, lonely, depressed, angry or fearful, it's so hard to pull ourselves out of it. In fact, we sometimes can't. Negative emotions are often a downward spiral, but the Lord tells us that He can turn our wailing into dancing, and He can have our hearts sing. So, we need to turn to Him to get us out of the dark places that we fall into. Think about how He can pull you out of your dark place. Can you trust Him to do that?

ACT: Joy is a choice, not just a feeling we can muster up. And God tells us how we can get that joy—through Him. Don't be silent. Ask Him right now to change your thoughts and emotions from sackcloth and wailing to joy, dancing, and praise! It's not an immediate transformation. It takes prayer, Bible reading and commitment. But, take a step right now and praise your God and give Him thanks - forever.

YOUR THOUGHTS:

SALVATION

WEEK SIXTEEN

Salvation comes from embracing the Good News of the Gospel. The Great Commission is to go out and tell the Good News to the people in our sphere of influence. But that's hard to do. This week we'll focus on the power, the joy and the eternal difference you can make by stepping out of your comfort zone and talking about Jesus, without freaking out.

DAY 1

GOD DRAWS US TO HIM

"No one can come to me unless the Father who sent me draws him, and I will raise him up at the last day."

John 6:44

"Orthodoxy, to me, is Jesus and him alone. But we need to not only invite Jesus into our hearts as a Savior but continue to invite Jesus into our lives as the creator and sustainer of the universe. Every heresy comes in a form of legalism, though sometimes it is disguised as "free for all" tolerance, and grace as universalism."

Makoto Fujimura

PRAY: Dear Jesus, I pray that the people whom I want to see become Christians will feel Your nudge and they will allow You to draw them to You. I ask that they will be in heaven – even if on their last day, so that they will be with me and You. Thank You for drawing my loved ones to You and that I can pray for their hearts to embrace You and for Your Holy Spirit to embrace them. Amen and Amen.

REFLECT: No one can come to Jesus unless the Father draws him. So, it takes BOTH our prayers, actions, and words AND the nudging, guidance, and transformation of the Father to draw others to Him. Reflect on how you're working in partnership with the Holy Spirit as you pray for other people to become Christians, and that He is the one who will raise them up. Isn't it amazing how perfect God is, to wait for our prayers and then to be the one to touch their hearts and make them ready to accept Him as their Savior? What a gift to be a part of God's perfect plan.

ACT: Today, don't just pray for your unsaved friends and family to become Christians, but ask your heavenly Father to melt their hearts, to nudge them to look up at Him, and to draw them into His Kingdom. Focus your prayers on the Lord to draw others to Him and ask Him to raise them up – even if it's on the last day. Your requests to the Lord are fulfilling His perfect plan.

YOUR THOUGHTS:

DAY 2

KNOW THAT YOU HAVE ETERNAL LIFE

"I write these things to you who believe in the name of the Son of God so that you may know that you have eternal life."   1 John 5:13

"It is vanity to wish to live long and then fail to live well."   Thomas a Kempis, 1425

PRAY: Lord, thank You for being so clear in not only telling us how to become Christians but then reconfirming to us that we are saved. Thank You for the Bible. You gave it to us as a gift, so that we know, without a doubt, that we are saved. Please let me never question my salvation and to tell other Christians Your promise that You gave us the Bible so that we KNOW we have eternal life. I praise You! Amen.

REFLECT: Have you ever questioned your faith? Do you know other people who question their faith? Have you thought about all the promises in the Bible? For you who believe in the name of the Son of God, the Bible is so much more than great stories, guidelines, and inspirational people. Most importantly, it confirms your salvation and promises you that you have eternal life. That is a comforting thought to reflect on.

ACT: Would you encourage someone today that the Bible tells us that there is no question that those who believe in the name of Jesus definitely have eternal life? Some people need to hear that, and you could give someone great peace today by passing on that promise. Pray about who needs to be confirmed in their salvation and just call or email them with this verse.

YOUR THOUGHTS:

DAY 3

CONFESSION + BELIEF = SALVATION

"That if you confess with your mouth, "Jesus is Lord," and believe in your heart that God raised him from the dead, you will be saved."   Romans 10:9

"Handle them carefully, for words have more power than atom bombs."

Pearl Strachan Hurd

PRAY: Dear Heavenly Father, so often I don't know how to explain to someone how to become a Christian. Please help me to memorize this verse so that I can clearly tell others the good news. You really make tough issues so simple, and I want to be better at telling others the good news with the promises of the scriptures. Thank You for Romans 10:9 and help me to express this life changing message to others clearly, calmly and with love. Amen.

REFLECT: Think about the times you wanted to tell someone about how to become a Christian, but you didn't because you didn't know what to say, or how to say it. Or you thought you'd sound silly or the other person really didn't want to hear it, etc. We must be prepared for spiritual battle every time we bring up the Gospel to a pre-Christian. Re-read this verse and think about the people you could talk to about this simple truth. Do you think you could express it clearly to another person? What would it take to have the complete confidence to explain this message about Jesus? It's really very simple

ACT: Memorize this verse! There are only two steps to become a Christian: 1) Confess with your mouth that Jesus is Lord, and 2) Believe in your heart that God raised Him from the dead. That's it, if you believe that, you will be saved! Don't allow the enemy's lies to talk you out of sharing this transforming hope. Don't think that you don't know enough or think you sound stupid, or convince yourself they aren't ready, or fear you'll be too pushy. If the Holy Spirit has nudged you to share Jesus, then don't listen to the condemning voice in your head. Memorizing these 2 steps could change your friend's life and your own! Don't miss this opportunity to be bold for the Lord. If you want help in sharing your faith, pick up a copy of our book—*How to Talk About Jesus without Freaking Out.*

YOUR THOUGHTS:

DAY 4

WE BRING HIS LIGHT TO OTHERS

"I will rescue you from your own people and from the Gentiles. I am sending you to them to open their eyes and turn them from darkness to light, and from the power of Satan to God, so that they may receive forgiveness of sins and a place among those who are sanctified by faith in me."'   Acts 26:17-18

"Aim at heaven when you pray and get earth thrown in. Aim at earth and you will get neither."   C.S. Lewis, from *The Joyful Christian*

PRAY: Dear Heavenly Father, I need to pray more for the people around me who don't yet know You. I ask that You use me to help open their eyes, so that they may turn from darkness to the light and from the power of Satan to You. And I pray that You send me to the pre-Christians in my life, so that I may help them to receive forgiveness for their sins and live among those of us who are sanctified by our faith in You. Send me Lord! Amen.

REFLECT: Have you considered that God personally sends us to talk to specific people who don't yet know Him? Can you imagine that there are people who can turn from the power of Satan to the power of God and receive forgiveness because of having you in their life? God tells us that He sends us so that we can be a part of rescuing people. Who do you think He is sending you to reach out to?

ACT: Choose one pre-Christian in your life to pray for EVERY DAY for the next month. Ask the Lord to show you how to pray for that person and what else you should do or say to open their eyes, turn them from darkness and offer them the hope of the Gospel and receive forgiveness. After the month of committed prayer, the Lord will reveal to you what He is doing in your friend's life and in yours.

YOUR THOUGHTS:

DAY 5

THE GOOD NEWS IS BEAUTIFUL

How beautiful on the mountains are the feet of those who bring good news, who proclaim peace, who bring good tidings, who proclaim salvation, who say to Zion, "Your God reigns!"

Isaiah 52:7

"Sitting in the pews wringing our hands about decay in the world is not being salt. Neither is decrying the evil without offering positive alternatives."

Bob Briner, from *Roaring Lambs: A Gentle Plan to Radically Change Your World*

PRAY: I pray for You, the God of Abraham, Isaac, and Jacob, to reveal Yourself through me to others as I proclaim peace and salvation and bring good tidings to those around me. I want to bring good news to the people in my life and I ask that You give me more opportunities to say to others, 'My God reigns'! Amen.

REFLECT: "How beautiful on the mountains are the feet of those who bring good news." Is that you? Are you bringing good news and good tidings to the people in your life? Are you proclaiming salvation to your friends, family members, neighbors, and co-workers? What would it take for you to become that beautiful person standing on the mountain top and proclaiming salvation?

ACT: Today is your day to be bold. Tell one person one good thing about Jesus! Tell him or her in a conversation, something wonderful about your Lord and Savior that will be good news to the person you're talking to. You can marvel at how much God loves you or tell them that He fills you with hope, joy, peace, or whatever you have experienced. Just one good tiding can make a person be hungry for more of Jesus, and it's beautiful!

YOUR THOUGHTS:

DAY 6

ALWAYS BE PREPARED TO GIVE AN ANSWER

"But in your hearts set apart Christ as Lord. Always be prepared to give an answer to everyone who asks you to give the reason for the hope that you have. But do this with gentleness and respect,"   1 Peter 3:15

"If only God would give me some clear sign! Like making a large deposit in my name at a Swiss bank."   Woody Allen

PRAY: Dear Jesus, whom I revere as Lord, I pray that You will give me and the Christians in influential cities, like Hollywood, the desire for, and the understanding of, how to clearly share the reason for the hope they have to those around them. And I ask that Christians in entertainment can make an eternal difference in the lives of the influential people around them; their co-workers, associates, and friends, by sharing their faith with love, gentleness, and respect. And I pray in Jesus' name, Amen.

REFLECT: Reflect on how you can give the people around you a reason for the hope that you have in you, to be a shining light in your world. Are you living every day with the confidence that God wants you to touch the hearts of your friends and co-workers, and are you asking Him to prepare you to give others hope, with gentleness and respect? Are you praying for our Christian culture-shapers, the Hollywood entertainment professionals, to be sharing their faith with those around them who have never been told about the reason for the hope we have?

ACT: Pray right now for the pre-Christian you've committed to pray for this month so that they will come to know Jesus. Decide to be a better friend to them by loving them, praying for them, and sharing your faith with them. Being a good friend to a pre-Christian, even in Hollywood, is giving someone a hope for eternity that they may never have known before. So, be ready! And, we would love to hear your stories! If you'd like to share them with us, email us at <u>info@hpnemail.org</u>

YOUR THOUGHTS:

DAY 7

BE ACTIVE IN SHARING YOUR FAITH

"I pray that you may be active in sharing your faith, so that you will have a full understanding of every good thing we have in Christ."   Philemon 1:6

"If I could just be like the salt and make people thirsty for the water of life -- that's all I ask."
                                                            Ruth Graham

PRAY: Oh Lord, I pray that I will be active in sharing my faith, so that I will have a full understanding of every good thing I have in Christ! I want to get excited about sharing my faith and not be intimidated, scared, insecure, or uncaring. Let me be so excited about You that I can't help but tell other people. And I pray this in Jesus' name, Amen.

REFLECT: Can you say that you like to share your faith? Are there other things in your life that you are so excited about that you talk more about those things than about Jesus? Maybe it's because you have a better understanding of those things than you do about Jesus. What would it take to be so aware of all the good things Jesus gives to you, and is to you, that you become excited to tell others about them?

ACT: Take out a piece of paper and make a list of ALL the good things you have in Christ…Your family, friends, job, neighborhood, house, food to eat every day, fun activities, joy, hope, comfort, etc. etc. As you make your list, pray about how much you would like to have your non-believing or pre-Christian friends experience the same joy and appreciation for the things in their life, and ask the Lord to open up opportunities for you to tell them about everything you're thankful for. Be bold and make an eternal difference in someone's life, the way someone did for you, so pray to be active in sharing your faith, and then do it!

YOUR THOUGHTS:

LONELINESS

WEEK SEVENTEEN

Loneliness is a part of the human condition, but the Lord tells us that we don't have to feel lonely if we trust in Him, seek Him, and let Him fill us up to overflowing. This week we investigate how to embrace His promises that He is always with us, so that we don't have to feel lonely!

DAY 1

I FEEL ALONE

"I lie awake; I have become like a bird alone on a roof."   Psalm 102:7

"But the man who loves God is known by God."   1 Corinthians 8:3

"Everybody has something that chews them up and, for me, that thing was always loneliness. The cinema has the power to make you not feel lonely, even when you are."

Tom Hanks

PRAY: Dear Lord, I lie awake feeling very alone, so I call out to You and ask that You put Your arms around me. I feel like a bird alone on a roof, and I want to feel secure as if in a warm nest. I love You God and I know that with You I'm not alone because I'm known by You. I need You now to comfort me and to remind me that You created me just like the birds, and that You are with me. In Jesus' name, Amen.

REFLECT: How often do you feel lonely, vulnerable, or lost like a bird alone on a roof? Scripture addresses our emotions so often, which we see when we stop to really listen to what we're reading. It's amazing that just by loving God we are intimately and eternally known by Him. And we never need to feel alone. How can you honestly believe this promise so that you never need to feel lonely? Every time you see a bird, it can be a reminder.

ACT: When you lie in bed tonight before falling asleep, remember that the Lord is with you, that you love Him and that He knows you and is right there in you, next to you, and around you. Make it a habit of saying a prayer every night before going to sleep, to thank God that you are not alone because He is always with you. What a beautiful routine to end each day.

YOUR THOUGHTS:

DAY 2

GOSSIP, CONFLICT, AND LONELINESS

"A perverse man stirs up dissension, and a gossip separates close friends." Proverbs 16:28

"He who covers over an offense promotes love, but whoever repeats the matter separates close friends."   Proverbs 17:9

"Hollywood is loneliness beside the swimming pool."... "Loneliness is the universal problem of rich people."..."Loneliness and the feeling of being unwanted is the most terrible poverty."   Liv Ullmann; Joan Collin & Mother Teresa

PRAY: Lord, thank You for showing me that we can cause ourselves and the people closest to us to be lonely and alone just by stirring up conflict or by gossiping. Would You show me how to bring peace to all my relationships so that I am the one who fosters love by covering over an offense? I don't ever want to separate close friends and isolate people because of responding poorly to conflict. I don't want to be a perverse person and I never want to be the person who brings on loneliness to another through a broken relationship. Amen.

REFLECT: Doesn't it make sense that one of the enemy's greatest tools is to separate believers and to isolate Christians so that we are weak and not effective? The way he does it is by encouraging people to stir up conflict, to gossip about others and to break relationships. If we all understood the ease of fostering love instead of separating people, the world would be a different place. And it's all a matter of how we respond. What type of person are you? Be a person who loves and fosters love, and you will never be separated from others or God.

ACT: Choose one person right now who you're separated from – either by their doing or yours, and pray for healing and reconciliation, asking God how to rebuild the relationship, for as long as it takes. He will show you how to bring peace to the relationship. Expect miraculous results! If they are indeed a perverse person, then your prayers for them could mend their heart and bring them back into community. As you foster love through your prayers, or through your words and actions, you could protect that person, and yourself, from being alone in your brokenness and separated from close friends.

YOUR THOUGHTS:

DAY 3

FEAR OF LONELINESS

"So do not fear, for I am with you; do not be dismayed, for I am your God. I will strengthen you and help you; I will uphold you with my righteous right hand."   Isaiah 41:10

"As much as we complain about it, though, there's part of us that is drawn to a hurried life. It makes us feel important. It keeps the adrenaline pumping. It means I don't have to look too closely at my heart or life. It keeps us from feeling our loneliness."   John Ortberg

PRAY: Father in Heaven, I thank You that when I get fearful, or dismayed over life's issues, I don't have to deal with them alone. You promise me that You are with me through everything and that You will give me strength and help me. Thank You for walking with me through all of the tough times in life so that I never have to go through anything alone. Amen and Amen.

REFLECT: What does God mean when He says He's holding us up with His righteous right hand? Think of what it could mean: that because He is righteous, He holds us up, that He is filling us with His righteousness, and that regardless of what we're going through, due to His righteousness, we never need to be afraid. We are never alone, and we have all the strength we need, all the time. That is a profound and comforting thought. Whatever is happening in your life, never forget that you are never alone, and God has given you everything you need to move forward.

ACT: Right now, think about one thing that you are most afraid of. Now think about God giving you everything you need to deal with that fear. Picture Him with you right now giving you strength, handling your fear and walking alongside you every step of the way. Doesn't it make the fear less powerful, less overwhelming, or maybe there's no longer any fear at all?

YOUR THOUGHTS:

DAY 4

ALONE WITHOUT GOD

"Yet they say to God, 'Leave us alone! We have no desire to know your ways."   Job 21:14

"For none of us lives to himself alone and none of us dies to himself alone." Romans 14:7

"While the resurrection promises us a new and perfect life in the future, God loves us too much to leave us alone to contend with the pain, guilt and loneliness of our present life."

Josh McDowell

PRAY: Lord, I pray for the people all over the world, especially in the entertainment industry, who have chosen not to embrace You, who want to live life on their own. It's such a lonely way to live! Would You put Your arms around them, melt their hearts and let them know that they do not live for themselves alone, and they don't have to die for themselves alone. Lord, You know that artists are often lonely people. Would Your Holy Spirit reveal Himself to them and fill them up to overflowing with Your hope, promises and love? Thank You for loving every single person You've created. Amen.

REFLECT: How many people do you know in Hollywood who are running away from Jesus, who are living for themselves, have no desire to know God, and are even proud of it? Have you even considered how lonely they must be? Wouldn't it be more powerful, instead of judging them or talking about them, that you pray for them, asking the Lord to do a miracle in their lives and fill up their loneliness with His Holy Spirit, so that their lives can be full to overflowing? Do you believe that when you pray for someone, their life changes?

ACT: Hollywood is a very lonely place. And creative people overwhelmingly struggle with loneliness. Choose two people in Hollywood whom you happen to know don't believe in God and commit to pray for them. Ask the Lord to help them fall in love with Jesus, to have God melt their hearts and humble them, so that they can turn to Him and love Him and never experience that deep loneliness again. You'll be making an eternal difference by your faithful prayers and maybe saving someone's life.

YOUR THOUGHTS:

DAY 5

YOU ARE NOT ALONE

"Be strong and courageous. Do not be afraid or terrified because of them, for the Lord your God goes with you; he will never leave you nor forsake you."   Deuteronomy 31:6

"Loneliness is a wilderness, but through receiving it as a gift, accepting it from the hand of God, and offering it back to him with thanksgiving, it may become a pathway to holiness, to glory and to God himself"
                                                                                    Elisabeth Elliot

PRAY: Oh God, I love it that You are empowering me all through the scriptures to be strong, bold, fearless, and You promise that I will never be alone. I want to fully embrace Your commands and Your promise in this verse so that I stand up tall and strong in every situation, every conversation and even when I'm alone in the dark. I praise You for never, ever leaving me or forsaking me. And I thank You that You go with me everywhere! Amen.

REFLECT: How humbling to realize that we are never fully living out the promises of God, even though we love Him, study His word, believe Him and follow Him. What will it take for you to truly be strong and courageous, never afraid, and never alone? What can you do to believe from the bottom of your heart and soul that God NEVER leaves you nor forsakes you? Do you live that way right now or are you afraid? We all struggle with feeling weak and scared or God wouldn't tell us so often in both the Old and New Testaments, "Do not be afraid!" Can you feel courageous in His presence right now?

ACT: Commit this verse to memory. Write it on an index card and carry it around with you, reading it, memorizing it, and pondering it. Make it a part of you so that you slowly realize that you are strong, you are courageous, and you are never lonely or afraid. Keep saying this verse out loud and quietly in your mind and heart until you are instinctively living it out in all circumstances, "for the Lord your God goes with you and He will never leave you nor forsake you."

Y**OUR** THOUGHTS:

DAY 6

THE GOOD SHEPHERD IS WITH YOU

"Even though I walk through the valley of the shadow of death, I will fear no evil, for you are with me; your rod and your staff, they comfort me."   Psalm 23:4

"The glorious, eternal, all-sufficient omnipotent Creator of the universe whose greatness surpasses anything we could ever imagine. Unlimited in resources, just as He is unlimited in love, He is the Good Shepherd who generously provides for our every need."

Dallas Willard

PRAY: Jesus, I don't want to go through dark valleys. That's when I feel the most alone, afraid, and insecure. It's scary to not see what's ahead and being powerless to do anything about it. But You tell me here that You ARE with me, You ARE guiding me and comforting me, and because of that, I am never alone. Thank you, Jesus, for this amazing and loving verse. I will fear NO evil for Your rod and Your staff are comforting me. I declare this truth in Your name. Amen.

REFLECT: God created us to be in relationship with Him and with others, so it must be the enemy who is lying to us, saying that we are alone in a dark valley, that evil is going to devour us, and that no one understands, or cares, or is there for us. Why is it that we believe the enemy much more often than we believe God and His Word? Here is one verse that can change your life if you honestly believe it and live it.

ACT: Are you currently walking through a dark valley? Are you fearful or do you need comfort? Then talk to God right now about the areas of your life that are driven by the lies of the enemy and ask Him to reveal His rod to guide you, His staff to comfort you, and His presence to take away your fear. Let this be the moment when you look at your life circumstances in a new light – with the promises of God in your heart.

YOUR THOUGHTS:

DAY 7

NOTHING CAN SEPARATE YOU FROM GOD'S LOVE

"neither height nor depth, nor anything else in all creation, will be able to separate us from the love of God that is in Christ Jesus our Lord."   Romans 8:39

"Look for yourself, and you will find in the long run only hatred, loneliness, despair, rage, ruin, and decay. But look for Christ, and you will find Him, and with Him everything else thrown in."   C. S. Lewis

PRAY: I praise You God, that NOTHING can separate me from Your love! I can't hide from You, I can't get too far from You, and nothing can get in the way of Your love for me through Christ Jesus. Thank You that whether I'm alone on a mountain top or deep below the sea, You are there. And right now, as I sit alone and talk to You, we are sitting together, for nothing in all creation can separate us. Praises to You! Amen.

REFLECT: Think about how frustrating it is when we're having an intense conversation on our cell phones and then suddenly the signal cuts off and the connection is dropped. We get the "failed call" message, and we have to wait until we get to an area with reception in order to try again. Can you imagine if that happened while we were talking to God? If we could only talk to Him in areas of good reception—like in a church, and certainly not on a mountaintop or while scuba diving—then He would only be available to us sporadically and inconsistently. But the truth is that NOTHING in all creation will be able to separate us from the Lord. That's awesome.

ACT: Each time you lose connection with someone on your cell phone, take a moment and thank God for always being with you, for never losing connection with Him, and for His faithfulness to stay with you, regardless of your distance from Him, physically, emotionally, and spiritually. Thank Him for never leaving you nor forsaking you. Then you can call your friend back...

YOUR THOUGHTS:

COMPASSION

WEEK EIGHTEEN

We think of God as a loving God, a good God, and a powerful God, but we don't often think of God as compassionate. We are going to spend this week seeing how amazingly compassionate God is to ALL of us, ALL the time. By the end of the week we should all be shouting for joy, rejoicing, and proclaiming thanks to our God of Compassion!

DAY 1

THE LORD HAS COMPASSION ON US

"Shout for joy, you heavens; rejoice, you earth; burst into song, you mountains! For the Lord comforts his people and will have compassion on his afflicted ones."   Isaiah 49:13

"Though the mountains be shaken and the hills be removed, yet my unfailing love for you will not be shaken nor my covenant of peace be removed," says the Lord, who has compassion on you."
                Isaiah 54:10

"His is a loving, tender hand, full of sympathy and compassion."   Dwight L. Moody

PRAY: Dear Father in Heaven, I shout for joy because You are a compassionate God. I rejoice and burst into song because You comfort Your people and have compassion on us – especially the afflicted ones. Thank You Father, that though the mountains be shaken, and the hills removed, Your unfailing love for us will not be shaken. I praise You for being full of compassion for all people. Praise to you, my heavenly Father. Amen and Amen.

REFLECT: Start this week by embracing the amazing, mind blowing truth that God has compassion on you – regardless of what you do or say or who you are. Do you shout for joy or burst into song because you are so grateful for your compassionate heavenly Father? Why not? God is a God of undeserved and unexpected compassion. He loves you so much and feels so deeply sympathetic for all your hurts, fears, struggles and heart aches, that His love will never be shaken. That should make us shout for joy!

ACT: Right now, think of times in your life when God clearly showed you His compassion. If you can't think of any, ask Him to reveal His love for you. Can you shout for joy to celebrate your creator who shows you mercy, grace, unconditional love and compassion? Re-read these verses and let the power and beauty of them sink into your heart, soul and mind. And then rejoice and shout for joy because of the compassion and His covenant of peace that He has poured on you!

YOUR THOUGHTS:

DAY 2

HIS COMPASSION NEVER FAILS

"Have mercy on me, O God, according to Your unfailing love; according to Your great compassion blot out my transgressions."   Psalm 51:1

"Because of the Lord's great love we are not consumed, for His compassions never fail."

Lamentations 3:22

"Compassion will cure more sins than condemnation."   Henry Ward Beecher

PRAY: O God, have mercy on me! According to Your unfailing love and Your great compassion, blot out my transgressions. Please let me not feel consumed, because You promise me that Your compassions never fail. I need You now, O God and I ask You to pour Your compassion on to me, Your weak, broken and sinful servant. Amen.

REFLECT: Do you ever feel that God can't forgive you for something you've done or that He can't wipe away your sins? Do you get consumed with discouragement, regret, or even despair and struggle with how in the world God could ever blot out your transgressions? Well, Psalm 51:1 and Lamentations 3:22 show you how to pray and then tells you God's response to that prayer. As we cry out for mercy, the Lord's great love for us stops us from being consumed. His compassions never, ever fail!

ACT: Make a list of one to three things you've said or done that you feel guilty about, regret or think can't be forgiven. Then read the prayer out loud in Psalm 51:1, followed by God's promise in Lamentations 3:22. Now you have given these burdens to the Lord and He has poured His compassion on you. They are over. He has mercy on you and has blotted out all of your transgressions. It is done. Now, you are not consumed by them anymore. He has just blotted out your sins and you are white as snow. And His compassions never fail. Continue your day with praise and thanksgiving, and don't look back!

YOUR THOUGHTS:

DAY 3

THE LORD IS COMPASSIONATE TO ALL

"The Lord is good to all; He has compassion on all He has made."   Psalm 145:9

"I will tell of the kindnesses of the Lord, the deeds for which He is to be praised, according to all the Lord has done for us— yes, the many good things He has done for Israel, according to His compassion and many kindnesses."   Isaiah 63:7

"It is the unseen and the spiritual in people that determines the outward and the actual."

Oswald Chambers

PRAY: Dear Jesus, there are examples all throughout the scriptures showing that You are good to all, You love every one of Your children and You have compassion on everyone You have created. Please help me to be more like You by being more compassionate. Let me not only tell others about Your kindness and compassion, but to live it out in my own life so that I will freely give compassion to others, the way You have so freely given it to me. Amen.

REFLECT: How compassionate are you to other people? Do you feel for others when they are hurting? Do you understand their pain, their anger, or their mean words, and respond with compassion? Or, do you respond to others in anger, impatience, or meanness? Maybe your compassion for others will grow if you focus on how compassionate the Lord is to you. As you realize His deep compassion and His many kindnesses to you it will be easier to be compassionate to others.

ACT: Choose a person who is in your life right now and to whom you need to show more compassion. Decide how you're going to do that and then plan out what kind words you need to say, or what loving action you need to take, to go out of your way to respond with non-judgmental acceptance and compassion. What they've done or said to you may have been wrong, but why don't you show them pure, Christ-like compassion in return. That may be exactly what they need to experience God's compassion and kindness through you.

YOUR THOUGHTS:

DAY 4

SHOW COMPASSION TO ONE ANOTHER

"This is what the Lord Almighty said: 'Administer true justice; show mercy and compassion to one another. Do not oppress the widow or the fatherless, the foreigner or the poor. Do not plot evil against each other.'"   Zechariah 7:9-10

"Now God had caused the official to show favor and compassion to Daniel,"   Daniel 1:9

"If anyone has material possessions and sees his brother in need but has no pity on him, how can the love of God be in him?"   The Apostle John

PRAY: God, You command us in Zechariah 7:9-10 and in Daniel 1:9 to administer true justice, to show mercy and compassion to one another. We are not to oppress the widow or the fatherless, the foreigner or the poor. And we are not to plot evil against each other. But we are to show favor and compassion to everyone. Help me to do that to people in authority or celebrities with whom I am angry, whom I disagree with, or whom I believe are hurting our nation. Lord, change me to be more like You. Selah! Amen.

REFLECT: We often can follow the Lord's commandments more easily to the kind people around us, but we don't think to show compassion to the people whom we read about in the paper, see on TV, or don't know personally. Many of us are very judgmental or show no mercy to our government leaders or our Hollywood celebrities because it's easier to form opinions and talk against people we're reading about in the news. What people in Hollywood do you need to show compassion to whom you may not like or with whom you disagree?

ACT: Are you judgmental about the celebrities and decision-makers who create our entertainment and shape our culture? Do you disagree with their choices of what they put on TV or in films, songs, or video games? Do you think they are negatively impacting our culture? Right now, stop and pray blessings on anyone in Hollywood who pops into your mind. Choose to speak words of compassion about them, not words of condemnation. Your compassion is what they need. Let the Holy Spirit take care of their hearts.

YOUR THOUGHTS:

DAY 5

A FATHER HAS COMPASSION ON HIS CHILDREN

"As a father has compassion on his children, so the Lord has compassion on those who fear him."
Psalm 103:13

"So he got up and went to his father, But while he was a long way off, his father saw him and was filled with compassion for him; he ran to his son, threw his arms around him and kissed him."
Luke 15:20

"Compassion is sometimes the fatal capacity for feeling what it is like to live inside somebody else's skin. It is the knowledge that there can never really be any peace and joy for me until there is peace and joy finally for you too."
Frederick Buechner

PRAY: Dear Jesus, just as the father had compassion on his prodigal son, thank You for having compassion on me. I want to have compassion on my children. Let me fear You and embrace Your unconditional compassion so I can be compassionate to other people. I want to be a loving and compassionate parent, boss, child, friend, and co-worker, so please help me to trust You for that. Amen and Amen.

REFLECT: The prodigal son story is about selfless compassion. The father, who represents God, not only accepted his son back home after he betrayed him, but he threw his arms around him and kissed him! Acting with compassion is a selfless act. We must put aside justice and act out of obedience to God toward people who hurt us. And if we fear God, we'll see that selfless compassion has eternal significance for both the other person and for us.

ACT: Re-read the story of the prodigal son and see that the son didn't deserve the compassion his father showed him, but because of it, his heart melted and he was able to accept his father's love – with no strings attached. Who do you need to selflessly embrace? Who do you need to show compassion to, instead of waiting for them to come to you for forgiveness? Show radical love and compassion today, run to someone who doesn't deserve it and offer Christ-like compassion and love. It will be life-changing for both of you!

YOUR THOUGHTS:

DAY 6

THE LORD HAS COMPASSION ON THE SICK

Jesus called his disciples to him and said, "I have compassion for these people; they have already been with me three days and have nothing to eat. I do not want to send them away hungry, or they may collapse on the way."   Matthew 15:32

"The first question which the priest and the Levite asked was: 'If I stop to help this man, what will happen to me?' But... the good Samaritan reversed the question: 'If I do not stop to help this man, what will happen to him?'"   Martin Luther King, Jr.

PRAY: Lord in Heaven, I want to have so much compassion for other people that I can even heal the sick and feed the hungry. Would You fill me with compassion today and show me how to resist the desire to get even or get justice. Help me trust that Your ways are better than my ways so that even when it seems to make no sense, I will choose compassion. Help me to do miracles because of my compassion for other people. I pray in Jesus' name, Amen.

REFLECT: Have you ever thought about the reason behind Jesus' miracles and His healings? He not only loved people, but He felt their pain, saw their struggles, witnessed their hurts, and then responded with compassion. And He fed the poor, clothed the naked, and healed the sick not because they deserved it, earned it, or even asked for it, but because He had compassion on them. Reflect on how God has that same unconditional love and compassion for you and that He wants you to have compassion for others. It's the first step toward healing.

ACT: Step out in faith today and ask the Lord to give you so much compassion for others that you can do miracles in His name. Set aside either your anger or your indifference and connect with those who are in pain, to the point of wanting to help alleviate their pain. That's a wild step of compassion, but Jesus did it all the time and we are made in His image. Maybe today is the day to step out of your comfort zone and see what the Lord can do in you and through you. You can do it!

YOUR THOUGHTS:

DAY 7

CLOTHE YOURSELF WITH COMPASSION

"Therefore, as God's chosen people, holy and dearly loved, clothe yourselves with compassion, kindness, humility, gentleness and patience."   Colossians 3:12

"If to be feelingly alive to the sufferings of my fellow-creatures is to be a fanatic, I am one of the most incurable fanatics ever permitted to be at large."   William Wilberforce

PRAY: Oh Father, You have allowed me to be grafted in to Your chosen people when I accepted You into my heart. Thank You that You have made me holy and I am dearly loved by You. I want You to clothe me with compassion, kindness, humility, gentleness, and patience. I can't do it without You. So, I come to You and ask You to touch my heart new and fresh, to renew me, change me, and transform me into the likeness of Your Son. I pray this in Your name, Amen.

REFLECT: Reflect on how much God loves YOU. He has made you holy and you are dearly loved by Him. Because of His unbelievable love, you can clothe yourself, wrap yourself up, and cover yourself with the fruits of the Spirit; compassion, kindness, humility, gentleness, and patience. If all of us could actually accept God's loving gift to clothe ourselves in these attributes the world would be a different place.

ACT: Commit to doing an experiment today: Only say words of compassion, kindness, humility, gentleness, and patience. Bite your tongue any time you want to complain, say something negative, get angry, frustrated, impatient, or mean. Tell someone close to you to help you and hold you accountable, if you think you'll need it. Can you make it through the whole day? How many times did you have to stop yourself? How many times did you show compassion? Just try it for one day and see if you can do it .

YOUR THOUGHTS:

TRUTH

WEEK NINETEEN

Truth is a controversial issue in today's divided world. What is truth? How do we stand firm in truth and yet not judge or offend people? This week we're focusing on God's Absolute Truth and how we can incorporate it into our everyday lives. Only His Truth will set us free!

DAY 1

CALL ON GOD IN TRUTH

"Guide me in your truth and teach me, for you are God my Savior, and my hope is in you all day long."

Psalm 25:5

"The Lord is near to all who call on him, to all who call on him in truth." Psalm 145:18

"I feel safe even in the midst of my enemies; for the truth is powerful and will prevail."

Sojourner Truth

PRAY: Dear Lord, I thank You for these Psalms and the reminders that You are guiding me in truth and teaching me Your truths. Thank you, Lord, that You are near to me because I call on You in truth. Help me to be committed to always seeking Truth and living by it my whole life. My hope is in You all day long and I am so thankful that Your Holy Spirit helps me to discern Your truth from lies and from the world's variations on Your absolute truth. Amen.

REFLECT: Truth is a crucial word, not only in the Bible but also in our culture. The dictionary definition says that truth is "the body of real things, events, and facts." But how we each define "real" or "facts" has become blurry and varied. As Christians, we must focus on Absolute Truth, which is defined as "a quality of truth that cannot be exceeded; complete truth; unvarying and permanent truth." As we spend this week on truth, we are focusing on God's Absolute Truth. The Lord will guide us in His truth, to never take His word of truth from our mouths. He is near to all of us who call on Him in truth. As we do this we begin to see a bigger picture of what it means to follow Him. Everything we read in the Scriptures is God's absolute truth. Let that fact sink into your heart and soul.

ACT: Are you clear about what God's Absolute Truth is? Do you believe that everything you read in the Bible is true, even if you don't fully understand it? Are you confident that God's scriptures hold absolute truth? As a Christian, are you confident in embracing God's truth to define your life, what you stand for and are willing to die for? These questions force you to go deep into your heart and soul to answer. Start your week in prayer, asking God to reveal His truth to you and show you what truths you may be struggling with, questioning, or avoiding. Maybe even get on your knees right now and ask God to reveal His truth to you.

YOUR THOUGHTS:

DAY 2

TRUTH THROUGH JESUS SETS YOU FREE

"For the law was given through Moses; grace and truth came through Jesus Christ."

John 1:17

"To the Jews who had believed him, Jesus said, "If you hold to my teaching, you are really my disciples. Then you will know the truth, and the truth will set you free. John 8:31-32

"God's truth judges created things out of love, and Satan's truth judges them out of envy and hatred."

Dietrich Bonhoeffer

PRAY: Dear God, I thank You that You sent Jesus to give us grace and truth. I ask that You help me to know the truth so that it will set me free. I don't want to live by just the law. I want to be like Jesus and live a life of both truth and grace. I want to use Your truth to set the captives free by lovingly speaking truth. God, I know that Moses gave us the law, but Jesus gave us Your truth and that truth will set me free and make me one of Your disciples. Thank you for giving me exactly what I need. I praise You, in Jesus' name! Amen.

REFLECT: Have you thought about how to simply define the Old and New Testaments with two concepts: Moses and the law and Jesus and truth and grace? How beautiful it is to understand that Jesus told us that if we hold on to His teachings of truth and grace, and allow ourselves to be transformed by them, that we will be His disciples. We can and should learn the Law that Moses gave us, but when we know Jesus' truth, that will set us free. Reflect on the power of Jesus' words. If you hold on to His teaching, you are not only His disciple, but you are free!

ACT: On a piece of paper write down a list of ways you are free because you know God's truths. How are you free in work? In relationships? In your actions and in your words? Are you free to go against the expectations of culture or peer pressure? Are you free to be confident in your beliefs and worldview, even though it goes against society's beliefs? Look at your list and praise God for the freedom in following His truths, with grace!

YOUR THOUGHTS:

DAY 3

JESUS IS THE TRUTH

"Jesus answered, "I am the way and the truth and the life. No one comes to the Father except through me."

John 14:6

"Truth lies in character. Christ did not simply speak the truth; he was truth; truth, through and through; for truth is a thing not of words, but of life and being."

Frederick W. Robertson

PRAY: Dear Jesus, I praise You for this promise. These verses are the foundation of my faith and they are so full of love. You are indeed the way to hope, joy, love, and salvation. You are the representation of absolute truth and You are not only the source of all life, but You give me my life. Thank You that I have access to the creator God through You and that You are the way and the truth and the source of all life. Amen.

REFLECT: Most of us know John 14:6 and yet have you ever really thought about each word? Jesus is the way. That means He gives us a path to follow that will bring us right where we need to go in life. He is the truth, which means everything He says is true and can be trusted, studied, understood, and embraced. He is the life, which means He is the source of everything we need and are; He gives us breath, strength, and purpose. We can't get to God without Jesus. That is His word of truth. Without Jesus we are nothing, we wouldn't exist, we wouldn't have life, purpose, meaning, or access to God. That is profound.

ACT: Right now, not only memorize this famous verse, but also memorize all that it actually means. Think through what it means when He says He is the way we should follow, that He is the truth of all that we should believe, say, and act, and that He is the source of life itself. Then think through the fact that you can't even get to God without Jesus. Do you recognize your need for Him? We are nothing without Him. Are you living your life based on these truths? What do you need to do to truly live out this short yet profound verse?

YOUR THOUGHTS:

DAY 4

THE HOLY SPIRIT GUIDES YOU TO TRUTH

"But when he, the Spirit of truth, comes, he will guide you into all truth. He will not speak on his own; he will speak only what he hears, and he will tell you what is yet to come."

John 16:13

"The Holy Spirit will always point people to the finish work of Jesus." John Paul Warren

PRAY: Oh, Holy Spirit. You are just as much a part of God as the Father and Jesus. Thank You that You are guiding me into all truth. I know that You speak to me only what You hear from the Father and yet, because You are in me, I am full of truth. Holy Spirit, tell me where I should go now and what I am to do next. You are my guide and You know what is yet to come. I need You and I thank You that You are always telling me the truth. I worship God through You and in truth. Amen.

REFLECT: These verses are a great description of the Trinity and especially helpful in understanding the role of the Holy Spirit. God is Spirit and He has given us a part of Himself, the Holy Spirit, so that He can guide us into truth and tell us only what God wants us to hear. In fact, the Holy Spirit in us is so powerful that He can even tell us what is yet to come. Have you thought about this amazing truth that the Holy Spirit is alive and living inside of you right now? If we could fully understand that truth, then we would all live different lives. We wouldn't be afraid, concerned, jealous, lonely, or selfish. Would we treat others differently, change the way we spend our time or our money? How would you be different if you utterly understood that the Holy Spirit is alive and well in your soul?

ACT: Commit in prayer to fully understand that the Holy Spirit is inside of you. Ask Him to reveal Himself to you, to guide you, and even to show you something that is yet to come. Then write down three ways in which you want to change as you fully embrace the power of the Holy Spirit living within you. What new truths will you believe? What actions and priorities will change? Keep your notes and in the days ahead, read them again to see how the Holy Spirit has changed you by the reality of His presence within you.

Y**OUR THOUGHTS:**

DAY 5

STAND FIRM IN THE TRUTH

"Stand firm then, with the belt of truth buckled around your waist, with the breastplate of righteousness in place,"

Ephesians 6:14

"The truth." Dumbledore sighed. "It is a beautiful and terrible thing, and should therefore be treated with great caution."

J.K. Rowling, *Harry Potter and the Sorcerer's Stone*

PRAY: Lord, thank You for the reminder that You want me to stand firm in any situation, with truth and righteousness. Help me to buckle the belt of truth around my waist and to put the breastplate of righteousness in place, regardless of what the people around me, or society, thinks. Even if everyone around me turns from truth, help me to stand firm in all situations, to endure hardship, and embrace Your truth. With You, Lord, all things are possible! Amen.

REFLECT: We are bombarded with messages every day that don't line up with God's word. In America most of it comes from Washington DC or Hollywood. We are told untruths in the news, in advertising, in public speeches, as well as in films, TV shows, and music. However, we also have great examples of God's truth in some leaders, and in some books, songs, films and TV shows. We have to stand with people who love God and His principals of love and grace. Do you pray for public leaders, culture-shapers and celebrities who lead our nation to stand firm in Truth? Every day, how do you discern God's truth from every source of information coming at you?   Stand firm!

ACT: Today is the day to begin asking God for wisdom, so you can discern His truth in all circumstances and stand firm in truth. Don't get angry at the people in Hollywood with whom you don't agree. Don't hate or talk against our leaders whom you believe are lying to you. Instead pray for the Lord to give you discernment in order to understand, not only what the truth is, but also how to respond with grace, love, and hope. Commit to start every day asking the Lord for wisdom, righteousness and truth, and He will reveal it. Stand firm, keep your head in all situations, even endure hardship, in order to speak God's truth in love, and pray for our leaders and celebrities who have not yet found God's truths. Today, you can start making an eternal difference.

YOUR THOUGHTS:

DAY 6

PEOPLE WHO OPPOSE THE TRUTH

"Have I now become your enemy by telling you the truth?"   Galatians 4:16
"Sanctify them by the truth; your word is truth."   John 17:17

"The very concept of objective truth is fading out of the world. Lies will pass into history...In a time of deceit telling the truth is a revolutionary act."   George Orwell

PRAY: Dear God, I want to be truthful to my friends, but sometimes when I speak God's truth it makes them angry. Please help me speak truth with love and grace, and to be sensitive to the right situation where You will be glorified and they will be blessed. I need You to guide me and give me the words and the wisdom to choose when the truth will sanctify someone else. Help me also to accept words of truth from my friends, so that I can learn, and grow with them, and not get defensive, angry, or hurt. Oh, I need You every moment! Amen.

REFLECT: Have you ever hurt a friend by speaking truth to them? Has anyone hurt you or made you angry because they were speaking truth to you? It's hard to hear truth. But God gives it to us in three ways: Through Scripture, through the nudge of the Holy Spirit, and through other people. We want to be sanctified as believers, set apart to do God's work, and we want the people we love to walk in His truth. But sometimes it hurts to face a truth that reveals our weaknesses, sin, or ignorance. Can you offer truth to others, in love, and can you accept truth that others offer to you? It is a huge step in maturity to walk in God's truth.

ACT: Sit quietly and ask the Lord to reveal to you if you have any enemies – either because you have pushed them away, or they have pushed you away. Was it because of truths or lies that were spoken? Be vulnerable and ask the Lord what to do about each person. Do you ask for or extend forgiveness, or open up about your hurt, anger, or pain? Do you pray about what is in your heart until the Lord brings peace or reconciliation? Choose what you need to do regarding anyone you have hurt, or who has hurt you, when speaking the truth. Maybe you spoke without grace or love. Maybe it was the wrong time, or words were spoken with anger. Whatever happened, ask the Lord to reveal your next step, so that you can walk in truth and have no enemies in the process.

YOUR THOUGHTS:

DAY 7

YOU HAVE GOD'S ANOINTING, SO PRAY

"I urge, then, first of all, that requests, prayers, intercession and thanksgiving be made for everyone--for kings and all those in authority, that we may live peaceful and quiet lives in all godliness and holiness. This is good, and pleases God our Savior, who wants all men to be saved and to come to a knowledge of the truth."   1 Timothy 2:1-4

"But you have an anointing from the Holy One, and all of you know the truth." 1 John 2:20

"Yes, if truth is not undergirded by love, it makes the possessor of that truth obnoxious and the truth repulsive."   Ravi Zacharias

PRAY: Oh Lord, I want to end my week embracing the anointing and the truth that You have given me. I just need to live it out every moment of every day. Help me to intercede for all people – for kings and those in authority, for friends and family, and even for neighbors and strangers. I want to have Your heart that desires all people to be saved and to come to the knowledge of the truth. I praise You and embrace all that You have for me. Amen.

REFLECT: Have you thought about having an anointing from God? Have you fully embraced the fact that God has given you His truth? How do we live out God's truth in our lives? God wants us to pray for others and thank Him for them, along with interceding for leaders, friends, family members, and strangers. We need to be quiet and pray, so that God can use us in His plan to bring all people to Him. Prayer is the key to living a Christ-like life and to understand all of God's truths that He has already given us. Prayer is what will impact the lives of the people around us. How is your prayer life?

ACT: End this week by sitting quietly now for 10 minutes and listen to God. Hear what truths He wants to reveal to you, what people He wants you to pray for, to serve, and to love. Be quiet and ask Him to envelope you in His peace and holiness. He wants you to come to a knowledge of the truth as you sit perfectly still. Try to spend 10 minutes every day listening, to God. He has anointed you with the truth already, so let Him reveal it to you. This time in God's presence can change your life. It is an exciting adventure!

YOUR THOUGHTS:

PATIENCE

WEEK TWENTY

This week's journal took me longer than any other week to write and I got so frustrated. Suddenly I realized the topic was patience! It made me laugh out loud. How often do we lose patience? Every day? Let's jump in and see what the Lord says about Patience, but don't be rushed about it! Take your time and be prepared for the Lord to teach you patience in unexpected ways....

Day 1

CHRIST HAS GREAT PATIENCE

"Here is a trustworthy saying that deserves full acceptance: Christ Jesus came into the world to save sinners--of whom I am the worst. But for that very reason I was shown mercy so that in me, the worst of sinners, Christ Jesus might display his unlimited patience as an example for those who would believe on him and receive eternal life."

1 Timothy 1:15-16

"Patience serves as a protection against wrongs as clothes do against cold. For if you put on more clothes as the cold increases, it will have no power to hurt you. So, in like manner you must grow in patience when you meet with great wrongs, and they will then be powerless to vex your mind."

Leonardo da Vinci

PRAY: Dear God, I thank You that You have immense patience for me, even though I am a sinner. Thank You, that because I believe in You and have received eternal life, that You are always showing me mercy. I don't deserve how good You are to me, but I accept Your promise that You love me and have great patience for me. I am humbled by Your unconditional love and I praise You for Your patient, saving grace. Amen.

REFLECT: It's amazing that no matter how good or bad we are, God loves us, accepts us completely as we are, and patiently responds to us with mercy. Do you really believe this? Paul thought that he was the worst sinner of all. Can you think of any times when you felt this way and yet experienced God's unconditional mercy and immense patience?

ACT: If you journal, write down a specific instance when you felt you deserved punishment or condemnation and yet God patiently showed you grace, mercy, and forgiveness. Put that reminder somewhere that you can read again when you feel unworthy, or like a horrible sinner. It's important to remember God's saving love, grace, unlimited patience and faithfulness, that He gives to those who believe on Him.

YOUR THOUGHTS:

DAY 2

PATIENTLY PREACH GOD'S WORD

"Preach the Word; be prepared in season and out of season; correct, rebuke and encourage--with great patience and careful instruction."   2 Timothy 4:2

"Wait on God and He will work, but don't wait in spiritual sulks because you cannot see an inch in front of you! Are we detached enough from our spiritual hysterics to wait on God? To wait is not to sit with folded hands, but to learn to do what we are told."

Oswald Chambers

PRAY: Dear Jesus, please give me a good attitude and a Christ-like approach to preaching Your word. I want to be correct and encourage others with great patience and careful instruction, and I don't want to judge others as I'm talking about You and Your word. Fill me with patience so that I can be an effective witness and not a hindrance or a stumbling block to others. I pray this in Your name, Amen.

REFLECT: Do you hear how some Christians often use God's word to rebuke others with judgment, anger or even hate? The Christians in Hollywood often feel that the Church is not "prepared" to encourage entertainment professionals, for they have no patience for Hollywood. Their anger and boycotts only cause an angry and defensive response. How can we be prepared in season and out of season and be more patient with people we don't agree with, so that we can lead them to Jesus with love, not judgment?

ACT: Have you ever talked against Hollywood or entertainment professionals? Have you thought that Christians should not be in Hollywood because it's evil and destructive? Or do you know anyone who feels that way? Could you look again at Hollywood with more patience and consider that those people need our prayers and our love in order to embrace Jesus? Choose now to help build a spiritual bridge between the Church and Hollywood by your response to the people and the projects coming out of the world's most influential mission field. Ask God to give you love and patience for them.

YOUR **THOUGHTS:**

DAY 3

GOD WILL REVEAL HIS GOODNESS

"I am still confident of this: I will see the goodness of the Lord in the land of the living. Wait for the Lord; be strong and take heart and wait for the Lord."

Psalm 27:13-14

"A waiting person is a patient person. The word patience means the willingness to stay where we are and live the situation out to the full in the belief that something hidden there will manifest itself to us."
Henri Nouwen

PRAY: Lord, I need Your help to be confident in believing that You are good. Help me to wait patiently for You, to be strong and to take heart. I want to see Your goodness here in the land of the living, but I need Your help. Thank You for being there for me so that I don't lose my confidence in You. Amen and Amen.

REFLECT: Have you thought that whenever God tells us to wait, it requires great patience? Joseph had to wait years to see his dream come to pass, Abraham and Sarah had to wait decades to see God's promised son, and the disciples had to wait for Jesus to reveal His truths to them. It took great patience for all of them. Can you say confidently that you will see the goodness of the Lord in the land of the living if you wait? It's all about patience!

ACT: Where, when, and with who do you struggle with patience? List three things that you are not patient with. Is it with annoying people? Is it with waiting for the Lord to answer your prayers, or waiting for family members to become Christians? Define where you need patience with just three examples and then be strong and take heart and wait for the Lord to answer. He will!

YOUR THOUGHTS:

DAY 4

HAVE PATIENCE FOR GOD'S PERFECT TIMING

"Be still before the Lord and wait patiently for him; do not fret when men succeed in their ways, when they carry out their wicked schemes."   Psalm 37:7

"They also serve who only stand and wait."   John Milton

PRAY: Oh dear God, I get so frustrated when crooked people get ahead, when liars get what they want, and when evil people get away with carrying out their wicked schemes. You have to help me to be still before You and to wait patiently for You to redeem me, so that I am okay about not succeeding when others around me are. I need to trust You more deeply and wait for You more patiently. But I can't do it without You. Please, Holy Spirit, fill me anew, give me wisdom in every situation, and patience to wait for Your perfect timing. Thank You. Amen.

REFLECT: When we get impatient, we start comparing our situations, our successes, even our lives, with other people. And often we get mad when people who aren't Christians, or are actually even wicked, get what they want while we are still waiting for our prayers to be answered. How often do we fret over comparing ourselves to the people around us and we don't match up? Do you know how to be still before the Lord and wait patiently for Him to answer your prayers to change your situation, or to transform you into His likeness?

ACT: Commit to setting aside 30 minutes sometime this week to be completely still before the Lord, in silence, and just wait patiently for Him. Just sit still, clear your brain of all the distractions of the day and listen. Don't allow yourself to fret or to compare yourself with others, but just enjoy being in His presence and waiting on Him. If you can do it for 30 minutes, then do it again next week. And then the week after. You could make this a weekly date with God – just 30 minutes a week of being still, sitting in His presence, and waiting patiently and lovingly for Him to fill you up new and fresh. That's a key to not fretting and becoming more patient!

YOUR THOUGHTS:

DAY 5

WISDOM BRINGS PATIENCE

"A person's wisdom yields patience; it is to one's glory to overlook an offense."

Proverbs 19:11

"Patience is the companion of wisdom."

Saint Augustine

PRAY: Lord, what a new concept for me to hear that wisdom yields patience. I want patience, so please give me wisdom. I don't want to take offense in anything that people say to me or do to me. I want to patiently understand the hurts and brokenness of other people and wisely choose to love them and pray for them instead of taking personal offense. I know it's not about me Lord, but about You and others. That's wisdom, and I am thankful it will produce patience in me and give me an un-offendable heart. I pray in Jesus name, Amen.

REFLECT: This is a huge, supernatural concept to embrace: "A person's wisdom yields patience." What does that mean practically and how does that help you to overlook an offense against you? Could it be that patience stops us from reacting to what others say, but allows us to respond by overlooking any ill intent and just praying for them, instead. This is a verse that requires great reflection. But it will help you to live with an un-offendable heart.

ACT: Plan how you are going to handle the next situation that arises where you would normally be offended? Decide now that you are going to patiently overlook the offense, ignore the words, and even the intention of what you hear, and choose instead, to respond in love and forgiveness with an un-offendable heart. Remember that it's most often not about you, but more about their hurts and pain. Practice what you might say to avert hurt, anger and division and ask the Lord to give you wisdom to overlook the offense. It will be life-changing!

YOUR THOUGHTS:

DAY 6

BE JOYFUL, PATIENT, AND FAITHFUL

"Never be lacking in zeal, but keep your spiritual fervor, serving the Lord. Be joyful in hope, patient in affliction, faithful in prayer." Romans 12:11-12

"What then are we to do about our problems? We must learn to live with them until such time as God delivers us from them. We must pray for grace to endure them without murmuring. Problems patiently endured will work for our spiritual perfecting. They harm us only when we resist them or endure them unwillingly" A. W. Tozer

PRAY: Dear Lord, I want to always have zeal and spiritual fervor serving You. Would You help me to stay joyful in hope, give me great patience when experiencing affliction, and keep me faithful in prayer? I pray that You fill me with joy, patience, and faith, for I know that would be the most beautiful way to live. I can't do this on my own, but I need to depend on You to change my heart, my attitude and my thoughts. Thank you, in Jesus name, Amen.

REFLECT: What does it mean to be full of zeal and spiritual fervor? It could be that if we asked the Lord to help us stay joyful in hope, patient in affliction, and faithful in prayer, that then we would never be lacking in zeal and we would keep our spiritual fervor serving Him! So, maybe zeal and fervor are not just a feeling, but also the result of trusting God in affliction and being faithful in prayer. Could being patient during times of affliction give you more zeal, or being joyful in hopeless circumstances fill you with spiritual fervor?...

ACT: Being patient is hard but being patient in affliction is even harder. Think of the last time you were afflicted, either physically in pain, emotionally distraught or mentally stressed. Were you patient? Pray right now, that the Lord will prepare you for times of affliction by giving you patience in all circumstances, so that ultimately you will be full of zeal for Him and overflow with spiritual fervor in everything that you go through in life, especially during hard times.

YOUR THOUGHTS:

DAY 7

BE PATIENT WITH EVERYONE

"Be completely humble and gentle; be patient, bearing with one another in love. Make every effort to keep the unity of the Spirit through the bond of peace." Ephesians 4:2-3

"Everyone feels benevolent if nothing happens to be annoying him at the moment."

C.S. Lewis

PRAY: God my Father, I want to be completely humble and gentle and patient. I want to bear with others in love and I want to make every effort to keep unity and peace in my family, in my community, and in my world. Would Your Spirit transform me so that I become a bond of peace? Thank you for allowing me to be used in such an amazing way in this world. I look forward to having You transform me. Selah! Amen.

REFLECT: What does it mean to keep the unity of the Spirit through the bond of peace? A mentor of mine once told me that being a peacemaker is a bloody business! It's hard to bring unity in our world, even in our own family or with our friends. It's also hard to bear with one another's burdens, struggles and brokenness. It takes tremendous patience, more than is humanly possible, to live as God wants us to. That's why we need Him desperately, at every moment, even as we make every effort, so that we can be humble, gentle and loving, yet strong, focused and intentional. If we could be patient on our own we wouldn't need God.

ACT: Choose one person with whom you have trouble and make the decision to be the peacemaker. Have your goal be unity, regardless of how humble, gentle, and patient you have to be. If you can reunite, or reconcile, or find peace with just one tough person, then you will have achieved the unity of the Spirit through the bond of peace! And remember, with God, NOTHING is impossible. Just be patient and pray as you make every effort to reach out in gentle love.

YOUR THOUGHTS:

WORSHIP

WEEK TWENTY-ONE

My friend and national prayer leader, Daniel Henderson, has three ideals for meaning and victory in our lives. He says Worship + Integrity + Nonconformity = WIN. This week we're focusing on WORSHIP, as the key ingredient to being a winner! Let's spend the week worshiping the Lord together and giving all the glory to Him.

Music is such an integral part of entering into worship, so we are going to include a suggested worship song each day. Whether you choose to listen to that one, or pick one of your own, be sure to enter into worship in some way each day!

DAY 1

HIS LOVE ENDURES FOREVER

"The trumpeters and singers joined in unison, as with one voice, to give praise and thanks to the Lord. Accompanied by trumpets, cymbals, and other instruments, they raised their voices in praise to the Lord and sang: "He is good; his love endures forever." Then the temple of the Lord was filled with a cloud,"   2 Chronicles 5:13

"Proper worship is central to our understanding of reality, the arts, and it affects everyone, Christians and non-Christians. Culture is affected by how we worship God. By "proper worship," I mean a distinctively Christological way of looking at God, the world and ourselves that is driven by understanding and experiencing God's grace."

Makoto Fujimura

PRAY: Lord, You are good and Your love endures forever! May the trumpets blare and the musicians play the cymbals and other instruments. Let the singers raise their voices in praise to You. And I sing out with them, "He is good; His love endures forever." Amen.

REFLECT: What a glorious week ahead. Have you ever spent a full week just worshiping the Lord? Experience it fully this week and notice how the rest of your days are impacted by starting each one with praise and thanks, all in an attitude of worship. Do you see a difference in your conversations, your attitude, and even your productivity? Get ready for a glorious week as you praise God with music, dance, art, creativity and love!

ACT: Commit to worshiping God all day, every day this week. Put aside any requests and complaining, and just worship the Lord. Take time to kneel, stand, sit, lay down, close your eyes, raise your arms, dance, play an instrument, read the scriptures and sing out loud. Be bold, adventurous, and even risky as you worship. Step outside of your usual worship habits. Worship is not just singing songs in church, it's using your entire body, mind, and soul, focusing on the Lord. Commit this entire week to WORSHIPING your GOD!

YOUR THOUGHTS:

SUGGESTED WORSHIP SONG: *You are Good,* by Israel Houghton & The New Breed

DAY 2

WORSHIP THE LORD WITH GLADNESS

"...for he is our God and we are the people of his pasture, the flock under his care. Today, if you hear his voice,...Exalt the Lord our God and worship at his footstool; he is holy....Worship the Lord with gladness; come before him with joyful songs."

Psalm 95:7; Psalm 99:5; Psalm 100:2

"Without worship, we go about miserable. We must never rest until everything inside us worships God."   A.W. Tozer

PRAY: Dear Lord my Maker, I come to You in an attitude of worship and I bow down to You and kneel before You. I praise You as a person of Your pasture. You are my God and I thank You that I am under Your care. I want to hear Your voice. I exalt You and worship at Your footstool; for You are holy. I worship You with gladness and I come before You with joyful songs. Selah! Amen.

REFLECT: It's awesome to think about God as our Maker, our Creator, and to think about being under His care. But what does it mean to you to say that your God is HOLY? Think about these synonyms and what they mean to you in referring to God: sacred, consecrated, hallowed, sanctified, sacrosanct, venerated, revered, divine, blessed, and dedicated. Some of these words may help you to hear the voice of your Holy God.

ACT: Can you physically worship God now by bowing down or getting on your knees? Use your whole body to worship God. If you're bowing, think about worshiping God at His footstool. If you're kneeling, raise your hands to heaven and sing out a joyful song. Don't be intimidated, just worship the God of the Universe. Bring all of your senses into your worship: visualize Him, reach up to touch Him, sing out to praise Him, smell His sweet aroma, and feel His presence. Worship your holy God with gladness!

YOUR THOUGHTS:

SUGGESTED WORSHIP SONG: *Come Worship The Lord*, by John Michael Talbot

DAY 3

WORSHIP GOD AS YOU EAT AND DRINK

"Worship the Lord your God, and his blessing will be on your food and water. I will take away sickness from among you,"   Exodus 23:25

"Worship is our response to the overtures of love from the heart of the Father."

Richard Foster

PRAY: My Father in Heaven, hallowed be Your name! I worship You today in everything I do, but especially whenever I'm eating or drinking. Would You focus my thoughts on You at every meal? I praise You for blessing my food and taking away sickness from me by keeping me well fed and healthy. I eat every meal today in an attitude of worship to You, not taking for granted one bite of the food that You provide for me. And I do it all in Jesus name, Amen.

REFLECT: Have you ever thought that eating meals and drinking can be worship? Every snack can be a worshipful meal to God. And have you thanked God every day for not being sick? What would it be like to worship God in everything that you do? Have you just limited worship to the singing portion of church each week? How can you turn every moment of your life into a worship experience? And how would that radically change your life?

ACT: Take a moment before each meal today to just stop and worship the Lord. And then worship Him with each bite, remembering that He is the one who supplies us our daily bread. Maybe you can say the Lord's Prayer as you eat. And every day, thank Him for your health. Remember that He tells you that as you worship Him His blessing is upon your food and water and He will take away sickness from you!

YOUR THOUGHTS:

SUGGESTED WORSHIP SONG: *When All Thy Mercies*, by Fernando Ortega

DAY 4

PRAISE THE FATHER TO THE FATHERLESS

"Praise the Lord , O my soul; all my inmost being, praise his holy name."   Psalm 103:1

"Sing to God, sing praise to his name, extol him who rides on the clouds – his name is the Lord – and rejoice before him. A father to the fatherless, a defender of widows, is God in his holy dwelling."   Psalm 68:4-5

"Worship changes the worshiper into the image of the One worshiped"   Jack Hayford

"It is in the process of being worshipped that God communicates His presence to men."
                                                                        C.S. Lewis

PRAY: I Praise You Lord, from my soul, from my inmost being, I praise Your holy name. I sing in praise of Your name, oh God, and I rejoice before You, who rides on the clouds. Thank You that You are a Father to the fatherless and a defender of widows. I worship you, God, in Your holy dwelling. Amen.

REFLECT: How big is your God? Does your God ride on the clouds? Is He a Father to the fatherless? Do you believe He defends the widows and orphans? Have you ever imagined what His holy dwelling is like? Think big today and believe in a God who is so much more amazing, personal, protective, loving, and all knowing than you ever before thought about. Praise Him in your inmost being and praise His holy name! Isn't that exciting?

ACT: Today, worship God with each person that you see, each conversation that you have, and everyone that you pass in your car, or on your bike, or jogging past on your run. Focus on worshiping and praising God out in the world where God is riding on the clouds above you. Turn every moment into a moment of worship to God in His holy dwelling.

YOUR **THOUGHTS:**

SUGGESTED WORSHIP SONG: *A Father's Prayer*, by James Covell

DAY 5

WORSHIP HIM WITH MUSIC

"Shout for joy to the Lord, all the earth, burst into jubilant song with music; make music to the Lord with the harp, with the harp and the sound of singing, with trumpets and the blast of the ram's horn – shout for joy before the Lord, the King."   Psalm 98:4-6

"A few minutes ago every tree was excited, bowing to the roaring storm, waving, swirling, tossing their branches in glorious enthusiasm like worship. But though to the outer ear these trees are now silent, their songs never cease."   John Muir

PRAY: Lord, I thank you for the gift of music as the language of the soul, because it is the most joyous way to worship You. I thank you for all kinds of music and how each different kind touches my heart in a unique way. I thank you for the gift of singing jubilant songs, and the joy of clapping our hands. You say even the rivers clap their hands and the mountains sing together for joy. Oh Lord, let the whole world sing in worship to You. Amen.

REFLECT: Reflect on what music means to you. Michael W. Smith says, *"I think worship is a lifestyle, first of all."* How does worship affect your everyday life? Have you ever thanked God for the musicians who perform the music you love? Have you prayed for them and asked the Lord to fill their hearts with love and worship? As professional musicians offer the world their gift of music, can you ask the Lord to fill them with His joy?

ACT: Choose three musicians or music groups who have impacted your life with their songs. Would you commit to pray for them and thank the Lord for them? If they aren't believers, pray for the Lord to come into their lives and transform them into people of worship. As you worship the Lord today, lift up the music professionals around the world and ask for them to have an encounter with the God of the Universe who created the joyful gift of music and gave them their gifts and talents. The music business offers God's gift to people across the globe, so when you pray for musicians, you are impacting the world.

YOUR THOUGHTS:

SUGGESTED WORSHIP SONG: *Sing a New Song,* by Glad

DAY 6

DON'T WORSHIP OTHER GODS

"Be careful, or you will be enticed to turn away and worship other gods and bow down to them." Deuteronomy 11:16

Jesus answered, "It is written: 'Worship the Lord your God and serve him only.'" Luke 4:8

"Human beings are at their core defined by what they worship rather than primarily by what they think, know, or believe. That is bound up with the central Augustinian claim that we are what we love." Dallas Willard

PRAY: Lord, please don't ever let me turn away from You to worship false gods. I never want to bow down to anyone or anything other than You – no idol, man, or image. Rather, help me to worship You, Lord, for it is You who will deliver me from the hand of all of my enemies. Thank You for Your protection and strength to keep my eyes only on You. I want to always just worship You and serve You only! And I pray this in the mighty name of Jesus. Amen.

REFLECT: Who are you worshiping? What encroaches on your time with God? Does your phone distract you from keeping your eyes on Jesus? Is technology or God your main passion? Who do you serve? Are there distractions or a misplaced passion that takes you away from spending time with God? Be careful not to turn away from God and worship other gods and bow down to them. Worship the Lord your God and serve Him only!

ACT: Write down the two things or people you are most passionate about. It could be a spouse, a hobby, a sport, a pastor, a spiritual mentor, or even a video game or your phone. After writing them down, ask the Lord to show you if they have become more important to you than Him. At first you will instinctively say, "Of course not, nothing is more important than my relationship with God!" But think again and allow the Holy Spirit to reveal to you if you are solid with Him or if those things have crept in to begin replacing your priority to seek the Lord. Be honest with yourself and be confirmed in either your service and faithfulness to Him or your need to readjust your heart and your priorities.

YOUR THOUGHTS:

SUGGESTED WORSHIP SONG: *I will Praise Him Still*, by Fernando Ortega

DAY 7

GIVE PRAISE TO THE LORD

"Give thanks to the Lord, call on his name; make known among the nations what he has done" "All the nations you have made will come and worship before you, O Lord; they will bring glory to your name."

Psalm 105:1

"There is plenty of television. There are plenty of talk shows. There are plenty of comedians. But there is not plenty of worship of the true and living God."

Charles R. Swindoll

PRAY: I worship You and give praise to You, oh Lord! I proclaim Your name and make it known among the nations what You have done for me and for the world. I pray that all the nations You have made will come and worship before You, Lord, so that they will bring glory to Your name! Amen and Amen.

REFLECT: Are you sharing your love for the Lord with other people? As you worship Him, does that overflow into your other relationships, conversations, and situations? Reflect on how you can be more effective in making your love for the Lord contagious to others! Lift up the name of the Lord to let all nations come to know Him and bring glory to His name. How perfect of God to have our worship for Him be a part of His great commission to the world.

ACT: Choose one practical way to share your love for the Lord with someone else, through your worship. Thank God for the people He's put in your life who don't yet know Him, invite one of them to church to experience the worship time in your service, and show you worship the Lord with your friends, neighbors, and co-workers. Tell someone about the worship music you love, or how you may worship Him in the car, in the shower, in any crazy place that someone wouldn't expect. Share your times of worship with others so that the nations will hear and give glory to the Lord. Be excited about worshiping the Lord!

YOUR THOUGHTS:

SUGGESTED WORSHIP SONG: *This is Living Now*, by Hillsong Young and Free

SERVING

WEEK TWENTY-TWO

Jesus came not to be served, but to serve. That's the mandate for this week. Can we serve others the way Jesus served us, with zeal, a spiritual fervor and with devoted faithfulness? It's worth seeing how we can be serving God and serving others the same way Jesus role-modeled for us over 2,000 years ago.

DAY 1

GOD HONORS THOSE WHO SERVE HIM

"Whoever serves me must follow me; and where I am, my servant also will be. My Father will honor the one who serves me."   John 12:26

"Faith is the first factor in a life devoted to service. Without it, nothing is possible. With it, nothing is impossible."   Mary McLeod Bethune

PRAY: Dear Jesus, I know You want me to serve You and to follow You all the days of my life. Please help me to do that so that Your Father, my heavenly Father, will honor me. I need Your help to understand how Your Father could ever honor me, but I trust that if I keep my eyes on You and serve and follow You, that I will see the full picture of this commandment. I am Your servant and am honored that Your Father, my God, honors me! Amen.

REFLECT: Is it possible that God, our heavenly Father, will honor us? What could that mean? He will honor those who honor Him. It's very honoring to God to be serving Him and following Him. So, to be honored by the God of the universe, follow Him and serve Him. He promises that where He is, we will be also. That's amazing to have that access to our God, while here on earth, as a mere human! How can we serve Him?... By serving others! And how can we follow Him, even when the world tries to pull us in a different direction? It's worth asking the hard questions in order to be in a place where God is honoring you.

ACT: List three ways that you can serve God. Then start putting those into practice. When you find yourself serving Him more naturally, you will find that you are following Him more closely and He will honor the one who serves Him. Pray that you become a faithful servant.

YOUR THOUGHTS:

DAY 2

SERVE HIM FAITHFULLY WITH ALL YOUR HEART

"But be sure to fear the Lord and serve him faithfully with all your heart; consider what great things he has done for you."   1 Samuel 12:24

"Being the Queen is not all about singing, and being a diva is not all about singing. It has much to do with your service to people. And your social contributions to your community and your civic contributions as well."   Aretha Franklin

PRAY: Dear God, I never want to forget what great things You have done for me. Your faithfulness to me makes me want to serve You more faithfully with all my heart. Teach me how to fear You more and serve You every day of my life. May my life be a testimony of Your faithfulness to me. Lord, let me consider all of the great things You have done and continue to do for me. I pray this in Jesus Name! Amen.

REFLECT: What does it mean to fear the Lord? We are not to be scared of Him, but we are to be in awe of His goodness, faithfulness and love, and then we should want to serve Him faithfully with all of our hearts. When you consider what great things He has done for you, what do you think of? Are you in awe of Him? Does it make you want to serve Him more?

ACT: Take a few minutes to sit in awe before God. Then thank Him for all of the great things He has done for you. Tell Him what you know He has done for you and thank Him for each one. Then ask Him if you are serving Him faithfully, with all your heart, or is there something else He wants you to do? He is an awesome God, so why don't you tell Him so?

YOUR **THOUGHTS:**

DAY 3

NO ONE CAN SERVE TWO MASTERS

"No one can serve two masters. Either he will hate the one and love the other, or he will be devoted to the one and despise the other. You cannot serve both God and Money."

Matthew 6:24

"If I could give you information of my life, it would be to show how a woman of very ordinary ability has been led by God in strange and unaccustomed paths to do In His service what He has done in her. And if I could tell you all, you would see how God has done all, and I nothing."

Florence Nightingale

PRAY: Oh Lord, I don't want to serve anyone but You. You tell me it's impossible to serve two masters, so I ask that you keep my eyes and heart only on You. I want to be devoted to You and stay away from evil, from the love of money or from any other temptations that will take me away from my love and devotion to You. I know that I can't serve two masters, so I need Your help to serve You only. Thank you, Lord! Amen.

REFLECT: We often think that we're only serving and following the Lord, but other idols or "masters" can slip in and take away our sincere service and faithfulness to our God. Who or what do you think you might be serving now, above God? Could it be money? Your job? The love of your life? God is so strong that He says we are to hate any other master other than Him and we should despise anything that comes in the way of Him. Who do you choose to serve? And how do you make sure you're not serving two masters?

ACT: Today is the day to draw your line in the sand. Choose, this day, whom you will serve. God has given us the freedom to choose who and what we want to serve, but if there is any chance that you might be serving money, or another person, or fame, or honor, or position, or anything else over God, then today is the day to repent. Ask Him to purify your heart and to faithfully, fully, serve only Him from this day forward. Put up a proclamation in your home "For me and my house, we will serve the Lord."

YOUR THOUGHTS:

DAY 4

KEEP YOUR SPIRITUAL FERVOR SERVING THE LORD

"Never be lacking in zeal, but keep your spiritual fervor, serving the Lord. Be joyful in hope, patient in affliction, faithful in prayer. Share with God's people who are in need. Practice hospitality."   Romans 12:11-13

"Experience proves that in this life peace and satisfaction are had, not by the listless but by those who are fervent in God's service. And rightly so. For in their effort to overcome themselves and to rid themselves of self-love, they rid themselves of the roots of all passion and unrest."   Saint Ignatius

PRAY: Jesus, You have laid out how to serve You, now I just need to do it. I want to be full of zeal, keeping my spiritual fervor as I serve You. Thank you for showing me how to share with Your people who are in need. I will be joyful in hope, patient when I'm afflicted, and faithful to pray. And now I need to share my faith with people around me, for they need the hope and truth of You and Your gospel. And I want to practice generous and loving hospitality. Thank you for this reminder. Amen.

REFLECT: God doesn't want us to be sad, grumpy or depressed Christians. He tells us NEVER to be lacking in zeal. How often do you have spiritual fervor while serving the Lord? Do you have an eternal hope that is joyful? Are you patient when things go wrong, when you're hurting or in pain? Do you pray faithfully? And harder yet, do you share your faith with others? How often do you have people over to your home, share a meal with someone in need or have a lonely person stay at your house? It's hard to serve God, both physically and emotionally, but God loves a cheerful giver. Do you need His help to be full of zeal and spiritual fervor? What kind of servant are you?

ACT: Do one thing this week to serve God with zeal. Invite a lonely person over for dinner, or share your faith with an unbelieving co-worker. Or, you can pray for someone who seems to be in need. Do something to help another person and do it with joy and spiritual fervor!

YOUR THOUGHTS:

DAY 5

IT IS JESUS YOU ARE SERVING

"Whatever you do, work at it with all your heart, as working for the Lord, not for men, since you know that you will receive an inheritance from the Lord as a reward. It is the Lord Christ you are serving."

Colossians 3:23–24

"If you have no opposition in the place you serve, you're serving in the wrong place."

G. Campbell Morgan

PRAY: Heavenly Father, today I want to pray for the people who are shaping our culture and our society. I want to pray for the decision-makers and cultural influencers in the Hollywood entertainment industry. May they work at whatever they do with all their heart. May they serve You and not human masters. And may You let them know that if they do, they can receive an inheritance from You that is far greater than an Academy Award, or their picture on a billboard, or their name on the credits of a great movie, song, or TV show. Lord, may the people in Hollywood serve You and You alone. Amen.

REFLECT: It's easy to judge people who don't live the way we do. And it's very easy to condemn the people in Hollywood for living godless, immoral lives. But have you thought how hard it is for you to work with all your heart, as working for the Lord? Just think how much harder it is for people who don't even know the Lord. It's possible that the people in Hollywood would want to receive an inheritance from the Lord as a reward for following Him, but they just don't know how. Maybe all they need to change their hearts and their behavior is for someone to lovingly pray for them to meet Jesus, trust Him, follow Him, and then serve Him. Maybe your prayers are all they need.

ACT: Pray right now that the decision-makers and the cultural influencers in Hollywood will come to know Jesus. Pray that they can learn about Jesus and want to follow Him and serve Him with zeal. Pray that their lives will be open to Him so that they can serve Him with all of their hearts, souls and minds, and find great joy in that. Your prayers will make an eternal difference and you will get the joy of sharing your inheritance with others who never knew Him and never knew the joy of serving Him until you prayed!

YOUR THOUGHTS:

DAY 6

SERVE OTHERS WITH YOUR SPIRITUAL GIFTS

"Each one should use whatever gift he has received to serve others, faithfully administering God's grace in its various forms." 1 Peter 4:10

"One of the principal rules of religion is, to lose no occasion of serving God. And, since he is invisible to our eyes, we are to serve him in our neighbor, which he receives as if done to himself in person, standing visibly before us." John Wesley

PRAY: God, would You show me what gift or gifts You've given me so that I can be a faithful steward of that gift, using it to help others and to glorify You? I want to be a faithful servant of Your grace in its various forms, depending on the gifts I have received from You. So, please show me and let me not miss anything that You have for me. Amen and Amen.

REFLECT: We are all given unique and special gifts and talents that we should use to give God the glory and to serve others. Have you thought about your gift or gifts? What are they? Are you using them? Are you serving others with them? Do you see that you're making an eternal difference in this world, in whatever form, to share God's grace through the use of your gifts? How can you become a more faithful steward of all that God has given you?

ACT: Why don't you take a Spiritual Gifts test today? If you have never taken one before, there are many options on-line. If you have taken one in the past, why not do it again and see if anything has changed? Once you know your spiritual gifts, then plan how to actively use them to serve others. You will truly have a more joyful and fulfilled life if you know your spiritual gifts and then use them to serve others, as a faithful steward.

Y**OUR THOUGHTS:**

DAY 7

TO BECOME GREAT YOU MUST SERVE

"Not so with you. Instead, whoever wants to become great among you must be your servant, and whoever wants to be first must be slave of all. For even the Son of Man did not come to be served, but to serve, and to give his life as a ransom for many." Mark 10:43-45

"We should always look upon ourselves as God's servants, placed in God's world, to do his work; and accordingly labour faithfully for him; not with a design to grow rich and great, but to glorify God, and do all the good we possibly can."　　　　　David Brainerd

PRAY: Dear Lord, this verse is the perfect one to end my week. The act of humbling myself before You and others so that I can become a willing and joyful servant is powerful. Don't let me want to be first, for I don't want to be a slave of all. Help me to remember that You came, not to be served, but to serve. Thank You for being the ultimate servant by giving Your life as a ransom for everyone, including me! Amen.

REFLECT: You've heard that "man's ways are opposite of God's ways." Well, this verse makes that very clear. "Whoever wants to become great among you must be your servant, and whoever wants to be first must be slave of all." This is the perfect example of God doing things so differently than man. Do you live your life this way? Serving others, not trying to be the first, or the best, or the most noticed? This goes against our culture but it's being like Jesus, who came, not to be served, but to serve. Are you willing to give your life as a ransom for many? This is a hard verse to live out, but with God, all things are possible for those who believe.

ACT: End this week by serving someone, sacrificially, as if you were giving your life for them. Go out of your way to do something radically generous or kind for someone who would not expect it. Surprise him or her with your servant's heart. Rock someone's world today by stepping out of your comfort zone and serving one person with the love of Jesus!

YOUR THOUGHTS:

FATHERS

WEEK TWENTY-THREE

There are so many verses in the Bible about FATHERS! This is a crucial issue in our nation and God knows it. Spend this week understanding our Heavenly Father's view of our earthly fathers, and in the process become better mothers and fathers.

Each day this week we are pleased to include videos of songs about fathers, written by Jim Covell. Find them all at
https://www.fathersongs.com/

DAY 1

GOD OUR FATHER

"Yet, O Lord, you are our Father. We are the clay, you are the potter; we are all the work of your hand."
Isaiah 64:8

"I will be a Father to you, and you will be my sons and daughters, says the Lord Almighty."
2 Corinthians 6:18

"He adopted a role called "Being a Father" so that his child would have something mythical and infinitely important: a Protector."
Tom Wolfe

PRAY: Dear Heavenly Father, I thank You that You are my true Father. Thank You that we are your true sons and daughters, and that though we are only clay, You are the potter and we are all the work of Your hand. I want to trust you and fall more in love with You more than I even trust or love my earthly father. I praise You, my eternal Father! Amen.

REFLECT: Have you ever thought about why God made Himself our father and not our mother? It's because a mother's love is instinctive, but a father's love is a choice. God chose to love each and every one of us. We can love because He loved us first. He is the ultimate, perfect Father whom earthly fathers try to be like, but only as a mere reflection of Him. God tells us that He creates us, molds us and completes us, as a potter does to a lump of clay. How perfect, powerful and precious is our God, our Father!

ACT: Do you have expectations of God your Heavenly Father, based on your relationship with your earthly Father? Do you have hurts, anger or numbness toward your earthly father that has hindered your relationship with God the Father? Right now, write God a love note, as your perfect Father, and thank Him for everything He is to you. How big and mighty is your God? Stretch out of your emotional comfort zone and thank God for being your creator, potter, supporter, supplier, care-giver, friend, advisor and more. Then save your love note and go back to it in the future. Never forget how amazing your Heavenly Father is.

YOUR THOUGHTS:

TODAY'S SONG: *A Father's Prayer* at https://www.fathersongs.com/

DAY 2

FATHERS, DON'T DISCOURAGE YOUR CHILDREN

"Fathers, do not embitter your children, or they will become discouraged" Colossian 3:21
"Do not exasperate your children; instead, bring them up in the training and instruction of the Lord." "...Be merciful, just as your Father is merciful." Ephesians 6:4, Luke 6:36

"When I come home, my daughter will run to the door and give me a big hug, and everything that's happened that day just melts away." Hugh Jackman

PRAY: Father, I pray for people who are deeply hurt by their earthly fathers. You tell fathers not to embitter their children or they will become discouraged, but to bring them up in the training and instruction of the Lord. Please come into the hearts of hurting children, of any age, heal them and fill them up with Your unconditional love and hope. I praise You for the fathers who are merciful and loving, like You, the Father to the fatherless. Amen.

REFLECT: Did you or any people in your life have bad or non-existent fathers? That is damaging to children. The role of the Father is crucial and yet many fathers embitter their children. What can you do to help in that desperate situation? Can you show mercy to hurting children or mentor prodigal children? Chuck Colson once said, "The problem of so many Americans being in jail is not because of too many guns, but because of too few fathers." What is your place in changing the fatherless crisis in our country?

ACT: Choose three people you know, including yourself, if it applies, who have been damaged by a bad father. Commit to pray for them every day this week, asking the Lord to come in as their Heavenly Father, to train and instruct them and show mercy to them. Pray for their hearts to heal, their emotions to be restored, and for the ability to embrace their Heavenly Father. Make an eternal difference in three people all week because of your prayers for them, inviting our God of mercy to take away their bitterness and discouragement!

YOUR THOUGHTS:

TODAY'S SONG: *Someday* at https://www.fathersongs.com

DAY 3

HONOR YOUR FATHER

"Honor your father and your mother, as the Lord your God has commanded you, so that you may live long and that it may go well with you in the land the Lord your God is giving you."
Deuteronomy 5:16

"My father gave me the greatest gift anyone could give another person: He believed in me."
Jim Valvano

PRAY: Heavenly Father, I want to pray for the people who have great fathers and for those who don't. It's easy to honor good fathers, and reap the results with a long life in the land. But would you help those who don't have great fathers to honor their fathers anyway? Heal broken fathers as You help their children show them Your love! Teach us the importance of honoring our fathers, how to love them more deeply, to forgive them and be patient with them. We all need Your help to love our fathers the way You have commanded us! Amen.

REFLECT: How hard it must be for angry, hurting, broken children of all ages to follow this commandment to honor their father? What does honor mean, in this context? We don't have to be buddies, spend lots of time, or even obey everything they say. The dictionary defines honor as "high respect; great esteem, adherence to what is right, or a conventional standard of conduct, fulfill an obligation or a contract." That's easy for great fathers, but what about abusive fathers? If your father was hurtful, then you can adhere to a right standard of conduct by not talking against him, or getting revenge, while honoring his position of father, versus his choices. And if your father breaks his contract with you, you can honor your end of the contract by praying for him. Is that possible in your relationship with your father?

ACT: Which part of the definition of HONOR above fits your relationship with your father? Reread "Reflect" and ask God to reveal to you if you're honoring your father. If not, ask how to honor him in a biblical way. Turn to Your Heavenly Father for guidance and direction on how you can fully honor your Father, regardless of how he has treated you.

YOUR THOUGHTS:

TODAY'S SONGS: *Thank That Man* and *Superman* at https://www.fathersongs.com

DAY 4

A LOVING FATHER'S DISCIPLINE

"And you have forgotten that word of encouragement that addresses you as sons: "My son, do not make light of the Lord's discipline, and do not lose heart when he rebukes you,... Endure hardship as discipline; God is treating you as sons. For what son is not disciplined by his father?... Moreover, we have all had human fathers who disciplined us and we respected them for it. How much more should we submit to the Father of our spirits and live!"   Hebrews 12:5,7, & 9

"Train up a child in the way he should go – but be sure you go that way yourself."
                                                                             Charles Spurgeon

PRAY: Dear Father, I know that as a father disciplines his children, You must discipline me. Help me to not lose heart when You rebuke me. Help me endure hardship as discipline, for I know that You are treating me as Your child. Help me to both accept Your discipline, and respect You for it, as I am to respect my earthly father when he disciplines me. Father, discipline me into a Christ-like child of Yours whom You are proud of. Amen.

REFLECT: It is so difficult to know how to discipline a child well. Should we "spare the rod," or use the spoon? Do we give time-outs, take things away, or give lectures on right and wrong? Human beings are still trying to figure it out. Only God knows exactly how to perfectly discipline His children. So why not seek insight on parenting skills by studying how God disciplines us: Read scripture, pray, and seek wise advice from Godly mentors.

ACT: Read Hebrews 12:5,7 & 9 again and pray over each verse. Seek wisdom about how you were disciplined and how you should discipline your children. Ask the Lord for insight into how He is disciplining you, for we need to submit when God is disciplining us to make us stronger or to learn a lesson. Seek Him for wisdom and ask God to help you not lose heart when He rebukes you. He loves you so much. Respect Him as your Heavenly Father!

YOUR THOUGHTS:

TODAY'S SONG: *Little Boys Are Wild At Heart* at https://www.fathers.com

DAY 5

ABBA FATHER

"Though my father and mother forsake me, the Lord will receive me."   Psalm 27:10

"Early on in my life, I had a broken soul. I was abused by my father, abandoned by my mother and ended up in a destructive first marriage. By the time I was 23, I was broken in my soul. I didn't know how to think right. I felt wrong about everything. But God stepped into my life, and I came out on the other side and didn't even smell like smoke."

Joyce Meyer

PRAY: Abba Father, I thank You that even though my father may forsake me, You will always receive me. Will You please fill up the holes in me that my father has not been able or has chosen not to fill? Will You be the father that I never had? Will you show the men in our world how to be good, strong, loving fathers to their children, even though their fathers never taught them how? Because You are my true Father, I turn to You to be a tangible father to me and all of the hurting children in the world. Come, dear Father and fill me up. Thank You for receiving me as your precious child. Amen and Amen.

REFLECT: It's amazing how God acknowledges that some fathers and mothers do forsake their children. That means that it's not that rare, and that if we're from families with broken fathers, the Lord knows it, loves us, and even tells us not to worry because He will receive us. This is important to encourage others, believe it ourselves, and pray for the broken fathers in our world. This might be why God has chosen to be our Father – because He knows how many fathers can't live up to the task and so He is our loving Father! What a revelation!

ACT: Reach out to one person you know who has no father, or is angry, hurt, or bitter because of a bad father, and tell them the good news that God knows, and that He receives them with open arms! He knows that many broken fathers and mothers forsake their children. And yet, He tells us in Psalm 27 that He is our loving father, and He is there for ALL of us. Encourage your friend, co-worker, or family member today with this loving promise of God.

YOUR THOUGHTS:

TODAY'S SONGS: *Daddy Please Hurry Home & Someday* at https://www.fathersongs.com

DAY 6

THE GREAT LOVE OF THE FATHER

"How great is the love the Father has lavished on us, that we should be called children of God! And that is what we are! The reason the world does not know us is that it did not know him." 1 John 3:1

"A father acts on behalf of his children by working, providing, intervening, struggling, and suffering for them. In so doing, he really stands in their place. He is not an isolated individual, but incorporates the selves of several people in his own self."

Dietrich Bonhoeffer

PRAY: God my Father, I know You have lavished great love on me, so please let me love others the same way. Many people live dark lives because they have never known You. Give me patience and understanding for the people in Hollywood who don't live according to Your laws, because they don't know You and they never had fathers to love them. I want to pray for them with the same love that You have shown me, in Jesus' name, Amen.

REFLECT: Have you thought about WHY people are sinful, nasty, abusive, or angry? Most often it's a spiritual issue. Because they don't know God and His ways, some people in Hollywood don't act or talk the way we want them to because of their broken backgrounds. That's why Christians need to pray for the Hollywood decision-makers and celebrities. Many come from broken homes and don't know the love of their Heavenly Father!

ACT: Would you join us at the Hollywood Prayer Network today and pray for the people in Hollywood who have bad, abusive, or distant fathers. Their earthly fathers are hindering them from embracing their Heavenly Father, so we pray for the Holy Spirit to grab their hearts with His unconditional love. We want God's love to transform them and set them free. Then their programming will also reflect His heart, His perspective, and His values. You can change the world by praying for Hollywood professionals to be healed from the hurts of their earthly fathers and for their acceptance of their Heavenly Father.

YOUR THOUGHTS:

TODAY'S SONG: *Tell Them That You Love Them Every Day* at https://www.fathersongs.com

DAY 7

THE PRODIGAL

"So he got up and went to his father. But while he was still a long way off, his father saw him and was filled with compassion for him; he ran to his son, threw his arms around him and kissed him... 'My son,' the father said, 'you are always with me, and everything I have is yours.' "

Luke 15:20 & 31

"There is nothing that moves a loving father's soul quite like his child's cry."

Joni Eareckson Tada

PRAY: Father, this story of the prodigal son is so powerful and shows unconditional love from the father as he tells his wayward son, "you are always with me and everything I have is yours," And that's just how You feel about me! Thank You that You ran to me and embraced me before I ever loved You. And now I see that my earthly father is only a mere reflection of Your unconditional love, even when I don't deserve it. In Jesus name, Amen.

REFLECT: This story is one of the best analogies of God's love in the Bible. The prodigal son is selfish, arrogant, foolish, and greedy – just like us. And his father is forgiving, loving, affectionate and embracing – just like God. It's humbling to see that the father is not judgmental or trying to get justice. He doesn't even mention the wrongs done to him. He is just overjoyed to see his son. How can we be that way to other people? We have to learn from our Father and choose to act and speak more like Him. How would you start to do that?

ACT: Are you a prodigal son or daughter, father or mother? As a parent, do you need to ask forgiveness for any of your actions or words. As the child, do you need to forgive your father for whatever he's done? This is the moment to trust in God and His love. Choose one relationship that needs to change and take action. First pray and confirm your choice. Next, forgive your prodigal self, child or parent. Then commit to write a note, make a call, or plan a meeting to offer your unconditional love to your child or your parent. You can change your most intimate relationships because God is with you every step of the way!

YOUR THOUGHTS:

TWO SONGS: The Prodigal Dad & Did I Ever Please Him at https://www.fathersongs.com

EXCELLENCE

WEEK TWENTY-FOUR

As Christians we want to be people of excellence. We should be doing everything as unto the Lord so that He is glorified through our work, our words and our actions. So, this week, let's strive to be excellent as Christians, brothers, sisters, parents, students, professionals, neighbors and friends, in everything we do and say!

DAY 1

DEVOTE YOURSELF TO EXCELLENCE

"He saved us through the washing of rebirth and renewal by the Holy Spirit, whom he poured out on us generously through Jesus Christ our Savior, so that, having been justified by his grace, we might become heirs having the hope of eternal life. This is a trustworthy saying. And I want you to stress these things, so that those who have trusted in God may be careful to devote themselves to doing what is good. These things are excellent and profitable for everyone."

Titus 3:5b-8

"The secret of living a life of excellence is merely a matter of thinking thoughts of excellence. Really, it's a matter of programing our minds with the kind of information that will set us free"

Charles Swindoll

PRAY: Heavenly Father, thank You that I am justified by Your grace and thank You for giving me Your Holy Spirit so that I can devote myself to doing what is good! I want to be excellent and profitable, for You, for myself, and for everyone around me, and I know I can only do it through You, with the guidance of Your Holy Spirit. Make me excellent! Amen.

REFLECT: What are the profitable things of God to which we should devote ourselves? Reflect on these things: The kindness and love of our God, His mercy and grace, our renewal by the Holy Spirit and the hope of eternal life. These things are excellent and profitable for everyone, so we must devote ourselves to learning this and then doing what is good. As you reflect on these eternally significant concepts know that your goal is EXCELLENCE!

ACT: Choose to act on the truths in Titus 3:5-8 today because they are excellent and profitable for everyone: Share God's kindness and love to someone, show mercy to someone who has hurt you, share the hope of eternal life with someone, or ask the Holy Spirit to renew you. Whichever you choose, commit to that action, choose your words wisely, and know that it is making you a more excellent child of God!

YOUR THOUGHTS:

DAY 2

HIS DIVINE POWER MAKES US EXCELLENT

"His divine power has given us everything we need for life and godliness through our knowledge of him who called us by his own glory and goodness. Through these he has given us his very great and precious promises, so that through them you may participate in the divine nature and escape the corruption in the world caused by evil desires. For this very reason, make every effort to add to your faith goodness; and to goodness, knowledge; and to knowledge, self-control; and to self-control, perseverance; and to perseverance, godliness; and to godliness, brotherly kindness; and to brotherly kindness, love."

2 Peter 1:3-7

"All labor that uplifts humanity has dignity and importance and should be undertaken with painstaking excellence."   Martin Luther King Jr.

PRAY: Almighty God, Maker of heaven and earth, Your divine power has given me everything I need to live a godly life. You allow me to participate in Your divine nature and to escape the corruption in the world. God, add to my faith goodness, knowledge, self-control, perseverance, godliness, and love between You and me, and between me and my brothers and sisters. I know that this will make me excellent in Your eyes. Amen!

REFLECT: These promises of God are both precious and overwhelming. Read through them again focusing on what He is offering us. Can you grasp the depth of His love for you, the miracles He offers you, and the transforming power He has given you? These qualities that Peter tells us to add to our faith is an almost impossible list of goals, but with God, NOTHING is impossible. How can you strive for excellence in all of these areas?

ACT: Pick one promise from this verse that you want to add to your faith and help you to become excellent. Don't try for them all at once. Just start with one. Do you want to be good? Do you want more knowledge? Self-control? Perseverance? Godliness? ... Whatever you choose, embrace it, pray about it, focus on it, and become excellent in it. And then, go on to another. You will be slowly transforming your mind and life. And remember, His divine power has given you everything you need to succeed and to become excellent!

YOUR THOUGHTS:

DAY 3

DON'T BE AFRAID; BE OF NOBLE CHARACTER

"And now, my daughter, don't be afraid. I will do for you all you ask. All the people of my town know that you are a woman of noble character."   Ruth 3:11

"We should not judge people by their peak of excellence; but by the distance they have traveled from the point where they started."   Henry Ward Beecher

PRAY: Dear Lord, will You help me to not be afraid? Thank You that You want to do for me all that I ask, according to Your will. May You help me do for You whatever You ask? I want to be known as a person of noble character and I want to be excellent in everything I do. So, please Lord, make me all that You've created me to be. In Jesus name, Amen.

REFLECT: While reading the Bible, don't let pronouns or gender labels stop you from getting the message of what the Lord is offering us. These words by Boaz to Ruth are reflective of God's heart for us. He wants to give us the desires of our hearts and He wants us to be people of noble character. We just have to trust Him. Are there any changes you need to make in your life to become a person of noble character? Look deep into your heart and ask the Lord to reveal anything that would stop the people in your life from calling you a "woman or man of noble character." And know that having a noble character is excellent!

ACT: Do you know someone whom you would say is a woman or man of noble character? If so, why don't you call them today and tell them that based on your morning devotional you were reminded of them and their noble character and you want them to know that you have given them that label of excellence. You will make your friend or co-worker's day, and your selfless words to them will be eternally significant.

YOUR THOUGHTS:

DAY 4

PRAY FOR OTHERS TO BE WORTHY

"With this in mind, we constantly pray for you, that our God may make you worthy of His calling, and that by His power He may bring to fruition your every desire for goodness and your every deed prompted by faith." 2 Thessalonians 1:11

"The test of the artist does not lie in the will with which he goes to work, but in the excellence of the work he produces." Thomas Aquinas

PRAY: Dear Jesus, help me to pray for others the way Paul prays for his friends in Thessalonica. May You make me, my friends, and the creative professionals in Hollywood all worthy of Your calling, and that by Your power You may bring to fruition the desires of our heart for goodness. May our every deed be prompted by faith in You. Jesus, I so desire to be excellent in Your sight and I want the same for my friends, family and for Hollywood leaders, who are impacting the world with their lives and work. Please make us all excellent and worthy of Your calling. Amen.

REFLECT: What does it mean to constantly pray for someone? Is there anyone you pray for constantly? That's a tremendous commitment. What do you think would change by praying constantly for the people in your life, or the people who influence your life? Probably their lives would change, and so would yours. Can you have a constant, ongoing conversation with your Savior a life's goal? Since practice makes perfect, you will surely become excellent at praying and worthy of His calling.

ACT: Who would be the one person whom you would like to be constantly praying for this week? Choose now and talk to God about that person as often as possible – as you start your day, during meetings and phone calls, lift up that person to Him. Take time at lunch to pray and then again at dinner and before bed. And don't be afraid to choose someone you don't know. Maybe it's your favorite movie star, singer, or celebrity… They need your prayers too, and by praying, you are being a person of excellence and God is pleased.

YOUR THOUGHTS:

DAY 5

SERVE WITH EXCELLENCE

"Those who have served well gain an excellent standing and great assurance in their faith in Christ Jesus."
1 Timothy 3:13

"If you give a good idea to a mediocre team, they will screw it up. If you give a mediocre idea to a brilliant team, they will either fix it or throw it away and come up with something better."
Ed Catmull, Creativity, Inc.

PRAY: Jesus, You are the ultimate servant. Would You please help me to serve well. I want to be in excellent standing with You and I want to have the great assurance in my faith in You, so I need You to help me to be a true servant in all I do. Help me to serve in my home, in the workplace, and with my friends. Would You make me a servant leader, Jesus? Thank You. Amen and Amen.

REFLECT: Think about the concept that in serving others you can gain both an excellent standing in God's eyes, but also a great assurance of your faith in Jesus. Have you ever thought about how serving can be so profoundly connected to the heart of Jesus? Serving others is actually a fun way to grow in your faith. The power of a servant's heart can go far! Would people describe you as being a servant?

ACT: Choose one person to serve today. Go out of your way to take the time to serve someone in a way you've never done before. Buy them lunch, help them at work, buy them coffee, fix their car, watch their kids…. Whatever it is, do it today, and then maybe go ahead and do it for someone else again tomorrow. Do you see the result? They will be blessed and you will be gaining an excellent standing and a great assurance of your faith in Jesus!

YOUR THOUGHTS:

DAY 6

YOU ARE THE MOST EXCELLENT

"You are the most excellent of men and your lips have been anointed with grace, since God has blessed you forever."
Psalm 45:2

"Perfection is not attainable, but if we chase perfection we can catch excellence."
Vince Lombardi

PRAY: Abba Father, I want You to think of me as "most excellent of men!" Would You anoint my lips with grace and bless me forever so that I will always be excellent in Your eyes. I need Your grace so that I can give grace to others, and I accept Your blessing so that I can be a blessing to others. I praise You for who You've made me, and who You're helping me to become. Oh Father, the desire of my heart is to have You see me as excellent! Amen.

REFLECT: Again, don't worry about this verse being just for men. In this Psalm it says, "You are the most excellent of men." In the Ruth verse this week it says, "You are a woman of noble character." In contemplating God's word, know that He is speaking directly to you with everything he says. He wants all of us to be excellent and have a noble character. So, embrace God's concepts, and do not get hung up on the unimportant things that can lead you off track. Today, think about being the "most excellent of people."

ACT: Would you focus today on your words and ask the Lord to anoint your lips with grace. Ask God, who has blessed you forever, to make you aware of everything you say today and ask Him over and over to guide your thoughts and control your tongue so that you will bless Him and others all day long.

YOUR THOUGHTS:

Day 7

FINALLY, THINK ABOUT THESE THINGS

"Finally, brothers, whatever is true, whatever is noble, whatever is right, whatever is pure, whatever is lovely, whatever is admirable--if anything is excellent or praiseworthy--think about such things."

Philippians 4:8

"Excellence is an art won by training. We are what we repeatedly do." Aristotle

PRAY: Dear Lord, help me to think about only good things, excellent and pure thoughts, lovely ideas, admirable dreams and give me a heart full of praise. Lord, I want to please You and to be so full of You that everything I do, say and even think, is excellent. Thank You for transforming me into a vessel of excellence. I pray in Jesus' name

REFLECT: What percentage of your thought life is focused on things that are true, noble, right, pure, lovely, admirable, excellent or praiseworthy? What would it take to stop thinking negative thoughts, thoughts against people, comparing yourself to others, jealous thoughts, feelings of insecurity, fear, hurt and pain? And what do you need to do to replace those thoughts with joyful, life affirming thoughts? Remember that we can't always completely change the way we are, but we can always manage our thoughts, words, and actions. Think about that…

ACT: Write down a plan to change and/or manage your thought life, and then prayerfully give that list to the Lord. In order to live a life of excellence, what needs to change? List the habitual thoughts you're stuck on and plan a way to change those thoughts into something positive and pray for help. Then put that plan in a place you see every day so that it will remind you to break the habit of negative thoughts and start a new habit of Christ-like thoughts of excellence. Changing your thoughts will change your whole life!

YOUR THOUGHTS:

DISCOURAGEMENT & DESPAIR

WEEK TWENTY-FIVE

Discouragement and Despair are two emotions with which the enemy attacks all of us. Would you spend time asking the Lord to deal with both your own discouragement and also the discouragement and despair of those who create our culture in the entertainment industry? The enemy attacks with isolation, discouragement and fear. Let's tackle discouragement and despair this week.

Day 1

BATTLE DEFEAT

"We are hard pressed on every side, but not crushed; perplexed, but not in despair; persecuted, but not abandoned; struck down, but not destroyed. We always carry around in our body the death of Jesus, so that the life of Jesus may also be revealed in our body."

2 Corinthians 4:8-10

"Transformation is a process, and as life happens there are tons of ups and downs. It's a journey of discovery -there are moments on mountaintops and moments in deep valleys of despair."

Rick Warren

PRAY: Lord, I want to be honest with You about what I'm going through; I know You can take it. You know that I am in process and that I feel fear, discouragement and sometimes even despair. Please show me that You are near when I am hard pressed on every side, when I feel persecuted, abandoned, and struck down. Could You remind me that You are holding me up and that You will never let me be destroyed. I thank You that Jesus' eternal life is in my body, giving me strength. I pray this in Jesus' name, Amen.

REFLECT: Think through the times when you honestly felt hard pressed on every side, crushed and in despair? Have you felt abandoned and struck down? Have you ever even felt destroyed or close to death? Now reflect on how you can focus on Jesus and His resurrection life that is within YOU. It may be through prayer, meditation, or praising Him – find what works for you and change your focus from defeat to believing His promises for you. This may be a lifetime commitment but never give up, never surrender!

ACT: Start thanking the Lord for everything that doesn't go your way! Thank Him for the job you didn't get, the bills you can't pay, your discouragements and disappointments. Thank Him that He will NOT let you down or allow you to be destroyed, for He is alive in you. Make this a daily habit and it will change you into someone who can handle anything, through Christ in you. You will see that you will not be in despair, you will not feel persecuted or abandoned, and you will not be struck down or feel death, because as you thank Him for ALL things you will feel victorious, regardless of your circumstances.

YOUR THOUGHTS:

DAY 2

PERSEVERE IN GOD

"So do not throw away your confidence; it will be richly rewarded. You need to persevere so that when you have done the will of God, you will receive what he has promised."

Hebrews 10:35–36

"Despair is a narcotic. It lulls the mind into indifference."   Charlie Chaplin

PRAY: Dear God, please fill me with confidence in You, in Your promises, Your love, protection, wisdom, and Your perseverance, so that I will be fulfilling Your will every hour of every day of my life. Thank You for Your rich rewards when I am faithful and that I will receive what You have promised me, because Your word is true and never changing. I don't want to throw away my confidence, but persevere through any storm, set-back or disappointment, because I have put my faith in You. Amen and Amen.

REFLECT: Where does your confidence come from? Do you struggle with insecurity? If so, maybe that's because your confidence is not in God, but in yourself, and you can never feel that you are good enough, strong enough, smart enough, or wise enough. Most people struggle with insecurity. And those who don't know the Lord are left to persevere through their own strength, which is exhausting and discouraging. The brokenness and poor choices of many people is because they don't know how to embrace the will of God. What a gift we have as Christians to be able to focus on building our confidence in Him so that we can see how He is richly rewarding us for our trust and dependence on Him.

ACT: Do not throw away your confidence for it will be richly rewarded. Ask the Lord to help you persevere so that you will receive what He has promised. In what area of your life do you need more confidence? Tell the Lord how you want to grow and ask Him to help you to persevere in achieving it, overcoming it or being healed from it. In order to not lose your confidence you must turn to Him. Then expect to receive what He has promised!

YOUR THOUGHTS:

DAY 3

LET GO OF FEAR

"He said: "Listen, King Jehoshaphat and all who live in Judah and Jerusalem! This is what the Lord says to you: 'Do not be afraid or discouraged because of this vast army. For the battle is not yours, but God's...You will not have to fight this battle. Take up your positions; stand firm and see the deliverance the Lord will give you, O Judah and Jerusalem. Do not be afraid; do not be discouraged. Go out to face them tomorrow, and the Lord will be with you.' "

2 Chronicles 20:15 & 17

"Do not abandon yourselves to despair. We are the Easter people and Hallelujah is our song."

Pope John Paul II

PRAY: Heavenly Father, would You show me where I am afraid and discouraged, so that I can identify the battles and ask You to fight them for me. I want to take up my position of prayer and praise, stand firm in my belief, and trust in YOU, and then watch the deliverance that You will bring. Thank You for how You take care of me and I don't have to be afraid or discouraged! Father, prepare me to "go out and face them" today, tomorrow and the next day. And You will be with me! Amen and Amen.

REFLECT: Sit quietly and ask yourself, and the Lord – "What am I afraid of?" Then ask the Lord to reveal to you what you're not trusting Him for. And when you see those issues, can you imagine giving them to God and knowing that He is fighting those battles for you? What does it mean to stand firm and take up your position? Is that physical, or emotional? Reflect on the practical meaning of this scripture.

ACT: Be vulnerable and jot down the things that bring you fear, anxiety, or worry. Is it finances, your relationships, your job, your career, your education, your insecurities? Choose one area of struggle and focus on giving that to God every day. Stand your position! Decide what you are going to do when that fear overtakes you and press into the fact that God wants to fight that battle for you. You have to give it to Him and walk away – both mentally, physically and emotionally. It is like developing a new muscle; it takes exercise, focus, prayer, and commitment.

YOUR THOUGHTS:

DAY 4

YOU ARE NEVER ALONE

"Have I not commanded you? Be strong and courageous. Do not be terrified; do not be discouraged, for the Lord your God will be with you wherever you go."   Joshua 1:9

"The friend who can be silent with us in a moment of despair or confusion, who can stay with us in an hour of grief and bereavement, who can tolerate not knowing...not healing, not curing...that is a friend who cares."   Henri Nouwen

PRAY: Oh Jesus, help me to be strong and courageous! I don't want to be afraid or discouraged, for YOU are my God and You will be with me wherever I go. Thank You that I can turn to You when I'm feeling weak and discouraged. And thank You that You are ALWAYS there for me, for You are with me wherever I go. Oh, Jesus, help me to understand how to apply Your commandments and promises to my daily life. In Your name I pray. Amen.

REFLECT: Think about God's commandment to be strong and courageous. If He gave us that command, then it must be possible. But how do you actually do that? Try focusing on the fact that Jesus is always with you; You are NEVER alone, even when you are by yourself. Moments of feeling weak are when you need Him desperately. Call out to Him. He will answer and give you strength, for He is with you wherever you go.

ACT: Memorize Joshua 1:9 so that it is in your brain and in your heart the next time you are discouraged. Say it over and over and let the truths of God's promise fill you up. Write the verse on an index card and start collecting a stack of cards to read over until they are a part of your being. You will feel less and less fearful or discouraged when this verse becomes a part of your DNA! Let this be the beginning of a lifetime of memorization.

Y**OUR THOUGHTS:**

DAY 5

HE RENEWS YOU

"Why are you downcast, O my soul? Why so disturbed within me? Put your hope in God, for I will yet praise him, my Savior and my God."   Psalm 42:5-6a

"The brave man is not he who feels no fear, for that were stupid and irrational; But he, whose noble soul its fear subdues, And bravely dares the danger nature shrinks from."

Joanna Baillie, Poet & Dramatist

PRAY: Oh, God, don't let me despair! Would You keep renewing my soul with Your Holy Spirit and don't let me get disturbed. Help me to hope in You for I want to again praise You for Your help, Your love, and Your constant presence in my every breathing moment. Why should I be downcast? For You are my Savior and my God! Selah! Amen.

REFLECT: Have you ever thought about your SOUL? What is it? How do you access it, understand it, change it, fill it, redirect it... He tells us that if we hope in God, we will again praise Him and experience His presence. So, it must be true that if you put your hope in the Lord and praise Him you will experience His presence in your soul, your mind and your emotions. So, why are you downcast, O my soul?

ACT: Praise God right now. Praise Him for His character, His promises, protection, His omniscience, His love, and for how He has given you life. And remember that praise is different than thanks. Today you are just praising and worshiping your Savior and your God. And whenever you are in despair, remember to start praising God for who He is. It will lift you out of that dark place and fill up your soul, giving you a hope that will not disappoint you. Try to commit to just praising God every day for a few minutes until it becomes not only a part of your day but a part of your nature.

YOUR THOUGHTS:

DAY 6

ENCOURAGE OTHERS

"We do not want you to be uninformed, brothers, about the hardships we suffered in the province of Asia. We were under great pressure, far beyond our ability to endure, so that we despaired even of life. Indeed, in our hearts we felt the sentence of death. But this happened that we might not rely on ourselves but on God, who raises the dead."

2 Corinthians 1:8-9

"The prayer power has never been tried to its full capacity. If we want to see mighty wonders of divine power and grace wrought in the place of weakness, failure and disappointment, let us answer God's standing challenge, "Call unto me, and I will answer thee, and show thee great and mighty things which thou knowest not!"' J. Hudson Taylor

PRAY: Hello Lord, I'm here with You again and I want to tell You openly about my troubles. I acknowledge that when I am under great pressure, You are here. Right now, my fears seem beyond my ability to endure, yet I don't want to despair because You promise me that I should rely on You, my God who raises the dead! Please remind me that I have no need to worry about anything. You want me not to rely on myself but on You alone. I praise You! Amen.

REFLECT: As in Corinth, Christians in Hollywood often feel very alone, even to the point of despair, as they work and live in this spiritually dark and challenging environment. They need to express their struggles to one another and inform them of what is going on in their lives and yet we are uninformed. We would see more breakthroughs in the media if the Christians working there had more supporters on the outside. Do you know Christians who are on the mission field in Hollywood? How can you encourage them to rely on God?

ACT: Are you connected to anyone in the media whom you can touch base with, pray for, encourage, or even save their life? If so, reach out to them and let them know you're praying for them. If not, pray for the Lord to connect you with a Christian in the media so you can be their prayer partner and intercede as they live the difficult life of a media/entertainment professional. We can match you up as a prayer partner with an industry professional through HPN by clicking on: www.hollywoodprayernetwork.org. Don't be uninformed!

YOUR THOUGHTS:

DAY 7

DON'T BE DISCOURGED

"Now to him who is able to do immeasurably more than all we ask or imagine, according to his power that is at work within us, to him be glory in the church and in Christ Jesus throughout all generations, for ever and ever! Amen."   Ephesians 3:20-21

"Now, God be praised, that to believing souls gives light in darkness, comfort in despair."

William Shakespeare

PRAY: Lord, I know that You can do immeasurably more than anything I can do on my own. So, help me not to get discouraged. I need to trust You completely with my thoughts, my words, and my actions so that I experience Your power that is at work within me. When I feel despair, I want to give You the glory both personally, and in the church, and pass on my praise and thanks to You to future generations, forever and ever! Amen.

REFLECT: Reflect on what it means to believe in the absolute power of God. Do you believe that He really is able to do far more abundantly than anything we ask or think? Our thoughts are pretty wild and yet He can do far more than even that. And He does it in us and through us because of His power at work within us. How much of God's power do you really feel within you? It should be enough to make you shake discouragement if you understand and embrace it fully. And would it be enough to pass it on to future generations?

ACT: PRAY for Christians you know across the world to be informed and prayerfully involved in what God is doing in their lives. Ask God to lift up people in churches all across the country to connect with your friends and family members and to stay informed about their needs and what they are doing—their struggles, victories, and battles. Your prayers for the Christians you know invites God in to do immeasurably more than all you can ask or imagine, according to His power! And your prayers have an impact through the generations!

YOUR THOUGHTS:

DOUBT

WEEK TWENTY-SIX

I think one of the greatest plights of man is this phrase: "I do believe; help me overcome my unbelief!" We believe God completely in some circumstances and then we doubt Him a moment later by getting fearful, angry, or discouraged. This week we're going to dig into doubt and ask the Lord to grow our faith so that we can move mountains!

DAY 1

WHY DO WE DOUBT?

"They were startled and frightened, thinking they saw a ghost. He said to them, "Why are you troubled, and why do doubts rise in your minds? Look at my hands and my feet. It is I myself! Touch me and see; a ghost does not have flesh and bones, as you see I have."

Luke 24:37-39

"Christ never failed to distinguish between doubt and unbelief. Doubt is can't believe. Unbelief is won't believe. Doubt is honesty. Unbelief is obstinacy. Doubt is looking for light. Unbelief is content with darkness."

Henry Drummond

PRAY: Dear Lord, as I start my week focusing on doubt, I want You to fill me up with peace and trust in You so that I do not question You and Your love. You told the disciples not to doubt. You knew that they were troubled by seeing You and You even had them touch You to show how real You are. Would You help me to KNOW, without a doubt, that You are real, all-loving, and the only one in whom I should put all of my trust? Thank you for proving Yourself to the disciples so that I don't have to doubt. I pray this in Your holy name, Amen.

REFLECT: Do you ever question why you would doubt Jesus? Read the definition of doubt: "To waver or fluctuate in opinion; to hesitate; to be in suspense; to be in uncertainty; to be undetermined." God tells us over and over again throughout the Bible that He is the Creator, all-loving, our help and salvation, and then He specifically tells us not to doubt His existence. And yet we doubt! What would it take for you to stop doubting God? Would you need to physically touch Him? Ask God to show you how to get rid of your doubt.

ACT: What are TWO areas of your faith where you find yourself doubting God's love? Is it in your finances, protection, security, relationships? Is it when you're alone in the dark, or when you're sick or angry? Choose the two most prominent areas and write them down on an index card. Then write this verse on the same card and as you memorize the verse, pray that the Lord takes control of those two areas so that you won't doubt anymore. When you believe the Lord's presence and promises have replaced those two areas of doubt, then define two more. Face your doubts and allow the Lord to heal you or help you manage them, once and for all!

YOUR THOUGHTS:

DAY 2

JESUS IS PATIENT WHEN WE DOUBT

"Then he said to Thomas, "Put your finger here; see my hands. Reach out your hand and put it into my side. Stop doubting and believe."   John 20:27

"Doubt discovers difficulties which it never solves; it creates hesitancy, despondency, despair. Its progress is the decay of comfort, the death of peace. "Believe!" is the word which speaks life into a man, but doubt nails down his coffin."   Charles Spurgeon

PRAY: Oh Lord, You understand us so well that You address the very issues with which we all struggle. We all doubt, we need proof of Your love and power, and You know that. Thank You that You are patient and You show us mercy when we doubt. Thank You for giving me Thomas as a role model whom I can relate to. You loved Thomas so much, knowing that he doubted You. So, I thank You that You love me the same way. I want to trust You more, lean on You, turn to You and rest in You more often. Help me to do that, in Your name. Amen.

REFLECT: Isn't Jesus lovingly patient when he says to Thomas, "… Reach out your hand and put it into my side. Stop doubting and believe." Can you imagine Him lovingly guiding Thomas's hand to the very spot on His side that revealed His divinity? He's not disappointed or mad at Thomas. He has no judgment in His statement. He wants to help Thomas through his unbelief. That's how He is with all of us. He loves us SO MUCH that everything He says and does is loving, patient, gentle, and kind. Isn't it amazing that Jesus loves you even as you doubt?! This should help you to let go of your doubt more easily. Be easy on yourself and choose, moment by moment, to trust Him. You'll watch the doubt slowly disappear......

ACT: Sit alone for 5 minutes and visualize Jesus holding your hand, guiding you through a storm, covering your head from the rain, wrapping his cloak around you to keep you dry, and constantly telling you not to worry, not to be afraid, not to question. Feel Him putting His arms around you and telling you how much He loves you. Rest in His love, know that He's keeping His eye out for you, He's walking with you wherever you go and He knows everything you're facing right now. Stay where you are until you can sense His presence and His love. Do you feel it? He's right there with you right now. There is no need to doubt!

YOUR THOUGHTS:

DAY 3

DO YOU DOUBT GOD'S LOVE AND FAITHFULNESS?

"Lord, if it's you," Peter replied, "tell me to come to you on the water." "Come," he said. Then Peter got down out of the boat, walked on the water and came toward Jesus. But when he saw the wind, he was afraid and, beginning to sink, cried out, "Lord, save me!" Immediately Jesus reached out his hand and caught him. "You of little faith," he said, "why did you doubt?" And when they climbed into the boat, the wind died down."

Matthew 14:28-32

"My coming to faith did not start with a leap but rather a series of staggers from what seemed like one safe place to another, like lily pads, round and green, these places summoned and then held me up while I grew. Each prepared me for the next leaf on which I would land, and in this way I moved across the swamp of doubt and fear."

Anne Lamott

PRAY: Lord, thank you for the reminder of Your presence and faithfulness when I am afraid. Just like Peter, help me to stop doubting that You are present in my life and in Hollywood. Don't let me doubt that it's a place that You can redeem, and that Christians are there. Help me stop talking against the people in Hollywood, and instead believe You love them and You are present there, just like you were with Peter in the water. I don't ever want You to say to me, "You of little faith." Lord, help my unbelief. Thank You Lord. Amen.

REFLECT: Christians trust Jesus when we're safe, but we doubt Him when we're in a scary place. Peter was staying afloat as long as he kept his eyes on Jesus. But the moment he looked down he started sinking. What's the place that you're afraid of? Is it Hollywood or another place where you think Jesus is not present? Can you trust that God is in control of our nation's culture creators? Don't doubt that He is there. He is working in the lives of the unsaved there through the Christian creative professionals and they need your prayers.

ACT: Take a moment to think honestly about the people who create our nation's entertainment. Is Jesus big enough to be in control of loving and saving the people in Hollywood? Are you walking on water right now and calmly looking up at Jesus, or are you looking down into the dark waters of Hollywood and sinking in doubt? Release your doubts about Hollywood and watch the waters become still, as the winds of anger and fear die down.

YOUR THOUGHTS:

DAY 4

QUESTION YOUR DOUBT

"Be self-controlled and alert. Your enemy the devil prowls around like a roaring lion looking for someone to devour. "
                                                                    1 Peter 5:8

"There was a castle called Doubting Castle, the owner whereof was Giant Despair."
                                                                    John Bunyan

PRAY: Dear God, I know that the enemy lies to me and fills me with doubt. I need Your help for me to be alert and have self-controlled to not believe his lies. As he prowls around me like a roaring lion I need Your Holy Spirit to give me discernment and confidence in You so that the enemy will not devour me. I need You to give me the strength to fight off his lies and to rest in Your truth. Thank You for keeping my eyes and heart on You alone. Amen.

REFLECT: Have you thought about the spiritual world in which we are all living and how it's even more powerful than our physical world? In that spiritual world the enemy is always attacking our heart, soul, mind, and emotions with his lies and temptations. How can you arm yourself with God's truths so that doubt won't take over in any area of your life? Be aware of the devil's schemes and pray to God to keep you strong and keep your mind clear in every situation, conversation, and decision. Your choice is either to doubt who God is and what He can do, or to be alert and sober of mind. The devil is prowling, but God has already won the battle and He loves you so much. There is nothing to doubt.

ACT: Take a piece of paper and make two columns. The top left says WHEN I DOUBT. The top right says WHEN I'M ALERT. Then write down whatever comes to mind in both columns. Know that when you are alert and of sober mind, you don't doubt, you make clear decisions and take direct action. But when you're doubting, things seem fuzzy, the options aren't clear, and the lines start blurring in your mind. So, write in your columns and see where you need prayer and where you can praise God for His definitive presence in your life. It will show you when you fully trust God and where you haven't let go of control. When we completely trust God we don't experience doubt. It's when the enemy is prowling around that the confusion and doubt creep or barge in. Pray over your list.

YOUR THOUGHTS:

DAY 5

DOUBT HELPS US BECOME STRONG IN FAITH

"Jesus replied, "I tell you the truth, if you have faith and do not doubt, not only can you do what was done to the fig tree, but also you can say to this mountain, 'Go, throw yourself into the sea,' and it will be done."

Matthew 21:21

"Don't dig up in doubt what you planted in faith."

Elisabeth Elliot

PRAY: Jesus, You are so powerful that You can look at a tree and say "May you never bear fruit again!" And immediately the tree will wither. You can move mountains, part seas and raise people from the dead. And yet I doubt You. You tell me to trust completely in You and You give me the power to throw a mountain into the sea. And yet I doubt. Oh Jesus, fill me new and fresh with Your Holy Spirit and take away my unbelief. I want to move a mountain and make a tree wither, but I need faith and confidence in You to do that. Right now, I ask that You change me so that I won't doubt. Thank You that You can do anything for me, through me, and in me. I praise You for that. Amen and Amen.

REFLECT: Have you ever walked up to a mountain and said, "Go, throw yourself into the sea," and it happened? Have you ever walked up to a tree and told it to stop bearing fruit and it immediately withered? That's the POWER Jesus has that we are working toward embracing. He told us that we can do even greater things than He did. But what stops us? DOUBT. What would it take for your faith to grow so much that you can move mountains and wither trees? Could doubt come from an inability to give up all of our control to God and truly believe that He has our backs? Pray about your faith and your doubt so that some day maybe even you can throw a mountain into the sea!

ACT: Read Matthew 21:18-21 and reflect on the power behind Jesus' words. It's almost overwhelming, and yet He tells us that we can do the same thing! Jesus' disciples were amazed and asked how that tree withered so quickly. Re-read the text and then question your own unbelief. Are you like the disciples or can you say that your God can wither trees and move mountains and you don't doubt Him for a second?!

YOUR THOUGHTS:

DAY 6

STAND FIRM, TRUST GOD

"But when he asks, he must believe and not doubt, because he who doubts is like a wave of the sea, blown and tossed by the wind...."   James 1:6

"Immediately the boy's father exclaimed, "I do believe; help me overcome my unbelief!"
                                                                   Mark 9:24

"Some say if only my fears and doubts will leave then I will get to work. But instead you should get to work and then your fears and doubts will leave."   Dwight L. Moody

PRAY: Lord, I ask that You help my unbelief. You tell us that if we doubt as we pray, we are like a wave of the sea, blown and tossed by the wind. I must trust Your word and stand firm in Your promises. I want to be solid in my walk with You, so please help my unbelief. The example of the boy's father saying, "I do believe; help me overcome my unbelief" is the desire of my heart, Lord. Amen.

REFLECT: Read the verse again. "I do believe; help me overcome my unbelief!" What does that mean to you? As Christians we all struggle with believing God, living for Him and yet doubting. Maybe our faith is "both/and." We believe but we doubt. We are strong but afraid. We trust God but we're unsure. Don't be hard on yourself when you pray as a wave that is blown and tossed by the wind. But you can change and come to know that God loves you too much to leave you as you are! What would it take to curb your doubt and try to stand firm in your faith and trust in God—in all circumstances?

ACT: What are you doubting this moment? Define your doubt and then say out loud: "I do believe; help me overcome my unbelief!" What else are you doubting? Define it and then again say out loud: "I do believe; help me overcome my unbelief!" Don't be like a wave blown and tossed by the wind. Stand firm and choose to nip your doubts in the bud the moment they creep up by proclaiming to the Lord, in an audible voice, "I do believe; help me overcome my unbelief!"

YOUR THOUGHTS:

DAY 7

WHEN YOU OR OTHERS DOUBT

"Be merciful to those who doubt."   Jude 1:22

The Lord appeared to us in the past, saying: "I have loved you with an everlasting love; I have drawn you with loving-kindness."
                                      Jeremiah 31:3

"Have the strength to explore the things you don't know, all the while holding on to the things you do know."
                                      Jeremy Hall, #DOUBT

PRAY: Dear Lord, I know that there are times when I doubt Your strength and even Your willingness to help me. So, how can I be merciful to others when they doubt? You are patient with all of us. I want to remind others and myself that You love all of us with an everlasting love and with unfailing kindness. May I show that same love and kindness to others? Thank You that though You tell me not to doubt, You also tell me that You are merciful, and that we need to show Your mercy to others. Thank You, Lord, for your consistent faithfulness. May I show that to others, just like You show it to me. In Jesus' name, Amen.

REFLECT: I've been told that what people are most frustrated about in the traits or behavior of others is what they're struggling with in their own lives. So, if I get frustrated with others for doubting God or His love for them, maybe that could be my own area of weakness. It's hard to fully trust God at all times. That's why He reminds us so often to pray and not doubt, and to be merciful to others who doubt. It's good to reflect on our own spiritual walk and check ourselves for areas of doubt. If we are honest about our own struggles, we will be much more patient with others. God loves us with an everlasting love. No doubt about it!

ACT: Take a moment to think about someone in your life whom you think doubts God's love. Does it frustrate you that they worry too much, or they don't trust that God will supply, heal or change their circumstances? If so, can you forgive them and show them supernatural mercy? Then ask the Lord where *you* doubt Him. Self-examine areas of fear, worry, control, or anxiety. Accept His mercy in your life and then give mercy to that person you see doubting God. Remember that He loves you with an everlasting love!

YOUR THOUGHTS:

POWER

WEEK TWENTY-SEVEN

We know that God is all-powerful, but did you know that we have access to that power? We can experience God's power in prayer, in being strong witnesses, in doing miracles, to fight Satan, and even in our suffering. We don't want to miss it, so this week we'll learn to access and embrace God's divine power. He did not give us a Spirit of timidity, but one of power!

DAY 1

OUR LORD IS THE REAL POWER

"Ah, Sovereign Lord, you have made the heavens and the earth by your great power and outstretched arm. Nothing is too hard for you."
Jeremiah 32:17

"There is a signature of wisdom and power impressed on the works of God, which evidently distinguishes them from the feeble imitations of men. Not only the splendor of the sun, but the glimmering light of the glowworm, proclaims his glory."
John Newton

PRAY: Dear Lord, You have POWER in Your name, in Your actions, in Your authority and in Your being! I thank You that I can experience the power of Your outstretched arm! I don't have to be afraid for nothing is too hard for You! I should never question the power I have available to me to overcome outside forces, internal demons, and relational obstacles. It's amazing and overwhelming to know that because of Your power, I can do ALL things through Christ who strengthens me. Amen.

REFLECT: Have you ever thought about how powerful God is? This verse focuses on the overwhelming power of our loving, creative God, who made the heavens and the earth, and nothing is too hard for Him. By His divine power God raised Jesus from the dead and He has given us everything we need, from food and work to knowledge and goodness. Jesus had power to heal and do miracles and the Holy Spirit has the power to transform us from the inside out. Let's praise Him for His acts of power and for His surpassing greatness.

ACT: Ask yourself these four questions and pay attention to your honest answers: Do you truly believe that absolutely nothing is too hard for God? Do you believe that by His divine power, He has given you everything you need to live a godly life? Are you an eyewitness of His majesty? Do you praise Him for His acts of power and surpassing greatness? How do you answer? Do you need to think through any and figure out how to change your answer to a powerful YES? Go through them again and keep them for your own personal spiritual growth. Once you can say YES to all of these questions, you will experience the abundant life He offers to each of us as we worship His majesty.

YOUR THOUGHTS:

DAY 2

THERE IS POWER IN THE NAME

"Praise him for his acts of power; praise him for his surpassing greatness." Psalm 150:2

"Our help is in the name of the Lord, the Maker of heaven and earth."   Psalm 124:8

"I will remain in the world no longer, but they are still in the world, and I am coming to you. Holy Father, protect them by the power of your name--the name you gave me--so that they may be one as we are one."   John 17:11

"To holy people the very name of Jesus is a name to feed upon, a name to transport. His name can raise the dead and transfigure and beautify the living." John Henry Newman

PRAY: Oh Lord, no one is like You! You are great and Your name is mighty in power. I praise You for Your acts of power. My help is in the name of the Lord, and You are the maker of heaven and earth. Jesus, I thank You for sending Your Holy Spirit to protect us, by the power of Your name. I praise You. Amen!

REFLECT: Have you ever thought about the power in a name? There are many people who change their name because they want a name with more meaning. Have you ever thought about why the name of God and Jesus are used so often as swear words? It's because they have power in them. No one says, "Oh Buddha" as a swear word or yells out "Hare Krishna" in anger because it has no power behind it. Yet without even knowing it, people all over the world use the name of God or Jesus in both heartfelt worship and in intense anger, because there is POWER in the name! How do you use the names of God, Jesus, and the Holy Spirit?

ACT: As you say the name of God or the name of Jesus, ponder the power behind those words. Be in awe that even with 2 billion other people in the world He loves *you* and He alone—no other entity—has the power to listen to you and answer your prayers. You, personally, can have conversations, arguments, and worship times with the One, True, invisible God—the most powerful being in the universe! Why? Because there is power in His name and you are trusting your life to Him. Talk to God right now and be aware of His power. Call out His name because you know your help is in the name of the Lord.

YOUR THOUGHTS:

DAY 3

POWER TO HEAL AND DO MIRACLES

"You are the God who performs miracles; you display your power among the peoples"

Psalm 77:14

"When Jesus had called the Twelve together, he gave them power and authority to drive out all demons and to cure diseases."

Luke 9:1

"When Jesus performed miracles, he wasn't demonstrating what God can do, but what God can do through a man...It is INCONSISTENT to have Jesus pay a price for healing and for us to believe it is not Gods intention to heal."

Bill Johnson

PRAY: God in Heaven, who performs miracles, You display Your power among all people, You heal the sick and make the lame walk and the blind see, and You can even drive out demons! Lord, I want to personally experience Your almighty, Divine power in my life. I want to see more miracles. I don't want to miss any miracles and healing You have for me. Please show me more of Your power. Thank You for Your faithfulness. I pray in the name of Jesus, Amen.

REFLECT: How are you doing with Jesus? Are you content with your relationship with Him right now or do you want more? One of life's great tragedies is that so many Christians never fully live the exciting, abundant life that God offers all of us. Sometimes we get complacent and drift along, going to church on Sundays, going to work during the week, and busying ourselves to death. Or worse yet, we've lost our awe of God and we don't even expect Him to show up, answer our prayers, or move in our lives. Where are you right now?

ACT: Right now, why don't you embrace God fresh and anew, and experience more of His power in your life? Re-commit your life to Him and ask Him to reveal more of Himself to you, including His healing, miracles, and power. And then expect Him to answer. Get ready for a new season with the Lord and don't stop telling Him that you want to see Him, feel Him, touch Him, hear Him, and have your life and the lives of the people around you transform, because of His POWER! He is all-powerful and He wants to share it all with you!

YOUR THOUGHTS:

DAY 4

PRAYER POWER

"I pray that out of his glorious riches he may strengthen you with power through his Spirit in your inner being, so that Christ may dwell in your hearts through faith. And I pray that you, being rooted and established in love, may have power, together with all the saints, to grasp how wide and long and high and deep is the love of Christ, and to know this love that surpasses knowledge--that you may be filled to the measure of all the fullness of God.

Ephesians 3:16-19

"Don't pray when you feel like it. Have an appointment with the Lord and keep it. A man is powerful on his knees."   Corrie Ten Boom

PRAY: God, I love to pray to You because there is power in Your name. You alone care enough to listen to everything I say or even think, and respond. Thank You for the gift and power of prayer. I can confess my sins and intercede for other people, and I can trust that my prayers are powerful and effective. Strengthen me out of Your glorious riches, through Your Spirit, so that I may be established in love and have power to grasp how wide and long and high and deep is the love of Christ. I pray in the powerful name of Jesus. Amen.

REFLECT: Why do you pray to God? Is it to get everything you want? Or is it because you understand the power of conversing with the Almighty Creator who loves you so much that He listens and answers! There is nothing more beautiful, exciting, and powerful than experiencing answered prayer—a healed friend, an unexpected check in the mail, a puppy found, a parent surviving an accident. Have you ever experienced the life-changing power of prayer? You will be filled to the measure of all the fullness of God!

ACT: Choose to focus on the power of prayer right now. Go to a sick friend, colleague, or neighbor and pray boldly for their healing, whether they believe in God or not. Pray for something you haven't had the guts to pray for. Pray for someone you care about to become a Christian. Pray for a miracle today, expecting answers and not doubting God. Get out of your comfort zone and grow in your prayer life by believing the power of prayer. Start now to praise, pray, and listen to God in ways you never have before. He will strengthen you!

YOUR THOUGHTS:

DAY 5

BREAKING SATAN'S POWER

"For our struggle is not against flesh and blood, but against the rulers, against the authorities, against the powers of this dark world and against the spiritual forces of evil in the heavenly realms."

Ephesians 6:12

"But have we Holy Spirit power – power that restricts the devil's power, pulls down strongholds and obtains promises? Daring delinquents will be damned if they are not delivered from the devil's dominion. What has hell to fear other than a God-anointed, prayer-powered church?"

Leonard Ravenhill

PRAY: Dear God, don't let me be afraid of the power of the enemy. Lord, You are more powerful than the devil! When a person turns on me, remind me it's not a struggle against flesh and blood, but against the powers of this dark world and against the spiritual forces of evil in the heavenly realms. As powerful as the enemy is, he is not more powerful than You, or You in me! Thank You that You can give me an unoffendable heart! Amen.

REFLECT: Christians believe that God is more powerful than Satan, but we get confused and often blame people instead of the devil. When someone hurts you, do you get mad at them, or do you realize it could be Satan using them to hurt or discourage you? Jesus said on the cross, "Father forgive them for they do not know what they are doing." He knew it was the enemy who causes people to do horrible things, not men. Can you stop blaming people for evil actions of the enemy? Our struggle is not against flesh and blood but against the powers of this dark world and the spiritual forces of evil.

ACT: What areas of your life does Satan have a hold on you? What or who are you afraid of or angry at? Write a list of anything the enemy is holding you back from or telling you lies about. Next to that list, write down how God is more powerful. Compare your list of what the enemy is doing and what God can do and then ask the Lord to break the power of Satan over you. Call on the power of your God, don't blame people, and never give Satan any room to try to use you, in the name of God the Father, Jesus the Son, and the Holy Spirit. And then you can have an unoffendable heart and be victorious!

YOUR THOUGHTS:

DAY 6

POWER IN SUFFERING

"He gives strength to the weary and increases the power of the weak." Isaiah 40:29

"I meditate and pray all the time. The faith and respect that I have in the power of God in my life is what I've used to keep myself grounded, and it has allowed me to move away from the storms that were in my life." Halle Berry

PRAY: Heavenly Father, I thank You that You give me power even in my suffering. You give strength to the weary and increase the power of the weak. I give You the glory in my sufferings, because my suffering produces perseverance; perseverance, character; and character, hope. That's Your power working in me and through me. So, I acknowledge Your power in my life always, even when I'm weak or suffering. Your promise gives me the strength to go on! This hope will not disappoint me, ever! Amen and Amen.

REFLECT: Do you believe that God is all-powerful and has poured out His love to you through the Holy Spirit? You can do all things through Christ who strengthens you. But have you ever thought about God's power both in and through your suffering? God continues to surprise us with amazing truths that defy worldly intelligence. He can even increase the power of the weak. God is with us always, in every situation—even when we're suffering. He tells us that we glory in our sufferings. Just like Jesus gloried in His suffering, we can do the same. How would your life change if you could truly praise God amid suffering?

ACT: Is there any area where you are suffering physically, emotionally, or spiritually? Can you visualize embracing God's divine power that would squelch any fear or weakness? God is offering to fill you with His power, love, and self-discipline anytime, especially if you are suffering for the gospel. Praise Him and thank Him that it is producing perseverance in you which creates character, and character, hope. And His hope does not disappoint you. Now that's power! You are a child of God who has access to His almighty power—even in your suffering! Accept His power right now!

YOUR THOUGHTS:

DAY 7

GOD'S POWER IN HOLLYWOOD

"You are awesome, O God, in your sanctuary; the God of Israel gives power and strength to his people. Praise be to God!"   Psalm 68:35

"But you will receive power when the Holy Spirit comes on you; and you will be my witnesses in Jerusalem, and in all Judea and Samaria, and to the ends of the earth."

       Acts 1:8

"The power of the Holy Spirit is completely opposite to the world's power. The power of the Holy Spirit gives God's children the ability to serve His purpose for our lives. The Holy Spirit's power is unlike any other in the world. Only the power of the Holy Spirit can transform us, relieve our guilt, and heal our souls."   Michael Youssef

PRAY: God, I am so thankful to end my week understanding Your amazing power in and through me! Thank You for giving me power through the Holy Spirit so that I can be Your witness wherever I am, including Jerusalem, Judea, Samaria, and Hollywood! We need more witnesses in Hollywood, who exude Your power. Please give the Christians there the Holy Spirit in order to lead the decision-makers to You. I pray right now that the non-Christian entertainment professionals will experience Your power and strength. In Jesus' name! Amen.

REFLECT: Christians need God's power and strength to be bold witnesses, even to the ends of the earth. Hollywood is surely between Jerusalem and the ends of the earth, so Christians should be there with God's power, to share their faith as His witnesses. Think of that kind of power! If we believe in, and don't question God's power, then we would never question sending His people to be witnesses anywhere, even to Hollywood.

ACT: Take 5 minutes and pray for the Lord to send powerful witnesses to Hollywood as excellent professionals and bold witnesses. Pray Jesus transforms Hollywood, the world's most influential mission field, through strong witnesses who love the people who live and work there. There are now over 10,000 Christians in Hollywood that need your prayers! Help them make an eternal difference through the power of the Holy Spirit and see God move!

YOUR THOUGHTS:

BETRAYAL

WEEK TWENTY-EIGHT

Betrayal is one of the worst things we can do to another person. What do we do when we feel betrayed by a friend or a family member? Jesus is the expert at understanding betrayal. Let's look into His response to His betrayal and actually become good at knowing how to handle this hurtful but human issue.

DAY 1

WOE TO THE BETRAYER

"The Son of Man will go as it has been decreed, but woe to that man who betrays him...
Jesus asked him, "Judas, are you betraying the Son of Man with a kiss?" Luke 22:22 & 48

"You can't betray yourself too often, or you become somebody else."   Ed Harris

PRAY: Dear Lord, I ask that you help me never to betray You. Please give me the strength to do what You ask of me, regardless of how hard or scary or sacrificial it may be. I want You to be proud of me and I want to stand firm as a faithful follower of Yours. I don't want to act like I'm obeying You, then turn on You instead. Lord, help me to learn from Judas and never to be like him. Thank you for giving me what I need each day to be faithful to You always. I pray in Jesus' name, Amen!

REFLECT: We always think that it will never be us! We'll never be the one to let God down. We'll never be the one to turn on Him, deny Him, disappoint Him, or run from Him. But we are all only one-step away from disaster at every moment. That's what keeps us needing the Holy Spirit, because we can't stay pure, honest or faithful without His help. When have you betrayed God out of fear, disappointment, anger, or frustration? Like Judas, did you try to trick Him by doing it with a kiss? We all have the potential to be Judas.

ACT: Focus in on one time that you may have turned against God—in words or actions—and ask forgiveness. Don't be ashamed, for we all do it at some point. It may be obvious or subtle, but either way, if you can recognize it then you have less of a chance of ever doing it again. God forgives us but we learn and grow by coming to Him with our sins and even our shortcomings. After asking forgiveness, ask the Lord to have His Holy Spirit nudge you the next time you're tempted. He'll answer that prayer and you are on the road to becoming more Christ-like.

YOUR THOUGHTS:

DAY 2

DON'T TURN AWAY; STAY FAITHFUL

"At that time many will turn away from the faith and will betray and hate each other."

Matthew 24:10

"What was there to be gained by fighting the most evil wizard who has ever existed?" said Black, with a terrible fury in his face. "Only innocent lives, Peter!" "You don't understand!" whined Pettigrew. "He would have killed me, Sirius!" "THEN YOU SHOULD HAVE DIED!" roared Black. "DIED RATHER THAN BETRAY YOUR FRIENDS, AS WE WOULD HAVE DONE FOR YOU!" J.K. Rowling, *Harry Potter and the Prisoner of Azkaban*

PRAY: Dear Heavenly Father, will You keep me growing in my faith so that I never turn away from You? For I know that turning away from You will lead me to betray and hate other Christians. If I can stay faithful to You, then I will stay faithful to other people and not betray or hate them. I want that! And I need You to help me. Thank You. Amen.

REFLECT: One of the biggest struggles for Christians is other Christians. We all have stories of being lied to, cheated and betrayed by other believers. Are you a victim of that as well? Have you ever done that to someone else? It's often the result of turning away from God. If you've been hurt or betrayed by another believer, can you forgive them and pray for them and their walk with the Lord? Even Hollywood has a reputation of betrayal being a part of the culture. And the stories of betrayal that they tell have a powerful influence on our culture. Australian singer Nick Cave says, *"Film seems to be a medium designed for betrayal and violence."* God knows that many will turn away from the faith and will betray and hate each other. We must choose to actively stop that from happening.

ACT: Take five minutes to pray for the Christians in Hollywood who struggle with betrayal and hate from other believers. As on any mission field, it's the believers who often turn on other believers. Would you pray for these people to seek Jesus more passionately and treat the other believers with love, honesty and respect? People hurt other people because they are broken, and Christians hurt others when they are not walking closely with the Lord. Your prayers for the Lord to heal the believers in Hollywood could change our whole culture.

YOUR THOUGHTS:

DAY 3

PASSIVE BETRAYAL

"Then he returned to the disciples and said to them, "Are you still sleeping and resting? Look, the hour is near, and the Son of Man is betrayed into the hands of sinners."

Matthew 26:45

"I've been on the floor and I've been heartbroken. I didn't know how I was going to stand up. But I just gave it time."

Sandra Bullock

PRAY: Jesus, have I ever betrayed You without knowing it? Have I fallen asleep when I should have been praying, obeying, serving, or giving? I want to be walking with You and not betraying You out of laziness, weariness, or complacency. Help me to always be there for You. I don't want to betray You with my passivity and put You or me into the hands of sinners. I need your help to stay awake, sharp and aware of obeying You and serving others so as not to betray You Lord. I pray this in Jesus's name, Amen.

REFLECT: Turning from God is not always an active, conscious choice. It is sometimes a passive, subtle or even unconscious choice. When have you let God down, even to the point of betrayal, just by not seeking Him, listening to Him or actively obeying Him? Have you sensed Him telling you something, but you haven't done it because you don't want to, or you're too tired? How can you be more pro-active with your faithfulness to your Lord? How can you stay awake when He needs you?

ACT: Remember a time when someone popped into your mind and you thought to call them, but you didn't. Or maybe a time when you wanted to check in on a friend or a co-worker, but you were just too busy, or too tired? Why don't you call that person now? Or stop by and let them know they are on your mind? And choose in the future to listen to the nudges of the Holy Spirit or to God's still small voice. For if you fall asleep or get tempted to rest when you know you should be responding to the Lord, you will be betraying God. Even Jesus was betrayed and put into the hands of sinners because His disciples fell asleep. Be aware, be sharp, and actively seek God's face and voice. Then step out to minister to your friend, family, or co-worker right now!

YOUR THOUGHTS:

DAY 4

GOSSIP IS BETRAYAL

"A gossip betrays a confidence, but a trustworthy man keeps a secret." Proverbs 11:13

"A gossip betrays a confidence; so avoid a man who talks too much." Proverbs 20:19

"To me, the thing that is worse than death is betrayal. You see, I could conceive death, but I could not conceive betrayal."   Malcolm X

PRAY: Dear God, I don't want to be a gossip for that is betraying the person I'm talking about. Help me to hold my tongue. The consequences are bigger than I had realized and so I need You to help me not talk against anyone else, even if it's to have someone pray. I need to bring my thoughts about other people to You and not talk about them to others, for I don't want to betray friendships or any personal relationships. But I can't do it without You. Thank you God, for holding me accountable for my words. I trust, because of Your guidance, I will be a person of integrity and trustworthiness. Amen!

REFLECT: When have you talked about a person behind their back and betrayed a confidence? Or when have you turned a frustration about another person into a prayer request, so that you could talk about your hurt? Gossiping is so easy and yet we don't realize it's a betrayal of a relationship. How can you stop saying anything negative or gossipy about others so that you will be a trustworthy friend, brother or sister, and a Christ-like believer?

ACT: Identify the last time you talked about another person without them knowing it. Were you betraying a confidence? If so, identify what you did and choose not to do it again. Don't justify or rationalize your behavior if you talk about other people in privacy. If we ever say something that we don't want to the person we're talking about to hear, then it's gossip and a betrayal. Choose right now to repent for any betrayals in your past and commit to seek God, catch yourself and hold your tongue from this moment on.

YOUR THOUGHTS:

DAY 5

DO NOT BETRAY THE REFUGEE

"Give us counsel, render a decision. Make your shadow like night at high noon. Hide the fugitives, do not betray the refugees. Let the Moabite fugitives stay with you; be their shelter from the destroyer." The oppressor will come to an end, and destruction will cease; the aggressor will vanish from the land."
                                                                    Isaiah 16:3-4

"I could never hurt him enough to make his betrayal stop hurting. And it hurts, in every part of my body."
                                                        Veronica Roth, *"Insurgent"*

PRAY: Father in Heaven, I call out to You to give me an understanding of refugees and my part in protecting them. I need You to show me how I can be their shelter from whatever is trying to threaten and/or destroy them. I need Your wisdom on the role that refugees play in my life. Do I pray for them? Do I actively help people who have been displaced? I don't want to betray them. I am crying out to You because I don't know what to do! Amen.

REFLECT: Christians in America are often sheltered from the injustices happening in other parts of the world. And yet, one of the great needs is to help refugees who have been betrayed by their governments. Christians and non-believers alike are thrown out of their countries and have nowhere to go. What do you think your place is dealing with the world's refugees? Are you called to take action? Can you pray? Have you thought about this as a betrayal? Jesus tells us that we are to help the orphans, widows, and refugees. How does this aspect of betrayal impact your life?

ACT: Can you start a discussion with people close to you about this new look on refugees? It's a timely hot topic in our nation, both in churches and in politics, and yet, has anyone ever thought of it as a betrayal? You may not know a refugee personally but you can bring up the conversation that as a Christian we need to pray for, protect and/or help refugees who have been betrayed by the very people who should be helping them. Even opening up the discussion can be a way for you to help with this problem in our world. Choose now who your first conversation will be with on this topic.

YOUR THOUGHTS:

DAY 6

BETRAYED BY A FRIEND

"If an enemy were insulting me, I could endure it; if a foe were raising himself against me, I could hide from him. But it is you, a man like myself, my companion, my close friend, with whom I once enjoyed sweet fellowship as we walked with the throng at the house of God."

Psalm 55:12-14

"Some people are willing to betray years of friendship just to get a little bit of the spotlight."

Lauren Conrad

PRAY: Oh Lord, heal my heart from the wounds of friends and family members. Your children, my family, my friends, my co-workers, and my neighbors have betrayed me. Would You forgive them for their betrayal and me for my anger? You have warned me that other people will betray me, just as many people betrayed You. Please give me the strength and the wisdom to not take it personally but to forgive those who have hurt me, pray for them and then move on, with my eyes on You. Amen.

REFLECT: We're not surprised when our enemies try to hurt us, but the wounds of a friend or a brother are painful and even heartbreaking. God warns us in Matthew 10:21 that "brother will betray brother, a father will betray his child and children will rebel against their parents." Can you recognize betrayals as spiritual battle and not as personal attacks? This will help you not to be hurt or to hide from the betrayer, but to forgive them and yourself, when you are either the victim or the cause of division, betrayal and personal offense. And we've been warned that it's often to or from a companion or close friend, so don't be surprised, but choose to enjoy sweet fellowship at the house of God.

ACT: Identify one friend or family member who has betrayed, insulted, or hurt you. Can you see from this verse that it has happened to God's people from the beginning of time, and choose now to forgive that person? God shows us through David to expect others to hurt us because we are all human. Forgiving the one who has hurt you will allow the Holy Spirit to heal both you and the other person's heart, and it will make it less likely that either one of you will do it again.

YOUR THOUGHTS:

DAY 7

RESCUE ME FROM TREACHEROUS BETRAYAL

"From the ends of the earth we hear singing: "Glory to the Righteous One." But I said, "I waste away, I waste away! Woe to me! The treacherous betray! With treachery the treacherous betray!"

Isaiah 24:16

"Have courage for the great sorrows of life and patience for the small ones; and when you have laboriously accomplished your daily task, go to sleep in peace. God is awake."

Victor Hugo, Poet, Novelist, Artist & Statesman

PRAY: Lord, protect me from treacherous betrayers. As others praise Your name, I am struggling to the point of death due to people around me hurting me, disappointing me, lying to me, and crushing me. I need You to lift me out from the pit. I need You to redeem me and give me hope. I need You to protect me from evil men. I need You every moment of every day. Thank you for hearing my cry. Amen.

REFLECT: Don't you feel this way sometimes? Like the whole world is turning against you and you can't handle it anymore. Isaiah 24 lays out all of the evil in the world that the Lord will punish and is even entitled "The Devastation of the Earth" and one of the things it lists is betrayal. Think about all the forms of betrayal and notice that it's only the Lord who can protect you from becoming angry, bitter and revengeful. Man is sinful and betrayal is rampant, so how do you make the world a better place, in the midst of betrayal all around you?

ACT: If you've been hurt by betrayal, you can cry out to the Lord right now. Our God understands your hurt and frustration. His own son was betrayed, so you can be open and honest with Him and call out to Him to take away your pain. God wants to hear from you and He wants to help you through all of the unfairness and injustice in your life. He is there for you this moment.

YOUR THOUGHTS:

TRUST

WEEK TWENTY-NINE

This is a joyful week, full of promises, rewards, and hope. We'll learn that when we can truly trust the Lord, and not lean on our own understanding, He has gifts that He gives to us in return. It is so important to the Lord when we let go and trust Him, looking to Him, not to others, for our strength and direction. Then He can shower us with blessings!

DAY 1

TRUST IN GOD

"Blessed is the man who trusts in the Lord, whose confidence is in him."   Jeremiah 17:7

"Do not let your hearts be troubled. Trust in God; trust also in me."   John 14:1

"Faith is deliberate confidence in the character of God whose ways you cannot understand at the time."
                                                                    Oswald Chambers

PRAY: Dear Lord, I start my week focusing on TRUST by filling myself up with your encouraging, loving, hopeful words in scripture. Thank You that as I put my confidence in You, You will bless me. If I trust you with all of my heart and do not lean on my own understanding and acknowledge You in all my ways, You will make my path straight, (Prov. 3:5-6). Oh Lord, You will love me, hold me up, guide me, comfort me, protect me, empower me, and welcome me into eternity! My heart is not troubled as I trust in You. I praise You Lord Amen.

REFLECT: Have you ever thought about the abundant promises, rewards, results, and joys God offers us if we just trust Him? It sounds simple, but it's harder than we think, or He wouldn't need to continue to encourage us to do so. God constantly reminds us to put our trust in Him, not in ourselves and not in other men. He tells us that when we trust Him our confidence will be in Him and He will bless us. You will start to see that trusting God is not only important because we need to keep our eyes and our hearts dependent on Him, but it also takes away any ego, confidence or arrogance from ourselves. We can't deceive ourselves that we are in control. Trusting God keeps us in perfect balance between who He's made us to be and how much we need Him.

ACT: Take a moment to write down what God promises if we completely trust in Him. We will be blessed if we trust in God and put our confidence in Him. What other promises do you find in the Bible if you trust in the Lord? Look up TRUST in your Bible App. Continue to add to this list every day this week as you discover more and more benefits to trusting God. By the end of the week you will be surprised how extensive your list is.

YOUR THOUGHTS:

DAY 2

TRUST ONLY IN GOD, NOT IN WEALTH OR POSSESSIONS

"Some trust in chariots and some in horses, but we trust in the name of the Lord our God....Do not trust in extortion or take pride in stolen goods; though your riches increase, do not set your heart on them."   Psalm 20:7 & 62:10

"The resource from which God gives is boundless, measureless, unlimited, unending, abundant, almighty, and eternal."   Jack W. Hayford

PRAY: Dear Father, I don't want to trust in anything besides You. Don't let me think that I can get enough stuff, money, power, or control on my own. And don't let me compromise my integrity or character to acquire more. Help me let go of worldly riches, power, influence, status, reputation, visibility, or fame and completely trust in You. You are all I need, and all I want to live an abundant life. You are faithful and I trust in You alone! Amen.

REFLECT: Oh how difficult it is to let go of all the things of this world and totally trust in God ways, provision and timing! David says to let go of the things of this world and simply trust in the NAME of the Lord. David knew to use those four examples of the fastest, biggest, and the best that the world had to offer to show us the contrast of trusting God. Today, it's the same way. Can you let go of your own ideas, control, and striving and instead trust that God loves you enough to not only supply your daily bread, but to use you to make an eternal difference in this world? Don't get tempted by the ways and things of this world.

ACT: What plans, goals or "stuff" do you believe allow you to "make it" in this world? List the things that you trust in to give you status or value in your community and acknowledge that they are all from God, including your fancy cars, nice house, high-end office, expensive jewelry or any activities you've done to get ahead. Evaluate your current financial and social status and ask yourself if they are gifts that you are grateful for, or are they longings to make you feel more important, more powerful, or even more secure? It's time to trust the Lord and let go of false idols, then see how He gives you the desires of your heart.

YOUR **THOUGHTS:**

DAY 3

BE TRUSTWORTHY

"Whoever can be trusted with very little can also be trusted with much, and whoever is dishonest with very little will also be dishonest with much."   Luke 16:10

Now it is required that those who have been given a trust must prove faithful."

1 Corinthians 4:2

"Whoever is careless with the truth in small matters cannot be trusted with important matters."   Albert Einstein

PRAY: Dear Jesus, help me to be faithful and trustworthy with everything You've give me. I don't ever want to be dishonest or greedy with anything, no matter how small, for if I'm tempted with a tiny thing, who will trust me with true riches? I have to prove myself in the most menial instances in order to be trusted with more. For only then will You place me over the people as a chief, a leader, and a role model. I want to be Christ-like in all that I do and I know it comes with trusting You. I commit to that today, in Your name. Amen.

REFLECT: We are always drawn to the Christian men and women of the past who have done great things. Mother Theresa, George Müller, and William Wilberforce were only a few of the many Christ-like people who did big things for God. But they did not become great until they proved themselves in little ways. Mother Theresa thanklessly and faithfully cared for the lowest, neediest people in India. George Müller began by helping one orphan and trusted God every day for even a loaf of bread. William Wilberforce was a mere government servant who earned the trust and respect of each leader, before stopping slavery. And they all did it by trusting God. They were trustworthy with a little and then lifted up with much.

ACT: Choose two great Christians leaders in past centuries who did big things for God. Then take time to research them and find out how they started and where they ended up. You will see they started with little; they obeyed God, served Him, and trusted Him with everything they had. Then they proved faithful and He opened doors, and set their path to greatness. It's beautiful and humbling to know that if you want to make an eternal difference you must prove faithful and trust Him for everything! Start by finding two role-models.

YOUR THOUGHTS:

DAY 4

TRUSTING IN GOD WHEN YOU ARE AFRAID

"Fear of man will prove to be a snare, but whoever trusts in the Lord is kept safe."

Proverbs 29:25

The Lord is good, a refuge in times of trouble. He cares for those who trust in him,"

Nahum 1:7

"When a train goes through a tunnel and it gets dark, you don't throw away the ticket and jump off. You sit still and trust the engineer."   Corrie Ten Boom

PRAY: Dear God, I thank You for these reminders that I can't trust in humans, and I can't even trust in our nation's leaders for refuge, security, or in times of trouble. I just need to trust in You. When I'm afraid I can call out to You God, and I can trust that You are there for me. Having a fear of man will prove to be a snare, but if I trust in You I will be kept safe. Thank You God, that You are good, You are a refuge in times of trouble, and You care for me as I trust in You. What a comfort and a joy. I pray in the name of Jesus. Amen.

REFLECT: In a spiritual sense, we can understand that we need to trust in God. But when we are afraid for our safety it's frightening to feel alone and vulnerable. Those are the times when we need to put our trust in God. We trust our lives to God when we become a Christian. But when we're on a dark street and hear strange footsteps behind us, is He the first one we call out to? When our plane starts shaking in midair, is our first instinct to ask God for help? When our child is sick, do we call out to Jesus and then call friends to pray? It's in the little things that reveal our trust in God. "He cares for those who trust in Him!"

ACT: Look back on last week to recall any times that you were afraid, unsure, confused, overwhelmed, or even indecisive. Did you trust God to get you through that moment, that decision, or that experience? If not, then define what your default response was and start to identify where your trust goes and how you can instinctively turn to God! Develop the habit now of trusting God in the little things and you will soon learn to trust Him in the big things. Remember to add God's promises to your list: hint – look at each day's scriptures!

YOUR THOUGHTS:

DAY 5

TRUSTING IN GOD BRINGS JOY, PEACE & HOPE

"You will keep in perfect peace him whose mind is steadfast, because he trusts in you."

Isaiah 26:3

"May the God of hope fill you with all joy and peace as you trust in him, so that you may overflow with hope by the power of the Holy Spirit."   Romans 15:13

"I believe that a trusting attitude and a patient attitude go hand in hand. You see, when you let go and learn to trust God, it releases joy in your life. And when you trust God, you're able to be more patient. Patience is not just about waiting for something... it's about how you wait, or your attitude while waiting."

Joyce Meyer

PRAY: Heavenly Father, I am learning so much about the results of putting my trust in You. Thank You that You will bring me joy, keep me in perfect peace, give me a steadfast mind, and fill me with peace. I will overflow with hope when I put my trust in You. By the power of Your Holy Spirit I will literally be filled to overflowing with hope. I want to put all of my trust into You, in all circumstances, all decisions, all conversations, all relationships, and every time I'm afraid, confused, alone, or in danger. Thank You for Your promises Father. I love You and want to put ALL of my trust in You. Amen and Amen.

REFLECT: Peace, Hope, and Joy. We all want these in our lives, so we seek them through prayer, by putting on the armor of God, or memorizing the Psalms. But these verses tell us that we can get all three of these gifts through simply trusting in God the Father, through the power of the Holy Spirit. The God of hope will fill us with joy and peace if we put our trust in Him. We will overflow in the power of the Holy Spirit. Every part of the Trinity wants us to Trust in Him and put our lives at His feet.

ACT: What do you need to put at the foot of the cross right now to have joy, perfect peace, and a hope that will not disappoint you? Right now, ask God the Father, the Son, and the Holy Spirit to renew your mind, fill you with joy and give you perfect peace. These are three beautiful and powerful gifts that He wants you to have. Let go of everything you're holding on to. It's scary but it's incredibly freeing and today is the day!

YOUR THOUGHTS:

DAY 6

GOD CARES THAT WE TRUST IN HIM ONLY

"Of what value is an idol, since a man has carved it? Or an image that teaches lies? For he who makes it trusts in his own creation; he makes idols that cannot speak."

Habakkuk 2:18

"Blessed is the man who makes the Lord his trust, who does not look to the proud, to those who turn aside to false gods."   Psalm 40:4

"The most important lesson that I have learned is to trust God in every circumstance. Lots of times we go through different trials and following God's plan seems like it doesn't make any sense at all. God is always in control and He will never leave us."   Allyson Felix

PRAY: Father in Heaven, this helps me see that what man creates is actually You creating through us. There is no value in an idol or image carved by a craftsman, for a man-made idol cannot speak. Blessed is he who trusts in the Lord. Help me to not look to the proud, to those who turn aside to false gods. Let me not idolize the creative people in Hollywood who are rich and famous because of their work, or their looks, or their money. Man should not get the glory for creative works. Help me to trust in You and give You the glory. Amen.

REFLECT: These verses help us understand why we shouldn't idolize people. We often look up to movie stars, directors, and writers almost as gods. And yet we're reminded to "trust in the Lord." There are many wonderful Christians in Hollywood, but there are also those who don't yet know God, so they take credit for the successful projects they've gotten famous for creating. Think of the eternal difference we could make if we prayed for those people to embrace God as the source of all creation and creativity. And in doing so they would find God! He will put a new song in their hearts and bless them and you!

ACT: Choose one creative person in Hollywood you look up to or follow their work. Then start praying for that person. Ask the Lord to help them to trust Him, to give the glory to Him for all of their creative accomplishments, and for the Lord to take away any pride. Also, pray that other people don't idolize this person and make him or her more important than God. Pray that both the Hollywood professional you admire, and their fans, trust in God for their gifts, talents, accomplishments, fame, money, and love.

YOUR THOUGHTS:

DAY 7

THE LORD IS TRUSTWORTHY

"Trust in the Lord and do good; dwell in the land and enjoy safe pasture. Delight yourself in the Lord and he will give you the desires of your heart. Commit your way to the Lord; trust in him and he will do this: He will make your righteousness shine like the dawn, the justice of your cause like the noonday sun."   Psalm 37:3-6

*"My trust in God flows out of the experience of his loving me, day in and day out, whether the day is stormy or fair, whether I'm sick or in good health, whether I'm in a state of grace or disgrace. He comes to me where I live and loves me as I am."*Brennan Manning

PRAY: Dear Lord, I want to always trust in You and do good. I want to dwell in the land and enjoy safe pasture. Thank You that as I delight in You, You will give me the desires of my heart. I commit my ways to You, Lord, and I will trust in You. And I thank You that You will make my righteousness shine like the dawn and the justice of my cause like the noonday sun. You continue to bless those who trust in You and I am so thankful for that. I re-commit my life to You today, Lord. I love You and trust You with my whole being! Amen.

REFLECT: Here in Psalm 37, God gives us a list of more things He will do for us if we trust in Him. Throughout the Bible He continually tells us to trust in Him and then we will be richly rewarded. So, it must be VERY important. If we trust in Him and do good, we get to dwell on earth and enjoy a safe life. If we take delight in Him we will get the desires of our heart. We won't get everything we want, but He will change our desires to match His. And if we commit to Him and trust in Him, He says that our righteousness will shine to others. Re-read these verses to soak up the truth and power of these promises. We are truly blessed!

ACT: From the first day of this week, pull out the list of promises you received from God when you trusted in Him. Add the promises from every other day. Now add these last four promises from today's verses and read through the whole list again. It's amazing how much the Lord pours into us when we shift our trust from ourselves to Him. End this week with a list to carry with you forever, so that you will never forget to TRUST IN THE LORD!

YOUR THOUGHTS:

FAMILY

WEEK THIRTY

I believe that one of the greatest needs in our country is not a financial, social, or legal need, but a moral need. Morality is taught within a family. The family unit is crucial to the health of a nation and so this week we are going to focus on the Family. Join us as we read God's Word for parents, children, and what He expects from us.

DAY 1

DO NOT FORSAKE YOUR PARENTS

"Children, obey your parents in the Lord, for this is right. "Honor your father and mother"--which is the first commandment with a promise – "that it may go well with you and that you may enjoy long life on the earth."   Ephesians 6:1-3

"God created marriage. No government subcommittee envisioned it. No social organization developed it. Marriage was conceived and born in the mind of God."

Max Lucado

PRAY: Oh Lord, I'm amazed how much importance You place on the relationship between our parents and ourselves. I know it's because that's the closest human relationship we have to reflect Your love, guidance and the care You have for us. Would You help me to obey the parents whom You've given me and be the parent You want me to be, so that my children will want to obey and honor me? I want "that it may go well" with me, that I may enjoy long life and that my family can be an inspiration to others! Thank You Lord! Amen.

REFLECT: It's hard to build a healthy family. Has it been hard for you to embrace the concept of obeying your parents? How are you doing with that challenge? Did you come from a good or a broken family? Is your immediate family following the Lord? Do you need to pray for your children and/or your parents? Think about what you believe the Lord would want your family to be and ask Him to show you how to get to that place. Have you thought about what it takes to earn the right to be obeyed by our children?

ACT: Why don't you gather a small prayer group of close friends or prayer partners to pray for your family—your parents or you as parents! Be vulnerable and tell the trusted group what the physical, emotional and spiritual needs are of your family. Ask them to walk the journey with you, so that you will experience God's desire for your family from Ephesians 6:1-3. Pray for their families as well. Families are the most impactful relationships in our lives, we need help understanding how to honor our mothers and fathers, and we all need prayer!

YOUR THOUGHTS:

DAY 2

LISTEN TO YOUR FATHER

"The righteous man leads a blameless life; blessed are his children after him."

Proverbs 20:7

"My son, do not despise the Lord 's discipline and do not resent his rebuke, because the Lord disciplines those he loves, as a father the son he delights in."   Proverbs 3:11-12

"You don't choose your family. They are God's gift to you, as you are to them."

Desmond Tutu

PRAY: Dear Father in Heaven, You are the true Father and we are Your children. I ask that my earthly father would be a righteous man so that his children would be blessed. And please make me a righteous parent so that my children will be blessed after me. May I hear the instruction of my parents, and even more so, Your instruction. Let me not forsake Your law so that I can be a child that You delight in. Let me embrace Your correction, just as I want my children not to detest my correction. Thank you for being my perfect Father. I want to learn from You. In Jesus' name, Amen.

REFLECT: Have you ever thought about how your heavenly Father is the perfect example for an earthly father? Our parents are a mere reflection of God the Father. Are you a perfect reflection of God your Father? What changes would you have to make as a parent to follow the Lord's instruction, to not forsake His law, to not despise His discipline, or to not detest His correction? Reflect on the parallels God gives between us being a parent and Him being our Father.

ACT: Re-read today's verses and the reflection questions. There are quite `a few instructions in there to be a good parent, to be a good child and to see God as our perfect Father. What is the main struggle you think of in yourself as you read these verses? Write it down and commit it to prayer. The first step to changing is to define the problem and then pray about it.

YOUR **THOUGHTS:**

DAY 3

OBEY YOUR PARENTS

"My son, keep your father's commands and do not forsake your mother's teaching. Bind them upon your heart forever; fasten them around your neck. When you walk, they will guide you; when you sleep, they will watch over you; when you awake, they will speak to you. For these commands are a lamp, this teaching is a light, and the corrections of discipline are the way to life."   Proverbs 6:20-23

"Each day of our lives we make deposits in the memory banks of our children."

Charles R. Swindoll

PRAY: Heavenly Father, help me to listen to my father and mother. Please take the wisdom they have given to me and bind them around my neck and in my heart. Let the things You have given to me through my parents guide me, watch over me and speak to me, so that I can grow in wisdom. Please let me look past the words they've said that are not from You and embrace the words that are from You, so that their commands and teaching will make me more Christ-like. I pray this in Your name. Amen.

REFLECT: How much of who you are is because of your parents? How much of what they've said to you through the years has become a part of you? Try to remember some of the teachable moments. Are you giving your children commands and teachings that they will fasten around their neck, walk with and sleep with? What words have you heard from your parents or said to your children that were possibly harmful? What words were empowering? Think about what conversations you have remembered. Have they hurt you or made you a better person? The power of words in a family is life-changing.

ACT: Choose one incredible conversation or word of advice that one of your parents had with you. Why don't you go back and thank them for those words. Let them know that their words have stayed with you and have made you a better person. Or, offer your children some life empowering words that they will hang on to for their lives. Pour into them as the Lord continues to pour into us. Either thank a family member for a godly command or teaching that they offered you, or give one to someone in your life. Your teaching will be a light.

YOUR THOUGHTS:

DAY 4

CHILDREN ARE A HERITAGE

"Sons are a heritage from the Lord, children a reward from him. Like arrows in the hands of a warrior are sons born in one's youth. Blessed is the man whose quiver is full of them. They will not be put to shame when they contend with their enemies in the gate."

Psalm 127:3-5

"I have no greater joy than to hear that my children are walking in the truth." 3 John 1:4

"What can you do to promote world peace? Go home and love your family."

Mother Theresa

PRAY: Lord, thank You that You cherish children. You say that they are a heritage from You, the fruit of the womb, a reward. You bless the man whose quiver is full of children. Please help me to teach children Your truths, so that they will not be put to shame. Lord, please give parents the great joy of hearing that their children are walking in the truth. Please help mine and other families in our nation. And will You help me to be a heritage from the Lord. I want my parents, my children and You to be proud of me. Amen and Amen.

REFLECT: Can your parents say that you are walking in the truth? Are your children walking in the truth? God says children are a heritage from the Lord. Are you part of a spiritual heritage? Evaluate the spiritual health of your family and bring peace to your children through your choices today. How can you find that incredible joy of experiencing your children walking in the truth? We should want to be godly parents, but we also must be aware of what's impacting their hearts at school, through TV, video games and the music they listen to. How can you "contend with these enemies in the gate?"

ACT: PRAY for our Christian families in the entertainment industry as they contend with the cultural influences around them. It's especially hard with professional child actors, for they become role models to other young people who are watching them in their films, TV shows, or their music. Be encouraged, for there is a growing community of Christians in Hollywood who are gathering for fellowship, prayer, accountability, and support, to keep their families spiritually strong as their children work in entertainment. These families need prayer, for the Lord has no greater joy than to hear that His children are walking in the truth.

YOUR THOUGHTS:

DAY 5

PROTECT YOUR CHILDREN

"And if anyone causes one of these little ones who believe in me to sin, it would be better for him to be thrown into the sea with a large millstone tied around his neck." Mark 9:42

"Family is not an important thing, it's everything."

Michael J. Fox

PRAY: Jesus, You love the little children and it breaks Your heart to see them hurt, abused or abandoned. I ask that Your Holy Spirit convicts the hearts of the parents who are not treating their children with love and care. Would You show me what I need to do to help any of the children in my life circle to be taken care of and nurtured? Thank you for the gift of precious children and I ask that You protect them from harm. I pray in Your name. Amen.

REFLECT: We think about the horror of child abuse and we can hardly imagine how someone can hurt an innocent child. But have you thought about the severe punishment the Lord has for the adults who hurt and abuse children? It's more serious than we realize. This scripture says that anyone who even causes a little one to stumble would be better off if they were "thrown into the sea with a large millstone tied around his neck!" What can you do to protect any children in your life who may need your help. Or what adults do you need to warn about the consequences of hurting children? It's a difficult conversation to have but it's true that evil thrives when good people do nothing.

ACT: Are there any adults in your life who are not good to children? If you know someone who is not treating a child with love and care, would you pray about what your part is in protecting that child and/or warning that adult? It's a difficult issue to get involved in, but the Lord wants us to protect the children from harm and we don't ever want to turn away from a situation that we could help to change. And we always want to protect little ones from adults who could cause them to sin.

YOUR THOUGHTS:

DAY 6

MARRIAGE SHOULD BE HONORED

"Marriage should be honored by all, and the marriage bed kept pure, for God will judge the adulterer and all the sexually immoral. Keep your lives free from the love of money and be content with what you have, because God has said, "Never will I leave you; never will I forsake you."   Hebrews 13:4-5

"They say marriages are made in Heaven. But so is thunder and lightning."

Clint Eastwood

PRAY: Lord, I pray today for the personal relationships of our nations entertainment and media professionals. I pray for the marriages and for families of the culture-shapers. Show them the importance of family and give them the desire and the discipline to put their families first. Lord, the high divorce rate in Hollywood breaks my heart. Would your Holy Spirit come in and melt their hearts toward their spouses, their children, and the sanctity of marriage? Oh Lord, I want marriage to be honored by all, and every marriage bed in Hollywood to be kept pure. And I ask the same for me and my family as well. Amen.

REFLECT: Re-read this verse and think about the deep truths in it. Two big reasons for many divorces are adultery and money issues. Both are addressed in this verse. We pray for the marriages in Hollywood because not only are they impacting our culture, but they also reflect our nation's values. So, praying for them will impact us as well. What do you need to change in your marriage, or in the marriages around you? If you could stay faithful to God and your spouse, not argue or panic over money, and be content with what you have, you can trust that God will take care of all your needs because He has promised He will NEVER leave you or forsake you. WOW!

ACT: Choose one celebrity person or couple in Hollywood whom you follow and enjoy and pray for their marriage, pray for the Lord to keep them content with their money, and pray for them to stay faithful. As you pray for that person or couple you are going to change as well. You will become more faithful, more content, and even more Christ-like as you eternally change their lives through your prayers.

YOUR THOUGHTS:

DAY 7

HONOR YOUR FATHER AND MOTHER

"Honor your father and your mother, as the Lord your God has commanded you, so that you may live long and that it may go well with you in the land the Lord your God is giving you."   Deuteronomy 5:16

"Both my study of Scripture and my career in entertaining children have taught me to cherish them. But I don't believe in playing down to children, either in life or in motion pictures. I didn't treat my own youngsters like fragile flowers, and I think no parent should."

Walt Disney

PRAY: Dear God, I thank You for this reminder to honor our parents. It is so clear what we must do, and yet we need Your help to do as You command. You make it so clear that we are to honor our fathers and our mothers in order to live long lives. But I can't do this without You. Help me to be patient, kind, loving, and obedient to my parents, and please have my children be that way to me. It's so humbling to be a child or a parent and yet You promise me that it's worth it. May it go well with me in the land that You gave me. I pray in Jesus name.

REFLECT: What does it mean to HONOR your father and mother? That doesn't mean to do every single thing they say or bow to their every wish. It means to "regard them with respect" and to treat them with "high respect or esteem." Are you honoring them as the Lord commanded? What would you need to change? Do your children honor you? If not, how do you need to change in order to earn their respect? Choose honoring your parents today, even if they are no longer alive. Your honoring attitude toward them will change you and allow you to "live long in the land!"

ACT: Take action: Choose now to honor one of your parents today! Say something or do one thing today that you know will show them honor. If you don't have your parents any more then choose another parent to honor. As you take that one step, you'll see how easy it is and you will hopefully choose to do it one more time, and then again, and again, until it becomes a habit.

YOUR THOUGHTS:

CHILDREN

WEEK THIRTY-ONE

There is something divinely miraculous about children. And as adults, we have a responsibility to love them, protect them, and train them in the ways they should go – whether they are physically ours or not. This week as we focus on God's children, let's keep singing, "Red and yellow, black and white, they are precious in his sight. Jesus loves the little children of the world."

DAY 1

CHILDREN ARE A GIFT FROM THE LORD

"Sons are a heritage from the Lord, children a reward from him."   Psalm 127:3

"Children's children are a crown to the aged, and parents are the pride of their children."
                                                                         Proverbs 17:6

"Like arrows in the hands of a warrior are children born of one's youth. Blessed is the man whose quiver is full of them."
                                                                         King Solomon

PRAY: Dear Father, As I look to You as my Father, I thank You that You have promised us that children are a heritage and a reward from You. Thank you that even our children's children are a crown to the aged. And I am so deeply grateful that I can experience Your promise that parents are the pride of their children. The greatest gift You have given me, besides my salvation and my spouse, are my children, and I start this week praising You and thanking You for the miraculous journey of having children. I thank You in Jesus name, Amen.

REFLECT: Based on these verses, we should all be treasuring the children in our lives. God so deeply loves children, and He wants us to love and protect them as well. Jesus defended the children multiple times in the Gospels and God tells us that they are a heritage, a reward, and a crown. Those are strong words, showing God's passion for children. Are we loving and valuing our children as we should be? Sometimes we confuse love with spoiling, not disciplining or guiding. How can you love the children in your life with God's love? Ask Him what more you can do to love, guide, protect, discipline and train up a child in the way He should go, as Jesus would do.

ACT: Take a moment and go to or call a child in your life and tell him or her how much they mean to you. Tell them that you love them, that you're thankful they are in your life, and tell them something particular you value about them. This one visit, call, or note could change their life and give them the confidence to move forward in something, to seek Jesus more, or to show love to someone else. Your words of love can make an eternal difference.

YOUR THOUGHTS:

DAY 2

TRAIN YOUR CHILDREN IN THE WAY THEY SHOULD GO

"Start children off on the way they should go, and even when they are old they will not turn from it."   Proverbs 22:6

"It is easier to build strong children than to repair broken men."   Frederick Douglass

PRAY: Father in heaven, may You help me to be the parent I need to be so that my children will go in the way they should go, and when they get old they will not turn from You. My children are a gift from you so help me put them in Your hands so that You will hold on to them, guide them and protect them. Give me wisdom in the process of raising my children, so that they will stay on the right path, and not turn from it. And if they do, Lord, then give me peace to know they are Yours and You love them more than I do. I can raise my children, but I must trust You to hold them in the palm of Your hand. Thank You and Amen.

REFLECT: Every parent makes mistakes while raising their children and yet every healthy parent wants their children to do well in life. Raising children is complicated and difficult, but as parents, we want to raise our children, training them to have God's principles, truths, and scripture in their hearts, but also hold them loosely. We pray for them to stay on God's path so that when they are old, they will be following Jesus. How do we completely put our children in God's hands? Regardless of their age or yours, you can start today!

ACT: If you are not yet a parent, would you memorize this verse so that you are prepared to follow it from the moment you become a parent? If you are raising children right now or caring for others, would you memorize this verse and commit daily to ask God for wisdom in raising them? If your children are grown, would you memorize this verse and pray for them to be the kind of parents who will seek Jesus and start their children off on the way they should go so that they will not turn from it? It's never too late to start anew.

YOUR THOUGHTS:

DAY 3

DO NOT EXASPERATE YOUR CHILDREN!

"Fathers, do not exasperate your children; instead, bring them up in the training and instruction of the Lord."   Ephesians 6:4

"The moment you have a child, in an instant your life is not for you, and your life is completely, 100 percent dedicated to another human being, and they will always come first. It changes you forever. It changes your perspective, and it gives you a nice purpose and focus."   Angelina Jolie

PRAY: Lord, I know that there are some things that my parents did or said that were hurtful to me. They exasperated me, instead of bringing me up in the training and instruction of Your Word. Those choices by my parents may even be why I am struggling with some issues today. So, would You make me the kind of person to break those chains and not exasperate my children. Would You start now to help me bring up my children wisely and with Your training and instruction? I trust You to make me a good parent. Amen and Amen.

REFLECT: Hollywood is a place that often attracts people who have broken relationships with their fathers. Many who come here are trying to find the love, acceptance, and value they never got from their fathers. Ironically, they have come to the worst possible "stepfather" for that. We all long for fathers and mothers who don't exasperate, frustrate or devalue us. Please have patience and understanding for the "exasperated" celebrities and decision-makers in Hollywood who never grew up with the Lord's training and instruction.

ACT: Would you pray for the people in Hollywood whose names come to mind right now? You may not realize that they didn't get the love of their fathers and their broken, sad, or even abusive childhoods have made them who they are today. If you don't like the decisions or content coming out of Hollywood, you can be assured that the people behind those decisions are probably from non-Christian, broken, or even dysfunctional homes, and they need our prayers. You can make an eternal difference by praying for culture-shapers in Hollywood. Pray also for their children! Listen to some songs about Fathers at: https://www.jamescovell.com/fathers

YOUR THOUGHTS:

DAY 4

DISCIPLINE YOUR CHILDREN

"He who spares the rod hates his son, but he who loves him is careful to discipline him."
"The rod of correction imparts wisdom, but a child left to himself disgraces his mother."

Proverbs 13:24 & 29:15

"If we never have headaches through rebuking our children, we shall have plenty of heartaches when they grow up."
Charles Spurgeon

PRAY: Dear God, I need wisdom to understand the fine line between disciplining my children and being too strict. I need Your help to let me discipline my children through love, not anger. Let me understand that a reprimand imparts wisdom and that a lack of discipline will disgrace me as a parent, teacher or guardian. I need Your Holy Spirit to lead me, teach me, and guide me. Lord, let me follow Your Word so I can raise Godly children. Amen.

REFLECT: Raising children is difficult. Every parent knows that. But we also all have varying opinions on disciplining our children, to the point to being divisive. What do you think God means when He tells us not to spare the rod, for that shows we hate our children? Or, that the parents who love their children are careful to discipline them? If a "rod" and a "reprimand" impart wisdom, and children who are not disciplined will disgrace their mothers, then how do we wisely implement that into our parenting? How did your parents do at it? What would you, or have you, done differently?

ACT: Did you or will you "spare the rod?" Do you need to seek God for answers on what that means? Do you need to seek wisdom from professionals or parents who are great parents? Do you need to give your parents grace, forgiveness, or a compliment regarding this issue? What is your next step in either becoming a better parent or evaluating your parents? Maybe you need to give them a compliment or ask their forgiveness? Maybe you need to ask your own children for forgiveness and give them a compliment on how well they turned out. Decide your next step in directly facing this difficult issue of discipline and do it right now.

YOUR THOUGHTS:

DAY 5

THE KINGDOM OF HEAVEN BELONGS TO CHILDREN

"Jesus said, "Let the little children come to me, and do not hinder them, for the kingdom of heaven belongs to such as these."

Matthew 19:14

"When our children see us clinging to the promises of God, they will grow up trusting in His goodness. If we fail as adults in praying for and praying with the next generation, then they will become spiritually unsure."

Michael Youssef

PRAY: Dear Jesus, You love little children and You tell us not to hinder them from coming to You, for Your Kingdom belongs to them. Help me to love little children, and to tell them about You, whether they be my neighbor's or mine, or my relative's. I want to never say or do anything to keep a child from knowing You. I never want to hinder them from loving You and experiencing the kingdom of heaven. And may I encourage others to do the same. You place such a high value on children that I want to be more like You and celebrate them, empower them and love them, just as You would, so that they will come to know You. I commit to do this, in Your name. Amen.

REFLECT: Have you ever considered that we are told it's up to us to lead children to Jesus? And He doesn't say, "Let only YOUR little children come to me..." Jesus told us to let all the little children in our lives come to Him and not to hinder them. That means it's our responsibility as believers to point all the children in our lives and in our kid's classes, clubs, sports teams and neighborhoods, to know about Jesus. How may we have been, or are being, a hindrance to any children in our lives coming to know Jesus? How do we prepare to bring more children to learn about Him? How can we more effectively obey this commandment?

ACT: Choose one child in your life whom you can tell about Jesus and then ask the Lord to show you the best, most effective way to do that. Could it be through getting them a children's Bible or book, writing a note, or spending more time talking with them? Is it to share your faith with their parents? Decide right now what child is on your heart to reach out to so that you won't be a hindrance to them learning about and falling in love with Jesus!

YOUR THOUGHTS:

DAY 6

TEACH GOD'S TRUTHS TO CHILDREN

"Fix these words of mine in your hearts and minds; tie them as symbols on your hands and bind them on your foreheads. Teach them to your children, talking about them when you sit at home and when you walk along the road, when you lie down and when you get up. Write them on the doorframes of your houses and on your gates, so that your days and the days of your children may be many in the land that the Lord swore to give your forefathers, as many as the days that the heavens are above the earth."

Deuteronomy 11:18-21

"Recommend to your children virtue; that alone can make them happy, not gold."

Ludwig von Beethoven

PRAY: God my Father, I want to fix Your words in my heart and my mind. Please tie them as symbols on my hand and bind them on my forehead. Let me be sure to teach my children Your truths, Your commandments, and Your promises. And I want to offer this wisdom to others as well. Let Your truths be so much a part of my every breathing moment that my days and the days of my children and their children may be many in the land that You swore to give me. Thank You my heavenly Father! Amen.

REFLECT: Our heavenly Father wants us to not only know His truths, but He commands us to teach them to our children and grandchildren. And that's for all of us – whether we are single, married, or parents. We all should have spiritual "children" in our lives whom we are teaching, loving, guiding, and encouraging. Do you have anyone in your life like that? Have you written God's commandments on your heart and everywhere in your house as a reminder to share them with others? How can you be sure that you and your "children" may have many in the land—as many as the days that the heavens are above the earth?

ACT: Make a list of the physical and/or spiritual "children" in your life. Then write down how you can touch each one with the love of Jesus. You could spend more time with them, write them a note, call them, and pray for them. Choose what would be most effective to touch as many children with the love of our heavenly Father as you can. And then make the first move. This could be your first step toward leaving a legacy and that's exciting!

YOUR THOUGHTS:

DAY 7

BECOME LIKE A LITTLE CHILD

"He called a little child and had him stand among them. And he said: "I tell you the truth, unless you change and become like little children, you will never enter the kingdom of heaven. Therefore, whoever humbles himself like this child is the greatest in the kingdom of heaven. "And whoever welcomes a little child like this in my name welcomes me. But if anyone causes one of these little ones who believe in me to sin, it would be better for him to have a large millstone hung around his neck and to be drowned in the depths of the sea."
                                                                    Matthew 18:2-6

"Little children are God's ongoing witness of His kingdom: a perpetual reminder of what it means to belong to the father. Children are an unspoken sermon in every home for simplicity, joy, and humility of that which makes the world worth living in. They remind us what it means to be a real Christian."
                                                                    Winkie Pratnie

PRAY: Dear Lord, As an adult and a follower of You, I want to be child-like in my spirit. Would You help me become like a little child so I can fully experience the Kingdom of Heaven! Lord, please never let me hinder anyone else from seeking You and Your Kingdom. I never want to stumble in loving and encouraging other people to come to know you and to grow deeper in their love for You. Thank You for your strength and wisdom. Amen.

REFLECT: We don't think much about changing to become a child in God's eyes. And we probably don't think enough about how to welcome others into God's Kingdom, whether they are children or adults. Knowing that God warns us about stumbling others to come to Him, what would you need to change to be used by the Lord to not hinder other "children" of His to find and follow Him? It's a responsibility with consequences so ponder the options.

ACT: Now is the time to change. Re-read this scripture and choose one thing that you can change about yourself to become more of a child in God's eyes and to reach out to others so that they can find Him and love Him as well. You can write it down and then check back to see how you're doing. And remember, we can't change ourselves on our own; we need the Holy Spirit to do the changing. So why don't you start with a prayer!

YOUR THOUGHTS:

COMMUNITY

WEEK THIRTY-TWO

What kind of community do you live in? Do you have strong Christians around you? Are you building up the body of Christ and reaching out to those who don't know Him? We're going to focus on the importance of community remembering that UNITY is the word that completes COMMUNITY.

DAY 1

LOVE YOUR NEIGHBOR

"My brothers, as believers in our glorious Lord Jesus Christ, don't show favoritism...If you really keep the royal law found in Scripture, "Love your neighbor as yourself," you are doing right. But if you show favoritism, you sin and are convicted by the law as lawbreakers."

James 2:1 & 8-9

"My job on my set, I believe, is to first just love people and gain that trust with people where they know that I really do love them and care about their well-being, so that when they are running into problems, they will hopefully, at some point, come to me and ask me, 'What is your peace all about? What is your comfort all about? Where do you get your love? Where do you get your talents?' And I can turn to them and say without blinking, 'Jesus Christ.'"

Zachary Levi

PRAY: Dear Lord, help me to love my neighbor as myself. Help me to love everyone I come in contact with, even if I don't like them, or disagree with them, or don't understand them. Teach me how to love so that I can fulfill Your greatest commandment and build a loving community around me. I need Your help to do that. Amen.

REFLECT: It's easy to show favorites and love some people more than others. In fact, that's expected in our society. Reflect on God's perspective on loving your "neighbors." What does it mean to follow a law that says to love literally everyone around you. And if you don't, you are showing favoritism and sinning. Our heavenly Father is so strong about that, so it must be vitally important.

ACT: It's interesting that UNITY is a word within the word COMMUNITY. So, what "neighbor" do you need to choose to love right now in your community? Ask the Lord to reveal that person to you and then do something to show your love, whether you feel like it or not. Remember, this is God's law.

YOUR THOUGHTS:

DAY 2

HELP OTHER PEOPLE

"To equip God's people for works of service, so that the body of Christ may be built up until we all reach unity in the faith and in the knowledge of the Son of God and become mature, attaining to the whole measure of the fullness of Christ."   Ephesians 4:12-13

"When facing the mad religionist or blind legalist, we have no recourse, no place to stand, if we do not have firsthand experiences of hearing God's voice, held safely within a community of brothers and sisters in Christ who also have such knowledge of God's personal dealings with their own souls."   Dallas Willard

PRAY: Heavenly Father, would You equip me for Your work, so that I can be used by You to build up the Body of Christ in my community? I want to attain unity with the Christians around me, and share my knowledge of the Son of God to the non-believers around me. Thank you for this verse that reminds me of Your command. Amen.

REFLECT: Is this verse a reminder for you, personally, to equip others for the work of the ministry in order to build up the Body? Do you need to be equipped to fulfill the task? Or are you already doing it and can now pray for others to join you in unity? Ponder this verse, and ask the Lord to reveal His knowledge to you, in order to fully understand what it means.

ACT: As you reflect on this verse, what conclusion did you come to? If you aren't equipped yourself or you want to help equip others, then it might help to read *"How To Talk About Jesus Without Freaking Out"* to learn how to share your faith, gain the knowledge of the Son of God, and build up the body of Christ. Make it a priority to equip yourself so you can equip the saints.

YOUR THOUGHTS:

DAY 3

TOGETHER WE ARE CHRIST'S BODY

"Now you are the body of Christ, and each one of you is a part of it."

1 Corinthians 12:27

"The presence of Christ in you makes all that He is available to others." Henry Blackaby

PRAY: Lord, I thank You that I am a specific and important part of Your Body and that my community needs me to make it complete. Would You show me what my particular part is in the body of Christ, so that I don't miss anything that You have for me to do, to say, to pray, or to accomplish? In Jesus' name, Amen.

REFLECT: It's amazing to think that every single person is a part of Christ's body. Reflect on what your part is. Have you thought about what part your family members and friends play in your community? Each Christian you know is a special part of Christ's body, making it whole. And each of us is important, whether it be a tiny screw or the main steering wheel. The body wouldn't work well without each of us doing our part.

ACT: Start a conversation with your Christian friends and family members about each of you being a part of Christ's body. Ask them if they know what their part is, and if they know what your part may be. Ask if the body of Christ you're all in is like a well-oiled machine or a broken-down contraption? What parts need to be fixed to make it run better? You could be the first one to start building or healing your community.

YOUR THOUGHTS:

DAY 4

RUN A GOOD RACE

"Therefore, since we are surrounded by such a great cloud of witnesses, let us throw off everything that hinders and the sin that so easily entangles, and let us run with perseverance the race marked out for us. Let us fix our eyes on Jesus, the author and perfecter of our faith, who for the joy set before him endured the cross, scorning its shame, and sat down at the right hand of the throne of God. Consider him who endured such opposition from sinful men, so that you will not grow weary and lose heart."

Hebrews 12:1-3

I hope everybody could get rich and famous and will have everything they ever dreamed of, so they will know that it's not the answer."
Jim Carrey

PRAY: Dear God, I pray for the active Christians and ministries in Hollywood. I ask that each of them fill a place in Your overall plan to bring Your love, hope, salvation, healing, and fellowship into the Entertainment Industry. May You bless the efforts of these ministries, and bring great fruit from the work of the Christian professionals who lead these groups and minister to their co-workers. And may they bring Christians closer to You, and closer to one another in community, and that they draw the non-believers to Jesus. Help them to run with perseverance, to fix their eyes on Jesus, and not grow weary and lose heart. Amen.

REFLECT: God tells us that we are ALL surrounded by a great cloud of witnesses, so we all need to get rid of everything that hinders our walk and our growth as Christians. We need to be aware that we are being watched. Think about how that feels. Have you ever thought about the cloud of witnesses watching the visible Christians in Hollywood? It's very difficult to be in the limelight. The Christians there endure great opposition and become weary and lose heart. Have you ever considered praying for them?

ACT: Go online to the HPN website: www.hollywoodprayernetwork.org and pray for the list of active Entertainment Ministries in Hollywood. Pray that they will run with perseverance, bear great fruit, and that the Christians in Hollywood won't grow weary and lose heart. Their community is on the spiritual front lines and they need our prayers.

YOUR THOUGHTS:

DAY 5

YOU ARE GOD'S FRIEND

"I no longer call you servants, because a servant does not know his master's business. Instead, I have called you friends, for everything that I learned from my Father I have made known to you."

John 15:15

"Coming together is a beginning; keeping together is a process; working together is success."

Henry Ford

PRAY: Lord, I want to make sure that I share my faith with the people around me so that I tell others all I know about You. I don't want anyone to be a "servant" of the world, but that they know You as their Master. Would You show me how to be salt and light, to be a good friend, and to be a loving Ambassador to all the people in my community, workplace, and city? Amen.

REFLECT: Our culture is very aware of not wanting to treat anyone as inferior. So, it's a challenge to realize that though we don't believe in having or being a servant, God says that anyone who doesn't know what his master is doing IS a servant. Reflect on the truth that we can be a friend of God, and pass on our knowledge of God to others, so that they no longer have to be servants, but rather, they too can be friends of God.

ACT: Now it's your turn to be able to say to the people closest to you, "All I have known about the Father I have passed on to you." Who do you need to tell that you are a follower of Jesus? Choose one person now and pray about what you might say and do. And pray for their heart to be prepared as you open your heart up to them.

YOUR THOUGHTS:

DAY 6

ENCOURAGE ONE ANOTHER

"Therefore encourage one another and build each other up, just as in fact you are doing."

1 Thessalonians 5:11

"I've worked with a lot of really fine actors, both on stage and on screen. The level of their game lifts me up and brings the level of my game up to theirs. Always. It's like a constant upgrade."   Gary Sinise

PRAY: Oh Lord, I want to encourage the people around me. I want to build each one up in their faith and let them know how special they are. I pray that I can be a person of encouragement and inspiration to others, both the Christians and the non-believers. Let me share the love I have from You, to everyone in my community. Amen.

REFLECT: Are you an encouraging person or a complaining person? Do you build others up in the Lord, or do you criticize and point out others' wrongs and weaknesses? Do you need to change your attitude, your approach, or your words, so that you will be known as a positive person, full of encouragement and inspiration?

ACT: Choose one person right now to encourage. Once you choose someone decide if you will call them, text them, write them a love note, or drive over to their house and give them a hug. Whatever it is, make it special, and be sure it's for no other reason than you want to build them up and fill them with a dose of great encouragement. Why don't you choose to encourage one person every week with a special effort to build them up and let them know they are loved by you and by God. Choose to be an encourager!

YOUR THOUGHTS:

DAY 7

THANK GOD FOR COMMUNITY

"We always thank God for all of you, mentioning you in our prayers. We continually remember before our God and Father your work produced by faith, your labor prompted by love, and your endurance inspired by hope in our Lord Jesus Christ".

1 Thessalonians 1:2-3

"I have a group of people, about 40, in a local church in Surrey in England, who pray for me regularly."

Cliff Richard

PRAY: Thank You God for the Christians in my life. I am grateful for each one. I want to lift them up to You and thank You for their work, their endurance and their lives. I want to encourage them and build each one up and ask You to help them to do the same. May I always be a source of inspiration and encouragement to the people I love. I pray this in the name of Jesus. Amen.

REFLECT: What people have you not thought to thank God for? Reflect on the people in your life whom you can be praying for—especially business leaders, community leaders, political and entertainment leaders, and cultural influencers. They need our prayers for faith, love, endurance, and hope.

ACT: Stop and choose three celebrities whom you know or like. Now pray for God to bless their lives, their careers, their families, and their friends. Pray that regardless of what they believe right now, they will come to know their blessings are coming from the God of Abraham, Isaac, and Jacob.

YOUR THOUGHTS:

Check out this video, "The Hollywood Community" to see that God is real and present in Hollywood!

https://youtu.be/OrCctEdCrgs

SHAME

WEEK THIRTY-THREE

This week's study on SHAME should be full of surprising revelations—insightful in showing how to avoid experiencing the heavy burden of shame, and practical in sharing how to pray for others to be free of shame as well. Feeling shame is a warning, like touching a hot stove; IF you are full of shame THEN you stop what you're doing and make different choices. Anyone can live shame-free!

DAY 1

SHAME, GUILT, AND DISGRACE CAN OVERWHELM US

"If I am guilty—woe to me! Even if I am innocent, I cannot lift my head, for I am full of shame and drowned in my affliction."   Job 10:15

Because the Sovereign Lord helps me, I will not be disgraced. Therefore have I set my face like flint, and I know I will not be put to shame."   Isaiah 50:7

"I feel shame, not for the wrong things I have done, but for the right things that I have failed to do."   Marcel Duchamp

PRAY: Father in Heaven, I need You to rid me of the shame that I am living in right now. Forgive me and make me clean. I want to be as clean as freshly fallen snow in Your presence. I don't want my face covered in shame. I want to be innocent and pure, and hold my head up high, with confidence in You! Thank You for forgiving me for everything in my life that is displeasing. Help me to forgive myself—even if others don't forgive me! I will not be disgraced for with You, I will not be put to shame. Amen.

REFLECT: So many people spend their whole life in fear, doubt and shame, even when they're innocent. Imagine the shame carried by those who have done terrible, hurtful things to others, or to God? Separate yourselves from worldly influences and from selfishly seeking personal gain. Be loyal to God and His Truth above all else. "Set our face like flint." Be disciplined, focused to follow in Jesus's footsteps. Regardless of what you've done in your life, whether you're innocent or guilty, God does not want you to carry shame. Know that the Sovereign Lord helps us so that we are not put to shame.

ACT: Do these verses ring true to you? Regardless of how bad your sins or guilt are, if you carry shame, you are crippling yourself. This is the week to rid yourself of that shame. You can end this week as a new creature, full of confidence in Him, with a clean heart and hope for the future, but you have to "set your face like flint". Turn right now to your Sovereign Lord and ask Him to define your shame and then remove it. Tell Him you accept His forgiveness, and know that you will no longer be put to shame! This is the week to walk away from shame.

YOUR THOUGHTS:

DAY 2

GOD CHOSE THE FOOLISH AND THE WEAK

"But God chose the foolish things of the world to shame the wise; God chose the weak things of the world to shame the strong." 1 Corinthians 1:27

"I just feel compelled to continue to be transparent. It just really levels the playing field and eradicates the shame that I have, or that one might have, about being human. So I'm going to just keep going." Alanis Morissette

PRAY: God, I love this verse! You can take us, even at our worst, and use us to make an eternal difference in this world. Would You choose me, as foolish as I may be, and use me to shame the wise? And choose me, as weak as I may be, to shame the strong, for "I can do all things through Christ who strengthens me!" How crazy and fabulous! Amen and Amen.

REFLECT: God doesn't see anyone as useless. He uses ordinary people in powerful ways. Sometimes the greatest impact comes from the last person we'd expect, challenging our conviction that certain qualifications and skills are necessary to be useful to society, or to be used by God. God so believes in you that He can use you even to shame others. Can you imagine that? Shame is defined as, "a painful feeling of humiliation or distress caused by the consciousness of wrong or foolish behavior." If God could send Jesus as a baby in a manger instead of sending a mighty warrior from a fortress, then God can use you to change the world. He chose you to be a part of His bigger plan, to bring others to Him and to do miracles! Are you willing and ready?

ACT: Make a list of people who intimidate you, people whom you think are much smarter, more powerful, richer, or who have more influence than you do. Now imagine God using you to put these people to shame. He doesn't give us this verse because He wants us to make others miserable. He wants to show us how much He believes in us and can use us for His good, with all of our limitations, insecurities, and weaknesses. God wants us to be a part of His plan to touch every person's heart on the planet. Don't let people intimidate you. Pray for them and ask God to use you to melt their hearts. Have confidence in Him, not in your abilities, and know that He is pleased with you.

YOUR THOUGHTS:

DAY 3

HOLD FAST TO THE LORD

"But those who trust in idols, who say to images, 'You are our gods,' will be turned back in utter shame."
                                                                Isaiah 42:17

"Multitudes who sleep in the dust of the earth will awake: some to everlasting life, others to shame and everlasting contempt."
                                                                Daniel 12:2

"Tell the truth and shame the devil."
                                                        Francois Rabelais

PRAY: Dear Lord, I realize that experiencing shame is a choice. Would you help me to make the right choices in my life so that I won't be turned away in utter shame! I want to wake every day to everlasting life and freedom, not shame! Help me to be a warrior in battle, Lord. I will fight to put the enemy to shame and everlasting contempt, and not be turned back in shame myself. Thank You Lord for Your love, help, and protection to give me everlasting life. Amen and Amen.

REFLECT: We are reminded in these verses again, that in order to avoid shame, we must trust in God. We should only fight if the Lord is with us and it is for righteousness. We can't trust in idols or false gods or we will be put to shame. We can either have everlasting life or everlasting contempt and shame. We make choices every single day and they all give us a different quality of life.

ACT: Is there anything in your life that could become more important than God? Can you identify any idols or false gods in your life? Try to identify them now so that you can ask God to help you rid yourselves of them. You don't want to fight unnecessary battles. You want to put the enemy horsemen to shame, not allow them to lead you to experience shame. Make choices now to live life everlasting and free of shame. You will succeed; Trust in Him, for if God is with you, who can be against you?

YOUR THOUGHTS:

DAY 4

JESUS OVERCOMES SHAME

"Let us fix our eyes on Jesus, the author and perfecter of our faith, who for the joy set before him endured the cross, scorning its shame, and sat down at the right hand of the throne of God. Consider him who endured such opposition from sinful men, so that you will not grow weary and lose heart."
Hebrews 12:2-3

"Repentance keeps sin from condemning us because Jesus died and scorned the shame."
Mark Driscoll

PRAY: I praise You, Jesus for being the author and perfecter of my faith. You are my role model for how to handle shame. You never sinned, and then when others tried to place shame on You, You scorned it. Thank You Jesus for the inspiration You are to me. I want to choose wisely and then not let anyone make me feel ashamed. I am a child of God and I will fix my eyes on You and not lose sight of the joy set before me. You endured the cross so I can handle anything and not grow weary and lose heart. I praise You, Jesus! Amen.

REFLECT: We sometimes place scorn (Def: to hold in extreme contempt; to despise; to condemn; to disdain) on ourselves, or allow others to scorn us, because of the shame we carry from our sin. But the feeling of scorn is a lie. God created us in His image, and we are His precious children. We need to scorn the enemy and his lies, so that we, like Jesus, can endure even our sufferings. We need the author and perfecter of our faith to help us be wise and to keep sight of the joy set before us. Don't allow shame to creep into your life. Keep your eyes fixed on Him. It will change your life and the lives of every person you encounter.

ACT: Fix your eyes on Jesus. Get everything else out of your mind. Be in a quiet place where you're not distracted and spend a few minutes just with the Lord. Thank Him for giving you your faith. Think about how your life has changed and improved since knowing and following Him. Now think of Jesus dying on the cross, just for you, and that He ignored the shame that He was going through; naked, bleeding, weak, powerless, and being mocked by people all around Him. Can you shed any or all of your shame right now? Let it go and keep your eyes fixed on Jesus. When you're looking at Him you can't feel any shame.

YOUR THOUGHTS:

DAY 5

SHAME IS A HEAVY BURDEN

"My guilt has overwhelmed me like a burden too heavy to bear."   Psalm 38:4

"O my God, I am too ashamed and disgraced to lift up my face to you, my God, because our sins are higher than our heads and our guilt has reached to the heavens."   Ezra 9:6

"People have pain—they do regrettable things, they feel shame, and shame equals pain."

Jennifer Garner

PRAY: Lord, I pray for entertainment industry professionals, and ask that You help them to be free of shame, whether they follow You or not. Please lift the burden of guilt and shame from their lives. It is too heavy a burden for people to bear. Some are so ashamed and disgraced by their choices that they can't even lift their faces to You. And Lord, please put on the hearts of Christians globally, to pray for the people in Hollywood who are creating our culture and our entertainment, to not be covered in shame. They need You to give them the strength to let go of the heavy burden of shame. Thank You, in Jesus' name! Amen.

REFLECT: Shame brings so much disgrace that we sometimes can't even lift our faces. And guilt can become a burden too heavy to bear. Leaders in Hollywood need our prayers rather than judgment. Many are already overwhelmed with guilt, disgrace, and shame, just like us. God says our kings, even princes and ancestors, are covered in shame and we all need God's grace. So, catch yourself before judging the lifestyles in Hollywood. They need our loving, life-changing prayers, not condemnation or anger. God loves us SO MUCH that He died for everyone, even the people in Hollywood!

ACT: Think of one person in Hollywood whom you dislike or disagree with regarding their actions or lifestyle. Say their name as if God were calling out to them, and imagine they respond by saying this: "I am too ashamed and disgraced, my God, to lift up my face to You, because my sins are higher than my head and my guilt has reached to the heavens." Doesn't that change your perspective of that person? Can you feel their shame? Pray for them right now and ask God to lift the burden of their shame and fill them with His love.

YOUR THOUGHTS:

DAY 6

REDEEMED FROM SHAME

"In you I trust, O my God. Do not let me be put to shame, nor let my enemies triumph over me. No one whose hope is in you will ever be put to shame, but they will be put to shame who are treacherous without excuse... Guard my life and rescue me; let me not be put to shame, for I take refuge in you." Psalm 25:2-3, 20

"When secularization has had its full sway, it will leave a generation devoid of shame. And if you show me a generation that lacks shame, I will show you a generation that is monstrous in its appetite... never satisfied." Ravi Zacharias

PRAY: Dear Heavenly Father, I trust in You. Do not let me be put to shame, and never let my enemies' triumph over me. I understand shame will come to those who are treacherous without cause, so don't let me make poor choices or foolish decisions. I know there are consequences to my actions, so I put my trust in You alone. Guard my life, for You guarantee that if I hope in You I will never be put to shame. Thank You Father, for that promise. With You all things are possible. I praise You for that, in Jesus' name, Amen.

REFLECT: This verse challenges us to understand that if we trust in God, and do nothing on our own, then we will never be put to shame. If we don't trust in God, our enemies will overtake us, we will do treacherous things, and we will be put to shame. That goes against what we learn in our culture. We're taught to be independent, reach our personal and professional goals above all else, and let no one stop us from succeeding. But God tells us that is the way to death, and instead we should trust *Him* for everything. Can *you* trust God with your goals, desires, relationships and jobs?

ACT: What are you afraid to totally turn over to God? Your spouse? Your dream job? That big house? What things have you done or said that you are ashamed of? What choices of yours have burdened you with shame? In God's crazy divine connection between trust and shame, can you see your choices that caused you shame are because you didn't trust God? You might have just broken through to an area of great spiritual growth and freedom. Write down this revelation in your journal.

YOUR THOUGHTS:

DAY 7

PRIDE AND FOOLISHNESS LEAD TO SHAME

"The wise inherit honor, but fools get only shame….When pride comes, then comes disgrace, but with humility comes wisdom…. He who ignores discipline comes to poverty and shame, but whoever heeds correction is honored….He who answers before listening— that is his folly and his shame."   Proverbs 3:35; 11:2; 13:18 & 18:13

"Whatever is begun in anger ends in shame."   Benjamin Franklin

PRAY: Dear God, I want to be wise. I want to inherit honor. I don't want to feel shame. Please help me with my pride and fill me with humility. Remind me to ask for wisdom every day so that I become humble in the process. You tell us what we can do to avoid poverty and shame, so help me to not disregard discipline, but heed correction so that I am honored. Don't let me answer before listening for that, too, is folly and shame. Thank You that I can avoid shame and be wise if I keep my eyes on You and obey Your commandments. Amen.

REFLECT: The Bible is full of actions and consequences, IFs and THENs. God doesn't impose unfair punishments on us, but He did create a world with natural results for our choices. And one of the best examples of the natural consequences of sin is shame. IF we're foolish THEN we will experience poverty, folly, and shame. However, IF we live life God's way THEN we will be wise, and will inherit honor and be truly humble. We can't fight how God set up the world, but if we choose wisely, we can benefit from our choices and not suffer from them. What choices do you want to change?

ACT: Look through all of this week's seven days of verses and discover how to avoid experiencing the heavy burden of shame in your life. Make two columns: IF and THEN. In the left IF column write down all of the actions listed in the verses—from "Fixing your eyes on Jesus" to being "Treacherous without cause." Then on the right THEN column write down the consequences to those actions—from, "I will not be disgraced" to "My face is covered in shame." It will become clear how you can avoid shame. Keep the list, practice trusting in Him and using self-discipline, and your watch your shame drop away.

YOUR THOUGHTS:

COMFORT

WEEK THIRTY-FOUR

We all live busy, hectic, stressful lives and sometimes we would do anything to just feel peace, rest, and comfort. God has sent us the Comforter to give us peace. He promises to take away our weariness if we trust in Him. As we look through the scriptures this week, let's see how we can find comfort in our lives.

DAY 1

ARE YOU WEARY AND BURDENED?

"Come to me, all you who are weary and burdened, and I will give you rest."

Matthew 11:28

"You may readily judge whether you are a child of God or a hypocrite by seeing in what direction your soul turns in seasons of severe trial. The hypocrite flies to the world and finds a sort of comfort there. But the child of God runs to his Father and expects consolation only from the Lord's hand."

Charles Spurgeon

PRAY: Dear Jesus, I come to You right now. I am weary and burdened and I need rest. I take Your yoke upon me and learn from You. Thank You that because You are gentle and humble in heart, that I can find rest in You for my soul. And I praise You that Your yoke is easy and Your burden is light. I find comfort in Your promises to me. Thank You Jesus. Amen.

REFLECT: Ponder the meaning of Jesus' yoke being easy and His burden being light. A yoke is a harness that an animal wears to be guided. Jesus tells us that we need to take His yoke, but that it is easy. He wants to train us, guide us and help us, but He says that it's a light burden. Can you trust Him to lead and guide you through each day, knowing that He will give you comfort and rest for your soul? That sounds pretty amazing!

ACT: Make a list of all the burdens that you are carrying with you right now. Then give that list to the Lord, even reading them out loud to Him and ask Him to take them from you and carry them Himself. Then thank Him for lifting your burdens, taking away your weariness, and giving you rest for your soul. Feel the Lord's comfort as you do this exercise.

YOUR THOUGHTS:

DAY 2

THE LORD IS MY SHEPHERD

"The Lord is my shepherd, I shall not be in want. He makes me lie down in green pastures, he leads me beside quiet waters, he restores my soul. He guides me in paths of righteousness for his name's sake. Even though I walk through the valley of the shadow of death, I will fear no evil, for you are with me; your rod and your staff, they comfort me."

Psalm 23: 1-4

"A carefully cultivated heart will, assisted by the grace of God, foresee, forestall, or transform most of the painful situations before which others stand like helpless children saying "Why?" Dallas Willard, *Renovation of the Heart*

PRAY: Oh Lord, You are indeed my shepherd and I thank You that You comfort me. This Psalm is like salve to my soul and I want to read it and say it as if it is brand new to me. Would You show me new and fresh, what this means and how You give me deep lasting comfort in my life because of Your promises. I want to fear no evil, even when walking through difficult times, but experience Your comfort instead. In Jesus name, Amen.

REFLECT: Have you ever read through Psalm 23 and prayed through each sentence, one at a time, in order to understand it in a new way? It's a powerful Psalm and the promise of God's comfort is rich and true. Could it be that God might mean "green pastures" to be laying in bed sick or with a broken bone, or stuck somewhere without your cell phone? Could walking "through the valley of the shadow of death" be a broken relationship, losing a job, or having no money to pay rent? See how relevant this Psalm is to your daily life. Notice how even a rod that pokes and a staff that guides can be used by God to give us comfort.

ACT: Psalm 23 is one of the most famous and powerful Psalms of the Bible. Memorize and meditate on it if you don't already know it. You can write it on an index card and carry it around with you as you memorize it. If you do know it then recite it out loud to someone else today to see how well you can say it. Having this Psalm in your heart and on the tip of your tongue will give you strength and comfort.

YOUR THOUGHTS:

DAY 3

SHOUT AND SING FOR JOY!

"Shout for joy, O heavens; rejoice, O earth; burst into song, O mountains! For the Lord comforts his people and will have compassion on his afflicted ones."

Isaiah 49:13

"My heart, which is so full to overflowing, has often been solaced and refreshed by music when sick and weary."

Martin Luther

PRAY: God, I want to shout for joy and rejoice by bursting into song, for You comfort me and all Your people. Thank you that You have compassion on all of us, especially Your afflicted ones, and You care about every single person whom You've created. I need comfort when I'm scared, stressed, confused or angry and You promise me that I can turn to You for comfort and You have compassion on me when I am afflicted. I praise You and shout for joy, oh Comforter! Amen.

REFLECT: Have you ever been so overwhelmed by God's love that you wanted to shout for joy? Can you imagine so much joy that the earth itself rejoices and the mountains burst into song? Now that's praise! If we fully understood that the Lord comforts His people and has compassion on us, then we too would shout for joy, rejoice and burst into song! Can you do that?

ACT: Go to a private place right now and shout out to the Lord with joy or burst into song for God. Express your love and praise to Him through music, song or even shouting, and see if you experience something new in the presence of the Lord. What you should feel is His comfort, His compassion, and His love. Shout with Joy to the Lord. Try it.

YOUR THOUGHTS:

DAY 4

WE COMFORT THOSE IN TROUBLE

"Praise be to the God and Father of our Lord Jesus Christ, the Father of compassion and the God of all comfort, who comforts us in all our troubles, so that we can comfort those in any trouble with the comfort we ourselves have received from God. For just as the sufferings of Christ flow over into our lives, so also through Christ our comfort overflows."

2 Corinthians 1:3-5

"We who lived in concentration camps can remember the men who walked through the huts comforting others, giving away their last piece of bread."   Viktor E. Frankl

PRAY: Praise be to You, God the Father of my Lord Jesus Christ, You the Father of compassion and the God of all comfort. Thank You that You comfort me in all my troubles and that You then let me comfort others who are in trouble, with the comfort that I've received from You. Lord, help me remember that though I share in your sufferings, I also receive Your abundant comfort whenever I need it, through Christ Jesus. Thank You for always being there for me. In Jesus name, Amen.

REFLECT: It's important to realize that God comforts us, not only for ourselves, but so that we can then turn around and comfort others. God gives us everything we need so we can be ministers of the Gospel to other people. Are there people around you who need comforting and you never thought that you could be the one to comfort them? God tells us that our comfort abounds through Christ. Have you fully understood that before? How will that change your response to those around you who are going through hard, stressful, scary or intense days? Reflect on how you can share all that Christ has given you.

ACT: Reach out to someone today who needs comforting and offer the compassion and comfort that God has so abundantly given to you. Show that friend or family member God's comfort through your actions and words. Even if you don't feel like it, remember that God has given you enough comfort to give it away. Let Christ's comfort overflow from you to someone you care about today!

YOUR THOUGHTS:

DAY 5

WE GET BEAUTY FOR ASHES

"The Spirit of the Sovereign Lord is on me, because the Lord has anointed me to preach good news to the poor. He has sent me to bind up the brokenhearted, to proclaim freedom for the captives and release from darkness for the prisoners, to proclaim the year of the Lord's favor and the day of vengeance of our God, to comfort all who mourn, and provide for those who grieve in Zion- to bestow on them a crown of beauty instead of ashes, the oil of gladness instead of mourning, and a garment of praise instead of a spirit of despair. They will be called oaks of righteousness, a planting of the Lord for the display of his splendor."

Isaiah 61:1-3

"Religion works. I know there's comfort there, a crash pad. It's something to explain the world and tell you there is something bigger than you, and it is going to be alright in the end. It works because it's comforting."

Brad Pitt

PRAY: Dear God, I want to experience Your Spirit upon me so that I can proclaim the good news to the poor, the captives and the broken hearted. I pray for the people in Hollywood who don't know You and proclaim freedom over them, in the name of Jesus. Please comfort all of who mourn and let them see Your splendor. Bestow on them a crown of beauty instead of ashes and a garment of praise instead of a spirit of despair. In Your righteous name, Amen.

REFLECT: Reflect on how God has given us the power to free the captives and comfort those who mourn. We are oaks of righteousness and we display His splendor! We can bring good news to those in our family, neighborhood, and even to those we don't know—even change the lives of media professionals by praying Isaiah 61:1-3 over them. Who can you pray for to receive a spirit of praise instead of despair? What captives can you set free?

ACT: Pray for one family member, one friend and one person in Hollywood who needs to be freed from some captivity, needs comfort or who is lost and needs Jesus. Spend 10 minutes right now praying for these three people—whether they are Christians or not, and ask the Lord to fill them with His Spirit, to comfort them and to bestow on them the oil of gladness instead of mourning, through the power of the Spirit in you!

YOUR THOUGHTS:

DAY 6

YOUR UNFAILING LOVE IS MY COMFORT

"My comfort in my suffering is this: Your promise preserves my life…May your unfailing love be my comfort, according to your promise to your servant."   Psalm 119:50 & 76

"If you're going through hell, keep going…This is no time for ease and comfort. It is time to dare and endure."   Winston Churchill

PRAY: Lord, thank You that You comfort me in my suffering and that Your promise preserves my life. Oh Lord, may Your unfailing love be my comfort, according to Your promise to me, Your servant. Amen.

REFLECT: Have you ever physically experienced God's comfort? Have you ever literally experienced God preserving your life? Can you imagine that His love is so deep for you and so consistently strong and steadfast that it will never fail to comfort you. And know that this is not just a thought, but it's a promise from the living God, to you, His servant.

ACT: Think about a time when you needed comfort. Did you feel it from God? If not, do you truly believe that He loves you so much that He promises to comfort you? Can you embrace His unconditional love right now, as a promise, that He will always be there for you, to comfort you? If not, then ask Him right now to reveal His love and comfort to you so that you will always know He's there and His promise is real.

YOUR **THOUGHTS:**

DAY 7

THE HOLY SPIRIT IS OUR COMFORTER

"But the Counselor, the Holy Spirit, whom the Father will send in my name, will teach you all things and will remind you of everything I have said to you. Peace I leave with you; my peace I give you. I do not give to you as the world gives. Do not let your hearts be troubled and do not be afraid."　　　　　　　　　　　　　　　　　　　John 14:26-27

"I think anytime in someone's faith journey, my faith journey also, you go through doubting... I think you kind of have to go through that, honestly, just to ask the tough questions... I mean, life is crazy, and to know that, honestly, a loving God is walking through it with me is very comforting for me." Tony Hale *(actor comedian Arrested Development)*

PRAY: Holy Spirit, You are my comforter. I'm so grateful that the Father has sent You to teach me and remind me of Your promises and to give me peace. Thank You that You do not give me shallow promises or a feeling of happiness, as the world gives, but You give me a deep peace in my soul, so that my heart is not troubled and I am not afraid. Oh Holy Spirit, fill me up with Your Divine comfort that stays deep down in my soul. Amen.

REFLECT: Reflect on the Holy Spirit. He is the most intangible of the Trinity, but He's our comforter! He teaches us all things, reminds us of God's promises, guides us and encourages us, and that's comforting. He also leaves His peace with us, not as a temporary feeling, as the world gives, but as an eternal presence that never goes away. Because of the Holy Spirit in you, you never have to let your heart be troubled and you never need to be afraid. Doesn't that give you great, lasting comfort?

ACT: Have a time of silence right now to focus on just the Holy Spirit – not God, the Father, or Jesus, the Son, but just on the Holy Spirit, the Counselor. Talk to Him, experience His presence, listen to Him, thank Him for being all of these things: your teacher, guide, advocate, consoler, intercessor, the revealer of truth and your comforter. Get to know the Holy Spirit much more intimately right now by spending time with Him, talking to Him, thanking Him, praising Him, listening to Him and feeling his peace. Your heart won't be troubled and you will not be afraid!

YOUR THOUGHTS:

FEAR

WEEK THIRTY-FIVE

Let's delve into a horribly destructive, yet common, emotion—
FEAR! It's never wise to make a decision out of fear, yet most of
us waste hours, days, even years of our lives, immobilized by fear.
So, let's break the spirit of fear this week, and seek the Lord for
deliverance, freedom and strength to push aside fear and be filled
with the power of joy, peace, and His unconditional love.

DAY 1

GOD IS OUR LIGHT AND OUR STRONGHOLD

"The Lord is my light and my salvation whom shall I fear? The Lord is the stronghold of my life— of whom shall I be afraid?"

Psalm 27:1

"Whether you like it or not, you're forced to come to the realization that death is out there. But I don't fear death, I'm a fatalist. I believe when it's your time, that's it. It's the hand you're dealt."

Clint Eastwood

PRAY: Dear Heavenly Father, I thank You that You are my light and my salvation. Thank You that because You are in my life that I have nothing to fear! Thank You that You are my stronghold and I can depend on You whenever I struggle with fear. Would Your Holy Spirit fill me up new and fresh every day so that I am not afraid? In Jesus' name, Amen.

REFLECT: What does it mean to say that God is our light and our salvation? Those are often "Christianese" terms that we say but don't really understand. What does it mean for Him to be a stronghold? Think of other strongholds in your life… they are all pretty powerful influences in our thoughts and choices. If God were your only stronghold, then would you ever be afraid?

ACT: Make a list of everything that you are afraid of and that is controlling you or pulling your focus away from the Lord. Is it a good stronghold or a bad one? Is it something that draws you toward God and the light or away from Him? Does it confirm and encourage your salvation? Pray over that list. Maybe it's time to make some changes…

YOUR THOUGHTS:

DAY 2

FEAR GOD AND BE WISE

"The fear of the Lord is the beginning of wisdom, and knowledge of the Holy One is understanding."   Proverbs 9:10

"There's two sorts of fear: one you embrace and one you should listen to and turn the other way."   Matthew McConaughey

PRAY: Lord, I want to have a healthy fear of You, an awe and respect that makes me wiser. I want to understand You, as Father, Son and Holy Spirit, so that I will be a wise Christian, not a fearful one. Please help me to understand how to have a wise, knowledgeable, and Christ-like fear of You that comes not from my own understanding, but from You, the Holy One. Amen.

REFLECT: It's confusing to think that we shouldn't be afraid, but that we should fear the Lord. Fearing our gracious God is a difficult concept to grasp, yet it's helpful to understand that the "fear of the Lord" is a healthy awe of God and His authority and power. He is our friend, and He is always with us, but He is also more powerful than we can ever understand, and therefore deserves our honor and respect. He loves us so much that we never have to "be afraid" of Him, but we do need to "fear" and revere Him.

ACT: Stop right now and pray—ask the Lord to give you wisdom. God tells us that we get wisdom by asking Him for it. If we want to have a deeper fear of the Lord and more understanding of Him, then we must gain wisdom and knowledge—and that comes only by asking! Stop right now and pray—ask the Lord to give you wisdom and knowledge. God tells us that we get both by asking Him.

YOUR THOUGHTS:

DAY 3

GOD IS OUR REFUGE AND STRENGTH

"God is our refuge and strength, an ever-present help in trouble. Therefore we will not fear, though the earth give way and the mountains fall into the heart of the sea, though its waters roar and foam and the mountains quake with their surging. Selah" Psalm 46:1-3

"I will not fear, for you are ever with me, and you will never leave me to face my perils alone."
                                                                    Thomas Merton

PRAY: Oh Lord, I know that You are my refuge and my strength, but I don't always feel that way. I know You are an ever-present help in times of trouble, but I forget that in the middle of adversity and depend on my own strength. Would You help me to keep my eyes on You so that I won't fear anything—from the earth giving way to any trouble that comes along? Amen.

REFLECT: What an awesome thought that we could actually go through life without experiencing any fear. That seems impossible and yet that's what He tells us. Do you consider God your refuge and your strength? Is He the first one you think of in times of trouble? How can you get to that place? Reading and memorizing scripture is usually the best way to have the Lord become the first thought on our minds.

ACT: Think of the times you've been in a scary situation— whether it be a natural disaster like an earthquake, a tornado, or a terrible storm; or if it was because of a bad person like a robbery, a murder, or a fight. How did you handle it? Were you fearful? What was your first thought? Commit to memorize Psalm 46:1-3 and you will find next time you're in trouble that scripture may be the first thought on your mind. How great would that be?!

YOUR THOUGHTS:

DAY 4

FEAR NOTHING AND NO ONE

"The chief priests and the teachers of the law heard this and began looking for a way to kill him, for they feared him, because the whole crowd was amazed at his teaching."
Mark 11:18

"Remembering that I'll be dead soon is the most important tool I've ever encountered to help me make the big choices in life. Because almost everything—all external expectations, all pride, all fear of embarrassment or failure—these things just fall away in the face of death, leaving only what is truly important."
Steve Jobs

PRAY: Dear God, remind me that people are afraid of You because You are SO powerful: You created the world, You teach radical ideas, You change people and You do miracles. Help me to remember that people killed You for being so life changing. Thank You for trusting me with the same truth that got You killed. Help me not to fear anything or anyone because I believe in You, the One who takes away all fear! Amen.

REFLECT: Are there people in your life who are afraid of God? Remember that Your God is scary to people because He is all-powerful, all-knowing, and omnipresent. Have you thought that you might be afraid of things you don't understand? Could you be afraid of someone whom you think is evil because that person is very powerful or influential? Many Christians are afraid of Hollywood and they hate the people there, due to their fear of the influence and power of the media. Hollywood is the world's most influential marketplace, so we often fear it. Jesus shows us that fear is so powerful it can get us to the point of wanting to kill! Don't be afraid of Hollywood. Be amazed at God's teaching!

ACT: Choose one Christian you know who hates Hollywood. Ask them if it could be out of fear. Fear makes us believe lies, and because Hollywood is the world's most influential industry, there are Christians who are very afraid of it. Their fear has made them hate a place that they should be praying for. Will you tell that one Christian the truth about the negative power of fear, and that this scripture tells us that nothing, and no one, is too bad for the Lord to redeem. They might just be amazed at your teaching!

YOUR THOUGHTS:

DAY 5

GOD WILL NEVER LEAVE YOU

"The Lord himself goes before you and will be with you; he will never leave you nor forsake you. Do not be afraid; do not be discouraged."   Deuteronomy 31:8

"Fear is faith in the Devil"   Bill Johnson

PRAY: Lord, will You help me to understand how You go before me. And please help me to truly believe that You will never leave me or forsake me. I don't want to be afraid or discouraged, but often times I feel alone or confused, and I don't know how to feel Your presence. Oh Lord, help me to not be afraid of the unknown or discouraged by what seems impossible. I pray in Jesus' Holy name, Amen.

REFLECT: How long has it been since you've been afraid of something or someone? When was the last time you were discouraged because a problem seemed insurmountable? When was the last time you actually felt God's presence in your life? Think about which emotions you feel more often: fear or peace, discouragement or comfort. Could fear be too much a part of your life?

ACT: Choose to face fear head on! Go to your best friend or spouse and ask them to hold you accountable so that every time you feel any level of fear you'll tell them and they'll pray for you or remind you that God is before you, behind you, and with you, that there is nothing to be afraid of and no reason to be discouraged. Let them remind you that He will never leave you or forsake you—ever! This will help both of you to put God above fear and His presence before discouragement.

YOUR THOUGHTS:

DAY 6

DO NOT BE AFRAID

"But even if you should suffer for what is right, you are blessed. "Do not fear what they fear; do not be frightened." But in your hearts set apart Christ as Lord. Always be prepared to give an answer to everyone who asks you to give the reason for the hope that you have. But do this with gentleness and respect, keeping a clear conscience, so that those who speak maliciously against your good behavior in Christ may be ashamed of their slander. It is better, if it is God's will, to suffer for doing good than for doing evil." 1 Peter 3:14-17

"My TV show had been cancelled; nothing else had gone anywhere; some alliances I had made petered out and nothing came of them and I was looking at a long, long year ahead of me in which there was no work on the horizon, the phone wasn't ringing. I had two kids, one of them a brand-new baby, and I didn't know if I would be able to keep my house."

Tom Hanks

PRAY: Dear Jesus, What a freeing thought that we have nothing to fear as Believers. Help me be bold in sharing my faith without any fear of what others may think. Please help me remember that I should always be prepared to speak to non-believers with gentleness, respect and a clear conscience, I don't have to be ashamed, no matter what unkind words are said to me. Thank You for the promise that I need not fear what anyone thinks of me! Amen.

REFLECT: Often the people around us influence how we think and act. Living in Hollywood, we are around a lot of people who are full of fear, insecurity, and shame. So, we have to choose to spend time with God so that He is a greater influence on us than our co-workers and industry friends. Are your friends having a greater influence on you than the Lord? Do you fear what they fear? How can you be "in the world but not of it?" How can you choose to live in freedom from fear even though people around you are living in fear?

ACT: Pray for the Christians who live and work in influential businesses like Hollywood. The people in the entertainment industry, or any position of power, shape our culture, but many of them don't know the Lord and are full of fear, and worse yet, have no hope. Your prayers will make an eternal difference and open the door for the Lord to come in and take away their fear. It is vital to live differently than those around us and pray for the people who are living in fear—especially those who are impacting our culture and us!

YOUR THOUGHTS:

DAY 7

GOD IS ALWAYS WITH YOU

"So do not fear, for I am with you; do not be dismayed, for I am your God. I will strengthen you and help you; I will uphold you with my righteous right hand."   Isaiah 41:10

"To win the war against fear, we must know the true God as He is revealed in the Bible. He works to give us lasting peace. He receives joy, not from condemning us but in rescuing us from the devil. Yes, the Lord will bring conviction to our hearts concerning sin, but it is so He can deliver us from sin's power and consequences. In its place, the Lord works to establish healing, forgiveness and peace.   Francis Frangipane

PRAY: Dear God, that is such a joyful passage from Isaiah. I thank You for strengthening me, helping me and holding me up. Thank You for the visual image of Your hand holding me up above troubles, sin and pain. I ask that this image never leaves me so that I won't fear, but always think of You walking with me in good times, and holding me up with Your righteous right hand in hard times. Amen.

REFLECT: Wow, God is with you right now. He's always with you. There's nowhere you can go that He is not there also. And He is giving you strength, protecting you, and taking care of you with His own hand. There is nothing to fear! Ponder this: The God of the universe, who knows all and created all, is with you right now and is holding you up with His righteous right hand. Can you feel Him?

ACT: Write this verse down on an index card, or a post-it note, and carry it with you today. Put it in a place where you will often look at it, so you are constantly reminded that God is with you every second of today, and there is nothing to be afraid of. Knowing that there is nowhere you can go without Him being with you should change how you act, what you say, and what you think about!

YOUR THOUGHTS:

We recommend listening to the song "Tremble" from the Mosaic worship team.

PERSEVERANCE

WEEK THIRTY-SIX

Life is hard and we need strength, wisdom, character, and hope to make it through and to end well. That takes perseverance. God talks a lot about perseverance and tells us how important it is and how to get it. This week, let's focus on strengthening our faith through building perseverance, so that we can run a good race.

DAY 1

REMAIN IN THE VINE TO BEAR FRUIT

"Remain in me, and I will remain in you. No branch can bear fruit by itself; it must remain in the vine. Neither can you bear fruit unless you remain in me."   John 15:4

"Becoming like Christ is a long, slow process of growth."   Rick Warren

PRAY: Lord, I start this week focusing on perseverance by asking You to remain in me always and forever. And I want to commit right now to You to remain in You always and forever. I understand that no branch can bear fruit by itself, so I need to persevere in my relationship with You and remain in the vine! Lord, I want to bear fruit, I want to become Christ-like, and I want to remain in You always. I pray this in Jesus' name, Amen.

REFLECT: Did you know that some synonyms for REMAIN are: exist, endure, last, abide, carry on, persist, stay, stay around, prevail, survive, live on. And synonyms for PERSEVERE are: persist, continue, carry on, go on, keep on, keep going, struggle on, hammer away, be persistent, be determined, see/follow something through, keep at it, press on/ahead, not take no for an answer, be tenacious, stand one's ground, stand fast/firm, hold on, go the distance, stay the course, plod on, stop at nothing, leave no stone unturned. They are practically the same! Do you see why Jesus tells us to remain in Him, as He also remains in us?! We must persevere in order to bear fruit. How do you remain in Jesus?

ACT: Choose one relationship or one circumstance where you want to flee, end it, or walk away. Have you prayed about what God would want you to do in that relationship or that circumstance? Why don't you remain in that situation and persevere until you get a clear understanding from God that it's time to leave, change, or shut that door? Right now, commit to "struggle on" or "hold on" and work that perseverance muscle until you know without a doubt what the next step is. Don't give up or walk away. Wait and persevere until the Lord guides your next step!

YOUR THOUGHTS:

Day 2

THE TESTING OF YOUR FAITH PRODUCES PERSEVERANCE

"Consider it pure joy, my brothers, whenever you face trials of many kinds, because you know that the testing of your faith develops perseverance. Perseverance must finish its work so that you may be mature and complete, not lacking anything... Blessed is the man who perseveres under trial, because when he has stood the test, he will receive the crown of life that God has promised to those who love him." James 1:2-4,12

"When you get into a tight place and everything goes against you, till it seems as though you could not hang on a minute longer, never give up then, for that is just the place and time that the tide will turn." Harriet Beecher Stowe

PRAY: Dear Jesus, I want to consider it pure joy to face trials, knowing that they are making me a better, stronger, more Christ-like person. I want perseverance to finish its work so that I can be more mature and complete, not lacking anything. I want to be blessed and You say that comes from persevering under trial. So, please help me to stand the test and receive the crown of life that You have promised. Amen and Amen.

REFLECT: Don't you love this verse? It's powerful, visual and empowering. And it promises more than we could actually even hope for or imagine. It's full of God's promises and it's life changing, if we can just do it. Who would have thought that we are supposed to consider it pure joy whenever we face trials? In our culture, we're encouraged to avoid trials! We need to take time to contemplate this counter-cultural concept, embrace it, and live it out. As you ponder it's full meaning, remember that those who persevere under trial will be blessed!

ACT: If we want to be joyful, mature, and complete and not lacking anything, we MUST learn to persevere. And the first step in persevering is to be joyful. We can't be joyful until we stop complaining. Commit right now to stop complaining about any difficult situation, relationship, or obstacle that you're going through. That will be a start to finding joy and persevering through any trials. You will be blessed!

YOUR THOUGHTS:

DAY 3

WATCH YOUR LIFE AND PERSEVERE

"Watch your life and doctrine closely. Persevere in them, because if you do, you will save both yourself and your hearers."
                                                    1 Timothy 4:16

"Our motto must continue to be perseverance. And ultimately I trust the Almighty will crown our efforts with success."
                                                    William Wilberforce

PRAY: Dear Jesus, I need Your help to both watch my life and watch what I believe. I need to persevere in both living a Christ-like life and in believing only what is from You, not what the Christian culture or the American culture tells me is true, because those are not always right. I also don't want to teach others wrong doctrine. So, would you help me to persevere in pursuing truth, both in action and in Your word? Thank You Jesus. Amen.

REFLECT: It's easy to get comfortable in our faith and our Christian walk and not stay sharp and clear with our choices, our beliefs, or our words. Paul warns us to watch our life and our doctrine closely, to persevere, and not get lazy about our faith, because if we don't keep persevering in our walk with the Lord, we will get off track and harm both others and ourselves. It's impossible to stay stagnant. We are either growing closer to the Lord or going farther from Him. Choose to keep your eyes on Jesus and never give up or surrender when it comes to walking and talking in the way you should go.

ACT: "Watch your life and doctrine closely." Now is the best time to evaluate how you're doing: Are you happy, satisfied, and proud of every part of your life? What might you want to change? Define the area and then ask God to help you to change. Then commit to persevere in doing everything you can to conquer that weak area. Remember you'll need the whole Trinity to overcome your defined area of weakness, and yet when you do, you will save yourself AND you "hearers", everyone else you influence in your daily life. That's worth persevering for.

YOUR THOUGHTS:

DAY 4

LOVE PERSEVERES

"I planted the seed, Apollos watered it, but God made it grow. So neither he who plants nor he who waters is anything, but only God, who makes things grow." 1 Corinthians 3:6-7

"Perseverance is failing 19 times and succeeding the 20th." Julie Andrews

PRAY: Lord, I thank You for reminding me that Love is the most powerful emotion of all and we are to delight in it – not in evil. We are to rejoice with the truth! Help me to remember to love all people, even those people I don't agree with or whom I feel are hurting others. Lord I ask to love the people in Hollywood who are creating all of our country's TV shows, films, music, video games and news. I want to delight in loving them and rejoicing in the truth that You love them as well. Lord would you protect them, and may they trust You, find hope in You, and persevere. And please help me to do that so that I can love others more powerfully and more deeply. Amen.

REFLECT: Did you ever think that when you choose love and persevere in your choice, that both parties benefit. When you pray for the people in Hollywood, you will delight in the truth and so will they. You will be protected and so will they. You will trust God more deeply, experience a hope that will not disappoint you, and be able to persevere in all you do. And so will they. And it all starts from choosing to love people you don't understand, don't agree with, or just don't like. You will be a different, more Christ-like person by persevering in your love for others.

ACT: Choose two people from Hollywood whom you don't really like and choose right now to love them. You don't have to like what they do or how they act, just choose to love them as fellow human beings whom God has specifically created because He loves them so much. Then persevere in that love; keep praying for them, never say anything but nice things about them, and bless them. You watch, for not only are you changing them, but also you will change. And you know if you pray for someone, you can't hate them!

YOUR THOUGHTS:

DAY 5

SUFFERING PRODUCES PERSEVERANCE

"Not only so, but we also rejoice in our sufferings, because we know that suffering produces perseverance; perseverance, character; and character, hope. And hope does not disappoint us, because God has poured out his love into our hearts by the Holy Spirit, whom he has given us."

Romans 5:3-5

"Permanence, perseverance, and persistence in spite of all obstacles, discouragements, and impossibilities: It is this, that in all things distinguishes the strong soul from the weak."

Thomas Carlyle

PRAY: Father, Son and Holy Spirit, I turn to the Trinity today to seek the strength and wisdom to understand that I can find joy, and experience glory, in my sufferings. Paul says that I must embrace my sufferings because they produce perseverance, which produces character, which gives me hope and that hope I get through suffering will not disappoint me. I know it's true, but I can't do it on my own. Change me and help me embrace my sufferings, so that I may persevere, gain character, and be full of hope. Amen and Amen.

REFLECT: How do you handle your sufferings? Do you complain, feel hopeless, afraid, or angry? I learned years ago to thank God in my sufferings, my heartbreaks, and even the jobs I lost! We can thank Him because we don't know how He's protecting us or guiding us to something better that wouldn't have happened without suffering. And through that, you will start to see that you have gained perseverance, you'll have a stronger Christ-like character and He will give you a hope in your future. God is in control and working out your circumstances for your benefit. This one verse, when lived out, will NOT disappoint you.

ACT: Make a list of your "sufferings"—anything you're struggling with or disappointed in, including your hurts, pains, and sorrows. Take that list and thank God for protecting you from something worse, or allowing them to happen so that you can grow stronger. Thank Him for loving you so much that He's walking through it all with you, holding you up, and giving you strength. Thank Him for building your perseverance and giving you a hope you didn't have before that will not disappoint, and a perseverance to carry you through your life.

YOUR THOUGHTS:

DAY 6

LET US RUN WITH PERSEVERANCE

"Therefore, since we are surrounded by such a great cloud of witnesses, let us throw off everything that hinders and the sin that so easily entangles, and let us run with perseverance the race marked out for us. Let us fix our eyes on Jesus, the author and perfecter of our faith, who for the joy set before him endured the cross, scorning its shame, and sat down at the right hand of the throne of God." Hebrews 12:1-2

"When I was about five, I gave my heart to Jesus Christ, and since then it's just been a stronghold in my life. Really, through the shark attack and all the hard times that my family and I went through, it gave us unity and perseverance to push through all this crazy stuff that we never knew was going to happen." Bethany Hamilton

PRAY: God, as Christians, we are all being watched. People know that we are different, and they are intrigued with who we are and what we do. I want to be a great witness with my faith. So, please help me to throw off everything that hinders me, and my sin, which so easily entangles me. I want to run with perseverance the race marked out for me. But I need Your help to keep my eyes fixed on Jesus and fill me with perseverance! Amen.

REFLECT: We must remember we are responsible to live out our faith without sin. People are watching. What does it take to run a good race, to keep our eyes on Jesus, and to do it with perseverance? We can't just assume that since we're Christians we have our act together or we are good witnesses. It takes commitment, hard work, and dependence on Jesus, the pioneer and perfecter of faith. What is hindering your Christian witness to others?

ACT: Think about the people whom you are around each day. The people at work, your neighbors, your family members, your friends and the people at the stores you frequent. Do they know you're a Christian? If so, are you a good witness? If not, what do you need to change that is hindering you? What sin is affecting your life? What do you need to do to run a good race, with perseverance? Ask God right now to reveal that to you so that you can make changes in your life that will not only make you run a better race, but will be noticed by the great cloud of witnesses around you. Do whatever it takes to keep your eyes on Jesus.

YOUR THOUGHTS:

Day 7

ADD PERSEVERANCE TO YOUR FAITH

"For this very reason, make every effort to add to your faith goodness; and to goodness, knowledge; and to knowledge, self-control; and to self-control, perseverance; and to perseverance, godliness; and to godliness, brotherly kindness; and to brotherly kindness, love. For if you possess these qualities in increasing measure, they will keep you from being ineffective and unproductive in your knowledge of our Lord Jesus Christ. But if anyone does not have them, he is nearsighted and blind, and has forgotten that he has been cleansed from his past sins."
                                                                2 Peter 1:5-9

"Life is not easy for any of us. But what of that? We must have perseverance and above all confidence in ourselves. We must believe that we are gifted for something and that this thing must be attained."
                                                                Marie Curie

PRAY: God my Father, what do I need to get more faith, goodness, knowledge, self-control, perseverance, godliness, affection, and love? I need You so that I won't be ineffective and unproductive in my knowledge of Jesus. I never want to forget that I have been cleansed from my past sins because of You. Help me to persevere so that I can possess these qualities in increasing measure and be cleansed from past sins! Amen.

REFLECT: Perseverance is presented in the Bible in many different contexts. We need to persevere in witnessing to others; we need to persevere in trials and in suffering; we need to persevere because a cloud of witnesses is watching us. Even our love has to persevere. Here in 2 Peter we're told that self-control leads to perseverance and perseverance leads to godliness. There are so many other references in both the Old and New Testaments, that perseverance must be PARTICULARLY important to God. Would you describe yourself as someone who perseveres? If not, what might you do about that?

ACT: Since perseverance is so important to God, take another week to study all the other biblical references for perseverance. It's worth the additional study. After reading all of the scriptures and asking God for insight and wisdom, you'll surely be more persevering, and it will become more natural to "remain in Him." It will be worth it!

YOUR THOUGHTS:

ANXIETY & WORRY

WEEK THIRTY-SEVEN

This week we're facing one of the most powerful and debilitating emotions that we experience: ANXIETY/WORRY. God tells us over and over again in His Word that we are not to worry, we're not to feel anxious, and yet we struggle with it every day. If we could truly trust God to give us wisdom, guide us in our thoughts and conversations, and have the faith to let Him take care of the details of our life, we would feel freedom and joy, despite our circumstances. Let's try to master a sense of peace by giving our anxiety and worry to Him this week!

DAY 1

GIVE YOUR ANXIETY TO HIM!

"Cast all your anxiety on him because he cares for you."   1 Peter 5:7

"An unpeaceful mind cannot operate normally. Hence the Apostle teaches us to 'have no anxiety about anything.' Deliver all anxious thoughts to God as soon as they arise. Let the peace of God maintain your heart and mind."   Watchman Nee

PRAY: Lord, would You fill me with Your peace and take away all of my anxiety? I know that You love me and don't want me to worry, but I need Your help to control my emotions and to trust completely in You. Thank You that You care so deeply for me and let me rest in Your arms. In Jesus' name, Amen.

REFLECT: Do you really believe that God truly and deeply cares for you? How does He show His care, His love, His concern? Are you aware of the little things that He does to encourage you, guide you, care for you? What does that feel like? How are you caring for others? Could it be that as we care for others we will feel more of God's love and care for us?

ACT: Try reaching out to someone today whom you know and show them in some way that you care. Then ask God to let you see the ways that He cares for you. If you know someone in the media or creative entertainment industry, they probably need to know that someone cares, and especially that God cares. We are all emotionally needy and when we reach out to others we truly feel less anxiety and more loved ourselves.

YOUR THOUGHTS:

DAY 2

DON'T WORRY ABOUT TOMORROW!

"Therefore do not worry about tomorrow, for tomorrow will worry about itself. Each day has enough trouble of its own."   Matthew 6:34

"Worrying always results in sin. We tend to think that a little anxiety and worry are simply an indication of how wise we really are, yet it is actually a much better indication of just how wicked we are. Fretting rises from our determination to have our own way. Our Lord never worried and was never anxious, because His purpose was never to accomplish His own plans but to fulfill God's plans. Fretting is wickedness for a child of God."   Oswald Chambers

PRAY: Dear Lord, You tell me not to worry and yet I keep doing it. Thank You for reminding me that each day will have its own troubles, that I can expect hard times, but I still don't have to worry. I need You every moment of every day to help me and change me so that I can replace worry with joy and peace. Please change my heart and my thoughts so that I will not worry about tomorrow, but only focus on today and Your provision for me. Amen.

REFLECT: What good does it do to worry about tomorrow – or to worry about anything, for that matter? Why do we keep worrying when God tells us over and over that we don't have to? There has to be some way that God can change our thoughts so that we can plan for tomorrow but not worry about it. What could that possibly be?

ACT: God tells us to live our lives today without worrying about tomorrow, but He doesn't mean that we shouldn't plan for tomorrow. So, we don't necessarily have to change our actions, only our thoughts. Worry is a state of mind that comes from a lack of trust or faith in God. What is one thing you worry most about that you can control by finding a verse that counters that worry? Go find it, memorize it, and bring it to mind each time you start to worry!

YOUR THOUGHTS:

DAY 3

DON'T BE ANXIOUS – SEEK HIM!

"And do not set your heart on what you will eat or drink; do not worry about it. For the pagan world runs after all such things, and your Father knows that you need them. But seek his kingdom, and these things will be given to you as well."   Luke 12:29-31

"If you ask what is the single most important key to longevity, I would have to say it is avoiding worry, stress and tension. And if you didn't ask me, I'd still have to say it."

George F. Burns

PRAY: Lord, don't let me focus on the things of this world when I could be seeking Your kingdom and all the things that You have for me. Please help me to stop worrying about money, my health, and the material things in my life. I don't want to be like the world. I want to trust you to supply all that I need. Thank You that You will supply everything that I need. Amen.

REFLECT: When you think of Hollywood, what do you think of? A pagan city? Creative TV shows, great music, and powerful films, or rich celebrities who stand for things you disagree with, compromising programming, and a city lacking God? Christians often focus on Godly thoughts in their own life, but they focus on the things of this world when it comes to our media and entertainment. Can you see loving, creative children of God in Hollywood? Can you imagine people of integrity offering creative stories to the world? Would you trust God that He is in Hollywood, supplying the people who impact our culture with everything that they need? Can you stop worrying about Hollywood?

ACT: Commit to focusing on the things of God, both in your own life and in the lives of others. Seek His kingdom. If God can give you everything that you need, then He is doing the same in the parts of the world that are pagan to you. As you set your heart, not on the things of this world, will you pray that the people in Hollywood will also not set their hearts on the things of this world, but on the God of the universe who knows what they need and wants to give it to them?

YOUR THOUGHTS:

DAY 4

HAVE CONFIDENCE IN HIM!

"But blessed is the man who trusts in the Lord, whose confidence is in him. He will be like a tree planted by the water that sends out its roots by the stream. It does not fear when heat comes; its leaves are always green. It has no worries in a year of drought and never fails to bear fruit."   Jeremiah 17:7-8

"Have you been propping up that foolish soul of yours with the idea that your circumstances are too much for God to handle?"   Oswald Chambers

PRAY: Dear Heavenly Father, I want to be blessed! I want to have more confidence in You. Please help me to be like a tree planted by the water. Show me what I need to do to have no worries in hard times and to always be bearing fruit. Change my thoughts so that I can trust fully in You and not have anxious thoughts. In Jesus' name, Amen.

REFLECT: Think about a beautiful tree in your neighborhood, or one that you've seen, and its beauty, perfection, or lush growth that has caught your breath. How can you be like that tree, even in hard times, dry seasons, or through a storm? Can you imagine having deep spiritual roots that are always fed by God's word and rich fruit that comes from your faith?

ACT: If you are going through a hard time right now, what can you do to shift your thoughts and actions so that you can continue to bear fruit, no matter how difficult your life situation is? How can you act in faith and not react to your circumstances, so that you break the cycle of anxiety and worry and start flourishing, despite your current struggles or hardships? Make a choice to break the cycle today by turning to God for guidance and strength. Put your confidence in Him and you will be blessed.

YOUR THOUGHTS:

DAY 5

GOD WILL TAKE CARE OF YOU!

"Therefore I tell you, do not worry about your life, what you will eat or drink; or about your body, what you will wear. Is not life more important than food, and the body more important than clothes? Look at the birds of the air; they do not sow or reap or store away in barns, and yet your heavenly Father feeds them. Are you not much more valuable than they? Who of you by worrying can add a single hour to his life?"　　　Matthew 6:25-27

"I am no longer anxious about anything, as I realize the Lord is able to carry out His will, and His will is mine. It makes no matter where He places me, or how. That is rather for Him to consider than for me; for in the easiest positions He must give me His grace, and in the most difficult, His grace is sufficient."

Hudson Taylor

PRAY: Dear God, I need help with my worry. I can't shake the fear of having no money, being in bad health, or losing close relationships. Can you please reveal to me today how to overcome my worry by truly embracing the truth that You are taking care of me? You are the one who supplies my daily needs, and I am wasting time by worrying about what You are already taking care of. Thank You that I am more valuable than the birds of the air! Amen.

REFLECT: Imagine being a bird who wakes up in the morning, flies to the ground to find breakfast, then spends the day flying through the beautiful sky with his/her family and friends. That bird has no worries, no obligations, no bills, no job to find. God tells us that even in our world we can feel that free. Can you imagine letting go of all of the heaviness that comes from obligations, bills, and responsibilities, and allowing yourself to feel free, despite your circumstances? God tells us that's possible.

ACT: Commit right now to stop your brain from thinking about anything that questions God's provision and His promises to take care of you. Find a way to train your brain to break old habits of worry and concern. You'll know what works for you, but don't allow the same patterns of question and worry to control your life. Today is the day to get your brain to find peace in God's care for you. You are SO valuable in His eyes and He doesn't want you to waste your life by worrying.

YOUR THOUGHTS:

DAY 6

THE HOLY SPIRIT IS WITH YOU!

"When you are brought before synagogues, rulers and authorities, do not worry about how you will defend yourselves or what you will say, for the Holy Spirit will teach you at that time what you should say." Luke 12:11-12

"Worry is a thin stream of fear trickling through the mind. If encouraged, it cuts a channel into which all other thoughts are drained." Arthur Somers Roche

PRAY: Dear Jesus, thank You that You are my defender. And thank You, Holy Spirit, for giving me the words to say when I stand before Kings—or my boss, or an angry neighbor—and try to talk about my faith. I want You to teach me to have complete confidence in You so that You will give me the words to say, and the steps to take, to clearly express my faith. If I can fully trust in You to guide me and give me all that I need in every circumstance, then I will not feel worried about any conversation I will have about You. Thank you, Jesus! Amen.

REFLECT: When was the last time you had to talk about Jesus or defend your faith in front of other people? Was it a private conversation or did you give your testimony in front of a crowd? How did you handle it? Were you worried? Can you say that God gave you the words or directed your thoughts? Do you feel that He prepared the listener to hear the truth? What would you do differently? How would you prepare to be even more effective next time? Or if you've never talked about your faith with someone, why not?

ACT: One of the greatest fears of the Christian faith is to tell others about Jesus. And yet it's a command. We are not to force Jesus on anyone, but we are to be prepared to give an account for the faith that we have within us. Pray for the Lord to bring someone into your life whom you can talk to about Jesus. And then ask the Holy Spirit to give you the words, and help you not to back down or stay silent out of fear. He will prepare you to stand before Kings if you ask Him. And then you can be a part of His work to reach everyone with the truth of His gospel.

YOUR THOUGHTS:

DAY 7

DON'T BE ANXIOUS – BRING GOOD CHEER!

"An anxious heart weighs a man down, but a kind word cheers him up." Proverbs 12:25

"Why worry? If you've done the very best you can, worrying won't make it any better."

Walt Disney

PRAY: Dear Father, thank You so much for the gift of words that can change lives and circumstances. Thank You that when I feel anxious You can send someone to me to cheer me up. Would you please use me to cheer up others with a kind word, so that I can be a part of helping them to feel less anxious? I don't want a heavy heart, and I don't want the people I love to have heavy hearts. Please guide my tongue and not let me be weighed down by anxiety. Amen.

REFLECT: Think about when someone changed your whole day by saying something kind to you. Do you know any people around you who have the gift of encouragement? Are you someone who lifts up others through your words? Reflect on ways you can lessen your anxiety, or others', by speaking words of kindness, truth, and joy to people around you, and to yourself.

ACT: Watch your words today and see if you can encourage a family member, a co-worker, or a close friend. We all feel anxious, and you could relieve the anxiety in others by going out of your way to say something encouraging and uplifting to them. And if you are feeling anxious today, don't spend time with people who are negative or complain, for that will heighten your anxiety. Use your words carefully, but be generous with kindness, and your kind words will cheer others up.

YOUR THOUGHTS:

FELLOWSHIP

WEEK THIRTY-EIGHT

Fellowship is not just being a part of a great group of loving friends; it's experiencing the grace of God, the love of Jesus, the intimacy of the Holy Spirit, and being a part of others' salvation. This week we focus on the extraordinary power of living in fellowship with God and with others and how it can change our lives and the lives of people all around us.

DAY 1

FELLOWSHIP WITH GOD

"Sacrifice fellowship offerings there, eating them and rejoicing in the presence of the Lord your God.
                                                            Deuteronomy 27:7

"We proclaim to you what we have seen and heard, so that you also may have fellowship with us. And our fellowship is with the Father and with his Son, Jesus Christ." 1 John 1:3

"You were put on this earth to have fellowship with the living God."   Judy Harrell

PRAY: Greetings Lord, I come today to seek more intimate fellowship with You. I want to offer you a Fellowship offering, knowing that You are offering me fellowship with You as my Father and with Your Son. Help me to spend more time with You, to be more open with You and to talk to You more. I want to also be in fellowship with You corporately, along with other Christians, so that together we can proclaim to You what we have seen and heard You doing and saying in our lives. Oh, may I feel Your presence in my life, every day! Amen and Amen.

REFLECT: Have you ever thought about why the Israelites sacrificed fellowship offerings to the Lord? We don't have to sacrifice through offerings anymore, but we do need to embrace God's priorities because they are always for our good. And fellowship with the Father, and with the Son, is an incredibly important priority to God. So, in what ways can you make it more important in your life?

ACT: Fellowship, as defined in the dictionary, includes eating together, spending time together, building relationships, and depending on one another during both good and bad times. To develop better fellowship with God, start now to bring Him into all your thoughts, your words, your actions, and your activities. Our goal is to be in 24/7 Fellowship with the God of the Universe! Start NOW!

YOUR THOUGHTS:

DAY 2

INTIMATE FELLOWSHIP

"Then the Israelites, all the people, went up to Bethel, and there they sat weeping before the LORD. They fasted that day until evening and presented burnt offerings and fellowship offerings to the LORD."   Judges 20:26

"It goes against the grain to give an image of oneself that is anything less than perfect, and many Christians imagine that they will be rejected by others if they admit to any faults. But nothing could be more destructive to Christian koinonia (fellowship) than the common practice today of pretending not to have any problems."   Ray C. Stedman

PRAY: Dear Father in Heaven, I thank You for giving us friends and family to live life with. I realize that I need fellowship in order to feel loved, to gain perspective and wisdom on issues in life, and to experience compassion and camaraderie as I laugh, cry, hurt and sing together in community. Please show me how I can be better in fellowship with others, who I should fast with, and how we can be more unified as the body of Christ. Amen.

REFLECT: In reading this verse, it shows the vulnerability of the Israelites as they sat weeping and fasting together before the Lord. Notice how they got through difficult times together. They didn't face life's struggles alone, but they had corporate praise and worship. Do you have healthy fellowship with your friends, family, work associates, and neighbors? Do you walk through life in fellowship? Do you spend intimate corporate times with God? If not, what do you need to do to create the fellowship that God intends for all of us?

ACT: Think about the times in your life that you got through because you could cry with others, fast with others, or just come before God with other people. Are you vulnerable enough to share your life in fellowship with others? If so, praise God for that and choose to intentionally spend more time in intimate fellowship with other believers. If not, take steps to open up more with the people you trust whom God has put in your life so that you can create richer, deeper fellowship with others and more times of vulnerable fasting, prayer and sacrifice in community.

YOUR THOUGHTS:

DAY 3

FELLOWSHIP WITH OTHERS

"How good and pleasant it is when brothers live together in unity!"   Psalm 133:1

"If a house is divided against itself, that house cannot stand."   Mark 3:25

"Our love to God is measured by our everyday fellowship with others and the love it displays."
Andrew Murray

PRAY: Jesus, it is so hard to live in unity. It's so hard to live in peaceful loving fellowship. I can't possibly do it without You. Would You help me to love the people around me, so that I am never the one to cause division, but to be the one who brings people together, with wisdom and peace? I know the difference between good and pleasant unity and a house that is so divided it cannot stand. May my house with my family and fellowship with my Christian friends never be divided. Let me be good and pleasant and always live in unity. Thank You for giving me what I need to live in loving fellowship. Amen.

REFLECT: God warns us all through the Bible, how we will suffer when we don't live in fellowship with Him or with other people. And just as often, He tells us how He will bless us when we love one another and live in peace and unity. So, why can't we do that? What is your part in living in unity and not division? Are you consciously helping to bring unity and love into your home and your community? Or could you possibly be the cause of a divided home?

ACT: Right now think of one person in your life whom you are not in good fellowship with. Regardless of whether it is your fault or theirs, choose to take a step toward peace and even reconciliation. Take an active step in order to live in unity and not be divided. Remember that a house divided cannot stand. Choose to step outside of your comfort zone in order to experience how good and pleasant it is when God's people live in unity.

YOUR THOUGHTS:

DAY 4

FELLOWSHIP OF THE HOLY SPIRIT

"May the grace of the Lord Jesus Christ, and the love of God, and the fellowship of the Holy Spirit be with you all." 2 Corinthians 13:14

"A habit of devout fellowship with God is the spring of all our life, and the strength of it."
Henry Edward Manning

PRAY: Loving Father, I love this prayer from 2 Corinthians that clearly defines the work of the Trinity in our lives. I see that true fellowship comes from God the Father, the Son, and the Holy Spirit all working together in our lives. I pray this prayer for people all over the world. Today I pray this prayer for the people in Hollywood. May you bring them to You and bring them together as a loving community, through the grace of Jesus, the love of God, and the fellowship of the Holy Spirit. I pray this in Your name. Selah, Amen.

REFLECT: Oswald Chambers said "Prayer is not preparation for the greater work, Prayer is the greater work." Reflect on how you could change the world by praying this prayer of grace, love, and fellowship over the people in Hollywood who are creating our culture. If they experience the grace of Jesus, the love of God, and the fellowship of the Holy Spirit, they will live changed lives. Asking the Holy Spirit to touch people, and inviting the Trinity into people's lives, makes an eternal difference. Do you believe you can change the world by praying this prayer over others?

ACT: Write down three names of decision-makers or celebrities in Hollywood and then say out loud this prayer of 2 Corinthians 13:14. Would you commit to saying this prayer over those three people every day for the rest of the week? Know that as you pray for the Trinity to come upon them with grace, love, and fellowship, you are changing their lives forever!

YOUR THOUGHTS:

DAY 5

FELLOWSHIP FOR ACCOUNTABILITY

"Now we ask you, brothers, to respect those who work hard among you, who are over you in the Lord and who admonish you."   1 Thessalonians 5:12

"Our love to God is measured by our everyday fellowship with others and the love it displays."
Andrew Murray

PRAY: Dear Jesus, You have set up the perfect plan as you tell us to live in fellowship with one another. Thank You that You do it not only to supply love and comfort for us, but You supply accountability through fellowship as well. Help me to live in unity with others so that I will not be idle or disruptive, but that I would allow others to admonish me, if needed. Also, help me to acknowledge those who work hard, to hold people in the highest regard in love, to help the weak, be patient with everyone, and make sure that I don't pay back wrong for wrong. And help me to always do what is good for others. I need to live in peace with others so that we will all experience beautiful, Christ-centered fellowship. I pray this in your name, Jesus. Amen.

REFLECT: Did you ever consider that God has put us in fellowship with others so that we will hold one another accountable? And did you realize that it goes both directions? We are told to hold others accountable for their wrongs, sins, and mistakes, but we also are to allow others to hold us accountable as well. Are you willing to do that? Do you see that happening in your personal relationships in your family and in your community?

ACT: In order to truly live in fellowship, choose today to be extra patient with one person in your life who frustrates you, annoys you, treats you unkindly, or outright drives you crazy. Practice godly fellowship by being visibly patient with that person. And not because they deserve it, but because God tells you to "always strive to do what is good for each other and for everyone else." You'll be glad you did!

YOUR THOUGHTS:

DAY 6

FELLOWSHIP FOR SPIRITUAL GROWTH

"As iron sharpens iron, so one man sharpens another."　　　　Proverbs 27:17

"The fellowship of true friends who can hear you out, share your joys, help carry your burdens, and correctly counsel you is priceless."　　　　Ezra Taft Benson

PRAY: Oh, God, this verse is hard for me. Iron sharpening iron is uncomfortable, it hurts, and it's extremely intimate. I understand this concept in theory, but I'm crying out to You now to show me how to live this out in reality—both by being willing to sharpen a fellow believer and by allowing other believers to sharpen me. In seeking true, godly fellowship I have to learn to do this and I need You desperately. Please make me a sharpened sword. Amen and Amen.

REFLECT: Have you ever thought of this verse in light of Fellowship? After reading it a few times, you will find that in order to allow two Christians to "sharpen" one another, you must know each other, trust each other, and be close enough to allow each other to speak the truth, in love. That's true fellowship and in time it will also make you both more Christ-like. That seems worth pursuing.

ACT: Start practicing true fellowship by choosing a close friend to approach with the challenge to purposely allow you both to sharpen one another spiritually. Have a conversation about how that would look, practically speaking, and then set out to become two sharpened swords. You could do that through honest conversations, through committed prayer, or both. Choose to pursue this challenging fellowship with another believer in Jesus, today.

YOUR THOUGHTS:

DAY 7

FELLOWSHIP FOR SALVATION

"They devoted themselves to the apostles' teaching and to the fellowship, to the breaking of bread and to prayer... Every day they continued to meet together in the temple courts. They broke bread in their homes and ate together with glad and sincere hearts, praising God and enjoying the favor of all the people. And the Lord added to their number daily those who were being saved."   Acts2: 42, 46-47

"When a Christian shuns fellowship with other Christians, the devil smiles. When he stops studying the Bible, the devil laughs. When he stops praying, the devil shouts for joy."

Corrie Ten Boom

PRAY: Father God, I want to devote myself to others and be a good witness so that I can lead others to You. I want to invite people over to my home, break bread with them and love others with a glad and sincere heart. Help me to praise You and enjoy the people around me so that pre-Christians will notice the fruit in my life and want that for themselves. Lord may my life of healthy fellowship daily add to the number of those who are being saved. Amen.

REFLECT: God has humans on this earth for one reason: Relationship. Our whole goal is to build our relationship with Him and then to build Christ-like relationships with other people. That's it. This verse is one of many in the scriptures where God tells us we will watch people being saved, not by convincing them to believe in Jesus, but by living a Christ-like life of relationships, with gladness and praise to God, and in fellowship and love with other people. It's not up to us to change others, it's up to us to love God and love people. Then other people will get saved. Reflect on this: if we do that, the Lord will add to our number daily those who are being saved.

ACT: As the last day of this week focuses on Fellowship, would you commit to the Lord to change your life priorities so that #1 is to LOVE HIM and #2 is to LOVE OTHERS. Living out these two goals will not only give you deep, loving relationships with others in beautiful fellowship, but it will bring others to commit their lives to Jesus and change the world!

YOUR THOUGHTS:

SORROW

WEEK THIRTY-NINE

The topic of sorrow is complex, real, and not pleasant. The Lord knows when we feel sorrow, and He promises us that He is walking through it with us, He is compassionate, loving, and He even turns it into joy and dancing! Let's all embrace sorrow this week, with trust and faith in the Lord.

DAY 1

HOW LONG, LORD?

"My eyes grow weak with sorrow; they fail because of all my foes....How long must I wrestle with my thoughts and every day have sorrow in my heart? How long will my enemy triumph over me?"
Psalm 6:7; 13:2

"As a saint of God, my attitude toward sorrow and difficulty should not be to ask that they be prevented, but to ask that God protect me so that I may remain what He created me to be, in spite of all my fires of sorrow."
Oswald Chambers

PRAY: Dear heavenly Father, my eyes grow weak with sorrow, and I feel that I'm failing in all that is coming against me. I'm not handling the stresses and discouragements in my life well, and I wonder how long must I wrestle with my thoughts and with all of the sorrow in my heart? Oh dear Father, how long will the enemy triumph over me? I need to overcome and I don't know how to do that on my own! I need You, God, to take away my sorrow and to triumph over the enemy. Help me, oh God. Thank You! In Jesus' name, Amen.

REFLECT: Reflect on the sorrow in your heart and how much it's inhibiting you from living an abundant life. Are you growing weak with sorrow? Are you unable to enjoy the Lord and others because the enemy is triumphing in crippling you? Are you asking the Lord to help you break through the bondage of sorrow? Maybe this is the day to wrestle with your thoughts in order to triumph over it. We can't fully embrace the life that the Lord has for us if we are full of sorrow. What would be the first step to break through and be free of the heaviness of sorrow in your heart?

ACT: This is the week to deal with any hindering sorrow that may be crippling you or preventing you from living the life that the Lord has for you. Right now, if you find that you are heavy with sorrow, would you get on your knees and ask the Lord to replace that sorrow with the joy of His Holy Spirit? Only He can reveal to you the cause of the sorrow and only He can replace it with Divine joy! We all need Him desperately, and that's right where He wants us. So, boldly go to the Lord right now and tell Him you're ready to let it go and no longer let the enemy triumph. This is the moment to start a new, beautiful season in your life.

YOUR THOUGHTS:

DAY 2

GOD IS OUR COMFORTER

"My soul is weary with sorrow; strengthen me according to your word." Psalm 119:28

"O my Comforter in sorrow, my heart is faint within me." Jeremiah 8:18

"Here bring your wounded hearts, here tell your anguish; Earth has no sorrow that Heaven cannot heal." Thomas Moore

PRAY: Jesus, my soul is weary with sorrow. Would you strengthen me according to Your Word and be my Comforter in my sorrow? Since I committed yesterday to break through the sorrow I've been feeling, I want Your word and Your Holy Spirit to lift my sorrow and give me strength so that my heart will not faint within me. This is my time to break through the sorrow and I thank You for your Word and that You are my Comforter. With You, my heart will not faint within me. Amen and Amen.

REFLECT: The Lord promises to strengthen us, according to His words in the Bible. He tells us that He is our Comforter in sorrow, even when our heart is faint within us. His promises are AMAZING. He knows that we feel sadness and sorrow in our lives, and so He addresses it head on and tells us He knows our pain, and He has a plan to get us out of it. What an incredible Creator God to not only allow us to experience sorrow but to promise us that it's not forever and there is hope for comfort and relief. Let that make your heart strong and full.

ACT: Now is the time to focus on asking the Lord to strengthen you, not to focus on your sorrow. Ask Him right now to push through whatever is making you faint of heart and to replace the sorrow with His divine, supernatural joy and peace. He will answer your prayer and you will begin to be comforted and not burdened! Praise God for His faithfulness.

YOUR THOUGHTS:

DAY 3

MY SOUL IS OVERWHELMED

"Then he said to them, "My soul is overwhelmed with sorrow to the point of death. Stay here and keep watch with me."   Matthew 26:38

"Jesus feels my sorrow greater than I, for His love is infinite, and He suffers in an infinite way."
                     Mother Angelica

PRAY: Jesus, this verse helps me to understand that when You were in a season of deep sorrow, You needed Your friends to help You get through the darkness. You called out to Your disciples and asked them to stay with You and keep watch. You couldn't go through it alone. Help me to swallow my pride or my embarrassment when I'm overwhelmed with sorrow so I can reach out to the people around me who can hold me up and love me through the valley of the shadow of death. Thank You for helping me to understand this truth. Amen.

REFLECT: Jesus is our only true role model and yet it seems so much of what He did was the opposite of our human instincts. We tend to back off from others when we're sad and yet Jesus reached out and asked for their help and support. He also was vulnerable enough to say that His soul was overwhelmed with sorrow, to the point of death. Can you embrace your sorrow and be open about it to the people closest to you? Can you ask for help in vulnerable times to "stay here and keep watch with me"?

ACT: Right now, would you commit to having a conversation with your closest friend or family member and tell them about any of the dark times you have been experiencing? Or will you ask them to walk with you through a current difficult time? Tell them you want to risk being vulnerable with them as you go through this time of pain. It will be hard, but it will deepen your love for one another and it will help you to get through a difficult time because you aren't walking through it alone. Jesus wants you to experience the intimacy of community, and sometimes He allows us to go through a time of sorrow in order to have us turn to the people He's given us as a gift. Have that conversation and watch how the Lord blesses both of you.

YOUR THOUGHTS:

DAY 4

GODLY SORROW VS. WORLDLY SORROW

"Godly sorrow brings repentance that leads to salvation and leaves no regret, but worldly sorrow brings death."   2 Corinthians 7:10

"Life has never been easy. Nor is it meant to be. It is a matter of being joyous in the face of sorrow. If we wait until our lives are free from sorrow or difficulty, then we wait forever. And miss the entire point."   Dirk Benedict

PRAY: Lord, as I look at people whose lives I don't agree with, I ask that You help me to see their choices and their lifestyles through Your eyes. I want to understand that if they knew You they would live lives with no regret. Help me to remember that worldly sorrow brings death, but that You can turn anyone's sorrow into gladness. Let me pray for those people to come to know You, instead of judging them for not knowing salvation through You. Amen.

REFLECT: So many Christians don't like the people in Hollywood. We gossip about celebrities and judge their lives, and yet we don't stop to think that they may be dying inside. My heart goes out to the people who seem to have everything: money, celebrity, influence, and yet they live with deep sorrow that brings regret and ultimate death. If we could pray for the people in Hollywood with compassion and love, wanting them to experience the repentance and freedom of Jesus, then we are blessing people who don't yet know the Lord to understand Godly sorrow instead of worldly sorrow. Our prayers for Hollywood professionals have eternal impact. Our gossip or anger just leads to regret and it brings death.

ACT: Write down two Hollywood professionals and/or celebrities who aren't yet Christians and commit to pray for them every day for a week. Then choose to pray for them to fall in love with Jesus, to experience His joy, hope and salvation. Ask the Lord to free them of worldly thoughts and sorrow and help them to experience God's repentance and joy. Ask that they would be free of regret and instead that they would embrace all the promises that God offers all of us. Your prayers for those two people for seven days will change their lives and yours!

Y**OUR THOUGHTS:**

DAY 5

GOD GIVES US JOY IN OUR SORROW

"Then maidens will dance and be glad, young men and old as well. I will turn their mourning into gladness; I will give them comfort and joy instead of sorrow."

Jeremiah 31:13

"And I will ask the Father, and he will give you another Counselor to be with you forever—

John 14:16

"Your sorrow itself shall be turned into joy. Not the sorrow to be taken away, and joy to be put in its place, but the very sorrow which now grieves you shall be turned into joy. God not only takes away the bitterness and gives sweetness in its place, but turns the bitterness into sweetness itself."

Charles Spurgeon

PRAY: I praise You Father, for being so loving, kind and comforting. You will bring joy, dancing, and gladness to all of us. You are the only one who can turn our mourning into gladness and our sorrow into joy! I praise You for giving us Your Holy Spirit to be our advocate, to help us in our time of sorrow and trouble and to be with us forever. Praise be to God! Amen!

REFLECT: The hardest thing for us to do is feel hope in a seemingly hopeless situation, or to feel joy when we are deep in sorrow. That's when we need scripture to let God's promises sink into our hearts and embrace His unconditional love, support, strength, and joy. He gave us the Holy Spirit to lift us out of our sorrow and pain. Praise God for His faithfulness, even in the darkest of times. He wants us ALL to dance and be glad. What would it take to refocus your thoughts and emotions so that we will always be praising our amazing God?

ACT: Take 5 minutes right now to push aside any sorrow, confusion, hurt, or fear and just PRAISE GOD. You can use the Psalms, or the words in Jeremiah 31:13 and John 14:16. Praise Him for turning our mourning into gladness and our sorrow into joy. Praise Him for giving us the Holy Spirit to live inside of us. Praise Him for His unconditional love, His hope, and His joy that is not dependent on our circumstances. Praise the Lord out loud so that you hear yourself praising, and everyone around you can hear. Praise be to God! Amen!

YOUR THOUGHTS:

DAY 6

A TIME TO MOURN AND A TIME TO DANCE

"There is a time for everything, and a season for every activity under heaven: ...a time to weep and a time to laugh, a time to mourn and a time to dance," Ecclesiastes 3:1 & 4

"Our vision is so limited we can hardly imagine a love that does not show itself in protection from suffering.... The love of God did not protect His own Son.... He will not necessarily protect us – not from anything it takes to make us like His Son. A lot of hammering and chiseling and purifying by fire will have to go into the process." Elisabeth Elliot

PRAY: Dear Heavenly Father, I thank You that it's OK to feel sorrow and that You have planned sorrow as part of our human experience. Thank You that You promise we will feel all kinds of emotions throughout our life and we don't have to be afraid of the negative emotions. In fact, how would we ever truly feel the richness of joy and laughter if we haven't felt the depth of sorrow and mourning? Help me to embrace my sorrow and not be afraid of it. I pray this in Jesus' mighty name. Amen.

REFLECT: The Western world is known for doing everything we can to avoid sorrow, pain, hurt, and despair. And yet, God created those emotions as well, so that we can understand the full range of human emotions and gain wisdom from living through different seasons. Are you afraid of feeling sad? Do you avoid it at all costs? Maybe it's time to look at the bigger picture and trust God that He will not only get you through the times of sorrow, but He will make you a richer, wiser person because of it. Don't run from sorrow, for you want to learn through this season and then fully embrace the coming seasons of laughter and dancing!

ACT: Write down the saddest season of your life and the most joyful season of your life. Then prayerfully compare what you learned from both. How did you grow? Did anything come out of both seasons that made you a better person? Are you more Christ-like, empathetic, or patient because of experiencing both seasons? Then thank God for giving you sorrow and joy, and ask Him to allow you to use them both to offer compassion and hope to someone else.

YOUR THOUGHTS:

DAY 7

GOD SHOWS COMPASSION IN OUR SORROW

"For men are not cast off by the Lord forever. Though he brings grief, he will show compassion, so great is his unfailing love. For he does not willingly bring affliction or grief to the children of men."   Lamentations 3:31-33

"We cannot understand. The best is perhaps what we understand least."   C.S. Lewis

PRAY: Jesus, I come to You now to give me hope. You promise me that You will never cast me off. Though I understand that life brings grief, I know that You show compassion because Your love for me is unfailing. I know that you don't willingly bring affliction or grief to anyone, but I'm feeling sorrow now, and I need to feel Your compassion. Jesus, would You put Your loving and comforting arms around me right now? Thank You for Your unending compassion. I pray this in Your name, Amen.

REFLECT: Lamentations is a powerful book to read when we are feeling sorrowful. It not only acknowledges the reality of our pain, but it gives us hope that God is with us in our sorrow, with love, compassion, and hope. It reminds us that though we do feel grief, we shouldn't pretend it's not there, or push it away. So, embrace the Lord in your grief because He will never leave you or forsake you. He will use that sorrow in your life so that you can grow stronger, help others, and expand your compassion.

ACT: End this week of studying sorrow by spreading the good news of God's unfailing love! Tell someone you love, who doesn't know Jesus, that He shows compassion to everyone and does not willingly bring affliction or grief to anyone. Give a person a hug who looks sad or who is going through a time of sorrow. Encourage them with God's promises to us that His love is unconditional and unending. Tell them that a time of joy, gladness and dancing is coming, for there is a season for everything under the sun!

YOUR THOUGHTS:

DOMESTIC VIOLENCE

WEEK FORTY

We chose to tackle this difficult issue because, "Domestic violence affects one in three women and one in four men, globally." We are praying you can get free of being a victim of domestic violence, or you will help a loved one get free. Please forward this to any friend or family member whom you know may need help!

I still wake up with your name stuck in my throat sometimes
Where it caught between your hands when you squeezed
I still wake up in fear most nights, your eyes follow me from every shadow,
every loud noise crowding the edges of my memory.
I still wake up.

Amber Koneval, Survivor

If you are in an abusive situation, please call either the U.S. National Domestic Violence Hotline at 1-800-799-7233 or call your local domestic violence hotline for help. You can find them by searching online under "domestic violence hotline" or go to TheHotline.org. Be safe!

DAY 1

NO UNWHOLESOME TALK

"Do not let any unwholesome talk come out of your mouths, but only what is helpful for building others up according to their needs, that it may benefit those who listen."

Ephesians 4:29

"The scars from mental cruelty can be as deep and long-lasting as wounds from punches or slaps but are often not as obvious. In fact, even among women who have experienced violence from a partner, half or more report that the man's emotional abuse is what is causing them the greatest harm."

Lundy Bancroft

PRAY: Lord, I don't want to have any unwholesome talk come out of my mouth, and I don't want to be the victim of others talking to me with words that cut me down, hurt me, or demean me. Show me how I may be allowing my spouse, parent, child, or anyone in my home, to speak to me with words that are not beneficial to me. Make sure that the words in my home are helpful for building others up according to our needs and that they will benefit those who listen! Thank You for Your help, wisdom, and discernment. Amen.

REFLECT: Words are a powerful tool of the enemy to steal, kill, and destroy lives. Ponder how people closest to you are speaking to you. Is it with love and respect, or with resentment and ridicule? Are the conversations in your home benefitting everyone involved? Are *you* in the habit of tearing down your loved ones rather than building them up? Verbal domestic abuse can be just as damaging as physical or sexual abuse. "Sticks and stones may break my bones, but words will never hurt me" is a lie.

ACT: Get on your knees and ask the Lord to reveal if you are allowing anyone in your home to speak to you with unwholesome talk. Ask Him for direction on how to stop allowing any disparaging words and instead fill your home with words of love and grace. God can open your eyes right now to reveal any level of abuse or mistreatment from anyone in the home, even you. Take steps for the abuse to stop RIGHT NOW.

YOUR THOUGHTS:

U.S. National Domestic Violence Hotline: 1-800-799-7233

DAY 2

DO NOT BE OVERCOME BY EVIL

"Do not be overcome by evil, but overcome evil with good." Romans 12:21

"You have a right against any forms of domestic violence. Protect your life. Protect your family and loved ones. Mutual respect and love are main keys to avoid violence."

Angelica Hopes

PRAY: Dear Lord, I do not want to be overcome by evil. I want to overcome evil with good. I need You to give me a bigger perspective on my situation and help me to act wisely, with strength and yet with truth and goodness. I need You to protect me from evil so that I am not overwhelmed. Give me Your grace to respond with dignity and discernment, so I can get out of danger. That is only possible with You. I pray this in Jesus' name, Amen.

REFLECT: Have you noticed that when you are overwhelmed and not in control, you are more tempted to do evil—just like someone in your house may be doing? We need the Lord to overcome evil with good. We need encouragement and hope! And we need Him to guide us, strengthen us, and give us wisdom and discernment so we can be empowered with a confidence only He can give us, even as our spouse or family member is acting in evil. That's a delicate balance when we're in the midst of adversity. But with God, nothing is impossible!

ACT: Are you being mistreated by anyone, in any way? Are you overcoming evil with good or are you tempted to lash back or do something wrong to stop the wrong that's being done to you? Write down what your spouse or someone has said or done to you in full detail and add anything that threatens your well-being. If children are involved, write that down as well. Then immediately get help from a mature Christian, a parent, a friend, or a professional, so that you won't respond with evil in your state of feeling overwhelmed. You need protection and wise, scriptural counsel. Showing someone safe what you've written is one way you can respond to evil with good – to help you be tough, take strong action and get help today.

YOUR THOUGHTS:

U.S. National Domestic Violence Hotline: 1-800-799-7233

DAY 3

THOSE WHO LOVE VIOLENCE

"The Lord examines the righteous, but the wicked and those who love violence his soul hates."   Psalm 11:5

"Domestic violence is any behavior involving physical, psychological, emotional, sexual or verbal abuse. It is any form of aggression intended to hurt, damage, or kill an intimate person."   Asa Don Brown

PRAY: LORD, please examine my heart and my spirit as I endure persecution and abuse. I want to stay IN You, through ALL situations and in ALL circumstances. Your Word says You hate with a passion those who love violence. I also hate the wicked, evilness, and abusive actions and deeds the person who commits violence does. Please deliver me from evil, and bring me to the place where Your safety, peace, and protection abound. Thank You for Your love Jesus... I will trust in You and in Your mighty Name and glorious will. Amen.

REFLECT: Have you allowed the Lord to examine your heart? As a victim, you can only do so much, but you can pray for God's protection and admit when you do not agree with what the abuser is saying, even if you can't talk about it with them. Acknowledging your needs to God and to yourself will clarify your fear or guilt. We need the Lord to examine the righteous, the wicked and us, so that we see the truth in our own hearts and minds of not only whom we are but also how we ought to be treated. You must protect yourself because it's not possible for a violent, hateful person to do that. What would it take for you to face the truth and take action to stop, or walk away from, any violence and hated in your home?

ACT: Examine your current living situation right now. You can even write on a piece of paper what's good and what's bad about your life, your marriage, and your home. If the bad side includes any abuse, sin, or evil, then it must stop now. Muster the strength to ask the Lord for wisdom and then reach out for help to change your situation. None of us deserves to be abused in any way, shape, or form. Ask God to show you the evil that's happening and to reveal the correct action to take or the way out – immediately!

YOUR THOUGHTS:

U.S. National Domestic Violence Hotline: 1-800-799-7233

DAY 4

EXPOSE THE DEEDS OF DARKNESS

"Have nothing to do with the fruitless deeds of darkness, but rather expose them."

Ephesians 5:11

"It takes immense courage to come to the realization that you're being abused. And ANOTHER level of courage to finally tell someone. If someone approaches you with the unfortunate news that they are being abused, ask how you can help. Don't question them."

Camren Bicondova

PRAY: Heavenly Father, You tell me to have nothing to do with fruitless deeds of darkness. The fruits of the Spirit are love, joy, peace, patience, kindness, goodness, faithfulness, gentleness, and self-control. Anything else must be exposed. Lord, please turn my abusers' heart to abhor their actions, repent from them and heal. Protect me from the fruitless deeds done against me in domestic violence. Please save me Jesus. Show me how to expose these deeds according to Your way that is in line with Your Word. This is so hard God, but what is impossible with man is possible with God. Direct me and help me. In Jesus' name, Amen.

REFLECT: Paul was very bold in not only naming the people for whom he was thankful, but he also called out the names of the people who made trouble. He believed in exposing the darkness so that others would be protected, and the truth would come into the light. In 2 Timothy 4:14 he says, "Alexander the metalworker did me a great deal of harm. The Lord will repay him for what he has done." Paul was not afraid to let everyone know who was not following the Lord, in word or in deed. Why don't we truthfully and boldly do the same thing and expose the fruitless deeds of darkness in our homes and our lives?

ACT: Right now, commit to exposing the fruitless deeds of darkness and call out the names of anyone who is treating you with disrespect, anger, evil, or abuse. Tell the Lord who they are. Now make a plan to have nothing to do with dark deeds and words. Talk to someone about your abuser and expose the truth of the fruitless deed of darkness. The Lord will give you the strength as you take one step at a time.

YOUR THOUGHTS:

U.S. National Domestic Violence Hotline: 1-800-799-7233

DAY 5

NO WEAPON FORGED AGAINST YOU WILL PREVAIL

"No weapon forged against you will prevail, and you will refute every tongue that accuses you. This is the heritage of the servants of the Lord, and this is their vindication from me,"
declares the Lord."   Isaiah 54:17

"Perpetrators of abuse often make their victims believe that they are somehow responsible for their own abuse. Such misplaced notions shift the blame of the abuse from the abuser to the abusee."
                                                                        Mallika Nawal

PRAY: ABBA Father, I stand firm on your truth that no weapon forged against me will prevail and that You will refute every tongue that accuses me. You know nothing will prevail against Your plan because it is perfect, and Your truth is my heritage as a servant of Yours. Increase my faith to believe that there is vindication for me, for You declare it! Protect me from people who try to twist the truth of my encounter with the abuse. The enemy hates it when his lies and plans are thwarted, but You rejoice Lord! In Jesus' name, Amen.

REFLECT: We're reminded here that nothing is stronger than God and He will vindicate anyone who suffers from evil weapons. Are you living as if you really believe it? There is a terrible problem of abuse in the entertainment industry. And yet it's all hidden because the abusers don't want the public to discover their evil deeds. There are verbal, physical, and emotional weapons being forged against many people in Hollywood whom the public thinks are living perfect lives. But God punishes the attackers, and He refutes every tongue that accuses. There is vindication for the victims. There is hope for healing and change!

ACT: Would you read this verse out loud as a proclamation and then pray for the protection and healing for all victims of domestic violence, including those in the entertainment industry. Pray that the Lord will stop every tongue that accuses them. And plead with God to stop every weapon that is forged against them. Just as we desire this in every home, we want the hidden evil to come to the surface in Hollywood and for the Lord to offer a new heritage for the people who are creating our entertainment and shaping our culture.

YOUR THOUGHTS:

U.S. National Domestic Violence Hotline: 1-800-799-7233

DAY 6

THE HIDDEN WILL BE MADE KNOWN

"For the Holy Spirit will teach you at that time what you at that time what you should say."   Luke 12:12

"An abuser isn't abusive 24/7. They usually demonstrate positive character traits most of the time.   Miya Yamanouchi

PRAY: Lord, we humans want to keep things secret that are not glorifying to You. But You want NOTHING concealed or hidden. You want to disclose the truth so that it will come into the light and be made known. Please make sure that my every act, every word, every relationship that I have is open and honest, so that nothing will be hidden. Please disclose everything going on in my home or in the homes of the people I love, so that You can come in with Your healing hand. I need you Lord, to make the truth known in all of my relationships! Amen and Amen.

REFLECT: Have you thought about the power of secrets? Reflect on anything in your life that you haven't told anyone. Or maybe it's an issue or experience that you have told one person not to tell anyone else. Think about the things in your home that are concealed, hidden, and never talked about. Are those things of the Lord? Are they representing love, joy, peace, patience, kindness, goodness, faithfulness, gentleness, or self-control? If not, then those things can't remain secrets any longer.

ACT: List anything in your life that you consider a secret. Pray about the right people to tell, so no dangerous thing remains hidden anymore. Now is the time to reveal the truth of any concealed thoughts, words, situations, or issues that you have been afraid to face. Today is the first day of healing for you and your home!

YOUR **THOUGHTS:**

U.S. National Domestic Violence Hotline: 1-800-799-7233

DAY 7

THE LORD SAVES

"You intended to harm me, but God intended it for good to accomplish what is now being done, the saving of many lives."   Genesis 50:20

"It's hard at first...really hard. You may even question if leaving was the right decision. It was the right decision. After the shock, when the fog lifts, things will start to get easier."

Domestic Violence Survivor

PRAY: My dear Father, thank You that You can turn even the worst of things into good. And even if my abuser intended to harm me, I know that You did not cause it, but You've allowed it only to accomplish what is now being done in my life. Save my life Lord! And stop the sin and evil that's been going on in my home. I need You to accomplish Your good plans and purposes and yet I feel helpless and afraid. Only You can save me Jesus. Amen.

REFLECT: Throughout the Bible men do terrible things to others and yet God allows it, then turns them into circumstances for good in order to accomplish His purposes. Joseph's brothers betrayed him, tried to kill him, and then sold him off into slavery, only later to find out that he was alive and actually rose to the highest level of government and now had authority over his brothers—the ones who did the evil! Read this story in Genesis 37, 39 – 47. The brothers tried to get away with abuse and murder and yet God used their evil deeds for good in order to put Joseph in a place and location to accomplish His plan to save MANY lives through Joseph. Praise God for protection and healing and for all the good that He intends for you, including the saving of your life and many other lives!

ACT: God allows things to happen for reasons that we don't always understand, but we still have to make every effort to stop being harmed. If you and your abuser can go to counseling, then do that immediately. If you are in danger, call 911 or leave your home now. If you have kept the abuse a secret, then you must tell safe people. You must act, and as you do, ask the Lord to accomplish what He has planned and to empower, protect, and heal you in the process. Trust in Him, then take action so that He can save many lives – including yours!

YOUR THOUGHTS:

U.S. National Domestic Violence Hotline: 1-800-799-7233

REST

WEEK FORTY-ONE

The word rest is used throughout scripture to show God's love, peace, and comfort. God is very clear on wanting us to have a day of rest. He commands us to observe the Sabbath and He even tells us that His Holy Spirit rests on us. How good are you at resting?

DAY 1

OUR DAY OF REST IS HOLY

"By the seventh day God had finished the work he had been doing; so on the seventh day he rested from all his work. And God blessed the seventh day and made it holy, because on it he rested from all the work of creating that he had done."   Genesis 2:2-3

"A world without a Sabbath would be like a man without a smile, like summer without flowers, and like a homestead without a garden. It is the most joyous day of the week."

Henry Ward Beecher

PRAY: Dear God, what a great reminder that even YOU rested! You created the entire world and everything in it and then You rested. Would You help me to remember that I was made in Your image and You want me to rest. And not only get rest, but rest in You, rest from the cares of the world and not strive to get things done or get ahead. How beautiful that You rested from all the work of creating and You called that day Holy. I praise You, Lord. Amen and Amen

REFLECT: Have you ever thought that God needs to rest? He stopped what He was doing and just got quiet and rested. Then Jesus tells us quite a few times in the Gospels, that He rested, He went away from the crowds to be alone with God. He was sleeping soundly when the storm came up in the ship. Rest is an important exercise for God, so much so that He made the day of rest a Holy day. The Bible says, "Be still and know that I am God." It doesn't say "Be busy and know that I am God." How often do you set aside a day to rest and call that Holy?

ACT: Study all of the passages in scripture that talk about God and Jesus resting or when God forces us to rest. Notice the verses when Paul talks about the Holy Spirit slowing him down on his travels. God forced him to rest when Paul would rather have gotten to the next town. Include Psalm 23 where it says "The Lord makes us lie down in green pastures." He is making us rest. What would it take to truly believe God's important commandment to rest? Put rest into your schedule as a priority. Don't wait until He forces you to lie down......

YOUR THOUGHTS:

DAY 2

OBSERVE THE SABBATH AND REST

"There are six days when you may work, but the seventh day is a Sabbath of rest, a day of sacred assembly. You are not to do any work; wherever you live, it is a Sabbath to the Lord."
Leviticus 23:3

"The command is "Do no work." Just make space. Attend to what is around you. Learn that you don't have to DO to BE. Accept the grace of doing nothing. Stay with it until you stop jerking and squirming."
Dallas Willard

PRAY: Lord, thank You that You have given us a day of rest. The Sabbath is a sacred day and I need Your help to observe it with rest. Help me to not work on Sunday (or take one day off each week), to slow down and enjoy the day with You and my family or friends. I know that's good for me, but in our busy culture I need Your Holy Spirit to give me the discipline to do it. I pray this in Your name, Amen.

REFLECT: In this hectic world, stop and ponder when was the last time you took a day off to just rest with no work being done. The God who loves you, died for you, and knows what's best for you, asks you to stop one day a week and keep that day different, set aside for Him. It doesn't matter if it's on Saturday or Sunday, or even a day during the week if you work weekends. His purpose is to offer rest away from the chaos of daily life and think on Him. Do you trust Him? Why not obey Him in this most neglected commandment and allow your body weekly peace, calm and rest?

ACT: Do you keep the Sabbath? If not, why not commit right now to start this week? Choose this as a way to develop your spiritual discipline and take advantage of a gift that God is presenting and asking you to follow – the gift of rest!

YOUR THOUGHTS:

DAY 3

MY SOUL FINDS REST IN GOD

"My soul finds rest in God alone; my salvation comes from him. He alone is my rock and my salvation; he is my fortress, I will never be shaken... Find rest, O my soul, in God alone; my hope comes from him."

Psalm 62:1-2 & 5

"Once I knew what it was to rest upon the rock of God's promises, and it was indeed a precious resting place, but now I rest in His grace. He is teaching me that the bosom of His love is a far sweeter resting-place than even the rock of His promises."

Hannah Whitall Smith

PRAY: My dear Heavenly Father, I thank you that my soul can find rest in You. And I have rest because I know I am saved. You are truly my rock and my salvation. You promise me so many good things, it's almost unbelievable to fathom that You take personal care of me and protect me like a fortress and that regardless of what I go through, I will not be shaken. I praise You that yes, my soul finds rest in You and my hope comes from You as well. This is incredible and I am in awe of Your mighty promises and love for me! Amen.

REFLECT: Have you ever really realized and accepted the amazing and miraculous promises that God gives us? In this one verse He promises us that He will give our souls rest, that we are given salvation and eternal life from Him, and that He protects us and loves us so much that He is our rock, our fortress, and we will never be shaken. And then when that's even more than we can imagine, He tells us that we have hope because of Him. It's overwhelming and amazing. But the key to this verse is that all of that ONLY comes from Him and through Him and In Him. For His love is more than we can even fathom!

ACT: Write God a note thanking Him for all of His promises, protection, care, love, hope, joy, peace, wisdom, discernment, salvation and even the rest that He gives to us as a free gift. Then can you just sit quietly and re-read your note and rest in the truth of His Word and His love for you. Do that until you truly feel rest in your soul! Then go start your day and see if it's different than any other day!

YOUR THOUGHTS:

DAY 4

HE PROVIDES FOR US WHILE WE SLEEP

"In vain you rise early and stay up late, toiling for food to eat—for while they sleep He provides for those He loves."   Psalm 127:2

"Our rest lies in looking to the Lord, not to ourselves."   Watchman Nee

PRAY: Dear Lord, I don't want to live any moment of my life in vain. I don't want to strive constantly for success and money, nor toil endlessly for food to eat. Would You help me to rest in You so that You can take care of me and I don't have to rise early and stay up late because of anxiety in trying to survive? Help me to put my trust in You so that I may find rest, for You promise me that while I'm sleeping You will provide for me. I thank You in Jesus name, Amen.

REFLECT: Can you see how your faith in God actually makes a tangible difference in how you live your life? Do you live differently because you are a Christian? How much of your life do you still live in vain? How much striving do you do? Are you in survival mode, worrying about not making enough money to pay your rent or put food on your table? Can you believe that you can breathe, slow down, and trust God to supply your daily bread, to help you make that next deal at work, or to provide for your children to get through college? He promises us that while we are sleeping, He provides for us because He loves us! Do you really believe that to the point of experiencing rest during financial struggles or tough times?

ACT: Choose one thing that gets you uptight. Then stop and sit quietly, resting in the presence of the Lord. You might even want to turn on worship music. Ask the Lord to take that burden from you and to allow you to rest in Him. It may take a while to truly relax but take the time to give rest to your body, mind, and soul. This is a great daily exercise!

YOUR THOUGHTS:

DAY 5

REST FROM WORK

"There remains, then, a Sabbath-rest for the people of God; for anyone who enters God's rest also rests from their works, just as God did from his. Let us, therefore, make every effort to enter that rest, so that no one will perish by following their example of disobedience."

Hebrews 4:9-11

"Work is a blessing. God has so arranged the world that work is necessary, and He gives us hands and strength to do it. The enjoyment of leisure would be nothing if we had only leisure. It is the joy of work well done that enables us to enjoy rest, just as it is the experiences of hunger and thirst that make food and drink such pleasures."

Elisabeth Elliot

PRAY: Dear God, we need to obey You and take the Sabbath rest, not only for ourselves, but to be examples of obedience to others. I pray for the Christians in Hollywood to make every effort to enter into the Sabbath rest, so that no one will perish by their disobedience. I know the work schedules of people working in film, television, and music are incredibly arduous, often 7 days a week, but would You nudge the Christians to take the Sabbath rest so their actions can be a witness to the non-believers all around them? Amen.

REFLECT: Work in Hollywood can be so demanding and so stressful that it seems impossible to rest one whole day of the week. It seems irresponsible and unfair to the rest people on the film who are working 7-day weeks. I used to be that way. My work demanded ALL of my week. And yet I burned out, and that's worse than stress! So, now, even with my pressured life in Hollywood, I have to take time on Sunday, not only for church, but to rest, either with family, friends, or just with a long nap. God truly knows what we need.

ACT: Are you following the Sabbath? What kind of witness are you to others because of your disobedience to God? Choose what you can change in your life to rest one day of your week. And would you pray for one Christian you know in Hollywood and ask the Lord to use them, through obeying the Sabbath, to lead others to Jesus. Ask the Lord to protect the Christians in Hollywood from being a bad witness through their actions and that they will choose to rest on the Sabbath so no one perishes by following their example of disobedience.

YOUR THOUGHTS:

DAY 6

GOD'S YOKE IS EASY AND HIS BURDEN IS LIGHT

"Come to me, all you who are weary and burdened, and I will give you rest. Take my yoke upon you and learn from me, for I am gentle and humble in heart, and you will find rest for your souls. For my yoke is easy and my burden is light."   Matthew 11:28-30

"Thou hast made us for Thyself, O Lord, and our heart is restless until it finds its rest in Thee."   Augustine of Hippo

PRAY: Oh Jesus, I love these words that You tell all of us. You want us to come to You, knowing that we get weary and we are so often burdened. And You promise us rest! You understand that we can't handle our own stress but You can. How beautiful that You tell us that You are gentle and humble in heart and we will find rest for our souls when we come to you. Thank You Jesus that Your yoke is easy and Your burden is light. Those are words to soothe my soul and give rest to my beating heart and weary bones. You are so unconditionally loving and I thank You that, through resting in You, I will find peace. Amen.

REFLECT: This is a pretty well-known scripture and yet it is powerful. Have you realized how personal Jesus is? He is aware of our emotional needs and He addresses our stress, anxiety, and burdens head on. Not only is He gentle and humble, He is an amazingly good communicator. He calls things out, talks about them directly, and gives us a solution to the problem. He knows our need for rest and peace. And He loves us so much that He offers to take our burdens from us. That's an incredibly loving and personal God!

ACT: What is burdening you? Have you given it to God? Have you been able to let go of it and pray for the Lord to take it from you, solve it, and give you rest? Take time to do that right now. And then every day this week pray the same prayer to give that burden to the Lord, who can take it from you and give you peace and rest. For with Him all things are possible!

YOUR THOUGHTS:

DAY 7

THE SPIRIT OF GOD RESTS ON YOU

"If you are insulted because of the name of Christ, you are blessed, for the Spirit of glory and of God rests on you."   1 Peter 4:14

"In place of our exhaustion and spiritual fatigue, God will give us rest. All He asks is that we come to Him...that we spend a while thinking about Him, meditating on Him, talking to Him, listening in silence, occupying ourselves with Him – totally and thoroughly lost in the hiding place of His presence."   Chuck Swindoll

PRAY: God, I thank You that if I am ever persecuted because of loving You, I am blessed. May the one who insults me or persecutes me realize how much You love him or her and chooses to embrace You and experience Your blessings. Lord, let all the people I love who don't know You come to believe in Your Spirit and feel You resting on them like a warm blanket. I pray this in Jesus' name, Amen

REFLECT: Have you ever been teased, insulted, or even persecuted because you believe in Jesus? Did you know that because God's Spirit rests on you, that He blesses you, especially in those moments of standing up for your faith? You never need to worry that you are different or not liked or weird because of your faith. Stand with confidence knowing that you are blessed and that the Holy Spirit is resting on you. What a beautiful visual that is!

ACT: We think of resting in God, but have you ever thought of God resting on you? Think of the times that you have been awkward, shy, or even afraid of being a Christian. Then imagine the Holy Spirit resting on you, comforting, and protecting you. Isn't that a warm, peaceful thought? Realize that at any given moment, you can rest in God and He is resting on you. Let that truth give you confidence and power in all circumstances.

YOUR THOUGHTS:

FORGIVENESS

WEEK FORTY-TWO

This week we're focusing on FORGIVENESS! When we forgive others, we become free. But it's a conscious choice to forgive, not just a feeling to get over. And let's also determine to seek the forgiveness of others for anything they may have against us. Most importantly, let's embrace the unconditional, complete forgiveness that Jesus offers all of us!

DAY 1

FORGIVE AS THE LORD FORGAVE YOU

"Therefore, as God's chosen people, holy and dearly loved, clothe yourselves with compassion, kindness, humility, gentleness and patience. Bear with each other and forgive whatever grievances you may have against one another. Forgive as the Lord forgave you."

Colossians 3:12-13

"I have to get to the point of the absolute and unquestionable relationship that takes everything exactly as it comes from Him. God never guides us at some time in the future, but always here and now. Realize that the Lord is here now, and the freedom you receive is immediate."

Oswald Chambers

PRAY: Dear Lord, thank You for the gift of forgiveness! I want to practice it, embrace it, give it, and receive it. Will You give me the wisdom and strength to forgive anyone in my life who has hurt me? I don't want to hold a grudge, so please fill me with compassion, kindness, humility, gentleness, and patience. I want to forgive just as You have forgiven me. I pray in Jesus' name, Amen!

REFLECT: Reflect on the people in your life you may need to forgive. Start as far back as you can remember and don't worry if the person is not around anymore, or not even alive. Just lift them up to the Lord and tell them you forgive them. Lift those people up to the Lord. Ask Him to give you complete forgiveness and peace and to release any negative feelings from your heart.

ACT: Who are the people you have just reflected on? Write down their names and decide how you are going to forgive them. It can be in your heart, through a letter, a phone call, or in your journal. As you forgive the people in your life, take the step to do it in person, if that's appropriate. How wonderful it would be for a friend or family member to get a call, a visit, or a letter from you, asking forgiveness and embracing them anew and fresh. Make it your goal today to deal with any unforgiveness actively and bravely in your heart and bring peace to all of your relationships, with compassion, kindness, humility, gentleness and patience.

YOUR THOUGHTS:

DAY 2

FORGIVE OTHERS

"For if you forgive men when they sin against you, your heavenly Father will also forgive you. But if you do not forgive men their sins, your Father will not forgive your sins."

Matthew 6:14-15

"We must quit bending the Word to suit our situation. It is we who must be bent to that Word, our necks that must bow under the yoke."   Elisabeth Elliot

PRAY: Dear God, I want to fully understand the power of forgiveness. Would You make me understand the process of forgiving others and how that impacts my relationship with You? Would You reveal to me whom I haven't forgiven? I may not be aware that I am holding unforgiveness in my heart. Please show me so that I am in good standing with others and with You. Thank You for revealing to me any unforgiveness in my heart. Amen.

REFLECT: If we study the word FORGIVENESS we see there are emotional and even health benefits to forgiveness. It is not condoning, excusing, or forgetting the wrong, and it doesn't mean that you have to reconcile. It's letting go of an offense and giving up the right to get back at the person who wronged you. In understanding God's Word, you will be better able to succeed at the task. It's not "forgive and forget," it's "forgive and be free!"

ACT: List the people or groups of people, organizations, committees, or even corporations who make you angry, or who have done something to hurt you, hinder you or humble you. Could it be the government for making you pay too much for health care? Is it your boss for working you too hard for too little pay? Is it your union for not supporting you? Is it your neighbor for making too much noise, or a friend who betrayed or bullied you? There are so many levels of hurt, abuse, or pain that need to be forgiven. Start with the macro and move down to the micro. You may unveil a deep need for forgiveness that you didn't even know was there. Or you may find you are freer than you realized. Either way is okay, as long as you are honest with yourself and God.

YOUR THOUGHTS:

DAY 3

GOD DELIGHTS TO SHOW MERCY

"Who is a God like you, who pardons sin and forgives the transgression of the remnant of his inheritance? You do not stay angry forever but delight to show mercy." Micah 7:18

"My Mama always said you've got to put the past behind you before you can move on."

Forrest Gump

PRAY: I praise You, God, for being so amazing! You pardon my sins; You forgive my transgressions; You do not stay angry at me, but You delight in showing me mercy. You are such a good God, and I am so thankful to be Your child. I praise You for Your unconditional love, grace, mercy, and forgiveness. Praise be to the Lord! Amen.

REFLECT: "Who is a God like You?" What a good question. We worship the God who created the world, raises people from the dead, heals, reconciles, transforms, and unites. There is no other God who pardons our sin and who shows every single human being supernatural grace and mercy. We serve an amazing God. If we genuinely believed that with our whole heart, soul, and mind, we would be different people. Think about who the God is that you follow? Thank Him, for He is the God of forgiveness.

ACT: Take this time to Praise our forgiving God. Praise Him for things you've never praised Him for before. Praise Him for forgiving you for everything you've done – even things you didn't realize were sins. Praise Him for His mercy. Praise Him for creating this world and everyone in it – even the people you don't like. Praise Him for forgiving our politicians, teachers, your doctors, and even Hollywood. Praise Him for the joy these people bring into your life through films, TV shows, music, video games, books, fine art, plays, concerts, and all forms of art and entertainment. Praise Him for His Divine creativity and His Divine forgiveness. Praise the Lord!

YOUR THOUGHTS:

DAY 4

GOD HEARS, FORGIVES, AND HEALS

"If my people, who are called by my name, will humble themselves and pray and seek my face and turn from their wicked ways, then will I hear from heaven and will forgive their sin and will heal their land."   2 Chronicles 7:14

"The great gift of human beings is that we have the power of empathy."   Meryl Streep

PRAY: To my God and Father, I am called by Your name. I humble myself before You and pray to You, and as I seek Your face I will turn from my wicked ways. I want to hear from heaven so that You will forgive me for all of my sins, and You will heal our land. As I forgive others, I pray that as a church, Christians all across America will seek Your face. Then You will forgive us and heal our households, our city, our states, and our nation. Amen.

REFLECT: This verse should make you wonder if we all need to be encouraging other believers around us to also seek God. He says that "if His people"—not just one person—so we all can be more active in challenging our friends, family members, and church community to be seeking God's face. Is this verse a personal prayer, or a call to action for all of God's people? How would you humble yourself before Him, and how can you encourage others who are called by His name to do the same?

ACT: Whom can you encourage to grow in their Christian faith? Who can you challenge to spend more time with Him and to actively seek His face? Who can you inspire to fall more in love with Him? Tell him or her that you want God to forgive your sins, and all Christians' sins, and to heal our land, and you can't do it alone! You can have an eternal impact on others, as well as on your own life, by reaching out to other Christians and asking them to take this verse seriously. We need each other!

YOUR THOUGHTS:

DAY 5

JESUS PRAYS FOR US

"Jesus said, 'Father, forgive them, for they do not know what they are doing.' And they divided up his clothes by casting lots."   Luke 23:34

"It's said in Hollywood that you should always forgive your enemies – because you never know when you'll have to work with them."   Lana Turner

PRAY: Dear Lord, please forgive me and other people of the sins we don't even know we're committing. Would You heal the sick and broken people who are hurting, abusing, neglecting, and betraying others because of their emotional, physical, and/or spiritual brokenness. And would You give me compassion and grace for those who have hurt me, for maybe they don't know what they're doing? Thank You. Amen.

REFLECT: We always assume that when someone hurts us, they know what they are doing and are choosing to sin. But Jesus makes us wonder if that is always the case. Maybe we do and say things out of habit, from what we learned growing up, or from what society says is okay. Because of these influences, we can tend to justify and rationalize our behavior and convince ourselves we're not sinning. We come to believe our actions are deserved, expected, and even accepted. That should make us look differently at the actions of other people and help us to forgive more readily.

ACT: God wants to give you His perspective on the words and actions of other people. He longs to give you compassion, insight, understanding, and peace for those who need forgiving. Jesus understood that people sin because they truly don't understand what they're doing, so we need to pray the same way. What do you need to do to change your perspective on the people around you? Ask Jesus to show you one thing He's forgiven you for so that you will be more like Him and respond differently to others.

For a beautiful story of forgiveness, check out Biblical Stories video, "Emily's Story- Freedom through Forgiveness," on YouTube.

YOUR THOUGHTS:

DAY 6

YOU CAN BE FORGIVEN

"Therefore, my brothers, I want you to know that through Jesus the forgiveness of sins is proclaimed to you."   Acts 13:38

"I will not ask for forgiveness. What I have done is unforgivable. I was so lost in hatred and revenge..."   Maleficent (Angelina Jolie) by Elizabeth Rudnick

PRAY: Jesus, it is only through You that I can find true forgiveness. Help me to seek Your face and spend more time with You. I want to get so close to You that I can hear You proclaim forgiveness to me in a very personal way. Thank You for forgiving my sins and for reminding me that I need You for true and lasting forgiveness. Amen.

REFLECT: As you think about forgiveness, think about wanting others to seek forgiveness who don't know Jesus. True forgiveness and the ability to forgive others only comes through a relationship with Jesus. So, maybe we need to pray for a person's salvation before we expect them to forgive others or seek forgiveness for themselves. Sometimes we get angry at people in Hollywood for being bad role models for our children or for creating immoral entertainment, but if they don't know Jesus, what should we expect?

ACT: Write down the names of the people you haven't yet forgiven, and then write: "I forgive you, in Jesus' name!" If you find you just can't forgive someone who has hurt you, remember that the ability to forgive only comes from Jesus. So, in Jesus' name, you can forgive. If you can't do it yet, then ask Jesus to soften your heart and to prepare you for complete forgiveness and freedom. As you pray over the names, you will know when you have let them go into God's hands. And it is done!

YOUR THOUGHTS:

DAY 7

GOD IS FAITHFUL TO FORGIVE

"If we confess our sins, he is faithful and just and will forgive us our sins and purify us from all unrighteousness."

1 John 1:9

"God will forgive me. It's his job."

Heinrich Heine

PRAY: Lord, I come to You now, in confession, for anything and everything in my heart. I know that You are faithful and just and will forgive me of all my sins, and I thank You for that. I also ask, Lord, that You purify me from all unrighteousness. I am at Your feet, asking for Your divine forgiveness for my sins, for You are the only one who can wipe away my sins and make my heart as white as snow. Amen.

REFLECT: Why do we sometimes have to go back to God, again and again, asking forgiveness for the same sin? Is it because we don't really believe He has forgiven us when we go to Him the first time to repent? What prevents us from embracing His immediate forgiveness? Could it be our own guilt? Have you forgiven yourself? Could it be that if we don't forgive others, we don't feel complete forgiveness from the Lord? 1 John 1 says "If we confess, then He is faithful. So, if we want Him to be faithful to us, we must confess our sins to Him. It's a difficult yet life-changing issue that is worth wrestling with.

ACT: Right now, sit before the Lord and lay out everything you need forgiveness for: a bad attitude, a mean word you said to another person, lying, cheating, pride, unforgiveness... Tell Him everything on your mind and in your heart, and ask Him to wipe your slate clean. Then, as you thank Him, do not doubt that you're forgiven. You are starting over as a new creature with a pure heart and a righteous spirit. And remember, He is faithful and just and will forgive you of your sins and purify you from all unrighteousness. Ahh, what a way to start your day and end your week!

YOUR THOUGHTS:

HEALING

WEEK FORTY-THREE

Do you roll your eyes at the thought of a Christian healer coming into town? I wonder if anyone rolled their eyes when Jesus started healing people. This week we're embracing the power of God's healing and asking God to have us experience His healing in our bodies, minds, and souls.

DAY 1

BY HIS WOUNDS YOU HAVE BEEN HEALED

"But he was pierced for our transgressions, he was crushed for our iniquities; the punishment that brought us peace was upon him, and by his wounds we are healed."

Isaiah 53:5

"He himself bore our sins in his body on the tree, so that we might die to sins and live for righteousness; by his wounds you have been healed."   1 Peter 2:24

"How sweet the name of Jesus sounds in a believer's ear! It soothes his sorrows, heals his wounds, and drives away his fear."

John Newton

PRAY: My Father in heaven, You remind me in these verses what Jesus went through for me. It was because He suffered that I am healed. He was pierced for my transgressions, crushed for my iniquities, and punished to give me peace. Because of Jesus' wounds, I am healed. It's an unbelievable sacrifice that You allowed Your only beloved Son to bear my sins and hang on a cross for me, just so that I would have eternal life. That is beyond my comprehension and I praise You for all You have done for me. Amen.

REFLECT: There is more to ponder here than seems possible to digest. Allow yourself to absorb all Jesus went through just to heal your body, mind, heart, and soul. You are a new creature because He suffered and died for you. If you really understood the sacrificial love that Jesus has for you, would you live differently or love people differently? Would you be more selfless and kind? Does eternal life mean more when you know what Jesus went through to give it to you? Try to absorb that profound and sacrificial act. How do you feel?

ACT: Try to walk in Jesus' sandals for just one day and do radical acts of love and kindness. Could you give a person in need some money or clothes? Could you do a kind act for someone who has been mean to you? Or, spontaneously go out and cut your neighbor's grass? Show people that you value them! Your actions have to be radical to even come close to what Jesus did for you. Choose a day, step completely out of your comfort zone, and try to be Jesus for a day. Die to your pride, to your desires, to winning, or embarrassment. It could be the most memorable and healing day of your life! By His wounds, we have been healed!

YOUR THOUGHTS:

DAY 2

SIN AND ILLNESS

"I said, "O Lord, have mercy on me; heal me, for I have sinned against you." Psalm 41:4

"Therefore confess your sins to each other and pray for each other so that you may be healed. The prayer of a righteous man is powerful and effective." James 5:16

"Listen to God with a broken heart. He is not only the doctor who mends it, but also the father who wipes away the tears." Criss Jami

PRAY: Lord, I am crying out to You in humility, confessing my sins, and I ask You to bring healing to me and anyone I may have sinned against. Please have mercy on me. I know that I need You and I need to confess to others. I want my prayers to be powerful and effective, but I will only be righteous if I am cleansed and healed by You. You are the only one who can heal me and make me whole. Help me to be a good friend and listener to those close to me. Lord, I confess to You my brokenness so that You can heal me. And I pray for my friends and family members, that they may be healed as well. Amen and Amen.

REFLECT: God tells us that we not only need to confess our sins to the Lord to be healed, but we also need to confess to one another. There are only two relationships that are crucial to our spiritual growth and healing: The vertical relationship between you and God, and the horizontal relationships between you and everyone in your life. God made us not only to need one another but to confess our sins to one another, and to forgive others when they confess to us. God gives us mercy when we walk with humility, honesty, and forgiveness in both our relationship with Him and with other people. What steps of healing do you need to take in both your vertical and horizontal relationships?

ACT: Make two healing columns: Put under the left column, titled FROM GOD, the ways you want healing from God. Be vulnerable with God about the healing you desire. Then on the right column, titled FROM MAN, list the ways you want healing from the hurts of others. Also write the names of people whom you want to forgive or from whom you want to receive forgiveness. Keep a copy of this list of two columns and pray over it, asking to experience total healing. The prayer of a righteous man is powerful and effective!

YOUR THOUGHTS:

DAY 3

CALL OUT TO THE LORD

"O Lord my God, I called to you for help and you healed me."   Psalm 30:2

When Jesus landed and saw a large crowd, he had compassion on them and healed their sick."   Matthew 14:14

"You pay God a compliment by asking great things of Him... However softly we speak, God is near enough to hear us."   Teresa of Avila

PRAY: Dear Lord, I am calling to You for help so that You will heal me. You are a healing God and I know that You have healed every disease and sickness among people throughout time. I want to see physical, emotional, and spiritual healings in my family, friends, co-workers, and neighbors. Thank You that You can heal anyone. You can even raise people from the dead. So, I call out to You to have compassion on me and other people today and heal me and the sick. I pray this in Your name, Amen.

REFLECT: Have you ever seen a miraculous healing? Do you believe God still heals? There are miraculous healings both in the Bible, and today. God is the same yesterday, today and forever and He continues to heal the sick and even raise people from the dead. There are documented stories in the US, and all over the world, of people being miraculously healed, physically, spiritually, and mentally. How can you expand your understanding of the love and power of God and all that He can accomplish? We can't minimize Him or what He can do. As we get older our God should get bigger!

ACT: Today is the day to embrace the incredible, miraculous healings that God still does through people, through doctors, or through the Holy Spirit. Don't question God's miracles. Ask Him right now to show you what He can do. If you have never seen a miracle, then ask Him to reveal a miracle to you. If you have experienced a miracle yourself, then go out and tell someone your story. We don't want to miss anything that God has for us! Believing in His miracles, and expecting them in your life, is one way to grow in your faith and in your relationship with Him. Pray big prayers today and step out in faith for the healing of others as well. God has compassion on us and He is a healing God!

YOUR THOUGHTS:

DAY 4

EMOTIONAL HEALING

"He heals the brokenhearted and binds up their wounds."   Psalm 147:3

"Dear friend, I pray that you may enjoy good health and that all may go well with you, even as your soul is getting along well."   3 John 1:2

"I've experienced several different healing methodologies over the years – counseling, self-help seminars, and I've read a lot – but none of them will work unless you really want to heal."   Lindsay Wagner

PRAY: Dear Jesus, thank You that You heal our hearts and souls, not just our bodies. I pray today for the people in Hollywood, whom many Christians have given up on. If they are hurting will You heal them? So many celebrities and decision-makers in Hollywood are broken, isolated, discouraged, and fearful. I know that though many Christians pray for our politicians, not many Christians pray for our cultural influencers. So, I ask You to bring healing to the brokenhearted in the world's most influential industry. Thank You that You love all those people and are binding up their physical and emotional wounds and that all will go well with their souls. Amen.

REFLECT: What an awesome thought to know that Jesus heals our bodies, our minds, and our souls! And we get the privilege to pray for people we don't even know, asking the God of the universe to heal them. You may never know the result of your prayers, but you can be assured that you are making an eternal difference for anyone God has put on your heart to pray for. So, what healing prayers do you want to pray for the people in Hollywood who are influencing the world? Realize the spiritual impact you can have on your favorite movie star, director, or songwriter. Embrace God's healing power as you pray!

ACT: Choose two people in Hollywood to pray for emotional healing. Many people have been sexually or emotionally abused, have severe anxiety, and even deep loneliness. Pray expectantly for healing for these people whom God has put on your heart. Your prayers can change their life! Be a part of a revolution of miraculous healing in Hollywood, just by choosing to pray—you may be the very first person to pray for those individuals! Thank you!

Y**OUR THOUGHTS:**

DAY 5

JESUS GAVE US AUTHORITY TO HEAL

"When Jesus had called the Twelve together, he gave them power and authority to drive out all demons and to cure diseases, and he sent them out to preach the kingdom of God and to heal the sick."

Luke 9:1-2

"In a futile attempt to erase our past, we deprive the community of our healing gift. If we conceal our wounds out of fear and shame, our inner darkness can neither be illuminated nor become a light for others."

Brennan Manning

PRAY: Jesus, You gave the disciples the power to heal the sick and You gave me the same power. As I read Luke, I want to pray for a lame man to walk and to offer someone a healing prayer to drive out demons and cure diseases. Help me to be a part of a miraculous healing. Would You stretch my faith so that I can embrace the power and authority to even drive out demons. Let me preach the kingdom of God and heal the sick, all in Your name, Amen.

REFLECT: Depending on your spiritual and church background, these verses may or may not be easy to embrace. If you have driven out demons or been a part of healings, then tell your story to others and preach the kingdom of God. If this scares you or makes you uncomfortable, then pray to be inspired this week to learn more about God's healing powers. Don't be afraid of any of God's gifts and don't make God too small. He raised His own son from the dead, and He gave His disciples the power and the authority to heal and drive out demons. And He has given us that same power. Are you ready to explore this gift from God?

ACT: Today is the day to step out of your comfort zone. If you have experienced God's healing, pray for healing for someone else. If you don't believe in the gift of healing, do a Bible study to see with new eyes what God says about healing. If you are uncomfortable with the thought, ask God to give you peace with the concept of supernatural healing. Commit now to step into a new season of growth, maturity, and experience with the Lord. He wants so much more for us than we can even hope for or imagine.

YOUR THOUGHTS:

DAY 6

GIVE THANKS FOR YOUR HEALING

"Praise the Lord, O my soul, and forget not all his benefits who forgives all your sins and heals all your diseases, who redeems your life from the pit and crowns you with love and compassion, who satisfies your desires with good things so that your youth is renewed like the eagle's."   Psalm 103:2-5

"One of them, when he saw he was healed, came back, praising God in a loud voice. He threw himself at Jesus' feet and thanked him--and he was a Samaritan."   Luke 17:15-16

"When we accept what happens to us and make the best of it, we are praising God."
                                                                        Teresa of Avila

PRAY: Lord, I praise You from my soul and I don't want to forget all of Your benefits – You forgive me all my sins and heal all my diseases. You even redeem my life from the pit and crown me with love and compassion. People in the Bible saw that they were healed and praised You in a loud voice. May I be healed and praise You today. I want You to say to me, "Rise and go; your faith has made you well." Praise the Lord! Amen.

REFLECT: These verses are full of hope and the stories remind us of God's almighty power. Be full of praise – not only for what God has already done for you, but because you know He has so much for you in the future. If we could all live lives of praise, we would experience more of God's love, compassion, redemption, and healing. The connection between praise and healing is amazing. But we often don't step out in faith and believe it. The more we praise God the easier it will be to believe in and experience His healing power. He wants to redeem your life, crown you with love and heal your soul. Can you believe that?

ACT: In this week on healing, take five minutes right now and just praise God for who He is and that He is in the process of healing you right now. Praise Him for your life, your family, your friends, your job, your opportunities, your wisdom, knowledge, joy, and peace. Even praise Him for the things that are not good in your life and for the people who have hurt you or been unfair to you. Praise Him because you know He has protected you from harm or pain. Give thanks to Him for the things you can't see, feel, or understand! Praise God!

YOUR THOUGHTS:

DAY 7

HEAL OUR LAND

"If my people, who are called by my name, will humble themselves and pray and seek my face and turn from their wicked ways, then will I hear from heaven and will forgive their sin and will heal their land."   2 Chronicles 7:14

"Prayer is not asking. Prayer is putting oneself in the hands of God, at His disposition, and listening to His voice in the depth of our hearts."   Mother Teresa

PRAY: God my Father, I am so grateful to end this week on healing by praying this beautiful prayer. I humble myself and pray, asking You to heal my land, my family, and my life. I am called by Your name and I seek Your face. Help me to turn away from my wicked ways, then I will hear from heaven and You will forgive my sins and heal my land. These verses are rich with promises, hope and healing. Thank You God, for your love, compassion, and healing hand on my life. I am honored to be called by Your name, Amen.

REFLECT: Read through each phrase of this verse and ponder their meaning. "If my people who are called by my name." That's you, a Christian, a follower of Christ. "Will humble themselves and pray and seek my face and turn from their wicked ways." Are you humble before the Lord? Do you pray and seek His face? Have you turned from all of your wicked ways? "Then I will hear from heaven, and I will forgive their sin and will heal their land." Do you believe that God hears every one of your prayers and forgives every single sin of yours? And do you believe that He will heal your land? What does that mean to you? Can you imagine what the world would be like if God healed our entire land? It's incredible!

ACT: End your week by memorizing this one verse. It's God's ultimate healing promise, but it takes work on our part. If you can memorize this whole verse and have it in your heart, it will soon become the steppingstone to living a Christ-like life and experiencing God's healing power. Put these words in your heart, mind, and soul, and then watch God do a healing work in your life and in your land! Remember is starts by humbling yourself.

YOUR THOUGHTS:

BEAUTY
WEEK FORTY-FOUR

This week let's tackle something that God gave us as a gift: BEAUTY. Beauty is a subject that opens the door for us to share our faith more deeply, to discuss the significance of God's creation, and for self-reflection. So, let's grasp the concept of beauty permeating our hearts, from the inside out, and also train ourselves to see beauty in the people and the world around us.

DAY 1

THE HOLINESS OF GOD'S BEAUTY

"Worship the Lord in the splendor of his holiness; tremble before him, all the earth."

Psalm 96:9

"We do not want merely to see beauty...we want something else which can hardly be put into words – to be united with the beauty we see, to pass into it, to receive it into ourselves, to bathe in it, to become part of it."   C. S. Lewis

PRAY: God, I want to be in the beauty of Your Holiness. Will You help me to worship You with joy and thanksgiving so that I tremble before You in Your majesty? Let me see You as beautiful. Help me to see Your beauty everywhere and to experience the splendor of Your holiness. I worship You, Oh Lord and ask that You bring me into Your glorious presence so that I am changed forever and can see the beauty in the world through Your eyes. In Jesus name I pray. Amen.

REFLECT: What would it mean to see God as beautiful? Is He beautiful to you right now? It could be that we can experience His splendor and beauty if we worship Him. You might need to change your definition of "beauty" to make it more internal and not just an external trait. Come before Him, asking to see the beauty in our world through His holiness. As you do, you may actually physically tremble before Him!

ACT: The media influences us all, and Hollywood has defined beauty to us as thin, sexy, pure skin, shiny hair, etc. We think of celebrities as beautiful people, and yet we don't know what's in their hearts. Change your definition of beautiful so that you are reflecting God's meaning. He cares most about our hearts, minds, and souls. As you take time right now to worship Him in the splendor of His holiness, ask Him to show the people in Hollywood what real beauty is and that they too can tremble before Him as they experience His splendor.

YOUR THOUGHTS:

DAY 2

EMPTY BEAUTY

"Woe to you, teachers of the law and Pharisees, you hypocrites! You are like whitewashed tombs, which look beautiful on the outside but on the inside are full of dead men's bones and everything unclean." Matthew 23:27

"As the excellence of steel is strength, and the excellence of art is beauty, so the excellence of mankind is moral character." A. W. Tozer

PRAY: Heavenly Father, help me to focus on having a pure heart, and not just on looking good or being impressive. For you tell us that we can be beautiful on the outside but full of dead bones and everything unclean on the inside. Please help me to stop worrying about what other people think of me, but only what You think of my heart. I don't want to be a hypocrite, like whitewashed tombs. I want to be a beautiful person more than just have a beautiful appearance. Thank You that You are making me beautiful from the inside out. Amen.

REFLECT: Look inside your heart and think about who you really are. Are there any areas where you are a hypocrite? Are you full of dead bones or unclean? Are you more concerned about how you look on the outside than how clean and beautiful you are on the inside? Could you possibly be living your life like a Pharisee? It's actually amazing how godly people are beautiful to others, even if they don't have a gorgeous outside appearance, because God's beauty is overflowing out of their hearts and that's what others see.

ACT: Look up what it is to be a "Pharisee" or a hypocrite. Also, research what God means when He says, "You are like whitewashed tombs, which look beautiful on the outside but on the inside are full of dead men's bones and everything unclean." Choose now to focus more on your heart than on your face, weight, or size. Would you get down on your knees right now and ask God to clean out your hypocrisy and to fill your heart, soul and mind with His beautiful promises and truths. You can choose to be more beautiful, this moment, both in the eyes of God and man.

YOUR THOUGHTS:

DAY 3

INNER BEAUTY

"Your beauty should not come from outward adornment, such as braided hair and the wearing of gold jewelry and fine clothes. Instead, it should be that of your inner self, the unfading beauty of a gentle and quiet spirit, which is of great worth in God's sight."

1 Peter 3:3-4

"The beauty of a woman is not in a facial mode but the true beauty in a woman is reflected in her soul. It is the caring that she lovingly gives, the passion that she shows. The beauty of a woman grows with the passing years."

Audrey Hepburn

PRAY: Lord, let me have a beautiful heart, mind, and soul so that I ooze beauty out of my every action, word, and thought. Help me understand I AM beautiful, not because of what I wear or how I look, but because I have great worth in your sight, a gentle and quiet spirit and a beautiful inner self. I want to radiate Your beauty and love, not just be disguised with gold jewelry and fine clothes. Thank you that I can have inner beauty just by walking in Your presence. Amen.

REFLECT: Reflect on how much time, money, and effort you spend on your OUTER beauty rather than your INNER beauty. Do you spend more time buying clothes, jewelry and skin products, primping in the morning, and getting expensive haircuts, or do you spend more time memorizing scripture, spending time with God, encouraging and serving others and praying? True beauty, that is of great worth to God, does not come from outward adornment. It comes from the inside. So how can you focus more on your heart than your body? Can you re-prioritize your goals to embrace the unfading beauty of a gentle and quiet spirit? Now *that* has great worth in God's sight.

ACT: Choose to do one thing today to make yourself more beautiful on the INSIDE. Decide to give up one thing you usually do to enhance your outer beauty, and spend that time getting more beautiful on the inside. You could memorize scripture, spend quiet time with God, do a random act of kindness to some unsuspecting neighbor. Take action on building up your heart and soul today, for that is of great worth in God's sight.

YOUR THOUGHTS:

DAY 4

HE MAKES YOU BEAUTIFUL

"He has made everything beautiful in its time. He has also set eternity in the hearts of men; yet they cannot fathom what God has done from beginning to end"   Ecclesiastes 3:11

"Never lose an opportunity of seeing anything beautiful, for beauty is God's handwriting."
Ralph Waldo Emerson

PRAY: Lord, would You please give me patience as I wait for You to make things more beautiful in my life in Your time? I want to have a greater understanding of eternity so that I'm not so frustrated with why things take so long in the present. May I seek beauty both in me and around me so that I can start to fathom what You have done and are doing in my life. Thank You that You make everything beautiful in its time! Amen and Amen.

REFLECT: Focus on what it means to "set eternity in your heart." God promises that and yet it's hard to tangibly experience. No one can fathom what God has done, but can you get a glimpse of what He's doing in your life? We know that He makes everything beautiful in its time, but how do we experience the eternity that He has set in our hearts? It's got to be beautiful but maybe it's so incredible that we can't fathom it...

ACT: List three things that God has done in your life—from beginning to end—that are hard to fathom. What miracles have you experienced? What changed lives have you seen? And how has He actually made you beautiful because of changing your heart? List the three top miraculous beautiful acts or things of God that you can praise Him for and that will help you to start to fathom what God has done from beginning to end, both in your life and in our world.

YOUR THOUGHTS:

DAY 5

YOU ARE ALTOGETHER BEAUTIFUL

"My beloved spoke and said to me, 'Arise, my darling, my beautiful one, come with me...You are altogether beautiful, my darling; there is no flaw in you'." Song of Solomon 2:10 & 4:7

"Taking joy in living is a woman's best cosmetic."

Rosalind Russell

PRAY: Lord, thank You that You call me Your beloved and You tell me that I am altogether beautiful, without even a flaw, for You created me in Your image. Oh, may I truly believe that and live that way, as a precious, beautiful child of Yours. You have given me the gift of beauty because You are proud of me. I know You want to make my life richer and more meaningful, with no flaws, and I praise You for that! Help me to believe that Lord so that I can have confidence in who You made me to be! Amen.

REFLECT: Can you honestly believe that you are truly beautiful, and that God calls you "darling" because you are so precious to Him? What would change in your countenance, your confidence, your stature, and your attitude if you really knew that God looks at you as His perfect love, without even a flaw? You can't convince yourself to have a better self-image, but you can depend on the Holy Spirit to change you from the inside out. He wants us to have the desires of our hearts, so if your desire is to truly feel beautiful then ask Him and He is faithful to answer.

ACT: Take today as the first day to not allow yourself to question your looks or God's unbelievable love for you. Ask the Holy Spirit to help you see yourself the way God sees you. Don't allow yourself to say anything negative about yourself. Don't beat yourself up or tear yourself down. Stop before you push away a compliment or a kind word from another and just say "Thank you." Embrace your beauty with joy and thanksgiving. And then if you succeed today, do it again tomorrow, and then the next day, and the next... Your goal is to fully believe that you are God's darling, His beautiful one, with no flaw in you—through the power of the Holy Spirit. WOW! Start right now!

YOUR THOUGHTS:

DAY 6

TRUE BEAUTY

"Finally, brothers, whatever is true, whatever is noble, whatever is right, whatever is pure, whatever is lovely, whatever is admirable--if anything is excellent or praiseworthy--think about such things."
Philippians 4:8

"In every heart there is a secret nerve that answers to the vibrations of beauty."
Christopher Morley

PRAY: Dear Heavenly Father, may I focus on everything beautiful in my life and especially in what I think about and talk about. You created the world and everything in it by thinking only thoughts that are true, noble, right, pure, lovely, admirable, excellent, praiseworthy, and beautiful. Help me to reflect you. Transform me from the inside out as I speak the truth about myself and everyone around me. I want to feel beautiful and see Your beauty all around me. I want You to fill me with beautiful thoughts and have them overflow to the people in my life. Oh Lord, show me Your beauty. Thank You! Amen.

REFLECT: What do you think or talk about that is untrue, ugly, negative, mean, cutting, or impure? Does something come to mind that is not praiseworthy or beautiful? If we want to think like Jesus, we have to change our thoughts. He saw the good and the beautiful in everyone and everything. Choose to form a habit to stop letting your carnal nature guide your thoughts, words, or actions.

ACT: Pinpoint one "negative" thought you struggle with and choose to stop thinking it by replacing it with something pure, noble, or beautiful. Decide what you're going to do any time that thought pops up and reprogram your brain to replace it with a beautiful image in your mind. Maybe it's a person whom you think badly of. Choose the positive, truthful thoughts and/or words that you want to think about and ask the Lord to help you change. You will become a more beautiful person and you will see more beauty in the people around you. Choose now to fill your life with God's beauty, in thought mind and deed.

YOUR THOUGHTS:

DAY 7

THE LORD IS BEAUTIFUL

"One thing I ask of the Lord , this only do I seek: that I may dwell in the house of the Lord all the days of my life, to gaze upon the beauty of the Lord and to seek him in his temple."

Psalm 27:4

"How much we need, in the church and in society, witnesses of the beauty of holiness, witnesses of the splendor of truth, witnesses of the joy and freedom born of a living relationship with Christ!"
Pope Benedict XVI

PRAY: Dear God, I ask You one thing, as the only thing I seek today—that I may dwell in Your house, close to You, and feeling Your presence, all the days of my life. Lord help me to dwell on You and Your beauty and that I may seek You everywhere I am and say, "Oh God, You are so beautiful!" May I keep gazing on You. In Jesus' name, Amen.

REFLECT: What does it mean to "seek" God? How can you do that more effectively? And what does it mean to "dwell in the house of the Lord" and to "seek Him in His temple?" And do you think of God as beautiful? Reflect on how to make these concepts real in your life, and how to personally make this scripture come to life for you so that you truly believe that God is beautiful.

ACT: Commit to actively SEEKING GOD in a new way. Either spend more time with Him or spend more time each day reading the Bible. Commit to talk to Him all day, bring Him into every conversation, meeting, and decision, and relentlessly pursue Him, because He is BEAUTIFUL!

YOUR THOUGHTS:

For further inspiration, check out Michael McClymond's audio interview, "Captured by God's Beauty," on John Piper's "Desiring God" website. He discusses understanding how God himself defines beauty. AND check out Tommy Walker's song, "I Fix My Eyes on You," on YouTube.

DECEPTION

WEEK FORTY-FIVE

"The enemy comes only to steal, kill and destroy." That's the foundation of why we are all hurt at some point in our lives by deception. This week we're looking into how to deal with the deceiver and those who deceive, including ourselves. Let's not let the enemy deceive us in any way or at any time!

DAY 1

ACCEPT RESPONSIBILITY FOR YOUR CHOICES

"Then the Lord God said to the woman, 'What is this you have done?' The woman said, 'The serpent deceived me, and I ate.'"   Genesis 3:13

"We like to be deceived."

Blaise Pascal

PRAY: Dear Lord, You know my heart and yet I have so much trouble accepting the responsibility for my actions. From the beginning of time man has blamed others for our personal choices and I ask You to please help me to be strong enough to acknowledge the wrongs that I do and to admit my mistakes. Then I can ask You for healing and change. I want to be more Christ-like and I need You to give me the strength to change my ways. Thank You for being there for me in times of fear and weakness. I pray in Jesus' name, Amen.

REFLECT: Like Adam and Eve, it's easy to see the weaknesses and sin in others, but it's so hard to see it in ourselves. What would it take for us to be able to ask the Lord to reveal our sins and our deceptions, embrace them, and then choose to do something to change them? That's probably the most difficult human task, but are you up for it? Reflect on how that would change your life. It can't be with shame, guilt, or blame, but with the desire to trust completely in the Lord, with humility and confidence in Him.

ACT: Take a moment and seek the Holy Spirit and ask Him to choose one trait or area of your life where you can honestly admit that you are either deceiving yourself or others. Once you define it, then bring that trait or issue to God and ask Him to reveal to you if you've been blaming someone else for that sin, instead of taking personal responsibility. Ask Him to heal you, or to show you how to handle it until you can release it to Him. This is an extremely difficult exercise and will probably take more time to fully deal with it. But keep asking the Lord to help you, with honesty and humility, and you will see breakthrough.

YOUR THOUGHTS:

DAY 2

DON'T DECEIVE OTHERS

"Do not steal. Do not lie. Do not deceive one another."   Leviticus 19:11

"No one who practices deceit will dwell in my house; no one who speaks falsely will stand in my presence."   Psalm 101:7

"The new freedom of expression brought by the Internet goes far beyond politics. People relate to each other in new ways, posing questions about how we should respond to people when all that we know about them is what we have learned through a medium that permits all kinds of anonymity and deception."   Peter Singer

PRAY: Dear Lord, I know we live in a culture of lies. We get used to white lies, lies to protect someone's feelings, and lies to protect ourselves from embarrassment. But You don't want me to deceive others. Your biblical view is often so different from our culture's views of truth, lying, and deception. Please reveal to me Your truth about how I'm practicing deceit so that I may dwell in Your house and stand in Your presence. Amen.

REFLECT: God is so vague in some areas and so clear in others. These verses couldn't be clearer on what we are to do and what we are not to do. It's easy to know that we're stealing or outright lying, but it's harder to be honest with ourselves about how we might be deceiving one another. But we must deal with this issue head on so that we may dwell in the house of the Lord and stand in His presence forever.

ACT: Right now, ask the Lord to reveal your heart to you and to help you never to speak falsely or deceive yourself or anyone else. Tell Him that you want to dwell in His house forever and that you want nothing to get in the way of being in His presence for eternity. Ask Him to reveal anything in you that may be getting in the way of standing before Him with a clean heart. Don't rush, just bask in His presence and wait on Him. Then thank Him for meeting you in that private place.

YOUR THOUGHTS:

DAY 3

DECEITFUL HEARTS DESTROY

"Everyone lies to his neighbor; their flattering lips speak with deception"..."The words of their mouths are wicked and deceitful; they fail to act wisely or do good."..."Your tongue plots destruction; it is like a sharpened razor, you who practice deceit."

Psalm 12:2; 36:3; 52:2

"I know how easy it is for one to stay well within moral, ethical, and legal bounds through the skillful use of words – and to thereby spin, sidestep, circumvent, or bend a truth completely out of shape. To that extent, we are all liars on numerous occasions."

Sidney Poitier

PRAY: Heavenly Father, I pray for the decision-makers in Hollywood who are choosing the messages and the stories in all of the films, TV shows and music we hear and watch. Would You touch their hearts so that their words are not wicked and deceitful? I know that many of them don't know You Lord, so I ask that You reveal Yourself to them and convict them so they turn from evil and do not practice deceit or harbor deception in their hearts. Amen.

REFLECT: Reflect on how much time we spend watching television and films, playing video games, and listening to music. Because many of the people creating our media and entertainment don't know Jesus, their hearts are deceived. Don't judge them or get angry, instead pray for the Lord to come into their hearts and give them the wisdom to do good. Your prayers could change both their lives and change the messages of the films, TV shows, music, and video games that we watch and listen to.

ACT: Choose one film, TV show, video game, or song that you think is immoral or crude. Now pray for the people who wrote it, directed it, acted in it, or produced it. You don't need to know their names. Ask the Lord to come into each of these people's lives and transform any deceitful hearts and flattering lips. Ask God to reveal their own wickedness and destructive tongues. Then ask the Lord to have them tell good, uplifting stories that celebrate the human spirit and tell God's truths. When you pray for them to meet Jesus, you are playing a role in changing the world through a positive influence of the media!

YOUR THOUGHTS:

DAY 4

WATCH OUT FOR DECEPTIVE PEOPLE

"Jesus answered: "Watch out that no one deceives you. For many will come in my name, claiming, 'I am the Christ, ' and will deceive many."   Matthew 24:4-5

"For I have sworn thee fair, and thought thee bright, who art as black as hell, as dark as night."   William Shakespeare

PRAY: Dear God, I pray for wisdom today. I want to watch out for anyone who may be trying to deceive me, especially those coming in Your name, claiming to be speaking Your truths. I don't want to be deceived by false teaching or follow false leaders, but I need Your Holy Spirit to give me discernment. Please, Lord, don't let me be deceived by the evil one through people who are using You for personal gain. Fill me with Your wisdom, God. Amen.

REFLECT: It's so easy to get to like someone and then trust everything they say. As Christians, we want to be wiser than that. But we need to pray for discernment and ask for wisdom. Jesus warns us about false leaders, but because He doesn't list who they are, we have to seek Him to know whom we should trust and whom to walk away from. We can't be untrusting of everyone or paranoid of liars, but we shouldn't place ourselves under the spiritual authority of anyone until we ask God for wisdom to see that person for whom he or she really is. Watch out. Don't be deceived.

ACT: Pray for your spiritual leaders right now. Ask the Lord to fill them with only His wisdom, truth, knowledge, and love. And ask Him to protect you from any false teachings. Commit to pray for your pastor, counselors, prayer leaders, and even government leaders. Ask the Holy Spirit to come into the hearts of the leaders in your life, and clean house, build truth, and fill them with words of truth, grace and love. And don't just pray today. Leaders, speakers, pastors, and teachers need our prayers every day, for many wolves in sheep's clothing will come in His name and will deceive many!

YOUR THOUGHTS:

DAY 5

DON'T DECEIVE YOURSELF

"If anyone thinks they are something when they are nothing, they deceive themselves...Do not be deceived: God cannot be mocked. A man reaps what he sows."　　Galatians 6:3, 7

"If the whole church goes off into deception, that will in no way excuse us for not following Christ."
　　　　　　　　　　　　　　　　　　　　　　　Leonard Ravenhill

PRAY: Oh, dear Father in Heaven, I come humbly before You and ask that You reveal my heart to me. I don't want to think that I am something that I'm not. I don't want to deceive myself into thinking I'm better, smarter, cooler or better looking than others. I don't want to mock You by taking personal credit for anything You've given me. I understand I will reap what I sow, and so I want to sow humility in my own heart with complete confidence in You. I want to celebrate what You've given me and yet, not take credit for it myself. Would You help me find that balance Lord? I pray this in Jesus' name, Amen!

REFLECT: How can we look at ourselves in the mirror and really see the whole truth of who we are? How can we honestly see areas where we are deceiving ourselves into believing what we want to believe, rather than understanding the truth of what is going on? It's only the Holy Spirit who can reveal this and keep us from our own deception. The Holy Spirit is our guide, our teacher, our comforter, and our mirror. This scripture says not to deceive ourselves, but that requires choosing to listen to the nudging on our heart and allowing the Holy Spirit to open our eyes.

ACT: Take some time to talk to God about your heart and your understanding of yourself. Ask the Holy Spirit to reveal to you what you are sowing and reaping so that there is no deception in your life. Tell Him that you don't want to puff yourself up, but you don't want to cut yourself down either. You want to be pure of heart and free of wrong motives or actions, but you need the Holy Spirit to do that. Ask God to reveal anything that you think about yourself that may not be accurate and then ask Him to help you see yourself through His eyes. Ah, what a freeing revelation that could be.

YOUR THOUGHTS:

DAY 6

DON'T MAKE TROUBLE

"A scoundrel and villain, who goes about with a corrupt mouth, who winks with his eye, signals with his feet and motions with his fingers, who plots evil with deceit in his heart he always stirs up dissension."..."There is deceit in the hearts of those who plot evil, but joy for those who promote peace."   Proverbs 6:12-14 & 12:20

"A little lie can travel halfway 'round the world while Truth is still lacing up her boots."
                    Mark Twain

PRAY: Lord, I ask that You protect me from evil people. Would You give me wisdom and discernment to know who is full of truth and who is trying to deceive others or me? Lord, I want to stay away from troublemakers and villains and those who are plotting evil, stirring up conflict, and deceiving people around them. Would You make me a person who promotes peace and is full of joy and open my eyes to people who aren't, so that I can be wise to their motives and pray for them? Thank You, Lord. Amen.

REFLECT: Being a Christian can be hard, especially when we're told to stay away from deceivers. We don't want to be on a witch-hunt and question the motives of everyone around us, but we don't want to be blind or naive to the evil around us. Reflect on how to find the balance between discerning a troublemaker and embracing those around us with the love of Jesus. And in the process, how might you promote peace and have joy?

ACT: Choose one person in your life, at work, in the neighborhood, at school, and even in your family, who creates conflict or who is deceptive, and commit to pray for him or her. Lift that person up to the Lord every day—even if just for a month—and ask the Lord to make him a peacemaker, not a troublemaker. Ask the Lord to melt his heart, to fall in love with Him and to no longer be able to plot evil or have malice. Your prayers for that person can completely turn around his life. **Don't judge, but pray with loving and healing prayers.**

YOUR THOUGHTS:

DAY 7

BE TRANSFORMED BY THE WORD

"He committed no sin, and no deceit was found in his mouth."   1 Peter 2:22

"Don't be deceived, my dear brothers... Do not merely listen to the word, and so deceive yourselves. Do what it says."

James 1:16, 22

"There is nothing more impotent than words which lie dormant in our brains and have no influence on our lives."

Alexander MacLaren

PRAY: Jesus, I praise You that You are and always have been sinless. You are my role model, my inspiration, and my encouragement. Don't let me be deceived. Let me read and learn Your word and then do what it says, so that I will not deceive myself into thinking that I am more righteous than I am. Please help me to be more like You and to depend on You for everything I do and say. Thank You Jesus. I pray this in Your name, Amen.

REFLECT: How humbling to realize that in our humanness we can deceive ourselves and others into believing and doing things that aren't true. Even when we think we're good people, doing good things and following Jesus, we can still say and do deceitful things. That's why we need a Savior. That's why Jesus died for us, even though He committed no sin, and no deceit was found in His mouth. Reflect on Jesus and what it means to follow His example in your life, in your words, and in your actions, not just in your thoughts. Ask Jesus to help you intentionally put the Gospel into practice.

ACT: Spend the next five minutes just praising Jesus. Praise Him for being sinless, for being your Savior, your role model, your inspiration, and your comfort. Thank Him for loving you so much that He is your example of truth. Praise Him for giving you His word to follow and His life as an example of how to live. Praise Him that no deceitful word has ever come out of His mouth. Praise be to His name!

YOUR THOUGHTS:

WISDOM

WEEK FORTY-SIX

One of the very specific commands God gives us is to ask Him for wisdom. This week we're going to focus on gaining God's wisdom versus worldly wisdom. And along with gaining wisdom, we will discover a list of other benefits that we receive. God says it's a hidden mystery until we ask for it and then it becomes life changing.

DAY 1

HOW TO GET WISDOM

"The fear of the Lord is the beginning of wisdom, and knowledge of the Holy One is understanding. For through me your days will be many, and years will be added to your life."

"For the Lord gives wisdom, and from his mouth come knowledge and understanding."

Proverbs 9:10-11 & 2:6

"Where then does wisdom come from? Where does understanding dwell? ...God understands the way to it and he alone knows where it dwells..." Job from the land of Uz

PRAY: Oh Lord, I am excited to start my week focused on WISDOM by thanking you that the beginning of wisdom is the fear of the Lord and the knowledge of You is understanding. Please help me to understand Your wisdom, for I want my days to be many and for You to add years to my life. Lord, I acknowledge that I can only get wisdom, knowledge of You and Your ways, and understanding from You, so I ask now that you can fill me up to the brim with all that You have to offer. I want to live a life of understanding Your ways and making wise decisions in all that I do. Thank You for being so faithful. I pray in Jesus' name, Amen!

REFLECT: What a humble but completely freeing insight to realize that we can't be smart enough, wise enough, or clever enough on our own. We could get a Ph.D. or study literature and great wise people of the past and still not gain wisdom. God is the only one who can give us Divine knowledge, understanding, or wisdom. And we only get more if we ask Him. So, how do we get smarter and wiser in His ways? First, we get to know God, then we fear Him—which means we are in awe of God and have tremendous respect for Him—and then we ask Him to give us His wisdom, knowledge, and understanding. The result? Ours days will be many, and years will be added to our life. What a profound and beautiful truth!

ACT: Start your week right now by asking God to help you fear Him and for Him to fill you with His wisdom, knowledge, and understanding. Ask Him to fill you up with more every day and commit to submit to His perfect plan for your life. If you ask God for wisdom every day, you will soon see the difference in your conversations, your relationships, your choices, and your actions. It's honestly a life-changing prayer!

YOUR THOUGHTS:

DAY 2

WISDOM IS BETTER THAN RICHES

"How much better to get wisdom than gold, to choose understanding rather than silver!"...
"for wisdom is more precious than rubies, and nothing you desire can compare with her."
Proverbs 16:16 & 8:11

"Life is wasted if we do not grasp the glory of the cross, cherish it for the treasure that it is, and cleave to it as the highest price of every pleasure and the deepest comfort in every pain. What was once foolishness to us—a crucified God—must become our wisdom and our power and our only boast in this world."
John Piper

PRAY: Dear Father, help me to remember that Your wisdom is much better than acquiring gold, and Your insight is better than getting silver. Your wisdom is more precious than rubies and nothing that I desire on this earth is better than wisdom. Oh Lord, fill me with understanding so that I will seek You and not strive for things that the world says are important or valuable. I want to be wise, for nothing compares to her. In Jesus' name! Amen.

REFLECT: These Proverbs are a great reminder of another of God's truths: man's ways are opposite of God's ways. Our culture teaches us that we need to make more money, build up our savings, set up a pension or 401K, acquire real estate and gain riches. And if we don't, we tend to be scared for our future. But that is the opposite of what God tells us. He says that His wisdom is better than gold or precious rubies, and to choose understanding is more important than having silver. People who seek God's wisdom are blessed.

ACT: Ask yourself if you have been caught up in the ways of the world, or have you been seeking wisdom over riches and understanding over success? Take inventory of your heart. Do you need to shift your priorities and commit to letting go of the world's goals and instead embrace God's? Saving is good but not at the expense and distraction away from seeking God. What are some things you can you do to invest in your relationship with God? Write those things down and take action today. You will be truly blessed!

YOUR THOUGHTS:

DAY 3

WALK IN WISDOM OR REMAIN A FOOL

"A fool finds pleasure in evil conduct, but a man of understanding delights in wisdom."..."Pride only breeds quarrels, but wisdom is found in those who take advice."..."He who trusts in himself is a fool, but he who walks in wisdom is kept safe."

Proverbs 12:15, 13:10 & 28:26

"The fool doth think he is wise, but the wise man knows himself to be a fool."

William Shakespeare

PRAY: Father in heaven, I don't want to be a fool. I want to listen to wise advice. I don't want to cause strife or be proud. You tell me that I will be wise if I take advice, and I will be kept safe if I walk in wisdom. Oh Lord, don't let me be a fool. Please give me understanding and let me delight in wisdom. I want to walk in wisdom and live a Christ-like life. Thank You for answering my prayer. Amen.

REFLECT: Have you ever realized that people who cause strife, or those who are proud, have no wisdom? Do you see that the difference between a fool who finds pleasure in wicked schemes and a person who has understanding, is WISDOM? We need to pray for the difficult people in our lives to know God so that they can grow in their understanding of Him and gain wisdom. Don't get angry at them and call them fools, rather pray that the Holy Spirit will come into their hearts and give them wisdom. Difficult people need to know God. They need to be prayed for, not judged. And in doing that, you are practicing wisdom.

ACT: On an index card write down two people you know who are not wise in their words or actions, or who make you angry, or cause you strife. Then start praying for those people to fall in love with Jesus, and for the Holy Spirit to give them wisdom. Pray they take wise advice, rather than trusting in themselves. Ask the Lord to reveal to them that they can find satisfaction in embracing His wisdom. Pray that they will no longer find pleasure in their evil conduct, but instead find delight in gaining understanding. Keep praying for these people and begin expecting less quarrels and more peace around you.

YOUR THOUGHTS:

DAY 4

LOVE THE LORD'S WISDOM

"Oh, how I love your law! I meditate on it all day long. Your commands make me wiser than my enemies, for they are ever with me. I have more insight than all my teachers, for I meditate on your statutes. I have more understanding than the elders, for I obey your precepts." Psalm 119:97-100

"Not until we have become humble and teachable, standing in awe of God's holiness and sovereignty. acknowledging our own littleness, distrusting our own thoughts, and willing to have our minds turned upside down, can divine wisdom become ours." J.I. Packer

PRAY: Dear Lord, how I love Your law! Help me to meditate on it all day long, for they are ever with me. And please make me wise. I want to learn your commandments so that I am wiser than my enemies, have more insight than all my teachers, and more understanding than the elders. I know that I need to obey Your precepts and to meditate on Your statutes. Thank You Lord, Amen.

REFLECT: Reflect on the difference between being a mighty warrior by physical training or a powerful leader through information and manipulation, versus being a mighty warrior by meditating on God's law all day long. The world tells us to work out, train, and become either physically or intellectually more powerful than the people around us. God says to love His law and to meditate on it. He wants us to get excited about His commandments in order to become wiser than our enemies. Contemplate God's statutes and obey His principles and gain God's WISDOM!

ACT: Upload your Bible and look up Wisdom in the search bar. Read every scripture God has about wisdom and study the strength, power, insight, and understanding we get from asking God for wisdom. Then be bold and ask God to give you so much wisdom that you will become more powerful than all the rulers in your city. Only God knows what He has in store for you to make an eternal difference in our world by the power you'll have through your prayers and meditations. Get ready and allow Him to do miracles through you.

YOUR THOUGHTS:

386 Wisdom – Week Forty-six

DAY 5

ASK FOR WISDOM FROM GOD

"If any of you lacks wisdom, you should ask God, who gives generously to all without finding fault, and it will be given to you."   James 1:5

"For I will give you words and wisdom that none of your adversaries will be able to resist or contradict."   Luke 21:15

"Before reading the Bible, ask the Holy Spirit to grant you the spirit of wisdom and revelation that you may spiritually discern the truth found in its pages."   Patricia King

PRAY: God, right now I'm asking you to generously give me wisdom, without finding fault with me. I am asking for wisdom that none of my adversaries will be able to resist or contradict. And please fill me again with Your Spirit and with wisdom, understanding, and knowledge. I want to be the best person and child of God that I can be. Since I know I lack wisdom, I'm coming to You to change that. I know that You will give it to me, and I thank You, in the name of Jesus. Amen.

REFLECT: The more scripture we study, seeking wisdom, the more things we find God giving us. Just like Solomon, who asked for wisdom and got everything the world had to offer and everything God had to offer, we find here that when we ask for wisdom, the same is available to us. We get wisdom that God gives us generously, without finding any fault in us. Isn't that amazing!? Ask and we can get wisdom our adversaries can't resist or contradict, and we can become filled with the Spirit of God, with understanding and knowledge! Why wouldn't we commit to ask for wisdom every single day?!

ACT: Do you know that you are filled with the Spirit of God? Have you asked for wisdom? Do you believe that God has given you understanding, knowledge, and even all of your skills? If so, praise Him for that. If not, ask Him right now, believing that He answers all of your prayers with joy, love, and abundant generosity. Pray this every day and then in return, generously give it all away to others, for you will never run out of God's wisdom. You can't out give God!

YOUR THOUGHTS:

DAY 6

WHAT IS WISDOM?

*"For where you have envy and selfish ambition, there you find disorder and every evil practice. But the wisdom that comes from heaven is first of all pure; then peace-loving, considerate, submissive, full of mercy and good fruit, impartial and sincere."*James 3:16-17

"In life, all good things come hard, but wisdom is the hardest to come by."　　Lucille Ball

PRAY: Dear heavenly Father, I want to be wise in praying for the people in Hollywood, who are known for being selfish, ambitious, and even for practicing every kind of evil. I pray today that You will pour Your wisdom down from heaven upon all of the TV and film actors, directors, writers, producers, editors, executives, cinematographers, video game creators, musicians, and agents. Please give them the desire to be peace-loving, considerate, submissive to You, full of mercy and good fruit, and to be impartial and sincere. Lord, I pray a prayer of blessing on all the people in Hollywood, in Jesus' mighty name. Amen.

REFLECT: It's easier to apply scripture to ourselves than to pray for others to follow God. Have you ever thought that James was also written for the people in Hollywood, California? All across the globe people are full of envy and selfish ambition. Yes, in Hollywood there is disorder and every evil practice. But wisdom that comes from heaven is pure, peace-loving, considerate, submissive, full of mercy and good fruit, impartial, and sincere. Will you pray for the people, projects and issues in the world's most influential mission field--Hollywood?

ACT: Choose one person, one issue, and one project in Hollywood and pray right now for God's wisdom to be over that person, issue, and project. It might be Angelina Jolie, the Disney+ streaming service, or the #MeToo movement. Ask the Lord to touch the hearts of the people involved in all of those endeavors and that He takes away envy, selfish ambition, disorder, and any evil there. Ask Him to reveal Himself to them and fill them with His heavenly wisdom so they would be pure, peace-loving, considerate, submissive to Him, and full of good fruit. By praying this prayer today, you could change the world!

YOUR THOUGHTS:

DAY 7

WISDOM IS HIDDEN IN CHRIST

"We declare God's wisdom, a mystery that has been hidden and that God destined for our glory before time began.."
                    1 Corinthians 2:7

"Let the word of Christ dwell in you richly as you teach and admonish one another with all wisdom, and as you sing psalms, hymns and spiritual songs with gratitude in your hearts to God."
                    Colossians 3:16

"Christ is the physical manifestation of God-given wisdom, and with our knowledge of the Word and by the power of the Holy Spirit, we have access to this wisdom." Andrea Lucado

PRAY: Lord Jesus, on my last day of studying wisdom I want to experience Your secret wisdom that has been hidden and that You destined for my glory. May the word of Christ dwell richly among my family, my friends and me. I ask that You help us teach and admonish one another with all wisdom through Your Psalms, hymns, and spiritual songs.. Help me, my family, and my friends to sing to You with gratitude in our hearts. Thank you, Lord Jesus. Amen.

REFLECT: In I Corinthians 2:7 Paul tells us that we have to declare God's wisdom because even today, it is often a mystery that has been hidden from man, but God has destined it for our glory, even before time began. In Colossians 3:16 He tells us to let the word of Christ dwell richly in you as we teach and admonish one another. It sounds like we're expected to do that with gratitude in our hearts, as we sing Psalms, hymns, and spiritual songs!

ACT: Choose a psalm, hymn, or song that you can read or sing to God. Now read it or sing it out loud, with gratitude in your heart, and praise Him for giving you the mysterious wisdom that most men never discover. Thank Him that He has destined it for your glory, for you to be filled with divine wisdom. Thank God that as you sing and read scripture and learn hymns, you are being filled up with wisdom and becoming mature. Maybe you can make a habit of doing this. Now go out into the world filled with God's rich wisdom that will make you more powerful than your adversaries and full of gratitude in your heart!

YOUR THOUGHTS:

THANKFULNESS

WEEK FORTY-SEVEN

Being thankful is one of the most beautiful qualities of a Christian and makes us stand out amongst our non-believing friends as they see us expressing a thankful attitude for all things in our life, for we have so much to be thankful for. This week we focus on being thankful to the Lord every day, so that we end the week overflowing with thankfulness, praise, gratitude, and joy.

DAY 1

REJOICE, PRAY AND BE THANKFUL

"Be joyful always; pray continually; give thanks in all circumstances, for this is God's will for you in Christ Jesus."   1 Thessalonians 5:16 -18

"The first thing I do when I start my day is, I get down on my hands and knees and give thanks to God. Whenever I go outside of my house, the first thing I do is stop at the church."   Mark Wahlberg

PRAY: Lord, I know this verse so well, but I ask that You give me deeper insight into it. I don't want to just read it again. I want to experience it. Please show me how to always rejoice, to pray continually, and to give thanks in ALL circumstances, for I want to be in the center of Your will, and I want to experience You in a more intimate way. Fill me with thanks so that my prayers will also be full of worship! Thank You Lord. Selah.

REFLECT: This is a tougher verse to live out than we sometimes imagine. The Lord says to rejoice ALWAYS—not just sometimes. He tells us to pray CONTINUALLY—not just once or twice a day. And He tells us to give thanks in ALL circumstances—not just when things are going well! And then He says that doing these three things is His will for us. So, this is a command. How are you doing with this command? Don't feel guilty, but reflect on how you can be more joyful, more prayerful and more thankful every day of your life.

ACT: Commit to one week of prayer time with the Lord where you don't ask Him for anything. You just rejoice, praise Him and thank Him for everything in your life—for seven days. Put aside your needs, your requests, and your questions until next week and just spend a week thanking Him. You'll find that next week you won't have as many requests and needs because they no longer seem as important. Rejoicing and thanking God on a regular basis will change your life forever!

YOUR THOUGHTS:

DAY 2

OVERFLOWING WITH THANKFULNESS

"So then, just as you received Christ Jesus as Lord, continue to live in him, rooted and built up in him, strengthened in the faith as you were taught, and overflowing with thankfulness."

Colossians 2:6-7

"I would maintain that thanks are the highest form of thought, and that gratitude is happiness doubled by wonder."   G.K. Chesterton

PRAY: Lord, I understand by this verse that just as I received You as my Savior, I am to be rooted in You so that You can build me up and strengthen me in my faith. And ultimately, I will be overflowing with thankfulness. I want that! Would You do that for me today? I want to go deeper with You so that I fall more in love with You, get stronger in my faith, and am filled to the brim with thankfulness. Thank You and Amen!

REFLECT: Have you thought about the process of growing in your faith? God teaches us that we are to be continually growing in our faith. How do you get to the point of being known as a thankful Christian? Maybe you need to be more rooted or strengthened in your faith. Maybe you need to go back and review what you've been taught about living the life of a Christian. Or maybe you need to choose to be thankful all the time, instead of being a habitual complainer, whiner, or worrier! What do you need to do?

ACT: Start a THANKFUL LIST. Start writing down every little and big thing that you are thankful for: people, situations, conversations, events, nature, experiences, lessons learned, insights, revelations, joyful thoughts, etc. etc. I was challenged last year to make a list of 1,000 things I'm thankful for and I'm already at 463! It's fun and it has changed my outlook on life. I now extend that challenge to you.

YOUR THOUGHTS:

DAY 3

THANK YOU FOR THE PEOPLE IN MY LIFE

"We ought always to thank God for you, brothers, and rightly so, because your faith is growing more and more, and the love every one of you has for each other is increasing."

2 Thessalonians 1:3

"In everyone's life, at some time, our inner fire goes out. It is then burst into flame by an encounter with another human being. We should all be thankful for those people who rekindle the inner spirit."   Albert Schweitzer

PRAY: Dear Father, I thank You so much for my family members, friends, co-workers, neighbors and all the people I come in contact with. You have put such amazing people in my life, and I want to always thank You for them. And I thank You that the love we all have for one another is growing. I never want to compare myself to others with jealousy in my heart, or wish them harm, so keep me thankful so that I never take one of my relationships for granted. I know that as I thank You for my loved ones, You are increasing our love for one another. Amen.

REFLECT: How many people do you have to whom you can turn for support, encouragement, advice, wisdom, or laughter? Sometimes we go to different people for different needs? Reflect on your community of loved ones. As your faith grows, does your circle of loved ones grow as well? Is your circle growing deeper as it grows wider? And can you say that your love for one another is increasing? Notice that happening as you practice THANKFULNESS as a priority in your life.

ACT: Why don't you encourage a friend or family member today to grow in their faith, to use their gifts to bring beauty into the world, and to pursue God with all of their body, mind and soul? And tell them that you are thanking the Lord that He created them to make a difference in this world.

YOUR THOUGHTS:

DAY 4

BE THANKFUL AND WORSHIP

"Therefore, since we are receiving a kingdom that cannot be shaken, let us be thankful, and so worship God acceptably with reverence and awe..."   Hebrews 12:28

"Let us thank God heartily as often as we pray that we have His Spirit in us to teach us to pray. Thanksgiving will draw our hearts out to God and keep us engaged with Him; it will take our attention from ourselves and give the Spirit room in our hearts." Andrew Murray

PRAY: Jesus, I thank You that I have nothing to worry about in my life because I am receiving a kingdom that cannot be shaken. Help me to remember that so I can be thankful every day of my life—regardless of my circumstances. I want to worship You with reverence and awe, despite how I feel or what I'm going through. I want to be filled up to overflowing with thankfulness as I walk down the bumpy road of life. I pray in Jesus name, Amen.

REFLECT: What does it mean to you when you read that God promises us we are receiving a kingdom that "cannot be shaken," Do you wonder if that will be in heaven or can we have that unshaken kingdom right here on earth? " Either way it's an amazing and precious promise for which you can be thankful! Let those words sink deep into your heart and soul, and worship God with reverence and awe. How can you get to that place in your relationship with Him? What will it take to be thankful and worshipful instead of shaken?

ACT: To experience one way of receiving a kingdom that can't be shaken, take a risk and do an act of thankfulness that is more heavenly than earthly: Make a list of Hollywood entertainment professionals whom you like and whose careers you follow, or better yet, those you don't like and perhaps condemn in your mind. While you are worshiping God with reverence and awe, start thanking the Lord for those people on your Hollywood list and ask the Lord to reveal Himself to them. As you pray for them you will gain a Kingdom perspective of God's love for us all. And notice how your heart changes as you pray for others instead of being shaken by focusing on envy, idolatry or hatred for those you disagree with. As we worship God our hearts can't help but be filled with more joy and thankfulness.

YOUR **THOUGHTS:**

DAY 5

SING TO THE LORD WITH PRAISE

"Let us come before him with thanksgiving and extol him with music and song... Sing to the Lord with thanksgiving; make music to our God on the harp... That my heart may sing Your praises and not be silent. Oh LORD my God, I will give thanks forever."

Psalms 95:2, 147:7 & 30:12

The thankful heart sees the best part of every situation. It sees problems and weaknesses as opportunities, struggles as refining tools, and sinners as saints in progress.

Francis Frangipane

PRAY: Heavenly Father, I thank You SO MUCH for the gift of music. I thank You that You find pleasure in us when we sing songs of praise and thanksgiving to You. Help me to use music more to praise You, knowing how it pleases You. Thank You for the musical artists that You have created. And may music be an instrument you use to grow my faith. Thank You that I have access to worship songs, hymns, Christian music, and all types of music to nurture my soul. Let me not be silent, rather let me be compelled to sing praises to You forever, Oh Lord! Amen.

REFLECT: What part does music play in your life as a Christian? Does your heart soar when listening to it? When you play an instrument or sing out loud, does it make you feel joy? Does it lead you closer to the Lord? Do you find yourself to be me more thankful when you have music in your life? Isn't it amazing that the Lord emotionally touches our hearts through music, and lets us also touch His heart through songs and thanksgiving. If you love music, thank the Lord for it, exalting Him with song as you worship Him.

ACT: Choose a song that touches your heart. Listen to it or sing it now. Then thank the Lord as you do. Embrace the music as an avenue for God to speak to your soul through the sounds. Listen again and practice using music as a spiritual language to draw you closer to the Lord, for He tells us to sing to the Lord with thanksgiving and grateful praise!

YOUR THOUGHTS:

DAY 6

HIS LOVE ENDURES FOREVER

"Give thanks to the Lord, for he is good; his love endures forever."   1 Chronicles 16:34

"Do not say, 'But it is hypocritical to thank God with my tongue when I don't feel thankful in my heart. Thanksgiving with the mouth stirs up thankfulness in the heart." John Piper

PRAY: Dear Jesus, can You help me to truly believe that You are good and that Your love endures forever?! I thank You right now for my life and for Your love for me. Continue to remind me of Your unending goodness and unconditional love for me. Fill me up Lord. I thank You for everything You're doing in me and through me, every day. Amen and Amen.

REFLECT: How often do you stop and just thank the Lord for something? How often do you think about how GOOD He is? And have you fully grasped that He loves you forever, regardless of who you are, what you do, or what you think or say? What would it take for you to remember to thank Him EVERY DAY for His amazing and forever enduring love for you?

ACT: Right now: Give thanks to the Lord, for He is good. Give thanks to the Lord for His love endures forever. Give thanks to the Lord because He is listening to you this very moment. Give thanks to the Lord for_____. Start your day by spending time giving thanks to the Lord, for He is good and His love endures FOREVER!

YOUR **THOUGHTS:**

DAY 7

GIVE THANKS AND PRAISE HIS NAME

"Enter his gates with thanksgiving and his courts with praise; give thanks to him and praise his name."
Psalm 100:4

"Of all the characteristics needed for both a happy and morally decent life, none surpasses gratitude. Grateful people are happier, and grateful people are more morally decent."

Dennis Prager

PRAY: Thank You Lord that as I enter Your gates by coming to You now in prayer, and walk into Your courts with praise, You are pleased. I want to keep thanking You and praising Your name always, so I can get closer to You, please You, and be a more thankful, joyful person to others in my life. Let my thanks and praise be contagious to the people around me and let me focus on You with thanks for giving me life with You. Amen.

REFLECT: "Enter His gates" could mean many things, but one meaning is entering into each of your times of prayer, worship, quiet, or meditation. As you enter the holy place of His gates, do you do it with thanksgiving and praise? If not, what can you do to remind yourself to begin each prayer time with thanks and praise? It will change you. And oh, what an amazing goal to reach!

ACT: Congratulations! You have spent a whole week thanking God, praising Him, and being thankful toward others as well. If it hasn't changed your life yet, then keep doing it. Skip a week of devotions and do this one again next week in order to alter your heart and soul to be more thankful. What a beautiful world it would be if we all entered His gates with thanksgiving and His courts with praise. Don't ever give up working at being a person who is known for being thankful, appreciative, grateful and full of praise!

YOUR THOUGHTS:

HOPE

WEEK FORTY-EIGHT

This week we're celebrating a topic that runs all through the entire Bible – God's life-changing promise of HOPE. God tells us to hope in Him, to not put our hope in the things of the world, that suffering produces hope and that hoping in our wealth is worthless but hoping in Him will never disappoint us. These commands and promises are thrilling, but so hard to do. Join us this week in letting go of what's comfortable and embracing God's promise to put all of our hope in Him!

DAY 1

RENEWED BY HOPE

"but those who hope in the Lord will renew their strength. They will soar on wings like eagles; they will run and not grow weary, they will walk and not be faint." Isaiah 40:31

"Darkness comes. In the middle of it, the future looks blank. The temptation to quit is huge. Don't. You are in good company... You will argue with yourself that there is no way forward. But with God, nothing is impossible. He has more ropes and ladders and tunnels out of pits than you can conceive. Wait. Pray without ceasing. Hope."   John Piper

PRAY: Lord, thank You for giving me strength each day. Help me to hope completely in You so that I will soar on wings like eagles. I need Your help to keep me from growing weary or getting faint. I know that life is hard, but I want to learn to hope in YOU in order to soar. I cry out to You today to show me how to put ALL of my hope in You and not in other people, my circumstances, or me. In Jesus' name, AMEN.

REFLECT: How would your life change by putting all of your hope in God, in Jesus, and in the Holy Spirit? Do you ever feel like you are soaring on wings like eagles? What would that be like? Do you believe it's possible? God tells us that it is so. The goal is to "hope in the Lord." Do you do that?

ACT: Evaluate the areas of your life where you are weary, or where you are growing faint. It could be because you don't have your hope in the Lord. Choose to focus on one area where you want to soar—regardless of the circumstances—and choose what you need to do to experience that freedom that only comes from hoping in the Lord. How thrilling it will be to soar through life as if on wings of eagles!

YOUR THOUGHTS:

DAY 2

LONGING FOR HOPE

"Hope deferred makes the heart sick, but a longing fulfilled is a tree of life."

Proverbs 13:12

"Why my soul, are you downcast? Why so disturbed within me? Put your hope in God, for I will yet praise him, my Savior and my God."   Psalm 42:5-6a

"When we have lost everything, including hope, life becomes a disgrace, and death a duty."

W.C. Fields

PRAY: Dear God, I need You to protect my heart and soul. I don't want a sick heart or a downcast soul. I want to hope in You and have my longings fulfilled. So, I praise You, my Savior and my God. Don't let me get downcast or to be disturbed within me. I need to put my hope in You. Will You help me to praise You more, my Savior and my God?! Thank You for allowing me to stand in this world as a tree of life! Amen.

REFLECT: Hope is an intangible emotion and yet we all have to choose what to put our hope in. God tells us that without putting our hope in Him we will have a sick heart and a downcast soul. Is your hope in anything other than God? Are you trusting God to fulfill your deepest hopes? Can you think of anything or anyone else in which you are putting your hope?

ACT: Write down one thing that you are hoping for that you are not yet getting. What one disappointment is giving you a downcast soul? A deferred hope makes your heart sick, so ask God to help you turn that desire over to Him and instead put your trust in Him. If we put our hope in God, instead of man, events or circumstances, we will be as strong as a tree of life, even in the face of disappointment! In whatever area today that you are losing hope, or feeling disturbed, choose right now to give it to God, trust Him, and focus your heart on praising your Savior. Putting your hope in God can take away your downcast soul, will lift you up, and fulfill your deepest longings.

YOUR THOUGHTS:

DAY 3

PUT YOUR HOPE IN GOD

"The Lord is good to those whose hope is in him, to the one who seeks him."

Lamentations 3:25

"May integrity and uprightness protect me, because my hope is in you."   Psalm 25:21

"Once you choose hope, anything's possible."

Christopher Reeve

PRAY: Lord, I ask that You help me to put all of my hope in You and to seek You first in my life. I believe that You will make me a person of integrity and uprightness and that You will protect me from the darts of the enemy. But I know it will only happen when my hope is in You alone. Would You transform my heart and my thoughts today? I thank You, in Jesus' name, Amen.

REFLECT: What is your greatest obstacle to letting go, and giving God control of everything in your life? What would it take to put all of your hope in Him and not rely on other people, circumstances or resources that you are in control of? Would your thoughts and actions change today if you honestly believed that you would be full of a supernatural hope by seeking Him first and putting all of your hope in Him?

ACT: Play a mind game today! Every time you start to worry or seek after some earthly thing, STOP and PRAY, asking God to be the one you are seeking. Ask Him to make you a person of integrity and righteousness, and to change your immediate thought to one of hope in Him. As you do this, at the end of the day ask yourself: How many times today did I have to STOP and PRAY?

YOUR THOUGHTS:

DAY 4

DON'T HOPE IN WEALTH

"Command those who are rich in this present world not to be arrogant nor to put their hope in wealth, which is so uncertain, but to put their hope in God, who richly provides us with everything for our enjoyment."   1 Timothy 6:17

"Hope is the struggle of the soul, breaking loose from what is perishable, and attesting her eternity."
                                                                                          Herman Melville

PRAY: Father, I come to you seeking humility and vulnerability as I ask You to reveal to me where I may be arrogant, and in what material wealth do I put my hope? Please show me areas of my faith where I have bought into the cultural belief that wealth is important, powerful, and freeing. I know that You are the one who will richly provide me with everything I need and want, but I need You to show me how to really live that out. Amen.

REFLECT: Can you recall the times when you have judged a rich person for being cheap, stingy, or arrogant? Did you ever consider that they were struggling with a spiritual battle, and that it is often more of a curse to be rich and not necessarily a blessing? What a thought to realize that the rich often depend on an uncertain faith in their money and don't realize that it will, at some point, disappoint them. Or does that describe you? Do you believe it when God says to put your hope in Him, not money, and He will richly provide your every need for your enjoyment?

ACT: Be radical with your wealth today—regardless of whether you have a lot or little. Give something away; give money to someone in need. Bring joy to someone else through your generosity, trusting that God is not only supplying for them through you, but He will give you everything that you need as well, including a richer hope in Him. You can't out-give God.

YOUR **THOUGHTS:**

DAY 5

SUFFERING PRODUCES HOPE

"...We also rejoice in our sufferings, because we know that suffering produces perseverance; perseverance, character; and character, hope. And hope does not disappoint us, because God has poured out his love into our hearts by the Holy Spirit, whom he has given us."

Romans 5:3-5

"We must accept finite disappointment, but never lose infinite hope."

Martin Luther King Jr.

PRAY: Jesus, I want to boast about You and the hope of Your glory! I also want to embrace my sufferings, knowing that they are a part of life. I want to believe that my sufferings produce perseverance, and by persevering I am building a Christ-like character, and that strength of character will give me a hope that will never disappoint me. Thank You for loving me SO MUCH and even giving me Your Holy Spirit. Thank You for answering my prayer! Amen.

REFLECT: Are you afraid of suffering? When have you ever thanked God in the middle of a crisis or looked back and thanked Him for how He turned your difficult season into good? Do you feel like you are a stronger Christian because of the suffering you have experienced? Like Job, allow yourself to wrestle with the question of whether you believe that God causes suffering or allows it for your own good. Ponder today's scripture in Romans 5 as you reflect on your own life experiences with suffering. Has your suffering given you Hope?!

ACT: Thank God right now for every difficult thing you're going through. Look at how your suffering is building your Christian character and thank Him that He loves you so much that He'll push you beyond your comfort zone in order to give you hope that will never disappoint you! And thank Him for giving you the Holy Spirit to hold you up through every hard day. Thank Him for loving you that much!

YOUR THOUGHTS:

DAY 6

MISPLACED HOPE

"Hopes placed in mortals die with them; all the promise of their power comes to nothing."
Proverbs 11:7

"Do any of the worthless idols of the nations bring rain? Do the skies themselves send down showers? No, it is you, O Lord our God. Therefore our hope is in you, for you are the one who does all this."
Jeremiah 14:22

Outside of the cross of Jesus Christ, there is no hope in this world. That cross and resurrection at the core of the Gospel is the only hope for humanity. Wherever you go, ask God for wisdom on how to get that Gospel in, even in the toughest situations of life.
Ravi Zacharias

PRAY: Dear Heavenly Father, show me who and what I am placing my hope in that will lead to emptiness and death. Let me see the reality of Your creation and Your hand on everything in my life so that I can put my hope in You only. Remind me that the promises of this world are meaningless and that I am surrounded by worthless idols telling me that they can fulfill me. I want my hope in you and to see the world through Your eyes. Amen.

REFLECT: How much of your faith is cultural and how much of your faith is biblical? It's easy to live out a Christian existence, thinking that we're doing all right, when our focus and our choices are dictated by the world around us. Even the church has accepted cultural beliefs that are not biblical. Seeking false idols can slip into our priorities and worshiping people over God can lead us astray. No idols can bring rain. Hopes placed in mortals dies with them.

ACT: Hollywood is the most powerful influence in our lives and we don't even know it. The messages and role models we embrace from Hollywood seep into our hearts. Without noticing we seek worthless idols over seeking God, believing cultural truths that come from our earthly influencers instead of God's biblical truths. Choose one entertainment celebrity that you look up to and instead of trying to be like them, would you pray for them? Ask God to transform their lives into His image and for them to embrace His hope for humanity—the Cross—because their power by themselves comes to nothing!

YOUR THOUGHTS:

DAY 7

HOLD ON TO HOPE

"Let us hold unswervingly to the hope we profess, for he who promised is faithful. And let us consider how we may spur one another on toward love and good deeds."

Hebrews 10:23-24

"Hope is being able to see that there is light despite all of the darkness." Desmond Tutu

PRAY: Lord, You say that if we profess our hope in You that You are faithful to fulfill that. So, I ask You now to help me hold unswervingly to the hope You offer me. And please use me to encourage others so that I can be a part of Your work, to spur on others to also love and do good deeds. I look forward to what You're about to do, In the name of Jesus. AMEN.

REFLECT: This verse brings up some great questions to reflect upon: Am I holding unswervingly to God's hope that will not disappoint me? Am I actually professing that hope to others? Am I holding unswervingly to the hope that I profess? Am I spurring on others to love people and to do good deeds? Do I believe I can actually be used by God to impact others to be more Christ-like? Do I believe that He who promised is faithful?

ACT: As the last day of our week on HOPE, today is your chance to spur on someone in your life to love more, and to do good deeds, all in the name of Jesus. Choose one person to pray for, and to reach out to with encouraging words. Maybe even challenge them to walk with you as a follower of Jesus, and make an eternal difference in their world. You can do it! Spur them on to hold unswervingly to the hope you profess, to love and to do greater things for God's glory.

YOUR THOUGHTS:

GENEROSITY

WEEK FORTY-NINE

One dictionary defines Generosity as "the quality of being kind and generous." That means that being generous can mean giving money and food to the poor and needy, but it can also mean being kind and generous of spirit. This week we'll look into different ways of being generous and the rewards that God gives us when we have generous hearts. Let's become Christ-like with generosity!

DAY 1

GENEROSITY LEADS TO THANKSGIVING

"You will be made rich in every way so that you can be generous on every occasion, and through us your generosity will result in thanksgiving to God."   2 Corinthians 9:11

"The gospel alone liberates you to live a life of scandalous generosity, unrestrained sacrifice, uncommon valor, and unbounded courage."   Tullian Tchividjian

PRAY: Father in heaven, I want to start my week with an attitude of generosity so that I will be enriched in every way and through my generosity, experience thanksgiving to God. Your ways are not our ways. They are so much more amazing and beautiful. So, please fill me with a generous spirit and thanksgiving for all that You have given me. I want to be known for my generosity so that I am pleasing You and blessing others at the same time. I'm excited for this week as I focus on generosity and thanksgiving. Thank You Father. Amen.

REFLECT: What would it look like to be generous on EVERY occasion? And how awesome is it to think that our generosity will bring both others and us a heart of thanksgiving. It's a WIN/WIN to be generous with our money, our stuff, our resources, our connections, and our hearts! Can you imagine that the Lord will enrich us in EVERY way and our generosity will increase? It's hard to fully embrace how our life would change but it's worth the effort to try to be generous on every occasion!

ACT: This week's goal is to be generous on every occasion. That means planning where you'll be, whom you'll be with, and what you'll be doing. Why not write in your calendar every day: BE GENEROUS! And then remember that's for every conversation, every meeting, every email, and every encounter with a neighbor or a stranger. Be generous with everyone you talk to and everything you do. Start right no on this adventure of GENEROSITY!

YOUR THOUGHTS:

DAY 2

GIVE OF YOURSELF TO OTHERS

"Give, and it will be given to you. A good measure, pressed down, shaken together and running over, will be poured into your lap. For with the measure you use, it will be measured to you." Luke 6:38

"The most obvious lesson in Christ's teaching is that there is no happiness in having or getting anything, but only in giving." Henry Drummond

PRAY: Lord, You are so amazing. When You tell us to do something, You always make sure it will benefit us. Thank You for Your generosity. Please help me to be a generous person – and not just because I will prosper. Help me to always remember that with the measure I use, it will be measured to me. I want to give generously without wanting anything back in return. I thank You for giving me a generous heart that runs over freely! Amen.

REFLECT: Think about how God created a world with consequences and rewards. If we follow Him, we experience more fruit, more abundance, and more peace and joy and blessings will be poured into our lap. If we choose to live life our way, we miss out on all the rewards God offers us, for with the measure we use, it will be measured to us. What better motivator to give, than to know what you give will be given back to you.

ACT: Do you consider yourself a generous person? How can you go above and beyond? How can you give more or refresh more people? Focus in on a person who is on your mind right now and choose to do some act of generosity for them. Would they need a note of encouragement, a call for you to pray with them, or a gift of money? Take that extra step right now to pour into another person. And then you will probably experience a blessing poured into your lap as well. Don't do it for that reason, but be ready for a subtle, or even an obvious, reward from the Lord for your selfless and generous act toward another person.

YOUR THOUGHTS:

DAY 3

GIVE WHAT YOU HAVE TO OTHERS

"The generous will themselves be blessed, for they share their food with the poor."

Proverbs 22:9

"If anyone has material possessions and sees his brother in need but has no pity on him, how can the love of God be in him?"   1 John 3:17

"We make a living by what we get; we make a life by what we give." Winston Churchill

PRAY: Dear Jesus, would You soften my heart toward the poor and the needy? Would You show me the widows and orphans in my life whom I haven't noticed or haven't gone out of my way to help and to pray for? Show me how I can share my food with others and be more generous even to my own family. I know Your love is in me, so help me to be a more generous person and have "the love of God" in my heart and with my wallet every day. Amen.

REFLECT: We often think of the word pity as a negative word. To pity someone sounds demeaning. Yet the definition of Pity is: "**the feeling of sorrow and compassion caused by the suffering and misfortunes of others.**" We need to show more godly pity on all the needy people around us—both our familial brothers and sisters and our Christian brothers and sisters—no matter who they are. We want to show the love of God to all people and that starts with a generous heart.

ACT: Choose one person you're worried about or you feel pity for. Reach out to that person today with a generous gift, or offer them resources, time, love, and your prayers. Make a Christ-like random act of kindness toward someone in need today by sharing a meal or anything that you have, and they need. You'll see how rich you really are and how easy it is to generously bless others. And as you share what you have with others, you will yourself be blessed!

YOUR THOUGHTS:

DAY 4

WE BENEFIT FROM OUR GENEROSITY

"Remember this: Whoever sows sparingly will also reap sparingly, and whoever sows generously will also reap generously." 2 Corinthians 9:6

"I do not believe one can settle how much we ought to give. I am afraid the only safe rule is to give more than we can spare." C.S. Lewis

PRAY: Lord in Heaven, please never let me be known for sowing sparingly. I don't want to be "fiscally conservative" or especially "cheap." Show me how to sow generously in order to help others, please You, and also reap generously in order to have even more to give away. It's exciting to know that You will help me to give to others as You have given to me. I look forward in anticipation for what You're going to do in me and through me. Amen.

REFLECT: The farmer's analogy of sowing and reaping is so clear when it comes to generosity. When a farmer works hard to sow his field, he receives a rich and large harvest as his reward. When we sow into others through our generosity, we can reap a rich harvest of fruit as well. But the opposite is also true. We can't be lazy or sow sparingly or we will reap sparingly and for farmers that means not having enough to get through that season. Have you ever experienced not having enough of God's peace, strength, joy, or fruits of the Spirit? If so, maybe that's because you have been sowing into others' sparingly...

ACT: Make a list of 5 people or families you can sow into. It could be family, neighbors, co-workers, parents of your children's friends, the teller at your bank…. Over the next month choose to sow into those five people. Be generous as you act out this commitment and see that by sowing generously you reap generously. Start now and have fun.

YOUR THOUGHTS:

DAY 5

GIVE WHEN YOU ARE IN NEED

"In the midst of a very severe trial, their overflowing joy and their extreme poverty welled up in rich generosity."
2 Corinthians 8:2

"Giving frees us from the familiar territory of our own needs by opening our mind to the unexplained worlds occupied by the needs of others."
Barbara Bush

PRAY: Dear Jesus, I need Your help when I am in the midst of a very severe trial, or when I'm lonely or depressed. Help me choose to be overflowing with joy and then watch my extreme poverty of emotions or finances well up into rich generosity. You tell us that when we are weak, through You we are strong. So, when I'm struggling financially or emotionally, I can choose to be generous and selfless and you will bless me. Even if it feels hard to do, I know that with You all things are possible! Amen.

REFLECT: This verse is so humbling. As we read about the Christians in the early days, they were selling property and giving it to one another, opening their homes for people to stay in, and giving away money and food to anyone in need. And today, we are taught to make sure we save up for ourselves: own a home and have a pension, and a college savings account, along with health and life insurance. If we truly believe that even in the midst of extreme poverty we can overflow with joy and well up in rich generosity, I think we would be more generous with what we have, without the fear of not having enough. God is faithful to supply our daily bread. It's up to us to be richly generous and overflow with joy in the process.

ACT: Ask God right now for a miracle in your life. Ask Him to show you how He can create joy in you when you don't feel it, or make you generous when you have little. Ask Him to change your heart, to take away your fear, and compel you to give to others from all that you have. And be sure to ask with an expectant heart. This verse is true, so live it out without doubt so you will enjoy the rewards He promises to those who obey. He's ready to give you a miracle in your heart and life, so just ask Him.

YOUR THOUGHTS:

DAY 6

GIVE WITHOUT A GRUDGING HEART

"Give generously to them and do so without a grudging heart; then because of this the Lord your God will bless you in all your work and in everything you put your hand to."

Deuteronomy 15:10

"If you haven't got any charity in your heart, you have the worst kind of heart trouble."

Bob Hope

PRAY: Lord, I'm so sorry that I do things sometimes with a grudging heart. Would You change my heart and my mind so that I am a generous person in everything I put my hand to? And even help me to be generous to people I don't like! I ask that I would be generous to the people in the government, or Hollywood, with whom I don't agree, who are creating policy or entertainment that I don't like. Let prayers be generous, without a grudging heart. Let generosity pour into my heart so that I don't judge anyone, but rather give everyone the benefit of the doubt. Take away my grudging heart and bless me in everything I do because I am blessing others. In Jesus Name I pray. Amen.

REFLECT: Giving generously doesn't always mean just with money or resources. We can have a grudging heart and not give people love, grace, mercy, or the benefit of the doubt. Are you judging your political leaders or your culture shapers with a grudging heart and not offering them your generous prayers or kind words? Giving generously to our culture's leaders can open you up to amazing possibilities and opportunities and allow God to bless you in all your work and everything you put your hand to.

ACT: Think about the cultural leaders in our country whom you have judged. Have you ever written an angry letter to someone in Hollywood? Have you talked against them to others, or cursed them in your heart? Why don't you give love generously to a cultural leader in our country and write them a letter of support, letting them know you are praying for them. We want to bless those who are impacting our culture and be generous to them with our words and our love! If you write to someone in Hollywood and need help getting the letter delivered, just email us at info@hpnemail.org and we'll help you get it to them

YOUR THOUGHTS:

DAY 7

BE GENEROUS IN DOING GOOD

"Command them to do good, to be rich in good deeds, and to be generous and willing to share."..."remembering the words the Lord Jesus himself said: 'It is more blessed to give than to receive.'"   1 Timothy 6:18 & *Acts 20:35b*

"In all of my years of service to my Lord, I have discovered a truth that has never failed and has never been compromised. That truth is that it is beyond the realm of possibilities that one has the ability to out-give God. Even if I give the whole of my worth to Him, He will find a way to give back to me much more than I gave." Charles Haddon Spurgeon

PRAY: Dear Father, You have commanded us to be good, to be rich in good deeds and be generous and willing to share. Would You check my heart so that I truly am a generous person? Help me to share everything, not just my extras or out of my abundance. Help me to be a sacrificial giver, because I know I can't out-give You. Thank You for stretching me outside of my comfort zone so that I can follow Your command to do good, the way You mean me to do it! I'm excited about what You will reveal to me about Your way of being generous. Amen.

REFLECT: You've probably heard the saying, "You can't out give God!" But have you ever thought of living that way? What would you need to change or adjust in your life to be RICH in good deeds and to be GENEROUS and willing to share? If you take this thought to the nth degree, it could be life-changing.

ACT: Choose today to be your DAY OF GENEROSITY. Commit to go crazy with your generosity, in your service to others, your words, your financial giving, and your prayers. And even be generous to God by giving more time and more of yourself to Him. Do more than seems rational or reasonable and trust Him to reward you for your efforts. Don't let fear or practicality stop you from going crazy with generosity. If people don't notice that you're different then you haven't done or said enough. How much fun it will be to have people thinking you've lost your mind with your selfless acts of Divine generosity. GO FOR IT!

YOUR THOUGHTS:

GRACE

WEEK FIFTY

Grace is one of the supernatural gifts from God to us. His grace is sufficient, Jesus is defined as grace, and we are to show grace to others. It's a poetic word with a powerful effect on everyone who practices it and accepts it from God. We'll spend this week grasping how wide, deep, and high grace can be in life if we embrace it and practice it every day.

Amazing grace
How sweet the sound
That saved a wretch like me
I once was lost
But now I'm found
Was blind, but now I see

DAY 1

JESUS IS GRACE

"The Word became flesh and made his dwelling among us. We have seen his glory, the glory of the One and Only, who came from the Father, full of grace and truth...From the fullness of his grace we have all received one blessing after another. For the law was given through Moses; grace and truth came through Jesus Christ."   John 1:14, 16-17

"Christ is no Moses, no exactor, no giver of laws, but a giver of grace, a Savior, He is infinite mercy and goodness, freely and bountifully given to us."   Martin Luther

PRAY: Dear Jesus, I am humbled to learn that you ARE grace. I have seen Your glory and know that You are full of grace and truth. And I thank You that out of Your fullness I have received grace! Thank You that not only did You bring grace and truth to me, but you ARE grace and truth. And because You are full of grace, I have received one blessing after another. Thank you, Jesus, for giving me grace and truth. Amen and Amen.

REFLECT: It was a profound revelation to me that GOD IS LOVE and JESUS IS GRACE. If we try to define both terms outside of God the Father and Jesus the Son, we limit the meaning of those words. I look forward to a week of studying grace and how it impacts my life, my thoughts, and my actions. And I want to be in a state of thanks to Jesus Christ, for offering Himself to me as grace. I want His grace to wash over me and sink deep into my heart and soul so that I will walk and talk in grace and truth all the days of my life.

ACT: Spend time thanking Jesus right now for all of the ways He has given you grace, taught you about grace and shown you grace through other people. Thank Him for the grace He shows you, especially when you don't deserve it, and the ongoing grace you receive without even naturally thinking about it. Because of Jesus you are living in grace and truth. Thank Him for that and then think of Jesus whenever you hear the word grace.

YOUR THOUGHTS:

DAY 2

IT IS BY GRACE THAT WE'VE BEEN SAVED

"But because of his great love for us, God, who is rich in mercy, made us alive with Christ even when we were dead in transgressions--it is by grace you have been saved. And God raised us up with Christ and seated us with him in the heavenly realms in Christ Jesus, in order that in the coming ages he might show the incomparable riches of his grace, expressed in his kindness to us in Christ Jesus. For it is by grace you have been saved, through faith--and this not from yourselves, it is the gift of God—"   Ephesians 2:4-8

"The law detects, grace alone conquers sin. For grace is given not because we have done good works, but in order that we may be able to do them."   Saint Augustine of Hippo

PRAY: Dear Heavenly Father, I praise You for Your great love for me. I know that You are rich in mercy and You gave me life through Christ, even though I'm a sinner. Thank You for sacrificing Jesus to show me the incomparable riches of grace. I praise You that it is by grace that I have been saved, through faith, and not by anything that I have done or could do myself. My salvation is a gift from You, not by any works of my own. And I know that I can never boast about the amazing gifts You've given me. Amen and Amen.

REFLECT: The concept of grace is beyond our human understanding. We can try to fathom what God has done for us by giving us Jesus so that we can live lives of grace, but can we embrace the "incomparable riches of His grace" or see that our salvation is a gift of God's grace? Have you ever thought of God as being "rich in mercy?" And though we are all sinners, He loves us SO MUCH that He overlooks our transgressions with His amazing grace. "Amazing Grace, how sweet the sound, that saved a wretch like me."

ACT: Take a few minutes and play a recording of "Amazing Grace" and listen carefully to the words. You may be so used to this song that you need to listen to it with fresh ears. As you listen, ask the Lord to reveal to you the truth of His amazing grace in your life. Here are a few artist suggestions: Bill & Gloria Gaither (live) with Wintley Phipps; Judy Collins; Chris Tomlin; Whitney Houston; Andrea Bocelli (live); The Tenors & Natalie Grant.

YOUR THOUGHTS:

DAY 3

WE ARE ALL UNDER GRACE

"For sin shall not be your master, because you are not under law, but under grace."

Romans 6:14

"Let us then approach the throne of grace with confidence, so that we may receive mercy and find grace to help us in our time of need."   Hebrews 4:16

"Your identity is not wrapped up in how right you get it or how perfect you can posture yourself. But, your identity is wrapped up in the grace of the Lord Jesus Christ."   Lecrae

PRAY: Abba Father, I am crying out to You to free me of the bondage of sin and to let sin no longer be my master. Help me to understand that I am not under the law, but under Your unconditional, loving grace. Help me to approach Your throne with confidence, so I may receive Your mercy and find Your divine grace to help me in my times of need. You offer so much. I want to embrace it and have Your grace change my life. In Your name, Amen.

REFLECT: Ponder this thought: We are all under the bondage of sin. Sin is our master as long as we live on this earth and don't die to self and live for God. But we can choose to get out from under the law and live freely by God's grace! We just have to mentally and emotionally approach God's throne of grace with confidence, so that we may receive mercy and find grace to help us in our time of need. This is all possible, if we are willing to commit to have only God as our master and no longer allow sin to rule our words, thoughts, and actions. That's a high order, but with God ALL things are possible.

ACT: Take a moment and sit quietly and after reading this. Close your eyes and think about physically walking in heaven toward the majestic divine throne of God. As you approach the throne, look into God's eyes and see that He is radiating forgiveness, love and grace. He is not judging you. He is so excited to see you. As you stand in front of Him, don't be shy. Be confident that you are worthy of His unconditional grace and though you can't be good enough on your own, His great love for you sees you as pure and good. This is a miraculous moment you can experience right now. When you can truly embrace His total love and grace, you will be a different person, full of peace and joy!

YOUR THOUGHTS:

DAY 4

BE FAITHFUL STEWARDS OF GOD'S GRACE

"Each one should use whatever gift he has received to serve others, faithfully administering God's grace in its various forms. If anyone speaks, he should do it as one speaking the very words of God. If anyone serves, he should do it with the strength God provides, so that in all things God may be praised through Jesus Christ. To him be the glory and the power for ever and ever. Amen."   1 Peter 4:10-11

"Grace is God acting in our lives to do what we cannot do on our own; it goes beyond unmerited favor."   Dallas Willard

PRAY: Dear Lord, I thank You for the gifts that You've given me. I want to use those gifts to serve others, as a faithful steward of Your grace. I also want to remember that people who have other gifts are also stewards of Your grace, just in different forms. Would You help me to grow in the grace and knowledge that You've given me so that I can use my gifts to make an eternal difference in our world, and give You all the glory, both now and forever, Amen.

REFLECT: Have you ever thought of yourself as a steward of God's grace? That sounds like an awesome responsibility, but if you know that God has specifically given you spiritual gifts and talents that He wants you to use to glorify Him, then you can joyfully serve others and grow in the grace and knowledge of Jesus, all at the same time. Wow! To Him be the glory both now and forever!

ACT: Do you know what your gifts are that God has given you? If you want to be a steward of grace in our world, you have to know your spiritual gifts. Right now, write down your spiritual gifts so that you remember them and consciously use them to serve others. If you don't know what they are, go to your pastor, small group leader, or go on-line and find a spiritual gifts test that can help you discover your gifts. Don't miss out on serving other people and growing in the grace and knowledge of Jesus.

YOUR THOUGHTS:

DAY 5

"MY GRACE IS SUFFICIENT FOR YOU"

"But he said to me, "My grace is sufficient for you, for my power is made perfect in weakness." Therefore I will boast all the more gladly about my weaknesses, so that Christ's power may rest on me."   2 Corinthians 12:9

"Man is born broken. He lives by mending. The grace of God is glue."   Eugene O'Neill

PRAY: God, it's hard for me to understand that Your grace is sufficient for me and that Your power is made perfect in my weakness. I want Your grace to be sufficient, so I ask that You reveal to me Your truths. And it sounds crazy that I should boast in my weaknesses. But I want Christ's power to rest on me and I want to be strong when I feel weak, so can You help me to understand Your truths even though they don't make sense. Thank You for making Your word real and tangible. In Jesus' name, Amen.

REFLECT: Have you ever meditated on the phrase "My grace is sufficient for you, for my power is made perfect in weakness?" I don't think we can ever be in the position to actually boast in our weaknesses, let alone with gladness, until we truly understand and believe that God's grace is ALL WE NEED. It's not works, a good attitude, the right words, or our own strength. It's the ability to completely embrace God's supernatural grace. Then and only then will Christ's power rest on you. Now that's worth working on.

ACT: Write down three poor choices or mistakes in your life that you still struggle with. Then tell the Lord each one and thank Him that His grace is sufficient for you and that His power is made perfect in those mistakes. Then out loud, boast to the Lord that those mistakes allowed His perfection to come through in your weakness. And tell Him that if you never made those wrong choices you would not get to see His unconditional grace and forgiveness at work in your life. Then thank God and glorify Him. You have just worked through a miracle of God's grace at work in your life.

YOUR THOUGHTS:

DAY 6

ALWAYS BE FULL OF GRACE

"He who loves a pure heart and whose speech is gracious will have the king for his friend."

Proverbs 22:11

"Let your conversation be always full of grace, seasoned with salt, so that you may know how to answer everyone.

Colossians 4:6

"Gratitude is what we radiate when we experience grace, and the soul was made to run on grace the way a 747 runs on rocket fuel."

John Ortberg

PRAY: Lord, I want to have my conversation always be full of grace and seasoned with salt, so that I may know how to answer everyone who talks to me about You. I know that You love a pure heart, and You love people who speak with grace so much that You promise us that we will have Jesus the King for our friend. Thank You for your promises and thank you for Your encouraging words that make me want to be a better person. I love You! Amen.

REFLECT: Reflect on what it means to have our conversation always full of grace and seasoned with salt. What do you need to do to make that happen? Do you need to watch your words, listen to what you say to others, and be sure to be encouraging and Christ-like in your conversations? What would have to change? What would it take to have a pure heart and to know how to answer people who ask you about Jesus? How do you speak with grace? These are all important thoughts to ponder.

ACT: Choose someone whom you may have trouble talking to about Jesus. Would you pray that you get a chance to have a conversation with them so that you can use words of grace and yet be seasoned with salt, which is truth. Before you talk to them, ask the Lord to give you a pure heart and to be overflowing with grace. Then trust that you will be led by your friend, the King, as you talk to the person. Pray for a divine appointment then watch as words and attitude of grace pour out from you from the Lord.

YOUR THOUGHTS:

DAY 7

"GRACE BE WITH YOU ALL"

"The Lord bless you and keep you; the Lord make his face shine upon you and be gracious to you; the Lord turn his face toward you and give you peace."   Numbers 6:24-26

"Grace and peace to you from God our Father and the Lord Jesus Christ. I always thank God for you because of his grace given you in Christ Jesus."   1 Corinthians 1:3-4

"I do not understand the mystery of grace – only that it meets us where we are but does not leave us where it found us."   Anne Lamott

PRAY: Dear Father, I ask that You bless me and keep me and that Your face will shine upon me and that You will be gracious unto me. Thank you for giving me peace. And Lord, will You help me to bless others and be gracious unto them. Will you help me to pray blessings on the people in Hollywood and to be gracious in my attitude toward them. Help me not to judge them, Lord. Instead I thank You for them and pray You reveal Yourself to them. Give them Your grace and peace. Thank You Father. Amen.

REFLECT: Do you pray blessings on people? Do you say words of blessings to them? Or do you talk against people and judge them? It's easiest to see our hearts by how we treat people we don't know. What is your attitude toward the celebrities and stars in Hollywood? Do you pray for them to prosper and to be instruments of peace or do you get angry at them? Reflect on the attitude of your hearts and then choose to pray prayers of blessings over the people you read about and hear about in Hollywood.

ACT: Choose one person you don't like in Hollywood, or one actor or celebrity whom you disagree with. Right now, pray words of blessings over that person. Pray for them to prosper and to experience the love, joy, hope, and peace of Jesus. And as you do that, the Lord will bless you and pour His grace upon you and give you peace. As you show grace to others, you too will receive grace. After you pray for that person in Hollywood, go out into the world and spread God's grace.

YOUR THOUGHTS:

CHRISTMAS

WEEK FIFTY-ONE

Christmas is our favorite time of year here at the Hollywood Prayer Network. It allows us to focus on the gift of Jesus, to send greetings and love to people, and to pray for those who struggle through this beautiful holy season. We hope to encourage you this Christmas by sharing this devotional that reminds you of the miracle of Jesus! And a very Merry Christmas to you!

DAY 1

OUR GREATEST CHRISTMAS GIFT IS JESUS

"She will give birth to a son, and you are to give him the name Jesus, because he will save his people from their sins."   Matthew 1:21

"Christmas Gift Suggestions: To your enemy—forgiveness, to an opponent—tolerance, to a friend—your heart, to a customer—service, to all—charity, to a child—a good example, to yourself—respect."   Anonymous

PRAY: Dear Father in Heaven, I thank You for giving me Your Son. I praise You and thank You for loving me so much that You sent Your Son to earth to give me hope, joy, peace and love. And it all started at Jesus' birth. Christmas is such a joyful reminder of what You have done for me and I don't ever want to forget that. My heart is overflowing with joy! Thank You so much. Amen.

REFLECT: Reflect on the overwhelming joy of knowing Jesus. We believe in the most radical person in history and we have the privilege of celebrating His birth. It's a miracle that it happened and a miracle that you believe it. Have you thought about what a gift it is that you are able to believe in Him and so many other people just can't embrace the truth of this whole season? Why you and not them?

ACT: Begin this Christmas week by praising God for what He did for you by sending His only Son to earth as a baby. Thank Him for the miracle of Christmas and how this one day has changed the world. Embrace the glory of both God the Father and Jesus the Son. And thank Jesus for giving you the Holy Spirit as His greatest gift.

YOUR THOUGHTS:

DAY 2

MONEY, POWER, AND CHARISMA

"But you, Bethlehem Ephrathah, though you are small among the clans of Judah, out of you will come for me one who will be ruler over Israel, whose origins are from of old, from ancient times." Micah 5:2

Christmas is a season not only of rejoicing but of reflection. Winston Churchill

PRAY: Lord, thank You that Christmas is a reminder that the things of the world are not important, they don't last, and I can't take them with me when I go to heaven. Jesus, please help me express my commitment to You, Your priorities and Your position as the ruler over all of Israel and the world! I don't want my focus or identity to be in my job, status, title or income. I don't want to forget the true meaning of this day! Amen.

REFLECT: Have you ever thought about the people of Bethlehem, that they were a small, weak community among the clans of Judah, and that Jesus came out of that town?! Just think of what YOU can do, even if you are an unknown, simple, quiet, weak person. None of that matters in God's Kingdom! Ask yourself, what are you capable of that you may never have thought of before? Let Jesus be your inspiration!

ACT: Dig deep into your heart this Christmas and write down your desires, your dreams and your goals—those that you have given up on or thought impossible. Trust that God gave you those thoughts and desires and He has plans for you that you may have given up on too soon. God loves to use those of us from small, weak clans, to do the unexpected. Write your list, pray about each goal, and take steps to walk into God's promises! What a Christmas gift that will be to you this year.

YOUR THOUGHTS:

DAY 3

HE IS THE GOD OF THE UNEXPECTED

"To the weak I became weak, to win the weak. I have become all things to all men so that by all possible means I might save some."   1 Corinthians 9:22

"Aren't we forgetting the true meaning of this day – the birth of Santa?" Bart Simpson

PRAY: Dear Jesus, You appeared so weak at first, as You did many times during your ministry on earth, and yet You did that to become all things to all people so that some, like me, might be saved. Thank You for Your sacrifice. Would You help me trust that when I am weak, You will make me strong? By all possible means help me be a part of saving some people in my life. I know that's ultimately what Christmas is all about. I pray in Jesus' name, Amen.

REFLECT: Think about the people who have no interest in Christmas or Jesus at all, because they don't see the power in His name, in His miracles or in His heart. How wrong might we be about people in our lives, whom we see as weak, unfocused, or purposeless? If we are all created in God's image, isn't it possible that everyone has the potential to make an eternal difference in this world? Don't be attracted just to celebrities, because they are more beautiful or more famous or bigger than life. Who are the seemingly weak people in your life? Could they have more eternal power and/or influence than you ever thought possible?

ACT: Hollywood celebrities look so powerful and Washington DC politicians seem so influential. Make a list of the people in your life who seem weak and the ones who are bigger than life. Then pray for each of them. Ask the Lord to show the ones who appear weak to see His strength in them. When you're praying for Hollywood celebrities, ask the Lord to reveal to them how He sees them and how He can use both their fame and weaknesses for His glory.

YOUR THOUGHTS:

DAY 4

LITTLE THINGS CAN CHANGE THE WORLD

"For to us a child is born, to us a son is given, and the government will be on his shoulders. And he will be called Wonderful Counselor, Mighty God, Everlasting Father, Prince of Peace."

Isaiah 9:6

"I will honor Christmas in my heart, and try to keep it all the year."   Charles Dickens

PRAY: Dear Father God, Your Son came into this world in the lowliest of circumstances and yet the government was, and still is, on His shoulders! Thank You that I can call Jesus my Wonderful Counselor, my Mighty God and my Everlasting Father. He truly is my Prince of Peace. I praise You for this Christmas day and for giving the world and me Your Son, Jesus! Amen.

REFLECT: This verse is MIRACULOUS! As you read it again think about the details that on the surface seem ridiculous, but because of God, are divinely perfect! God gave us a baby, His son, who is born of a poor, unknown young girl, and then suddenly, all the governments of the world will be on His shoulder?! He will go from being a weak, tiny, gurgling baby to God in the flesh: Wonderful, Counselor, Mighty God, Everlasting Father, Prince of Peace. Isn't that mind-blowing?

ACT: First, ask the Lord to reveal to you all of the profound truths of this verse. Then, read this verse three more times to yourself, then read it twice more, out loud. Do you see the miracles all through it? Jesus is a baby, He's a son, but governments are scared of Him, men are worshiping Him, and He is known for His strength, power and love. And, it all started on Christmas day. Tell the Lord that you never want to look at Christmas the same way ever again!

YOUR THOUGHTS:

DAY 5

GOD IS A GOD OF THE IMPOSSIBLE!

"Mary was greatly troubled at his words and wondered what kind of greeting this might be. But the angel said to her, "Do not be afraid, Mary, you have found favor with God. You will be with child and give birth to a son, and you are to give him the name Jesus. He will be great and will be called the Son of the Most High. The Lord God will give him the throne of his father David, and he will reign over the house of Jacob forever; his kingdom will never end."

Luke 1:29-33

"A virgin birth I can believe, but finding three wise men???"   Anonymous

PRAY: Lord, can You please help me to grasp the full meaning of this verse. What was Mary thinking? Can You help me to understand the full background and meaning of Christmas and the birth of Jesus? I want to know what Mary and Joseph went through to bring Jesus into the world. And then He became the Most High, reigning over all of us. I need Your help to completely embrace the power of what You're telling me here. Amen and Amen.

REFLECT: From Mary learning she was miraculously pregnant, to Jesus reigning over all men forever, this is the greatest, most profound, most controversial story of all time. This verse in Luke has caused wars, divided families, and transformed lives, and it's told over and over again every Christmas. Can you ponder the words and meaning of this verse so that you can embrace the full magnitude of what God has done for us, through the birth of Jesus?

ACT: Tell one person this story sometime this Christmas holiday. Choose someone who may never have heard it, or needs to hear it a new way, through your perspective, but with God's words. If you don't know whom to tell, ask the Lord to put someone's name on your heart or direct you to a person who will ask you what Christmas is all about. Don't go through this season without telling someone the true, powerful, life-changing story of Jesus! It will be a Divine Appointment!

YOUR THOUGHTS:

DAY 6

PRAISE GOD AND SPREAD CHRISTMAS CHEER

"Suddenly a great company of the heavenly host appeared with the angel, praising God and saying, "Glory to God in the highest, and on earth peace to men on whom his favor rests." When the angels had left them and gone into heaven, the shepherds said to one another, "Let's go to Bethlehem and see this thing that has happened, which the Lord has told us about." Luke 2:13-15

"Christmas, my child, is love in action. Every time we love, every time we give, it's Christmas." Dale Evans

PRAY: Dear Jesus, thank You for making Your birth so theatrical and so miraculous. You brought Your heavenly hosts to the most simple and poorest of people, to announce the birth of Your Son. You didn't have Jesus born in a palace with the King. It was the hardworking shepherds who were the first ones to see You. You care about everyone! May I see Your angels as well, as I praise You and sing out about Your Glory? In Your mighty name. Amen.

REFLECT: Can you imagine the scene in Bethlehem when suddenly the heavenly hosts showed up over the fields? Can you visualize how they were all praising God and giving Him the glory as they presented Jesus to the world? It's amazing that God created this scenario for His son. Think about how God wants us to experience Him within our community. Have you ever talked to other Christians about Jesus and then got so excited you just had to give Him the glory? We often rave about our earthly experiences to other people, such as a great book, white water rafting, a new "crush," etc. But do we ever talk excitedly to others about "this miraculous thing that has happened on Christmas night?"

ACT: When was the last time you got excited about the Lord and talked to other people about Him? Have you ever? Right now, call or see your best friend, neighbor or child and tell them how amazed you are by the birth of Jesus. That it's so incredible, you actually committed your whole life to following Him, obeying Him and falling more in love with Him. Put into words the miraculous fact that Jesus was born for you and you have chosen to follow Him forever! Shout it from the mountaintops and talk about it on the phone.

YOUR THOUGHTS:

DAY 7

GOD LOVES YOU SO MUCH, HE GAVE YOU HIS SON

"For God so loved the world that he gave his one and only Son, that whoever believes in him shall not perish but have eternal life."   John 3:16

"And know that I am with you always; yes, to the end of time."   Jesus Christ

PRAY: Father in Heaven, I thank You that You loved me, and every single person in the world, so much that You gave us Jesus. You gave us Your one and only Son, and when we believe in Jesus we will NEVER perish, instead we will live forever with You in Heaven. Thank You for this promise. And please help me to make this not only a favorite verse, but also a reality that I embrace every day. Amen.

REFLECT: This verse is so familiar to Christians that we often don't even think about the words anymore. We have it memorized and we can even tell it to our non-believing friends, but have you recently taken the time and effort to go through it word by word and study the implications, the miracle of it, and the amazing promise in it? Imagine what it will be like to live in heaven for eternity. What thoughts and images do you come up with?

ACT: Get out a pen and paper and dig deep into your soul to answer these questions:
- Can you imagine what it would have been like to be miraculously impregnated and then find out that your child is the Son of God?
- How did you get to believe in Jesus when most of the people around you don't believe?
- Can you commit to expressing God's unconditional love to someone this Christmas?
- You are promised eternal life in heaven and you have chosen to believe that. How does that affect your everyday life? Or does it?
- Do you live differently because of Jesus in your life?

That is your preparation for Christmas. Now you're ready to enter the season, with the right heart, right priorities and a deeper love for your Savior.

YOUR THOUGHTS:

YOUR MISSION FIELD

WEEK FIFTY-TWO

Have you ever thought of yourself as a missionary? Have you ever defined the place where you live or work as your mission field? This week we're going to focus on God's plan for all of us to be missionaries in our own marketplace mission field. We don't have to go overseas. We can spread the gospel to the people around us, just by loving them!

DAY 1

WHAT IS YOUR MISSION FIELD?

"Therefore go and make disciples of all nations, baptizing them in the name of the Father and of the Son and of the Holy Spirit, and teaching them to obey everything I have commanded you. And surely I am with you always, to the very end of the age."

Matthew 28:19-20

"Give your hands to Him for His work, your feet to walk His path, and your ears to hear Him speak."

Priscilla Shirer

PRAY: Dear Father, I want to obey this commandment to go out and make disciples of all nations. I want to share my faith with people, baptize them and teach them about You. Don't let me forget that You are always with me, to the very end of the age! Thank you for Your promise to be with me, and to use me wherever I am. Lord, reveal my mission field to me. Where do I start, who shall I reach out to, and what shall I say? I need You to speak through me in Jesus's name, Amen.

REFLECT: As we spend this week focusing on our mission field, have you thought about what it actually means to be a missionary? Do you have the old fashioned thought that we have to go to some miserable location on the other side of the world, and tell all the those people that they are going to hell if they don't believe in Jesus? Or can you think of it as using your gifts and talents in a specific place where God has called you to serve people, while being loving Ambassadors of Jesus along the way? Every day of our lives we want to make disciples by pouring into people's lives and investing in to their spiritual journeys!

ACT: Take out a piece of paper and write down what you believe your mission field is. Is it your neighborhood, school, workplace, or somewhere else you need to move to in order to be in the place God wants you to be? As Christians we are all missionaries, and we should all be discipling people, sharing our faith, baptizing people, and believing with confidence that God is with us always, to the very end of the age. Are you right where God wants you to be so you can start pouring into other people? Or should you make plans to move to where you know God wants you to go? He is always with you, so define your mission field today!

YOUR THOUGHTS:

DAY 2

PRAY, SERVE, LOVE, GIVE, SACRIFICE

"I have become its servant by the commission God gave me to present to you the word of God in its fullness-- the mystery that has been kept hidden for ages and generations, but is now disclosed to the saints. To them God has chosen to make known among the Gentiles the glorious riches of this mystery, which is Christ in you, the hope of glory." Colossians 1:25-27

"Preach the gospel at all times, and if necessary use words." St. Francis of Assisi

PRAY: Dear God, as Your servant I want to present Your Word to the people around me. To many, You are still a mystery that has been kept hidden for ages and generations. I want to talk about You to the people so that they can see, "the glorious riches of this mystery, which is Christ." Let me share Your hope and glory, so that I may present everyone Your hope, Your joy, and Your salvation. Thank You my God! Amen and Amen.

REFLECT: It's easier to embrace the concept of being a missionary in a mission field if we get excited about the riches of God's mystery, which is Christ. It's not our job to change people, but only to let others know the hope that we have within us. If we are confident in our faith and excited about whom we love, then it will be very natural to talk about God. St. Francis said, "Preach the gospel at all times, and if necessary use words." Do you love Jesus enough to want others to experience what you have? That's the key to being an effective missionary. And wherever you are becomes your mission field!

ACT: God commissioned us to present His word, His truth, and His love to other people. Think of the ways you can present His word to the people around you. Here are some possibilities: Pray for people, by name, to embrace the love of Jesus. Serve people, give them gifts in love, sacrifice for them, be a listening ear, don't judge them, show compassion and care for them. Each of these ideas is how you can be eternally significant in your mission field. Go out today and prayerfully do or say something to someone in your mission field that shows you love them. Be an example of Jesus' love.

YOUR THOUGHTS:

DAY 3

NO PERSON OR CITY IS HOPELESS

"Go to the great city of Nineveh and proclaim to it the message I give you." Jonah obeyed the word of the Lord and went to Nineveh. Now Nineveh was a very important city-a visit required three days."   Jonah 3:2-3

"Every Christian is either a missionary or an imposter."   Charles Spurgeon

PRAY: Lord, there are places that don't seem right for Christians to go to. And yet You call us to reach everyone across the globe. Please change my heart about what cities I don't like and help me embrace anything You have for me. Jonah didn't want to go to Nineveh, but when he finally obeyed You, the whole city was saved in the greatest revival in the history of the world! Please let us love people everywhere, even though we may not agree with their lifestyle. Let us love the people in Hollywood and pray for them to know you. Stop us from running from what You have for us and let us pray for the people in Hollywood and any other place we don't like or don't agree with. Help me embrace people everywhere I go as a mission field and every person as someone worthy to know You! Amen.

REFLECT: Are you one who doesn't like Hollywood? If not, do you know people like that? Would you think about the duplicity in sending missionaries around the world to all kinds of scary people groups, like cannibals, terrorists, etc. and yet not want to reach out to the people in Hollywood? Ponder how much God loves every single person on the planet and He wants each one to know Him and love Him. He cared about the people in Nineveh and He cares about the people in Hollywood! Can you believe that?

ACT: What cities, people groups, or areas do you *not* like? What places do you not want to live in? Would you pray right now for God's blessings on those people and those cities? Ask the Lord to help you to embrace the people in Hollywood or any other place you don't like. God's first commandment is to love Him and love other people. Would you pray to love the people in Hollywood? They need your love and your prayers. Be praying for people groups in mission fields all over the world and that includes Hollywood as it is the world's most influential mission field.

YOUR THOUGHTS:

DAY 4

FAMILY IS YOUR FIRST PRIORITY

"Jesus... said, "Go home to your family and tell them how much the Lord has done for you, and how he has had mercy on you."   Mark 5:19

"I do not know anything that would wake up Chicago better than for every man and woman here who loves Him to begin to talk about Him to their friends, and just to tell them what He has done for you. You have got a circle of friends. Go and tell them of Him."

D.L. Moody

PRAY: Oh Jesus, I may want to see the people in my workplace become Christians, but am I loving the people in my own home? Have I shared my faith with my own family members or extended family? Have I told them how much You have done for me, and how You have shown so much mercy to me? Help me to start by being in right standing with my own family. Let me be bold to tell them what You've done in me and through me and with me! I don't need to make them believe, but I can't put my light under a bushel. Help me to be transparent with my own family, for my home is my most important mission field. Amen.

REFLECT: Have you thought about how God has specifically put you in your family. As messed up or dysfunctional as your family is, God put you there for a reason. Maybe it's to pray for them, or to be Jesus to them! Jesus wants us to love Him, then ourselves, then our family, and then our friends, acquaintances, co-workers, neighbors, and strangers. But let's start with our own family members. Sometimes that's the hardest mission field of all! Who do you need to pray for in your family? Is there anyone with whom you need to mend the relationship, or tell them how much and you and Jesus love them? Reflect on how to proactively reach out more to your family with the unconditional love of Jesus.

ACT: Choose one family or extended family member and start praying for them, asking the Lord to show you how to share your faith with them, how to love them, support them and even sacrifice for them. After you feel you have broken through in that relationship then choose someone else, until you can say that you have been truthful about your faith, as well as loving, supportive, and brave with every member of your family.

YOUR THOUGHTS:

DAY 5

FOR SUCH A TIME AS THIS

"For if you remain silent at this time, relief and deliverance for the Jews will arise from another place, but you and your father's family will perish. And who knows but that you have come to royal position for such a time as this?"   Esther 4:14

"Every day you are witnessing. What are you witnessing to? Your witness is the total package of your attitudes, character, and actions. It does not lie."   Winkie Pratney

PRAY: Dear Heavenly Father, I no longer want to remain silent. I want the people in my life to know You, and I don't want anyone to perish, so I must be bold and faithful for such a time as this. I believe You have called all of us to make an eternal difference, and just as You sent Esther into the King's palace to represent You, I believe that You have sent me into my mission field to represent You. Prepare me to love the people around me. Amen.

REFLECT: Do you realize that God created each and every one of us to do at least one big thing in our lives here on earth? You don't want to miss making an eternal difference in this world and it's no coincidence that you are here at such a time as this. Author Phil Cooke wrote in his book "One Big Thing" that we were all born to do at least one big thing to make the world a better place. What would be your one big thing? Ask God to reveal your eternal purpose to you, then go fulfill your "royal position for such a time as this!"

ACT: Commit to pray to God every day, to show you what He has for you, until you know what it is. Ask Him to use you in the lives of the people around you, to fulfill any plan He has for you and not to miss anything that you can do to make our world a better place. You are a mighty Ambassador of the living God, sent to this very place as your mission field, and you have a mission to fulfill. Ask Him what that is and then, with great joy, do it!

If you'd like some tips on how to more naturally share your faith, or if you want to lead a 6 week Bible study on the topic, then be sure to get Karen and Jim Covell, and Victorya Rogers' book, "How To Talk About Jesus Without Freaking Out" or their newest edition, "The J Bomb" on amazon.com, at your local bookstore, or email us at info@hpnemail.org to receive a copy.

YOUR THOUGHTS:

DAY 6

PUT DOWN ROOTS: LOVE & BUILD WHERE YOU ARE

"This is what the Lord Almighty, the God of Israel, says to all those I carried into exile from Jerusalem to Babylon: "Build houses and settle down; plant gardens and eat what they produce. Marry and have sons and daughters.... Increase in number there; do not decrease. Also, seek the peace and prosperity of the city to which I have carried you into exile. Pray to the Lord for it, because if it prospers, you too will prosper."   Jeremiah 29:4-7

"It is the duty of every Christian to be Christ to his neighbor."   Martin Luther

PRAY: Lord in Heaven, sometimes I feel like You have put me in exile. Work is hard, I have many challenging obstacles. But, You have sent me to this city, in this neighborhood, and to my job for a specific reason. I want to see this place as my mission field, to build a house, plant a garden, put down roots, and call this my home. Help me to develop my friendships, share my faith, and seek the peace and prosperity of the city where You've carried me! And I must pray for it, because if it prospers, I too will prosper. Amen.

REFLECT: Reflect on how God's words tells us to put down roots where we are – even if we feel like we're in exile. We can't have an impact on people if we don't settle in and get to know them, plant seeds and watch them grow. How are you settling into your community? Are planting gardens, having a family and calling this place home? And most importantly, are you praying for the peace and prosperity of the city to which God has brought you? Do you love the people in your mission field and believe God brought you here for a purpose?

ACT: Make a mental checklist with the following questions: Do you consider where you live right now home? Are you building rich relationships in your neighborhood and workplace? Are you praying for the peace and prosperity of the city in which you're living? If any of these answers is NO, then you need to reevaluate for your life. Seek counsel on how you can love the place and the people where you are planted. Ask the Lord to change your heart and then take active steps to make an eternal difference right where you are.

YOUR THOUGHTS:

DAY 7

THEY WILL KNOW YOU BY YOUR LOVE

"A new command I give you: Love one another. As I have loved you, so you must love one another. By this all men will know that you are my disciples, if you love one another."

John 13:34-35

"What an incredible witness it is to a lost and fearful society when the Christian acts like a child of God, living under the loving sovereignty of the Heavenly Father." Henry Blackaby

PRAY: Jesus, I want to Love other people with all my heart, soul, and mind. I want to be known as one who loves other people. My greatest job as a missionary is to love You and other Christians unconditionally, but I need Your help to do that. I want to embrace Your commandment, for when I do, then non-believers will know that I am Your disciple. And I want to be so loving that others are attracted to You because they want what You've given me. Thank You for filling me up with Your love each day. I pray this in Your name, Amen.

REFLECT: John tells us that the best way to have others get to know Jesus is to love other Christians! Then we don't have to preach, share a gospel tract, or make pre-Christians pray the sinner's prayer. They will see our love for one another and that will lead them to Jesus, as they see that we are His disciples. It's actually easier than we think. You don't have to go knocking on doors and sharing the gospel with all of your neighbors. Just be a person of prayer and integrity, be excellent in all that you do, and love the Christians and other people around you with all your heart. Then the Holy Spirit will take care of the rest.

ACT: Congratulations, you have finished the year! Now – Go out today and change the world. LOVE SOMEONE with God's love, especially other Christians. Do intentional acts of kindness in your mission field and watch how people will want to know why you did that. You will stand out as a loving person as you live in your neighborhood, workplace, and city with a purpose. Don't hesitate, don't be afraid, don't cower. Just radically love other people and you will be one of God's most effective "missionaries" and Ambassadors. They will know you are one of God's disciples if you love ALL people. HAPPY NEW YEAR!

YOUR THOUGHTS:

APPENDIX A
THE NEXT STEP:

HOW TO KNOW GOD
A PRAYER FOR SALVATION

If you have read through this devotional and realized that you don't really know Jesus, or you believe in Him but you don't understand how to have a personal relationship with Him, now is the time to take the next step and give your life over to Him.

There is no one way to pray to receive Jesus and become one of His followers. Whatever words you say, it's about a heartfelt prayer of salvation—to be saved from the consequences of sin. Some people call it "the sinner's prayer" but it's simply a prayer to give the control of your life over to God, so He comes in to your heart and you are living for Him from this day forward. Jesus becomes your Savior, you are "born again" and you have eternal life.

When you're ready to take that step, you can say something like this:

"Dear Jesus, I want to know You personally. Please forgive me for all the things I've done wrong. I believe that You died on the cross to pay for my sins, and that You rose from the dead to give me eternal life. Please come into my life now, Jesus, and take over for me. Thank You for making me the kind of person You want me to be. Now, Jesus, show me what to do next. Amen."

Congratulations, you are now a Christian!

We would like to help you grow as a new Christian. Please email us at info@hpnemail.org and let us know you've made this commitment. We will then help you to get plugged into a local church and find a small group to disciple you as you grow in your faith. We look forward to hearing from you!

ABOUT THE AUTHOR

KAREN COVELL

KAREN COVELL is an independent Producer of films, TV Specials and Documentaries, Co-Founder of JC Productions, an active member of the Producers Guild of America and the Founding Director of the Hollywood Prayer Network (HPN).

Karen challenges Christians around the world to pray for the people, the projects and the issues in the Hollywood entertainment industry. She also speaks and teaches around the country on how to pray for the people in the world's most influential mission field; the entertainment industry. She is a published co-author of two books with her husband Jim and their writing partner Victorya Rogers, entitled, *"How To Talk About Jesus Without Freaking Out"* (the young people's version called *"The J Bomb"*) and *"The Day I Met God,"* all available at Amazon.com. Karen is married to her best pal, James Covell, a composer, and they have two awesome sons, Christopher and Cameron, who are both filmmakers in Hollywood.

You can reach Karen at: www.KarenCovell.com – www.hollywoodprayernetwork.org

KIMBERLY ROBERTS, CONTRIBUTOR

Kimberly Roberts is a Project Manager, Online Support and Development Professional, and Director of Logistics for several national companies. She has also produced a TV pilot, as well as several Christian teaching seminars, and coordinated numerous large events. Recently, her most fun and rewarding endeavor has been working with Karen Covell as the developer and coordinator of the YouVersion™ online Hollywood Prayer Network Devotional! Happily married, with three adult sons and four amazing grandchildren, she enjoys worship, book clubs, cooking, natural healing, spiritual formation, and connecting deeply with people.

ABOUT HOLLYWOOD PRAYER NETWORK

Hollywood Prayer Network (HPN) was founded in 2001 as a nonprofit 501(c)3 organization seeking to build a bridge of love and respect between Christians in the Church and professionals in Hollywood, through prayer. We are committed to mobilizing Christians around the world to pray for the people, the projects and the issues in the entertainment industry, with an attitude of love. It is our passion to challenge global Christians to engage in culture, pray for the media, and help transform the spiritual climate of Hollywood with hearts of love and compassion. Whether you're an industry professional who wants prayer and support or a Christian with a heart for prayer, we want to build bridges, light the way, and bring a message of love, hope and healing to an industry that dramatically shapes our world.

As a defined group of over 10,000 strong, the Christians working in this marketplace are growing as a community and experiencing God's presence here more than ever before. We encourage industry Christians to be professionals who use their gifts and talents to bring God's love to our community, and we are committed to have each one covered in prayer by an intercessor outside of Hollywood. To find out more about HPN, order more copies of Hollywood, Jesus, and You, or join our movement of prayer, visit our website:

www.HollywoodPrayerNetwork.org

CPSIA information can be obtained
at www.ICGtesting.com
Printed in the USA
FSHW020650241120